KABBALISTIC METAPHORS

KABBALISTIC METAPHORS

JEWISH MYSTICAL THEMES IN ANCIENT AND MODERN THOUGHT

SANFORD L. DROB

JASON ARONSON INC.
Northvale, New Jersey
Jerusalem

The author gratefully acknowledges permission to reprint portions of the following:

S. Drob. "Freud and the Chasidim: Redeeming the Jewish Soul of Psychoanalysis" in *Jewish Review* 3:1. Reprinted by permission of the Jewish Review, Inc. Copyright © 1989.

S. Drob. "The Mystic as Philosopher; An Interview with Rabbi Adin Steinsaltz" in *Jewish Review* 3:4. Reprinted by permission of the Jewish Review, Inc. Copyright © 1990.

R. Elior. *The Paradoxical Ascent to God: The Kabbalistic Theosopy of Habad Hasidism.* Reprinted by permission of the State University of New York Press. Copyright © 1993. All rights reserved.

G. Filoramo. *A History of Gnosticism.* Reprinted by permission of Blackwell Publishers. Copyright © 1990.

G. W. F. Hegel. *Lectures on the Philosophy of Religion.* Reprinted by permission of the University of California Press. Copyright © 1985.

C. G. Jung. *Memories, Dreams, Reflections.* Copyright © 1962, 1963 by Random House, Inc. Reprinted by Pantheon Books, a division of Random House, Inc. Reprinted by permission of the publisher.

C. G. Jung. *Mysterium Conjunctionis, The Collected Works of C.G. Jung,* Vol. 14. Copyright © 1963. Reprinted by permission of the publisher.

Plotinus. *The Six Enneads.* Reprinted from Great Books of the Western World. Copyright © 1952, 1990.

J. M. Robinson. *The Nag Hammadi Library,* third, completely revised edition. Copyright © 1978, 1988 by E.J. Brill. Reprinted by permission of HarperCollins Publishers, Inc.

I. Tishby and F. Lachower. *The Wisdom of the Zohar.* Vols. I, II, and III. Reprinted by permission of The Littman Library of Jewish Civilization. Copyright © 1989.

H. Zimmer. *Philosophies of India.* Reprinted by permission of the publisher. Copyright © 1971.

This book was set in 10 pt. Galliard by Alabama Book Composition of Deatsville, AL, and printed and bound by Book-Mart Press, Inc. of North Bergen, NJ.

Copyright © 2000 by Sanford L. Drob

10 9 8 7 6 5 4 3 2 1

Library of Congress Cataloging-in-Publication Data

Drob, Sanford L.
    Kabbalistic Metaphors: Jewish mystical themes in ancient and modern thought/ by Sanford L. Drob.
      p.   cm.
    Includes bibliographical references and index.
    ISBN 0–7657–6125–4
    1. Cabala—History. 2. Cabala—Comparative studies.   I. Title
BM526 D76 2000
296.1'6—dc21   99–044511

Printed in the United States of America on acid-free paper. For information and catalog, write to Jason Aronson Inc., 230 Livingston Street, Northvale, NJ 07647-1726, or visit our website: www.aronson.com

To my children,
Elliot, Robin, Amarilla, and Martín

Contents

Preface

This work places the symbols and ideas of the Kabbalah into a dialogue with several systems of ancient and modern thought. The opening chapters provide the rationale for such comparative study and present an outline of the history and basic concepts of the theosophical Kabbalah. Later chapters study the relationship between the Kabbalah and Indian philosophy; Platonism; Gnosticism; and the thought of Hegel, Freud, and Jung. As with my *Symbols of the Kabbalah*, my goal in this work is to provide a philosophical and psychological interpretation of the kabbalistic symbols that is relevant and vital to the contemporary reader.

As a philosopher and psychologist, I am indebted to those authors, including Gershom Scholem, Isaiah Tishby, Moshe Idel, Rachel Elior, Elliot Wolfson, Immanuel Schochet, and many others, whose works have made the Kabbalah accessible to those who are nonspecialists in Hebraic studies.

I am also indebted to the late Professor John Findlay whose modern Neoplatonic philosophy and personal inspiration have continually informed my efforts at a rational understanding of the Kabbalah. I would also like to thank Rabbi Shimmon Hecht for teaching me *Tanya*, Rabbi Joel Kenney for guiding my exploration of Chayyim Vital's *Sefer Etz Chayyim* and sharing with me his knowledge of kabbalistic and Hasidic symbolism, Harris Tilevitz for encouraging me to begin this project, and Arthur Kurzweil for encouraging me to complete it.

Introduction

I n this book I place the major symbols of the theosophical Kabbalah in the context of several familiar trends in the history of Eastern and Western thought. My goal is to show how the Kabbalah of Isaac Luria articulates a basic metaphor regarding God, cosmos, and humanity that can be understood as a template for much of modern philosophy and psychology. Although I believe that kabbalistic ideas have had considerable impact on more exoteric modes of Western thought, my argument in this book is not that such thinkers as Hegel, Freud, and Jung simply borrowed kabbalistic ideas and used them for their own purposes, but that through a combination of influence and convergent thinking, the major themes of the Lurianic Kabbalah are present, active, and alive in these later authors. Recognition of the parallels between the Kabbalah and modern philosophy and psychology can provide us with valuable insight into both the Kabbalah and modern thought, and help pave the way for a "New Kabbalah," one that is spiritually and intellectually relevant to contemporary man.

As I will demonstrate, many of the ideas and themes of the Lurianic Kabbalah are also present in systems of thought (Indian philosophy, Platonism, Gnosticism) that themselves antedate the Kabbalah. In the case of Platonism and Gnosticism, their impact upon the Kabbalah can hardly be gainsaid.[1] The Kabbalah, however, is unique in its position in the history of Western thought, acting, as it were, as a "switching station" in which the biblical tradition, Near Eastern mysticism, and Western philosophy converge. In the Kabbalah of Isaac Luria these traditions combine with Luria's profound spiritual insight and intense mythical imagination to produce a comprehensive philosophical and psychological vision of the nature of God and humankind that was only imperfectly represented in the prior traditions.

As in my previous book, *Symbols of the Kabbalah*, my goal in the present work is to provide an interpretation of certain basic kabbalistic ideas, which renders these ideas comprehensible and relevant to the modern reader. It is my conviction that the theosophical Kabbalah, particularly the Kabbalah of Isaac Luria, provides a symbolic matrix through which the "ultimate questions" regarding God and the world, and the meaning of human existence, can be provided with satisfactory solutions. Rather than being an antiquated mystical and theosophical system, the Lurianic Kabbalah provides us with a dynamic conception of God, world, and humanity that encompasses all happenings and all things, and that enables us to understand even the daily activities of men and women as vital to the redemption of the world.

The Kabbalah articulates a dynamic of being and nothing, revelation and concealment, destruction and restoration, and exile and redemption,[2] which not only serves as a powerful guide to human existence, but which embodies and reflects essential dynamics of logical (dialectical) thought, human history, and the development of both the individual and collective human psyche. As such, the dynamic described in the theosophical Kabbalah, while appearing to

---

1. Scholem, for example, has gone so far as to state that the Kabbalah can be defined as resulting from an interplay between Neoplatonism and a Jewish form of Gnosticism. Gershom Scholem, *Kabbalah* (Jerusalem: Keter, 1974), p. 45.

2. In characterizing the Lurianic Kabbalah as a philosophy of exile and redemption, I am adopting the interpretation of Gershom Scholem. This notion is not explicitly stated by the Kabbalists themselves but is rather fully implicit throughout their writings. My own view is that the Lurianic symbols do not simply reflect the historical exile and redemption of the Jewish people, but rather reflects a fundamental ontological alienation in the cosmos itself. See my *Symbols of the Kabbalah: Philosophical and Psychological Perspectives.* (Northvale, NJ: Jason Aronson, 1999), Chapter One. For a discussion of Scholem's understanding of exile and redemption in the Lurianic Kabbalah see also Moshe Idel, *Messianic Mystics* (New Haven: Yale University Press, 1998), pp. 179 ff.

be peculiar to Jewish mystical thought, actually adumbrates a perennial philosophy that is relevant to humanity as a whole.

The comparative studies that make up the core of this book seek to shed light on the philosophical vision that is embodied in the symbols of the Kabbalah. Each of these studies begins a dialogue between the Kabbalah and an influential spiritual or intellectual tradition—Indian philosophy, Platonism, Gnosticism, Hegelian philosophy, Freudian psychoanalysis, and Jungian analytical psychology—and each attempts to shed light both on the Kabbalah and these various other traditions.

The drawing of parallels between presumably unrelated religious and philosophical traditions can readily lead to premature and misleading conclusions about unidirectional or mutual historical influence. In this work I have pointed to the evidence of such influence, e.g., the impact of Platonism and Gnosticism on the Kabbalah or the influence of the Kabbalah on Hegel, Freud, and Jung, wherever warranted. However, my intent is not primarily one of uncovering and tracing influences. My purpose is rather the study of parallel ideas and the enrichment of understanding that such comparative study and mutual dialogue can afford. In discussing the kabbalistic notion of *Kelippot* together with the Jainist concept of Karma, for example, my purpose is simply to show that two traditions, separated greatly in both place and time, arrived at similar conclusions regarding the problem of "evil"—and that a dialogue between these respective traditions can enrich our own approach to "evil" as well. With respect to the relationship between Kabbalah and Gnosticism, the temptation to draw historical conclusions is far greater. However, even in this instance my goal is largely the same, i.e., to place kabbalistic ideas into a long-overdue dialogue with similar concepts in other religious and philosophical traditions. In the case of the psychology of C. G. Jung, the evidence for a powerful kabbalistic influence is overwhelming, but here too I am less interested in showing that Jung is a "modern Kabbalist" than I am in exploring the possibilities of mutual dialogue and enrichment between kabbalistic and Jungian thought. Indeed, because Jungian psychology mirrors so many aspects of the Kabbalah, it provides us with a unique opportunity to understand the Kabbalah in contemporary psychological terms.

An effort to bring kabbalistic ideas into dialogue with those of other traditions is actually as old as the Kabbalah itself. As Yehuda Liebes has pointed out, an outstanding feature of the Zohar is its "receptiveness to ideas from other sources and its ability to adapt them to its own particular style and way of thought."[3] However, in the more recent past, there have been several impediments to dialogue between the Kabbalah and other traditions. The first of these has been the traditional Jewish view that the Kabbalah is a self-contained ancient tradition that was part of the legacy to Moses at Sinai. Such a viewpoint hardly admits the possibility of comparative studies—and it was precisely this point of view that prevailed among the only serious students of the Kabbalah (orthodox Jews and, particularly, Hasidim) until at least the nineteenth century. A second factor limiting the comparative study between the Kabbalah and other disciplines has been the viewpoint of Gershom Scholem, who, while rejecting the orthodox "from Sinai" approach, treated the Kabbalah largely as a circumscribed, independent system of ideas. As Scholem once put it: "These are the four generations at the beginning of Kabbalah [R. Jehudah ben Barzilai, R. Abraham ben Isaac, R. Abraham ben David, and R. Isaac the Blind]. Before them, it does not exist."[4] For reasons that are somewhat unclear to me, Scholem (in spite of his recognition, for example, of the close relationship between the Kabbalah and Gnosticism) largely eschewed comparative studies, instead concentrating on the texts and ideas of the Kabbalah outside of their possible connections to other systems of ideas. Scholem has even been accused of failing to recognize the connections between Kabbalah and other traditions within Judaism, preferring to see the Kabbalah as the "underground" carrier of a unique mythical and mystical Jewish element, which served as a counterpoint to the legalisms of normative religion.

Whatever the reasons for the failure of scholars to do so in the past, the time is now ripe for comparative kabbalistic studies.[5] In the following

---

3. Yehuda Liebes, "Christian influences on the Zohar," in his *Studies in the Zohar*, trans. Arnold Schwartz, Stephanie Nakache, Penina Peli (Albany: State University of New York Press, 1993), p. 139.

4. Gershom Scholem, *The Kabbalah in Provence* [Hebrew], ed. R. Schatz (Jerusalem, 1963), p. 52. Quoted in Yehuda Liebes, *Studies In Jewish Mysticism*, trans. Batya Stein (Albany: State University of New York Press, 1993), p. 68.

5. An interesting exception to the lack of earlier work in this area is to be found in the writings of Maurice Fluegel, whose *Philosophy, Qabbala and Vedanta* (H. Fluegel & Company, 1902) is an early if superficial effort to tie together Indian philosophy, Spinoza, Philo, Schelling, and others through a knot forged by the Kabbalah. Although the task he set before himself was ambitious and, in my view, laudable, it was not one with which he was very successful. His knowledge of the Kabbalah, as well as the other traditions he treats, is very limited and he seems to equate these traditions almost exclusively on the grounds of their purported

chapters, I make a number of comparisons between the Kabbalah (particularly Lurianic Kabbalah) and other systems of ancient and modern thought. Some of these comparisons (e.g., with Gnosticism) have been made before; others (e.g., with Indian philosophy and Hegelianism) have been hinted at, but not, to my knowledge, explored in any detail by contemporary scholars. In the case of Platonism, a number of Kabbalists saw the close relationship between the Kabbalah and Platonic philosophy, some going even so far as to suggest that the Kabbalah was the source for Plato's ideas. Nonetheless the link between the Kabbalah and Platonism has not provided much stimulus to contemporary Jewish philosophers. Finally, comparative study of the Kabbalah and the contemporary psychologies of Freud and Jung has for the most part been absent or superficial. In particular, the important and rather obvious connections between the Kabbalah and Jungian psychology have not been adequately explored.[6]

As a result of insufficient comparative studies in Jewish mysticism and the tendency of such prime expositors of the Kabbalah as Scholem and Isaiah Tishby to deny that kabbalistic symbols have serious philosophical content, the Kabbalah has yet to earn its deserved position in contemporary intellectual discourse. This book is meant to go part of the distance in correcting this state of affairs.

It is my hope that those who give careful study to this work, in particular, to the chapters on the Kabbalah, Plato, and Hegel, Freud, and Jung, will find important vehicles for bringing discussion about such kabbalistic symbols as *Ein-Sof* (the Infinite), *Tzimtzum* (Concealment, Contraction), *Sefirot* (the Archetypes of Creation), *Shevirat ha-Kelim* (the Breaking of the Vessels), and *Tikkun ha-Olam* (the Restoration of the World) into contemporary philosophy and psychology. Further, it is my view that both Hegelian philosophy and Freudian (as well as Jungian) psychology express variations on basic themes that are most fully articulated in the theosophical Kabbalah. Therefore, a careful reading of the Kabbalah should

---

pantheistic views. The only kabbalistic concepts he considers are *Ein-Sof* and *Adam Kadmon*. Nonetheless his treatment is historically significant for its "early" positive treatment of the Kabbalah and the effort to link the Kabbalah to both Eastern and Western thought. Among contemporary scholars Moshe Idel has made some tentative steps in the direction of comparative studies. See, for example, his *Messianic Mystics*, Chapter 8, esp. pp. 290–292.

6. See Sanford Drob, "Jung and the Kabbalah," *History of Psychology*, Vol. 2, No. 2 (May 1999), pp. 102–118.

provide us with important insights into the basic structure and themes of modern philosophy and psychology.

The basic metaphors of the Kabbalah not only appear in such thinkers as Hegel, Freud, and Jung, but as I have argued in my *Symbols of The Kabbalah*, are discernible in such manifold arenas as historical development in the arts and sciences, individual human development, and the structure and dynamics of madness.[7] That these metaphors appear in so many disparate systems of thought and are reflected in so many human developmental processes argues for their archetypal status and significance.

Some readers will likely be of the opinion that in passing the kabbalistic symbols through the prism of ancient and modern systems of philosophy and psychology, I have in effect transformed as opposed to interpreted the Jewish mystical tradition. Such a conclusion, is in one sense, inevitable, for the very process of interpreting centuries-old texts and ideas inevitably transforms them in a manner that accords with the author's own conceptual schema. The reverse is true, of course, as well, as an encounter with such ideas can impact upon and alter contemporary schema and theory. This possibility is particularly salient with respect to the concepts of a tradition like the Kabbalah, which, for a variety of doctrinal and historical reasons, has yet to have considerable direct impact upon contemporary thought. Indeed, a major goal of this work is simply to bring kabbalistic ideas into a dialogue with contemporary philosophy and psychology.

It is my view that a variety of trends in both ancient and contemporary thought provide a context in which the age-old insights of the Kabbalah can be readily understood. The time is ripe, one might say, not only for a new-found appreciation of the Kabbalah, but for a *New Kabbalah*, one that will take into account both ancient esoteric wisdom and modern exoteric knowledge to the mutual enrichment of both.

Chapter One of this book provides a brief overview of the history of Jewish mysticism and a more detailed review of the basic symbols and ideas of the theosophical Kabbalah.

Chapter Two provides an overview of a variety of non-Jewish traditions in the history of religion, philosophy, alchemy, and psychology that have

---

7. I have discussed several of these themes in Chapter Seven of my book, *Symbols of the Kabbalah*. A discussion of the relationship between the kabbalistic myths and insanity is found in Chapter Seven of the current volume, in the section entitled "Freud and Mysticism: The Case of Daniel Paul Schreber," p. 272.

interacted with Jewish mysticism and that can be the subject of fruitful comparison with the Kabbalah.

Chapters Three, Four, and Five treat of the relationship between the Kabbalah and three ancient traditions whose symbols and concepts parallel and shed considerable light upon Jewish mystical ideas. Indian philosophy and religion represents the most developed form of mystical thought in the ancient world. Its notions of the Infinite God, the significance of "nothingness," the illusory nature of creation, the meaning of evil, and the essence of the human soul are clearly echoed in the Kabbalah and can provide much to enhance our understanding of Jewish mystical thought. Platonism is the foundation of Western philosophy in general, and idealist philosophy in particular, and such idealism serves as the conceptual foundation for several key kabbalistic ideas, including the *Sefirot*, which are in many ways equivalent to the Platonic "forms." Finally, Gnosticism provides us with a symbology so close to that of the Kabbalah as almost to force us to the conclusion of a historical influence. A comparison between Gnosticism and the Kabbalah provides an opportunity for us to examine a direction that the Kabbalah could have taken but did not, and to thereby highlight the Kabbalah's unique path and significance.

Chapter Six is a comparative study of the Kabbalah and the philosophy of G. W. F. Hegel. Such study can deepen our conceptual understanding of the Kabbalist's metaphors because large portions of Hegel's philosophy can be read as a philosophical treatment of the kabbalistic myths. Nearly all of the major symbols of the Kabbalah reappear in Hegel as pure concepts or moments in his dialectic, and a study of Hegel can reveal how much conceptual content actually lays hidden in the Kabbalist's mystical metaphors.

The final two chapters of this book are comparative studies of Kabbalah, Hasidism, and the psychological theories of Freud and Jung. I have touched upon the parallels between the Lurianic Kabbalah and psychoanalysis in my book, *Symbols of the Kabbalah*. It is my hope that the chapters in the present volume will further clarify the link between these seemingly remote spheres of endeavor, and, along with the chapter on Hegel, point in the direction of a "New Kabbalah," one that is specifically relevant to our own age.

It is my thesis that the "basic metaphor" of the Lurianic Kabbalah can provide us with a template through which we can understand much of Western intellectual thought of the past two centuries. The Kabbalah, I believe, not only sheds new and fascinating light on such thinkers as Hegel,

Freud, and Jung, but also provides us with a perspective through which these thinkers can be understood in relation to each other. That Jung (both directly and via his study of alchemy) was greatly influenced by kabbalistic ideas is beyond any doubt; that such an influence is present in Hegel and Freud is likely but less obvious. My belief, however, is that regardless of any historical influence, the morphological parallels in the ideas of these great thinkers can be profitably understood through reference to the myths of the Lurianic Kabbalah.

The Kabbalah articulates a logical, historical, and psychological dialectic via its symbols of the Infinite God (*Ein-Sof*), divine contraction (*Tzimtzum*), emanation (*Sefirot*), deconstruction (*Shevirat ha-Kelim*), and restoration (*Tikkun*). Whether translated into philosophical terms (Hegel), psychological terms (Freud), or "archetypal" terms (Jung), this dialectic has been integral to Western intellectual life of the past 175 years. Although beyond the scope of this book, this same dynamic of alienation, construction, deconstruction, and restoration is also present in Marx and the existentialists, each of whom provide a contemporary variation on the Gnostic/kabbalistic (and ultimately, Jewish) theme of exile and redemption.

THE LURIANIC KABBALAH AS A "BASIC METAPHOR"

The Lurianic Kabbalah is an extremely complex system of thought[8] that integrates a variety of symbols into what appears, at least on the surface, to be a purely mythological account of the creation and the ultimate destiny of the world. In its essential outline we can summarize this account as follows:

Before and beyond time there is only *Ein-Sof* (the infinite) whose identity is *Ayin* (nothing) and All. *Ein-Sof* becomes the source, substance and goal of everything that is; its "light," the *Or Ein-Sof*, becomes the energy of the cosmos.

In an act of *Tzimtzum* (concealment and contraction) *Ein-Sof* withdrew

---

8. Idel has stated "There can be no doubt that Lurianic Kabbalah is one of the most complex intellectual systems ever produced by a Jewish author—indeed, as Gershom Scholem has correctly asserted, by any human mind." See Idel, *Messianic Mystics*, p. 170; also David Biale, "Gershom Scholem's Ten Unhistorical Aphorisms in Kabbalah: Text and Commentary," *Modern Judaism* 5 (1985), pp. 67–93. Scholem's point, however, is that the Lurianic Kabbalah is more "hidden and occult" than nearly any other system of thought.

from a point within itself, thus yielding a finite, independent, and yet illusory series of worlds (*ha-Olamot*).

Acts of contraction alternate with emanations of divine light, and the cosmos comes to consist of *Adam Kadmon* (Primordial Man), who in turn emanates the ten *Sefirot* (archetypes or dimensions), which become *Kelim* (vessels) for containing the further emanations of *Or Ein-Sof* (the divine, infinite light).

These *Sefirot* are the archetypal values (Will, Wisdom, Understanding, Kindness, Judgment, Beauty, Endurance, Splendour, Foundation, Kingship), and hence the basic molecular components of the cosmos. They are alternately conceived of as complimentary to or identical with the *Otiyot Yesod*, the "Foundational Letters" of divine speech.

The *Sefirot* are organized into five basic *Olamot* (worlds), each of which contains varying proportions of each of the ten *Sefirot*, as well as into countless lesser worlds and several divine personalities (*Partzufim*), representing masculine and feminine aspects of God. Our world, *Assiyah* (the world of "Making"), is the most remote from the infinite God.

The *Sefirot* were disunified and incomplete, and hence shattered under the impact of the infinite light. This shattering, known as the *Shevirat Ha-Kelim* (the Breaking of the Vessels), results in a condition in which all being is in a state of *galut* (exile): everything is out of place and the lower worlds are riddled with spiritual, moral, and psychological antinomies. The masculine and feminine aspects of God, which had hitherto been in a state of *coniunctio*, turn their backs on one another.

Shards from the broken vessels tumble through the *Tehiru* (metaphysical void) and in the process capture *Netzotzim* (sparks) of divine light, forming *Kellipot* (Husks), which are comprised of a lifeless shell and divine inner core, which is, however, estranged from its source in the Infinite Light. These *Kellipot* constitute the dark realm of the *Sitra Achra* (the "Other Side"), the place of evil in man's soul and the world, but also the source of ultimate redemption.

Contemporaneous with the Shevirah, the *Sefirot* begin to reorganize themselves into the *Partzufim* (Visages or Personalities), which in archetypal fashion represent the developmental stages of man from birth to old age. The *Partzufim* restore the world by re-engaging in conjugal relations. However, this restoration, which is known as *Tikkun ha-Olam* (the Restoration of the World), must be completed by mankind. It is mankind's divinely appointed task to gather the captured sparks of divine light, free them from their shells, and raise these sparks so they may once again rejoin the infinite. In so doing, mankind completes creation and, in a fashion, gives full actuality to God himself. The restored world of *Tikkun* is the very meaning of creation and the ultimate destiny of the universe.

This, in bare outline, is the "basic metaphor," the fundamental "myth," the significance of which is the subject matter of this book. The basic elements of this myth are as follows:

(1) An original, all-inclusive source of being and energy (*Ein-Sof*)

(2) contracts and conceals itself from itself (*Tzimtzum*), and

(3) becomes alienated in seemingly independent yet illusory realms (*Ha-Olamot*).

(4) Through a series of self-alienations and emanations, the source of being embodies itself in an abstract, Primordial Man (*Adam Kadmon*),

(5) who is composed of and himself emanates structures of ideas and values (the *Sefirot*) that are embodied in language.

(6) These structures are inherently unstable and break apart (*Shevirat ha Kelim*),

(7) causing a further alienation of the divine light in a negative "counter-world" (*Kelippot, Sitra Achra*), and

(8) a rending apart of opposites (symbolized by male and female) that had hitherto been joined.

(9) The divine light undergoes a developmental process (the *Partzufim*) and is ultimately returned to its source, where

(10) it is reorganized and restored (*Tikkun*), resulting in the fulfillment and actualization of the original, all-inclusive, being.

In purely abstract terms this myth can be restated as follows: (1) a primal being, energy or "Absolute" (2) initiates a self-negation, which gives rise to (3) an alienated and illusory realm (4) in which a created, personal manifestation of the Absolute arises. (5) This personal manifestation embodies the fundamental structures, ideas, and values of the human world, which are (6) inherently unstable and deconstruct, leading to (7) a further alienation of the primal energy from its source, and (8) a rending apart of opposites, resulting in the antinomies and perplexities of the world. As a result of (9) a spiritual, intellectual, and psychological developmental process, (10) the ideas and values of the world are restored in a manner that enables them to structure and contain the primal energy of the Absolute.

As I will show in detail in subsequent chapters, many of the elements of this structure are to be found in Indian philosophy, Platonism, and Gnosti-cism. More significantly, however, this structure constitutes a basic metaphor that is essentially repeated by Hegel in the nineteenth century, and again by Freud and Jung in the twentieth. By way of anticipation, I will briefly examine this metaphorical structure as it appears in Hegel, Freud, and Jung.

HEGEL

We can begin by briefly examining the philosophy of Hegel. There is, of course, something presumptuous in an attempt to summarize the work of Hegel in a few short paragraphs. However, Hegel's conception of the "Absolute" and its development as the "World-Spirit" is relatively simple and straightforward; it is the precise philosophical interpretation of this concep-tion and his explication of the development of the World-Spirit in history, philosophy, and the various fields of human endeavor that makes Hegel's thought controversial and complex.

For Hegel, the origin, substance, purpose, and direction of the universe is the realization of an infinite knowledge, consciousness, or mind. Like the Kabbalist's, Hegel held that the world's beginning, substance, and end is to be found in an infinite, all-inclusive, absolute being. This Absolute, which is analogous to the Kabbalist's *Ein-Sof*, is conceived of by Hegel as the Absolute Reason or Idea, a notion that is itself present in many kabbalistic works,[9] including the Zohar, where *Ein-Sof* is at times described as the "supernal thought."[10]

Like *Ein-Sof*, Hegel's Absolute is compelled to contract or alienate itself in the concrete particulars of a created world. This "self-alienation of the Absolute Spirit" is a direct parallel to the Kabbalist's *Tzimtzum*, the concealment and contraction of *Ein-Sof*. According to Hegel, this negation or alienation is a logically necessary event, for the Idea, any idea, must necessarily fulfill itself by becoming particular and concrete. The concepts of

9. For example, the early kabbalistic text *Sefer ha-Iyyun* (The Book of Contem-plation) holds that God is *united with* and created all things through the power of Primordial Wisdom (*ha-chochmah aa-kedumah*). See Mark Verman, *The Books of Contemplation: Medieval Jewish Mystical Sources* (Albany: State University of New York Press, 1992), pp. 41–42.

10. Zohar I:21a, as translated in *The Zohar*, trans. Harry Sperling, Maurice Simon, and Paul Levertoff, (London: Soncino Press, 1931–1934).

"horse" or "kindness," for example, are empty and abstract without actual horses and real acts of kindness. Thus, like the Kabbalist's *Ein-Sof*, Hegel's Absolute only *becomes itself* by negating itself, and particularizing itself in a world. However, the world, according to both Luria and Hegel, is in other respects an illusion, for while it appears to have an existence independent of the "All," it is in reality simply an aspect, indeed a concealed aspect, of the Absolute itself.

For Hegel, as for the Kabbalists, the Absolute negates itself in order to enter into a finite, natural realm, but begins the return to itself through the formation, within nature, of the World-Spirit, which is embodied in man. Like the Kabbalist's Primordial Man (*Adam Kadmon*), Hegel's World-Spirit creates, and is, in effect, composed of the sum total of ideas and values that define mankind. Indeed, for Hegel, mankind's progress in philosophy, religion, politics, ethics, and the arts marks the development of the Absolute in history, much as the Kabbalist's *Sefirot*, their shattering, and restoration by humanity mark the development of *Ein-Sof* in an historical world. Hegel, like the Kabbalists, holds, in effect, that God's sojourn into a finite, alien realm, and His manifestation in the spirit of humankind is a logically necessary aspect of God's very being and perfection.

Hegel's dialectic provides a philosophical parallel to the Lurianic Breaking of the Vessels. According to Hegel, man's original values, ideas, and institutions are insufficient to contain the full breadth of the Absolute, and these structures, values, and ideas break down or fall apart, and must be reorganized into ever-widening schemas that transcend and yet incorporate the original broken ideas. Thus, for example, in the realm of logic, "being" and "nothingness" dialectically break down in favor of "becoming," and in the realm of politics "abstract rights" and "morality" break down in favor of a "social ethic." Further, in the "broken" state, which Hegel refers to as the "Understanding," the oppositions of this world (e.g., between good and evil, truth and error, being and nonbeing, etc.) are rent apart and their mutual interdependence goes completely unrecognized. Luria's dynamic of *Sefirot* (original idea), *Shevirah* (shattering of that idea), and *Tikkun* (restoration of the original idea on a higher level) can be readily understood as a symbolic representation of the very dialectical reasoning that is later given conceptual form in Hegel.

For Hegel, the dialectic proceeds through all forms of thought, life, and historical expression, expanding itself into greater and deeper possibilities and antinomies, even into realms that are regarded as negative and evil. It is only through the process of "speculative reason," most perfectly manifest in the philosophy of Hegel itself, that the Absolute Idea, having alienated itself into a realm of Nature, can now, through the vehicle of mankind, return to itself and, having traversed nature and history, perfect itself in the union of Logic, Nature, and Spirit. In "Speculative Reason" the oppositions that had been broken apart by the Understanding are rejoined and are seen to be mutually dependent conceptions. This, of course, is Hegel's equivalent to the Kabbalist's *Tikkun*. The Absolute, which, of necessity, was exiled and alienated, has now been redeemed and fulfilled.

Hegel provides a radically cognitive or rational interpretation to our "basic metaphor." Absent from his philosophy, for example, is any serious consideration of the erotic, which is so prominent in the Lurianic myths. This is, in part, because Hegel conceived philosophy as providing a rational explanation for the cosmos, as answering the question of "Why does the world exist?". Hegel's answer to this question (and his entire system is but the development of this answer) is that the world exists as an arena for the fullest possible realization of Reason, Mind, or Spirit. For Hegel, Reason, is the one self-sufficient, independent principle that can be posited as the foundation of the world. In short, it is the one principle that can serve as its own explanation. (If we ask for the reason for "reason" we can only answer reason itself.) Reason is both the beginning and end of the world's development. Philosophy is both a rational explanation of the development of the "World-Spirit," and (because philosophy is the supreme rational expression) the ultimate manifestation of the World-Spirit itself.

Hegel's point of view corresponds to one moment in the Kabbalist's interpretation of *Ein-Sof*. As Scholem has pointed out, the entire history of the Kabbalah involves a struggle between views of the Absolute, which see *Ein-Sof* and the world-creative process in intellectual versus volitional terms. Indeed, two schemes for the ordering of the ten *Sefirot* developed, one that understood the highest *Sefirah*, the highest manifestation of *Ein-Sof* as *Chochmah* (Wisdom/Thought); and a second that understood it as *Keter* (Crown), which is embodied in Will or Desire (*Ratzon*) and *Tinug* (Delight). Though Hegel indeed has much to say about desire, the basic thrust of his philosophy is so rational that from a kabbalistic point of view it can be said to express the "basic metaphor" under the aspect of *Chochmah*.

FREUD

The opposite is, of course, the case when we turn to Freud. Freud's shift in the direction of the irrational, erotic, and "darker" aspects of man's psyche was an understandable reaction to the unbridled rationalism and optimism of the nineteenth century. Freud, of course, was a physician, not a philosopher, and the problems he considered were necessarily those of man as opposed to God and the world. Nevertheless one should be amazed at the extent to which the Lurianic metaphors seem to find their way into Freud's theory of the human mind. Even more amazing, however, is the fact that in spite of numerous studies on the Jewish origins of psychoanalysis, including David Bakan's well-known *Sigmund Freud and The Jewish Mystical Tradition*,[11] no one, to my knowledge, including Bakan (whose book scarcely even mentions Luria's ideas), has articulated the parallels between Luria's basic metaphor and the theories of Freud. This is all the more surprising because, according to Bakan, Freud himself is purported to have exclaimed "This is gold" when, in the 1930s, he was presented with a draft of a German translation of one of the works of Luria's chief disciple, Chayyim Vital.

Jung, who later took a lively interest in the Kabbalah, once commented that the Jewish roots of psychoanalysis are to be found in the recesses of Kabbalah and Hasidism.[12] Jung also held, however, that the Gnostics, Alchemists, and Kabbalists projected their unconscious onto the heavens and that the parallels between these religious phenomena and dynamic psychology arose because each is ultimately speaking about the depths of the human mind. It is worth noting that the Kabbalists themselves acknowledge this possibility in their doctrine that the microcosm mirrors the macrocosm, that the structure of the world is reflected in the psyche of man. Yet they refused to give primacy to one over the other: the Lurianic metaphor is meant to apply *both* to the world at large and to the human soul.

For Freud, at least in his earlier formulations, the original source of psychic energy, the libido, represents itself in man's consciousness as desire. The Freudian libido is, in effect, the psychological equivalent of the Kabbalist's *Ein-Sof*, which is frequently spoken of as the "supernal will,"[13] and which is said to embody a cosmic form of eros. According to Freud, as a result of the prohibitions of civilized life, the libido is repressed—i.e.,

---

11. David Bakan, *Sigmund Freud and the Jewish Mystical Tradition* (Boston: Beacon Press, 1971). (Originally published in 1958.)

12. Carl Gustav Jung, *Letters*, ed. Gerhard Adler (Princeton, NJ: Princeton University Press, 1975), 2:358–359.

13. Zohar II239a. As translated in Isaiah Tishby and Fischel Lachower, *The Wisdom of the Zohar: An Anthology of Texts*, trans. David Goldstein (Oxford: Oxford University Press, 1989), Vol. 1, p. 257.

concealed from the ego—much as the divine light of the Kabbalists is concealed through the *Tzimtzum*. For Freud, such repression provides sustenance to an alien, independent realm of primitive drives and fantasies, the unconscious. The repressed, because it prompts the phenomena of sublimation is, according to Freud, the seat of "character" and "culture," and it is precisely because his desire is concealed from himself that man becomes who he is. Just as, for the Lurianists, the world and Primordial Man are formed as a result of *Ein-Sof*'s self-concealment (and, for Hegel, Nature and, ultimately, the World-Spirit, are created through the Absolute's self-alienation) character and culture, for Freud, are formed as a result of man's self-deception, via *repression* and sublimation. This is achieved through the channeling of libidinous energy into structures—the ego and superego—whose function is to contain and modulate further emanations of the individual's libido, much as the *Sefirot* were designed as vessels for channeling the light and energy of God's will.

For reasons that are inherent in the nature of the conflict between instinct and culture, these psychic structures are unstable and are not consistently able to maintain and modulate the libidinous energy in ways that are most adaptive to the individual. There is, one might say, a partial "shattering" of each of these structures and a splitting off (exile) of ideas and emotions from the main fabric of the individual's personality, just as in Luria's system, the *Sefirot* are shattered and divine sparks are separated from the main source of light in God. This "splitting off" occurs, for example, when an individual becomes aware of an impulse, thought, or desire that his conscious self finds unacceptable. The impulse or idea and its associated affect creates a further repression and subsequently dwells in the nether psychological realm known as the "dynamic unconscious," which is quite analogous to Luria's *Sitra Achra* or Other Side. Once in the unconscious these "complexes" of thought and affect, which are akin to the kabbalistic *Kelippot,* are inaccessible to the individual. They become, in a sense, "exiled" and are the source of all manner and variety of psychological mischief, which the individual experiences as depression or other neurotic symptoms, in the same way as the *Kelippot* are the source of negativity and evil on the cosmic level. Furthermore, these repressed ideas and impulses disrupt the individual's erotic life in such a manner that he or she becomes incapable of true genital sexuality and union, just as the Breaking of the Vessels, for Luria, had forced a disjunction in the erotic unions on high. The erotic disruption conditions a whole series of other conflicts in which the individual is desperate in his neurotic efforts to keep opposing ideas, such as male and female, right and wrong, clean and dirty, strictly apart.

The job of the analyst is to make these unconscious complexes conscious, and, more importantly, to free the libidinous energy attached to them so that it can be made available to the individual for his own erotic and other life goals just as, in Luria, the "sparks" must be raised, i.e., the energy trapped in the *Kelippot* must be freed and made available to reunite the masculine and feminine aspects of God. From a kabbalistic perspective the psychoanalytic endeavor is itself a form of *Tikkun* (restoration), which brings an end to a *galut* ("exiled" aspects of the individual's personality) and ushers in a *geulah* or psychological redemption. Thus as in Hegel, the Absolute (empiricized in Freud as the "libido"), once alienated and exiled, is restored and redeemed. Also, as in Luria and Hegel, the redeemed man, by virtue of the formation of his "character," is far more complete than the purely instinctual man who (at least theoretically) existed prior to the original alienation (repression).

JUNG

Jung, for his part, takes the Freudian enterprise as his point of departure and ends with a psychology that, through his excursions into Gnosticism and Alchemy, essentially reconstructs the Lurianic Kabbalah in almost its original form. The Gnostics provided Jung with a symbolic structure very similar to Luria's, but for the Gnostics' hatred for, and desire to escape from, this world. The alchemists, who borrowed heavily from kabbalistic sources, provided Jung with a "material" version of the Kabbalah, which Jung, somewhat inadvertently, reconstructed through his psychological and spiritual interpretation of alchemy.

Jung, in his final years, described a psychic structure that originates in a primal, undifferentiated psyche (the Gnostic's "pleroma," the Kabbalist's *Ein-Sof*) that is concealed from itself (*Tzimtzum*) in a collective unconscious of archetypal values (the *Sefirot*) and partial personalities (the Kabbalist's *Partzufim*). These archetypal structures, in turn, embody oppositions, particularly male and female, persona and shadow (analogous to the Kabbalist's *Sitra Achra* or "other side"), which it is the individual's task to reunite. Jung borrows the *coniunctio* (celestial wedding) imagery of alchemy and the Kabbalah to express this unification. He also makes use of the kabbalistic symbol of *Adam Kadmon* to express the notion of an individuated "Self," which is realized through the unification of the opposite tendencies in the human psyche, and like the Kabbalists he equates this symbol with (the archetype of) God. For Jung, the completion of the Self can only occur via a sojourn through chaos (the Kabbalist's Breaking of the Vessels), and he utilizes the kabbalistic image of the "raising of the sparks" to symbolize the reconnection to the archetypes that occurs in the process of individuation. If Hegel translates the "basic metaphor" into rational terms and Freud expresses this metaphor in the realm of sexuality and emotion, Jung, in his archetypal psychology, provides a version of the kabbalistic symbols that remains closest to their original, spiritual form.

Much more can and, in subsequent chapters, will be said regarding the parallels between the myths of Isaac Luria and the theories of Hegel, Freud, and Jung. However, what these four thinkers have in common is a philosophy of exile and redemption, in which the alienation of man and/or God is a necessary stage toward their ultimate realization. It is precisely because the dynamic of exile, alienation, restoration, and redemption so pervades modern consciousness that the metaphors of the Lurianic Kabbalah are likely to have great appeal today, not only to Hegelians, psychoanalysts, and Jungians, but to Marxists, Existentialists, and Deconstructionists. While a little over a century ago the great Jewish historian Heinrich Graetz could call the Kabbalah "the babble of a semi-idiot,"[14] today we are in a position to appreciate the Kabbalah on a deeper, more profound level than perhaps at any other time in the past. Our task in the following chapters will be to secure such an appreciation and understanding of the kabbalistic symbols by relating (and contrasting) them to more familiar symbols and notions in the history of ideas.

---

14. Heinrich Graetz, (1817–1891), the greatest historian of Judaism in the nineteenth century, also referred to Isaac Luria's "fantastic mysticism" and "the absurdities" of the *Zohar*, concluding that "the Lurian cabala wrought great mischief to Judaism" and "had a deteriorating effect upon morals." Heinrich Graetz, *Popular History of the Jews*, fifth ed. (New York: Hebrew Publishing, 1937), 4:442–450.

The Basic Symbols and Doctrines of the Kabbalah

THE HISTORICAL CONTEXT

Jewish tradition traces the Kabbalah into the far reaches of antiquity. While contemporary scholars date its origins to the last quarter of the twelfth century in the Jewish communities of Provence and Languedoc, France, it is clear that the early Kabbalists drew upon Jewish mystical traditions that were then at least centuries in the making. The Kabbalists, while devout Jews, drew freely upon Greek and Hellenistic thought as well, and a full understanding of both the origins and nature of the Kabbalah must draw upon Jewish and non-Jewish traditions and philosophies that antedate the Kabbalah by many centuries. My approach in this book is both historical and theoretical, and the reader should be familiar in general terms with the historical development of Jewish mysticism,[1] as well as the basic symbols and ideas of the theosophical Kabbalah. These topics are the subject of the present chapter. A general review of those traditions outside of Judaism with which the Kabbalah likely interacted is the subject of Chapter Three.

---

1. The historical development of the Kabbalah is discussed by Gershom Scholem in his *Origins of the Kabbalah*, trans. R. J. Zwi Werblowski (Princeton, NJ: Princeton University Press, 1987), originally published in 1962; Gershom Scholem, *Major Trends in Jewish Mysticism* (New York: Schocken, 1941); Scholem, *Kabbalah*, pp. 8–86; cf. Moshe Idel, *Kabbalah: New Perspectives* (New Haven: Yale University Press, 1988), and Idel, *Messianic Mystics*.

Table 1–1:
Some Important Dates in the History of Jewish Mysticism

Historical Phase	Original Source
Prophetic Judaism	eighth to sixth centuries B.C.E. Isaiah, Ezekiel, and Zechariah
Apocalyptic Judaism	third to second centuries B.C.E. I Enoch, Book of Daniel
Rabbinic Mysticism	c. first century C.E. Johanan Ben Zakkai and his disciples Early Christian Jewish Mystics
Merkaveh/ Hekhalot Mysticism	first to second century C.E. Book of Enoch, *Hekhalot Rabbatai* (The Greater Palaces), *Hekhalot Zutari* (The Lesser Palaces), and *Merkaveh Rabbah* (The Great Chariot)
	prior to the sixth century C.E. *Shi'r Koma* (Measure of the Body)
Pre- or proto- Kabbalistic Thought	third to the sixth century C.E. *Sefer Yetzirah* (The Book of Formation)
The Early Kabbalah	c. 1175–1200 C.E. *Sefer ha-Bahir* (The Book of Illumination)
	c. 1175–1200 C.E. School of Isaac The Blind
Hasidai Askenaz	Early thirteenth century C.E. Eleazar of Worms
Scholarship	Early thirteenth century C.E. The School of Gerona Azriel of Gerona, Ezra ben Solomon, Jacob ben Sheshet, Moses ben Nachman (Nachmanides)

Zohar	c. 1286, *Sefer ha-Zohar* (The Book of Splendor) is distributed by Moses deLeon, d. 1305. Traditionally attributed to Shimon bar Yochai (second century C.E.). More recently attributed to deLeon and his circle in thirteenth-century Spain.
	c. 1290, Joseph Gikatilla (1284–1325), *Sha'are Orah* (Gates of Light).
Christian Kabbalah	1517 Johannes Reuchlin (1455–1522) publishes *De Arte Cabalistica*, an early work of the Christian Kabbalah.
Safedian Kabbalists	c. 1550, Moses Cordovero (1522–1570), *Pardes Rimmonim* (The Orchard of Pomegranates), Safed.
Lurianic Kabbalah	c. 1569 Isaac Luria (1534–1572) arrives and begins teaching in Safed.
	c. 1620, Chayyim Vital's (1542–1640) works, including those that will later be edited as *Sefer Etz Chayyim*, begin to circulate in manuscript form.
	1666, Sabbatai Sevi (1626–1676) a Lurianic Kabbalist from Smyrna, and his "prophet" Nathan of Gaza, declare Sabbatai to be the Messiah.
	1730s, Moses Chayyim Luzzatto (1707–1746) writes *Kelah Pithei Chochmah*, a succinct outline of Lurianic Kabbalah.
Chasidism	1760, (d. 1772) Dov Baer of Mezhirech assumes leadership of early Hasidic movement after the death of the Baal Shem Tov. Author of *Maggid Devarev le-Ya'aqov*.
	1797 Schneur Zalman of Lyadi (1745–1813), the first Lubavitcher rebbe (Chabad) publishes *Likutei Amarim—Tanya*.

Table 1–1: (*continued*)
Some Important Dates in the History of Jewish Mysticism

	1821 Aharon Halevi Horowitz of Staroselye (1766–1828), Chabad theorist, publishes *Sha'arei ha-Avodah* (Gates of Worship).
Jewish Scholarship	1941 Gershom Scholem publishes his *Major Trends In Jewish Mysticism*.

DEVELOPMENT OF THE KABBALAH

Table 1 presents an outline of the important dates in the history of Jewish mysticism. According to contemporary scholarship, the Kabbalah evolved out of the mixture of the *Merkaveh* mysticism and Neoplatonism that dominated Jewish religious speculation during the early centuries of the Common Era. However, Jewish mysticism itself has its roots in the biblical tradition. For example, we find as early as Exodus 24:10, a description of God's abode that is relevant to the development of the kabbalistic doctrine of the *Sefirot*: "And they saw the God of Israel: and there was under his feet as it were a paved work of a sapphire (*Sapir*) stone, and as it were the body of heaven in his clearness." The earliest kabbalistic text, *Sefer ha-Bahir*, suggests an etymology of the term *Sefirah* in the Hebrew word for Sapphire (*Sapir*), reinterpreting the Psalm (19:2), "The heavens declare the glory of God" as "the heavens are radiant in the sapphirine radiance of the glory of God."[2]

In the Book of I Kings (22:19) and in the prophet Isaiah (e.g., 6:1–3) we find descriptions of the Lord resplendent on His throne and attended by His hosts, who fill the world with His praise. Such descriptions of the heavenly throne played an important role in the prophetic literature of the eighth to sixth centuries B.C.E. Descriptions of the seraphim and other heavenly beings in the "likeness of a man" (Ezekiel (I:4–28) not only had a direct impact upon the *Merkaveh* (chariot) mysticism of the early centuries of the common era, but provided proof-texts for later kabbalistic speculations.

---

2. *Sefer ha-Bahir*, sec. 87, *Book Bahir* (Scholem edition), trans. Joachim Neugroschel. In David Meltzer, ed., *The Secret Garden: An Anthology in the Kabbalah* (Barrytown, NY: Stanton Hill, 1998), p. 75.

Verman has distinguished among four periods of early Jewish mysticism.[3] The first, which extended from the eighth to the sixth centuries B.C.E., was the era of visionary experience, evident in the prophets *Isaiah, Ezekiel,* and *Zechariah.* The second period begins with the end of the Babylonian exile in the sixth century B.C.E., and reaches a high point in the third and second centuries B.C.E. During this period we see a growth in angelology, speculation on the origins of the universe and the creation of man, talk about the "end of days," and descriptions of the afterlife. Such mystical and apocalyptic themes are evident in the book of Daniel and first book of Enoch.

The third period of early Jewish mysticism reaches an apex in the middle of the first century C.E., and is evident not only in Jewish sources but also in the writings of the Christian Jew, Paul, and in the revelation of St. John. According to Verman the mystical ideas attributed to such Mishnaic teachers as Johanan ben Zakkai, Eliezer ben Hyrkanos, Akiva ben Joseph, and Ishmael, the "High Priest," belong to the same tradition of speculation as those of the early Christians. While mystical themes were certainly entertained by the rabbis of this period, the compiler of the Mishnah, Rabbi Judah, made every effort to exclude them, and they are therefore far more apparent in the *Tosefta,* a second mishnaic collection from this same period. The rabbis of the mishnaic and talmudic periods were reluctant to discuss mystical themes in public or commit them to writing. They held that there was a serious danger associated with mystical activity. In Tractate *Chagigah* 14b we find this famous warning:

> Our rabbis taught: Four men entered the garden, namely Ben Azzai and Ben Zoma, Acher and R. Akiba. R. Akiba said to them: When you arrive at the stones of pure marble, say not: Water, water.[4] For it is said: He that speaketh falsehood shall not be established before mine eyes (Psalms 101:7). Ben Azzai cast a look and died. Of him Scripture says: Precious in the eyes of the Lord is the death of His saints (Psalms 116:15). Ben Zoma looked and became demented. Of him Scripture says: Hast thou found

---

3. Verman, *The Books of Contemplation,* p. 8.

4. This is a veiled reference to the trials that the mystical adept experiences in his approach to the heavenly throne. One is provided with an illusion that he is being bombarded by millions of waves of water when he is only witnessing the glittering marble of the heavenly palace. If the adept asks about the meaning of the "water" he is deemed unworthy of the ascent and he is struck and wounded with iron bars. See Scholem, *Major Trends,* pp. 52–53.

honey? Eat as much as is sufficient for thee, lest thou be filled therewith and
vomit it (Proverbs 25:16). Acher mutilated the shoots [i.e., brought about
heresy]. [Only] R. Akiba went up unhurt, and went down unhurt.

While the Talmud is virtually silent on the nature of the mystic's visions
of ascent, other contemporary texts provide detailed accounts of these
matters. The major extant texts belonging to the period of *Merkaveh* or
Hekhalot (Palaces) mysticism probably date from the first and second
centuries C.E. However, they reflect traditions that are at least two centuries
older. Among the literary legacy of this period are the (Jewish) *Book of Enoch*,
Hekhalot Rabbati (The Greater Palaces), *Hekhalot Zutari* (The Lesser
Palaces), and *Merkaveh Rabbah* (The Great Chariot).[5] These texts, which are
variously said to show the influence of Greek, Persian, and Gnostic themes,
treat of the splendor, beauty, and transcendence of God, who reposes on a
celestial throne, attended by His heavenly hosts who sing His praise. Here we
learn of the *yored merkaveh*, the spiritual adept who ascends (literally and
paradoxically "descends") on the chariot, through the seven gates, past the
gatekeeping angels who attempt to deter him with fantastic and terrifying
illusions, to a vision of the throne and the countenance of God Himself.
Numerous angels are here described; in the *Book of Enoch* seven angelic
princes are said to be in charge of the seven heavens, and the angel Metatron
is the attendant to the throne, and the intermediary between God and the
world. We learn that Metatron receives a "crown" on which God, with a
finger like a flaming stylus, engraves the letters of creation. This notion of
God engraving the letters of creation will later play an important role in both
Sefer Yetzirah and the Zohar.

In *Hekhalot Zutari* we also see, in anticipation of later kabbalistic
themes, an emphasis on the theurgic and magical power of divine names. The
"transmission of the mystery" in *Merkaveh Rabbah* is indeed a mystical
knowledge of God's names. Further, in these works there is a description of
divine robes or garments, the vision of which, according to *Hekhalot
Rabbati*, is the goal of the mystical adept. In the Kabbalah divine "garments"
become an important metaphor for the *Sefirot*. Finally, in this literature we
find a development of the rabbinic theme that God is mystically dependent

---

5. See Peter Schaefer, *The Hidden and Manifest God: Some Major Themes in
Early Jewish Mysticism*, trans. Aubrey Pomerantz (Albany: State University of New
York Press, 1992).

upon man's liturgical praise, an idea that anticipates the Zohar's dictum that man can be said to "create" God.

The notion of a Primordial Man, which was later to play an important role in the Kabbalah, makes its first appearance in Jewish thought in the literature of *Merkaveh* mysticism.[6] A work entitled *Shi'ur Koma* (The Measure of [the Divine] Body), which dates from before the sixth century C.E., describes the ascent to the celestial throne and the vision of a gigantic supernal man imprinted with magical letters and names.[7]

Scholem regards the *Merkaveh/Hekhalot* literature as a Jewish form of gnosticism, parallel but not identical to the Christian (and other non-Jewish) Gnosticism of the second century C.E. According to Scholem, in the Merkaveh mystics we find "a Jewish variation on one of the chief preoccupations of the second and third century gnostics and hermetics: the ascent of the soul from earth, through the sphere of the hostile planet-angels and rulers of the cosmos, and its return to its divine home in the 'fullness' of God's light, a return which, to the gnostics' mind, signified redemption."[8] The earliest kabbalistic texts sought to establish a foundation in this older "Jewish gnosticism," borrowing many of its images and vocabulary, but grafting these upon a new cosmological and theosophical point of view, derived from Greek,[9] particularly Neoplatonic, thought.

The influence of Greek philosophical thought is evident in a pre-kabbalistic work, *Sefer Yetzirah* (The Book of Formation), written in Palestine in the third to sixth centuries C.E.,[10] and later the subject of

---

6. On Merkaveh mysticism see Gershom Scholem, *Jewish Gnosticism, Merkabah Mysticism and Talmudic Tradition* (New York: Schocken, 1965).

7. *Shi'ur Koma*, secs. 2 and 5. Translated as "Shiur Qoma" in Meltzer, *The Secret Garden*, pp. 23–37.

8. Scholem, *Major Trends*, p. 49.

9. The most important Jewish Neoplatonic philosopher, Philo of Alexandria (15–10 B.C.E.–C.E.), may have actually had little impact on the development of the Kabbalah. Philo was a Greek-speaking Jew who made efforts to synthesize the revealed religion of the Bible with Greek, particularly Platonic, thought. He proclaimed the unknowability of the divine essence and spoke of the mystic identification of man with the divine. Though Philo was unlikely to have been read in Jewish mystical circles, he was an important influence on Christian theology, and therefore a possible vehicle through which Platonic thought was indirectly transmitted to the Kabbalists.

10. Gershom Scholem, "Yezirah, Sefer," *Encyclopedia Judaica* (Jerusalem: Keter, 1972), 16:782ff.

numerous commentaries by the Kabbalists themselves. It is here that the doctrines of the *Sefirot* and the *Otiyot Yesod* (the Foundational letters), which later become central symbols of the Kabbalah, make their first appearance. As will be detailed in later chapters, these doctrines bear the stamp of the Platonic ideas. In *Yetzirah*, the *Sefirot* are supersensible numbers or metaphysical principles from which the world is created. The twenty-two *Otiyot Yesod* are conceptualized in similar terms, as archetypes from which God formed the cosmos. Together the *Sefirot* and the letters form the "thirty-two paths of wisdom" from which the world was "graved and hewed."

The Kabbalah proper is most often said to originate in the anonymously authored *Sefer HaBahir*, which appeared in Provence late in the twelfth century.[11] The *Bahir* is steeped in language mysticism and contains a further qualitative elaboration of the *Sefirot* doctrine. Here the *Sefirot* are described as "the highest crown," "Wisdom," "the quarry of the Torah," "the throne of splendor," etc. In this work *Merkaveh* and Greek elements are woven together in an almost *ad hoc* manner, and such familiar kabbalistic themes as the cosmic tree, *coincidentia oppositorum*, and the identification of God with the "All" make their appearance.

The Kabbalah of the school of Isaac the Blind also dates from this period. Isaac the Blind[12] is the first Kabbalist consistently to use the word "*Sefirot*" and to relate these cosmic archetypes to the biblical enumeration of God's traits in Chronicles 29:11, where reference is made to God's greatness, power, beauty, victory, majesty, and sovereignty. Each of these was eventually adopted (by at least some Kabbalists) in the ordering of the lowest seven *Sefirot*.

While the Kabbalah was first developing in France, another influential Jewish pietistic movement in Germany, the *Hasidai Ashkenaz*, developed mystical themes in a direction different than that of the Kabbalah. The most important figure in this movement, Eleazar of Worms (d. c. 1230) put forth a mystical theology in which the supreme *Kavod* ("Divine Glory") or *Shekhinah* ("Divine Presence") is a holy being issuing from God and which acts as a divine intermediary in directing the world. The Hasidai Ashkenaz developed a detailed demonology, placed an emphasis on magic, and

---

11. On *Sefer ha-Bahir* and the early Kabbalah in general see Gershom Scholem, *Origins of the Kabbalah*, esp. Ch. 2, pp. 49–198.

12. Joseph Dan, ed., *The Early Kabbalah*, texts trans. by Ronald C. Kieber (New York: Paulist Press, 1966), p. 94.

preached divine immanence in all things. Their influence was short-lived, but is detectable in certain of the Kabbalists, particularly those of the *Iyyun* circle.[13]

From Provence, the Kabbalah rapidly spread to Gerona and then Castille. Among the first Geronese Kabbalists of the early thirteenth century were Azriel, Ezra ben Solomon, Jacob ben Sheshet, and Moses ben Nachman (Nachmanides). In Azriel of Gerona we find a developed philosophical conception of the *Sefirot*, according to which they are the finite manifestations or powers of *Ein-Sof*, the Infinite Godhead. For Azriel, the *Sefirot* are a necessary part of God's totality and perfection, and they provide God with finite power to complement his infinite divine power.[14] They are "the force behind every existent being in the realm of plurality,"[15] and are one with *Ein-Sof*, in the sense that the flame, the sparks, and the aura are one with the fire. In Azriel we find a sophisticated doctrine of *coincidentia oppositorum*: the *Sefirot* and even *Ein-Sof* are regarded as the "union of everything and its oppposite."

Among the earlier Spanish Kabbalists, Joseph Gikatilla (1249–c.1325) of Castille and Moses de Leon (1240–1305) are the most significant. Gikatilla provided a detailed exposition of the *Sefirot*, connecting each with a biblical name of God. He further explored their metaphysical and ethical meaning through detailed exegesis of what he regarded to be hidden references to the *Sefirot* in scripture.

The Zohar, the *locus classicus* and, according to tradition, the most holy of kabbalistic works, was presumably "discovered" by Moses de Leon in 1286. De Leon attributed this work to the second-century rabbinic sage Shimon Bar Yohai, but many felt, as do most scholars today, that de Leon was its major author.[16] The main section of the Zohar is composed as a commentary on the Five Books of Moses, and this and several other additions (e.g., *Tikkunei ha-Zohar*) contain theosophical discourses on such topics as

---

13. On the *Iyyun* circle, see Verman, *The Books of Contemplation*.

14. Dan, *The Early Kabbalah*, p. 90.

15. Ibid., p. 91.

16. The main body of the Zohar, translated into English, appears in Sperling, Simon, and Levertoff, *The Zohar*. A more accessible treatment, in which translated sections of the Zohar have been grouped topically and explained through extensive introductions and annotations, is to be found in Tishby and Lachower, *The Wisdom of the Zohar: An Anthology of Texts*.

the hidden and manifest nature of God; the processes of creation; the *Sefirot* (which the Zohar calls by an abundance of other names); the nature of good and evil; the masculine and feminine aspects of the divine; the nature of death, sleep, and dreams; and the essence of the human soul.[17] The Zohar is not a systematic treatise, and its ideas must be pieced together from fragments from its numerous sections. Many of the ideas of the Lurianic Kabbalah are dynamic developments of concepts and symbols that first appear in the Zohar.

Much of the later history of the Kabbalah involves commentary, explication, and elaboration upon various zoharic themes. However, in the sixteenth century, in the town of Safed in Palestine, there developed a revival of kabbalistic speculation that is unparalleled in the history of Jewish mysticism. First, Moses Cordovero (1522–70), and later Isaac Luria (1534–1572) developed theosophical systems, which, though based in the Zohar, were highly original. Cordovero developed a standard ordering of the *Sefirot* and a sophisticated theory in which each of the *Sefirot* were said to be contained within each of the others. According to Cordovero, each entity in the world obtains its identity through the relative admixture of sefirotic elements from which it is comprised. Further, since the *Sefirot* are created in the image of God's divine traits, individuals are enjoined to develop the sefirotic qualities within their own souls.

While Cordovero left numerous writings, Luria wrote comparatively little, and it is through the works of his disciples, most notably Chayyim Vital (1543–1620) that we are aware of Luria's unique system of thought, the most complex, insightful, and difficult version of kabbalistic theosophy.

Among Luria's original contributions to the Kabbalah are the doctrines of *Tzimtzum* (Divine contraction and concealment), *Shevirat ha-Kelim* (The Breaking of the Vessels), and *Tikkun ha-Olam* (The Repair and Restoration of the World). In contrast to prior Kabbalists who had put forth either a linguistic or "emanationist" view of creation, Luria held that the world was created through a negative act of divine concealment, contraction, and

---

17. The main section of the Zohar is indeed a Torah commentary. Many other additional sections, however, that do not follow this outline are appended to or interspersed within the main commentary, some of which, such as *Tikkunei ha-Zohar* and *Raya Mehemna*, appear to anticipate certain Lurianic themes that are not present in the Zohar proper. On the various sections of the Zohar, see Tishby and Lachower, *The Wisdom of the Zohar*, Vol. 1, pp. 1–12.

withdrawal. Originally God's infinite being is "all," and it is only through a divine contraction that a void is formed within which finite things can subsist. This void becomes the metaphysical "space" in which *Ein-Sof* emanates an infinity of worlds and beings, the first and most significant of which is the Primordial Man (*Adam Kadmon*).

According to Luria the *Sefirot* are emanated as "lights" from the ears, nose, mouth, and eyes of the Primordial Man. These lights emanate and return, leaving behind a residue from which the "vessel" for each *Sefirah* is formed. A second light projected from the eyes of *Adam Kadmon* fills these vessels, completing the formation of each of the ten *Sefirot*: *Keter* (Crown) or *Ratzon* (Will), *Chochmah* (Wisdom), *Binah* (Understanding), *Chesed* (Loving-kindness), *Gevurah* (Strength) or *Din* (Judgment), *Tiferet* (Beauty) or *Rachamim* (Compassion), *Netzach* (Glory), *Hod* (Splendor), *Yesod* (Foundation), and *Malchut* (Kingship). The *Sefirot*, which are also conceptualized as the crown, brains, torso, and limbs of the Primordial Man, are the ten archetypal elements of the world. They are organized into a series of five "Worlds" (the Worlds of Primordial Man, "Nearness," "Creation," "Formation," and "Making"), the lowest of which, *Assiyah* or Making, provides the substance of our earth.

According to Luria the sefirotic vessels are unable to contain the light that was meant to fill them, and a majority of them are shattered, with the remainder (the upper three *Sefirot*) being "displaced." The result of this "Breaking of the Vessels" is that exile and discord holds sway throughout the cosmos. Shards from the broken vessels fall through the metaphysical void, entrapping sparks of divine light in "evil husks" (the *Kellipot*) that form the basis of the *Sitra Achra*, "the Other Side," a realm of evil, darkness, and death. Chaos reaches throughout the cosmos, as the masculine and feminine aspects of the deity, the Celestial "Mother" and "Father," represented by the *Sefirot Chochmah* and *Binah*, turn their backs on one another, disrupting the flow of divine energy throughout all the worlds.

Luria held that the restoration and repair of the broken vessels is largely in the hands of humankind. In freeing the divine sparks from the "Kellipot" and restoring them to God, and reestablishing the flow of masculine and feminine divine energies, man acts as a partner in the creation and redemption of the world, and is actually said to complete God Himself. *Tikkun ha-Olam*, the Restoration of the World, involves the reorganization of the broken vessels into a series of *Partzufim*, "Visages" or personality structures of God. According to Scholem, the *Partzufim* actually represent the evolution of the Primordial Man (*Adam Kadmon*) as it evolves toward a restored and redeemed world.[18]

Lurianic ideas were prominent in the seventeenth-century messianic movement surrounding Sabbatei Zevi in Poland.[19] They are clearly articulated in the kabbalistic works of Moses Chayyim Luzzatto (1707–1747)[20] and were also highly influential among the Hasidim, who interpreted the Kabbalah in philosophical and psychological terms. Such early Hasidim as Dov Baer of Mezhirech, who assumed leadership of the Hasidic movement from its founder, Israel Baal Shem Tov, in 1760; Schneur Zalman of Lyady (1745–1813), the first Lubavitcher rebbe; and his pupil Aharon Halevi Horowitz of Staroselye (1766–1728); made important contributions to and original elaborations upon the Lurianic symbols.[21]

THE BASIC DOCTRINES

The Kabbalah is not a single system of thought. If we conservatively date the advent of the Kabbalah to the appearance of *Sefer ha-Bahir* in Provence in the year 1180, the Kabbalah has evolved over eight centuries, has derived from the pen of hundreds of authors, and has been embodied in, perhaps, thousands of texts. It should therefore come as no surprise to learn that there is no single Kabbalah, but a diversity of *Kabbalahs* that vary according to individual authors and schools. Indeed, given the Kabbalah's vast range and diversity, it would be misleading to regard the Kabbalah as a single doctrine or philosophy. Nevertheless, looking back over the centuries one can point to a remarkable coherence in basic problems, symbols, and ideas. This is

---

18. Scholem, *Kabbalah*, p. 142.

19. Gershom Scholem, *Sabbatai Sevi: The Mystical Messiah*, trans. R. J. Zwi Werbloski (Princeton, NJ: Princeton University Press, 1973), Chapter I.

20. In English see Moses Luzzatto, *General Principles of the Kabbalah*, trans. Phillip Berg (Jerusalem: Research Centre of Kabbalah, 1970).

21. Many regard the Hasidic elaborations upon Lurianic themes to constitute a virtually new form of mystical thought. My own position, as outlined in my *Symbols of the Kabbalah*, is that the Hasidic interpretations, particularly those of Chabad, remain within the meaning structure of Lurianic theosophy. At any rate, their philosophical and psychological interpretations of Lurianic symbols are of great relevance to any modern attempt to find significance in these symbols.

especially true with regard to the main object of the present study, the *theosophical* Kabbalah; the Kabbalah of the Zohar, Moses Cordovero, Isaac Luria, and their adherents; a Kabbalah that seeks to *understand and describe* the divine realm and its relationship to the finite world. However, even the *ecstatic* Kabbalah, which seeks to achieve *a mystical union* with God, and the *magico-theurgical* Kabbalah, which seeks to influence the divine realm, share a basic theological and theosophical vocabulary and symbolology that forms the basis for their practice.[22] While there are certainly major differences in both symbols and doctrine even among the theosophical Kabbalists, there is nonetheless a discernible common tradition, and it is thus possible to speak of the "Kabbalah's" basic doctrines and symbols without being overly misleading.

Scholem has spoken of two major stages in the development of the theosophical Kabbalah. The first, which focused upon the theory of the ten divine archetypes, the *Sefirot*, includes all of the Kabbalists through Moses Cordovero (mid-sixteenth-century Safed). Major works in this stage include *Sefer ha-Bahir*, the Zohar, Gikatilla's *Sh'are Orah*, and Cordovero's *Pardes Rimmonim* (Garden of Pomegranites). The second stage of the theosophical Kabbalah, which is identified with Isaac Luria (1534–1572) and his followers, is firmly rooted in the earlier accounts of the Infinite God (*Ein-Sof*) and the *Sefirot*, but adds a distinctive dynamic dimension to these accounts, one that was only implicit in the Zohar and related works. This dynamic dimension involves the introduction of the symbols of *Tzimtzum* (the divine contraction/concealment that permitted the emergence of a separate, finite world), *Shevirat ha-Kelim* (the destruction of the originally emanated *Sefirot* that resulted in our current world of alienation and evil), and *Tikkun* (the restoration and redemption of the world, in part through the spiritual and ethical activities of mankind). In spite of their differences, these two stages in the development of theosophical Kabbalah also have a great deal in common. According to Moshe Idel:

> If we disregard academic rhetoric . . . Lurianism and zoharic Kabbalah are much closer than we expect . . . The fascination with a complex theology haunted by syzygies, sexual couplings, emanations, and questions

---

22. The useful distinction among theosophical, ecstatic, and magical-theurgical Kabbalah is found in Moshe Idel, *Hasidism: Between Ecstasy and Magic* (Albany: State University of New York Press, 1995), p. 31.

of good and evil, is common to the two forms of Jewish theosophy. They are two forms or versions, of one basic structure.[23]

To Scholem's two stages in the development of the theosophical Kabbalah I would add a third, and perhaps even a fourth. The third stage is found in the interpretations, both philosophical and psychological, that were given to the Kabbalah by the Hasidim during the eighteenth and nineteenth centuries. The Hasidim are said to have simplified the Kabbalah for the masses, and to have frequently used kabbalistic terminology to express ideas that were foreign to the Kabbalists themselves.[24] However, many of their interpretations, particularly of such notions as *Tzimtzum, Shevirah, Kellipot*, and *Tikkun*, can be said to have uncovered or distilled much of what was most profound in the Lurianic tradition.[25]

The fourth stage in the development of the Kabbalah is our own. The advent of modern Kabbalah scholarship in the twentieth century has led to the opening of the Kabbalah to those who, in previous ages, would never have been exposed to its doctrines and symbols. For better or worse, the Kabbalah is for the first time interacting significantly with popular and scholarly secular thought. While the Kabbalah had earlier been brought to the attention of certain European intellectuals through the writings of the so-called Christian Kabbalists, e.g., Johann Reuchlin and Knorr Von Rosenroth, it is only in our century that the Kabbalah has had an opportunity to interact significantly with Western culture. The writings of Gershom Scholem, Isaiah Tishby, Moshe Idel, and numerous others have begun to bring kabbalistic symbols and ideas into common intellectual discourse, and dozens of popular books on the Kabbalah have brought (sometimes distorted) kabbalistic ideas into both Jewish and secular popular culture. The present work is part of this "fourth stage," and it is the author's hope that the kabbalistic tradition will both enhance and be enhanced by the wider cultural currents to which it is now being exposed.

Here I will provide a general overview of the symbols and ideas of the theosophical Kabbalah. My overview does not claim to be completely

---

23. Idel, *Hasidism*, p. 234.

24. Rachel Elior, *The Paradoxical Ascent to God: The Kabbalistic Theosophy of Habad Hasidism*, trans. J. M. Green (Albany: State University of New York Press, 1993), p. 5.

25. I have considered the relationship between Kabbalah and Hasidism in Chapters One and Three of my *Symbols of the Kabbalah*.

objective. Rather, it is modeled upon my reading of the Lurianic theosophy, and its development in the hands of both the later Kabbalists and Hasidim. In particular, I have been greatly influenced in my reading of the Kabbalah by the writings of such *Chabad* Hasim as Schneur Zalman of Lyadi.[26] While I have also drawn extensively upon the Zohar and other pre-Lurianic material, especially in my discussion of *Ein-Sof* and the *Sefirot*, I have integrated these perspectives (as the Lurianists themselves did) into the overall Lurianic scheme. This scheme not only provides the best vehicle for the comparative studies that comprise this book; but it is the Lurianic Kabbalah that, on my view, is the most relevant to the spiritual concerns of contemporary man. I have, as will become evident, been unavoidably and gratefully influenced by the authors of the "fourth stage" in the development of the Kabbalah, for it is contemporary scholarship that has made this complex material accessible to the kind of philosophical and psychological examination and critique that I have pursued here and in my other works.

EIN-SOF: THE KABBALIST'S ABSOLUTE

Any discussion of the ideas and symbols of the Kabbalah must begin, and also end, with the Kabbalist's absolute, *Ein-Sof*. The Kabbalists of Provence and Spain adopted the term *Ein-Sof* (roughly, "without end") to denote what they conceived to be the infinite, completely unknowable God. Although a number of other words were used to designate the kabbalistic absolute, including the terms "superfluity" (Hebrew: *Yitron*, a translation of the Neoplatonic "hyperousia"), "indistinguishable unity" or the "complete indistinguishability of opposites" (Hebrew: *ha-achdut ha-shavah*), and "the essence" (*ha-mahut*),[27] *Ein-Sof* became the appellation of choice in the Zohar and the later theosophical Kabbalah.

The Kabbalists formally practiced what is known today as "negative theology," utilizing several expressions (e.g., "the concealment of secrecy," "the concealed light," "that which thought cannot contain," etc.[28]) to signify that *Ein-Sof* is beyond human knowledge and comprehension. According to the Kabbalist R. Azriel of Gerona (early thirteenth century), it

26. See, for example, Schneur Zalman, *Likutei-Amarim-Tanya*, bilingual edition (Brooklyn, NY: Kehot Publication Society, 1981).

27. Scholem, *Kabbalah*, p. 88.

28. Ibid., p. 89.

is *Ein-Sof*'s very infinitude that makes it incomprehensible: "*Ein-Sof* cannot be an object of thought, let alone of speech, even though there is an indication of it in everything, for there is nothing beyond it. Consequently, there is no letter, no name, no writing, and no word that can comprise it."[29] God is unknowable, according to Azriel, precisely because he is "without end," and hence there is no outside point of view from which he can be circumscribed and made into an object. Some Kabbalists adopted the Neoplatonic view that *Ein-Sof* is unknowable even to itself. The Zohar, which at times identifies *Ein-Sof* with the first *Sefirah*, *Keter*, speaks of *Keter* as "that which knows but does not know," and holds that none of the *Sefirot* are in a position to perceive *Ein-Sof*.[30]

Like the Kabbalists before them, the Lurianists affirmed the total unknowability of the absolute. According to Vital the very word *Ein-Sof* "indicates that there is no grasping Him, neither by apprehension nor by any thought whatever; He is abstracted and separate from all thoughts."[31] Nevertheless, the Kabbalists frequently made use of a variety of phrases that characterized their absolute in more positive terms, e.g., "Root of all roots," "Indifferent Unity," "Great Reality,"[32] such terms signifying that *Ein-Sof*, like the God of the biblical tradition, is the *origin* of the world, the *reality* of the world, or the *totality* of all things. For a variety of reasons, including a desire to bridge the gap between *Ein-Sof* and the personal God of traditional Judaism, the Kabbalists were quite daring in their speculations regarding the inner workings of the Godhead, sometimes paying little heed to the admonition of the proto-kabbalistic work *Sefer Yetzirah*, which had advised that with respect to the absolute one should "restrain your mouth from speaking and your heart from thinking, and if your heart runs let it return to its place."[33] None of the Kabbalists openly take issue with this axiom, but

29. Tishby and Lachower, *The Wisdom of the Zohar*, Vol. 1, p. 234.

30. Zohar II, 239a; Tishby and Lachower, *The Wisdom of the Zohar*, Vol. 1, p. 257; see also p. 233.

31. Chayyim Vital, *Sefer Ez Chayyim*, as translated by Immanuel Schochet in "Mystical Concepts in Hasidism," appendix to Zalman, *Likutei-Amarim-Tanya*, p. 830, note 12.

32. Scholem, *Major Trends*, p. 12.

33. *Sefer Yetzirah*, I, 8. As translated in Tishby and Lachower, *The Wisdom of the Zohar*, Vol. 1, p. 234. See also Aryeh Kaplan, *Sefer Yetzirah: The Book of Creation*, rev. ed. (York Beach, ME: Samuel Weiser, 1997), p. 66. *Sefer Yetzirah* is also translated in Meltzer, *The Secret Garden*, pp. 41–48.

many, particularly the Lurianists, outline a theosophy that purports to set forth the inner nature of the godhead. We thus arrive at the first of many dialectical tensions in kabbalistic thought, between God's total ineffability and his knowability to humankind.[34] It is typical of the Kabbalah that rather than choosing between two poles of an apparent opposition, both are accepted as words of the living God, on the principle that God himself is *ha-achdut ha-shavah*, a coincidence of opposites.

The majority of Kabbalists held that the personal, creator God of the Bible is at some remove from *Ein-Sof*, and many refer to *Ein-Sof* as an impersonal "that," rather than a personal "thou" or "who."[35] According to one anonymous Kabbalist: "*Ein-Sof* is not even alluded to in the Torah or in the prophets, or in the hagiographers or in the words of the sages; only the mystics received a small indication of it."[36]

EIN-SOF AND NOTHINGNESS

The Kabbalists frequently identify *Ein-Sof* with "Nothingness."[37] There is, according to the Kabbalists, an awesome power in negation. According to Azriel, in mystical prayer the individual is able to "lead the world back to its origin—literally to its Nought," a nought that provides the self with the "power for its own existence."[38]

The Kabbalists, however, also identify *Ein-Sof* with the totality of all worlds and all being, and the *coincidentia oppositorum* that follows from the Kabbalist's identification of *Ein-Sof* with both nothing and everything led

---

34. On the dialectic between *Ein-Sof*'s ineffability and knowability see Steven T. Katz, "Utterance and Ineffability in Jewish Neoplatonism," in *Neoplatonism in Jewish Thought* ed. Lenn E. Goodman (Albany: State University of New York Press, 1992), pp. 279–298.

35. Scholem, *Kabbalah*, p. 90.

36. Scholem, *Origins of the Kabbalah*, p. 443. Cf. Scholem, *Kabbalah*, p. 88. The anonymous author of the kabbalistic work *Ma'arkhelut ha-Elohut* went so far as to say that *Ein-Sof* cannot be identified with God or serve as an object of religious thought.

37. Strictly speaking it is not *Ein-Sof* itself but *Keter*, the first *Sefirah*, and *Ein-Sof*'s primal manifestation, which is identified with nothingness. Of *Ein-Sof* not even "nothing" can be predicated. However, the Kabbalists speak in a manner that suggests the predication of "nothingness" to the essence of the deity itself.

38. Scholem, *Origins of the Kabbalah*, p. 416.

them to hold that *Ein-Sof* includes and transcends both existence and nonexistence.[39] The Zohar affirms that apart from its connection with creation *Ein-Sof* "has no name of His own at all."[40] However, this nameless God who, as such is a "nothingness" *without significance* is also "the cause of all causes,"[41] and the source of all meaning and significance whatsoever.

A *coincidentia oppositorum* between being and nothingness is referred to directly in Azriel's work on the *Sefirot*:

> He who brings forth Being from Nought is thereby lacking nothing, for the Being is in the Nought after the manner of the Nought, and the Nought is in the Being after the manner [according to the modality] of the Being. And the author of the Book of *Yetzirah* said: He made his Nought into his Being, and did not say: He made the Being from the Nought. This teaches us that the Nought is the Being and Being is the Nought.[42]

Both being and nothingness are also equally present in the creation of the world. According to the Kabbalist R. Joseph Ben Scholem of Barcelona (c. 1300) there is no change, alteration, transformation, or creation, in which the abyss of nothingness is not crossed and for "a fleeting mystical moment becomes visible."[43]

THE ETERNAL WILL

The Kabbalists identified the deity with the Supernal Will and associated this will with their characterization of *Ein-Sof* as "Nothingness." The Kabbalist Joseph Gikatila held that the relationship between nothingness and "will" is present in the Hebrew words meaning "nothingness" and "I." As we will see

39. See Moshe Idel, "Jewish Kabbalah and Platonism in the Middle Ages and Renaissance," in *Neoplatonism and Jewish Thought* ed. Lenn E. Goodman (Albany: State University of New York Press, 1992), p. 344. See Sarah Heller-Wilinsky, "Isaac ibn Latif—Philosopher or Kabbalist," in *Jewish Medieval and Renaissance Studies* ed. Alexander Altmann (Cambridge, MA: Harvard University Press, 1967), p. 344.

40. Zohar III, 225a, *Raya Mehemma*; Tishby and Lachower, *The Wisdom of the Zohar*, Vol. 1, p. 259.

41. Zohar I, 22b *Tikkunei ha*-Zohar, as quoted in Tishby and Lachower, *The Wisdom of the Zohar*, Vol. 1, p. 258.

42. Scholem, *Origins of the Kabbalah*, p. 423.

43. Scholem, *Major Trends*, p. 217.

later in this chapter, the Kabbalists held the essence of a thing to be embodied in the letters of which its name is composed. Gikatilia points out that the same consonants (AYN) enter into *Ayin* (nothing) and *Ani* (I), suggesting that *Ayin*, nothingness, undergoes a dialectical transformation to become *Ani*, the primordial "I" or will.[44] The Zohar itself identifies the nothingness of *Ein-Sof* with the Supernal Will: "that which knows but does not know (i.e., *Ein-Sof*) is none but the Supernal Will, the secret of all secrets. *Ayin* (nothing)."[45]

THOUGHT AND WISDOM

According to Scholem the history of the Kabbalah involves a struggle between views that see *Ein-Sof* in intellectual as opposed to volitional terms. While the earlier Kabbalists, such as the author of *Sefer ha Bahir* and Isaac the Blind, generally gave priority to "thought," later Kabbalists, beginning with the Zohar, placed a primary emphasis upon "will." However, in the Zohar we find both trends. For example, in its commentary on Genesis, the Zohar suggests that *Ein-Sof* is the "hidden recess of thought," and that its first manifestation is the "hidden Supernal Thought."[46] In another Zohar passage, Rabbi Simon relates that all the "lights which proceed from the mystic supreme thought are called *Ein-Sof*." Here the Zohar proclaims that *Ein-Sof* actually proceeds from an intellectual absolute and that *Ein-Sof* is the "nine lights of thought" that emanate from a certain fragment of the "unknown."[47]

"Will" and "Thought" are given equal status in the following zoharic passage: "Desire, which is Thought, is the beginning of all things . . ."[48]

THE PRIMORDIAL POINT AND "FAITH"

There is considerable speculation in the Zohar and other kabbalistic works regarding the "primordial point" of being, which presumably arose when *Ein-Sof* thought or willed the world into existence. This point is equated with

44. Ibid., p. 218.

45. Zohar II, 239a, Tishby and Lachower, *The Wisdom of the Zohar*, Vol. 1, p. 257.

46. Zohar I, 21a, Sperling and Simon, *The Zohar*, Vol. 1, p. 89.

47. Zohar I, 65a, Sperling and Simon, *The Zohar*, Vol. 1, p. 213.

48. Zohar I, 200a, Sperling and Simon, *The Zohar*, Vol. 2, p. 259.

the "beginning" spoken of in the first word of Genesis. According to the Zohar, in the beginning "there shone forth a supernal and mysterious point."

> Beyond that point there is no knowable, and therefore it is called *Reshith* (beginning), the creative utterance which is the starting-point of all.[49]

In the Zohar and other kabbalistic writings this point is identified as the "mystical seed of creation"[50] or equated with Divine Wisdom (*Chochmah*). According to the Zohar: "When the most Mysterious wished to reveal Himself, He first produced a single point which was transmuted into a thought."[51]

An interesting interpretation of the mystical point is provided by Azriel, when he says:

> . . . the place at which the Being is linked to the point where, from the Nought, it begins to have existence is called "faith" (*emunah*). For faith is not related to a visible and apprehensible Being, nor to the invisible and unknowable Nought, but precisely to the place where the Nought is connected to Being.[52]

For Azriel, "faith," which is normally spoken of as an interior, psychological act, is elevated to the primary principle of creation.

COINCIDENTIA OPPOSITORUM: THE INDISTINGUISHABLE UNITY OF OPPOSITES

In discussing the nature of *Ein-Sof*, Azriel states that "it is the principle in which everything hidden and visible meet, and as such it is the common root of both faith *and unbelief*" (my italics).[53] According to Azriel *Ein-Sof*, in its infinity, is the union of all opposites and contradictions, and the *Sefirot*, the archetypes through which *Ein-Sof* emanates the world, involve the union of

---

49. Zohar I, 15a; Sperling and Simon, *The Zohar*, Vol. 1, p. 63. See also Scholem, *Major Trends*, p. 219.

50. Scholem, *Major Trends*, p. 219.

51. Zohar I, 2a, Sperling and Simon, *The Zohar*, Vol. 1, p. 6.

52. Scholem, *Origins of the Kabbalah*, p. 423.

53. Ibid., pp. 441–442.

"everything and its opposite."[54] Johann Reuchlin, who was one of the first to introduce the Kabbalah into the Christian West, placed special emphasis on Azriel's conception that "non-Being is Being, and that Being is non-Being." On Reuchlin's paraphrase of Azriel, *Ein-Sof* is "all that to our rational minds seems contrary and self-contradictory."[55]

The idea that *Ein-Sof* is a union of opposites is given (by Azriel and others) the Hebrew term *ha-achdut hashawah*, which denotes a *coincidentia oppositorum*, an equivalence of the divine substance in all aspects of the cosmos including those that are opposed to or contradict one another.[56] This concept plays a major role in kabbalistic, and later in Hasidic, theology. It suggests an equivalence and reciprocity between such opposites as faith and unbelief, theism and atheism, man and God, the absolute and creation, the world and the mind, and a whole host of other contraries that in nondialectical systems of thought are held to be mutually exclusive.

According to Elior, the concept of "equalization" of opposites in the godhead, while present throughout the Kabbalah, achieves a complete expression in Chabad Hasidism where the *ha-achdut hashawah* is understood to be characteristic of all things and all time. According to the Chabad thinker R. Aaron Ha-Levi :

the revelation of anything is actually through its opposite[57]

All created things in the world are hidden within His essence, be He blessed, in one potential, in *coincidentia oppositorum* . . .[58]

According to Rabbi Dov Baer:

"within everything is its opposite and also it is truly revealed as its opposite."[59]

---

54. Dan, *The Early Kabbalah*, p. 94.

55. Johann Reuchlin, *De Arte Cabalistica* [On the Art of the Kabbalah], trans. Martin and Sarah Goodman (Lincoln: University of Nebraska Press, 1993), p. 122.

56. See Rachel Elior, "Chabad: The Comtemplative Ascent to God," in *Jewish Spirituality: From the Sixteenth Century Revival to the Present*, ed. Arthur Green (New York: Crossroads, 1987), p. 164.

57. Quoted in Elior, *The Paradoxical Ascent to God*, p. 64.

58. Quoted in Elior, "Chabad," p. 163.

59. Rabbi Dov Baer, *Ner Mitzvah ve-Torah Or* II, fol. 6a. Quoted in Elior, *The Paradoxical Ascent to God*, p. 64.

For the Chabad Hasidim, it is precisely the unity of opposites that provides for the *shelemut* or completeness of *Ein-Sof* itself: "For the principal point of divine completeness is that . . . in every thing is its opposite, and . . . that all its power truly comes from the opposing power, and, according to the strength of the opposing power, thus the power of its opposite will be found truly."[60] Within the godhead, the contradictory nature of earthly oppositions are nullified. According to R. Aaron: "He is the perfection of all, for the essence of perfection is that even those opposites which are opposed to one another be made one."[61] It is interesting to note that these Chabad authors (Dov Baer, Aaron Ha-Levi) writing in the Lurianic tradition were contemporaries of Hegel, who through his version of the dialectic, sought to overcome logical and historical oppositions in a philosophy of the "Absolute." In later chapters we will see how close the Kabbalah and Hasidim come to achieving a fully Hegelian conception of the dialectic.

THE *COINCIDENTIA* BETWEEN GOD AND WORLD

The Kabbalists held that just as God sustained the existence of all the worlds, the world we live in is absolutely necessary for the "completion" of God. In the opening of *Sefer Etz Chayyim*, Vital quotes the view that

> The purpose for the creation was that the Blessed One had to complete in all of his deeds and His powers, and all of his names of greatness, perfection and honor. If he had not brought forth his deeds and his powers, He could not have been called complete, so to speak, either in his actions or in His names or in His attributes.[62]

On the Kabbalists' view the divine essence is an abstract nothingness until the divine traits, represented in the *Sefirot*, are actualized in a finite and material world. It is, for example, only when a living Abraham expresses hospitality to strangers that the divine attribute of *Chesed* (Kindness) goes from a potential to an actual trait.

---

60. Rabbi Dov Baer, *Ner Mitzvah ve-Torah Or* II, fol. 6a. Quoted in Elior, *The Paradoxical Ascent to God*, p. 64.

61. Quoted in Elior, "Chabad," p. 166.

62. *Sefer Etz Chayyim* 1:1. Donald Wilder Menzi and Zwe Padeh, trans., *The Tree of Life: Chayyim Vital's Introduction to the Kabbalah of Isaac Luria, The Palace of Adam Kadmon* (Northvale, NJ: Jason Aronson, 1999), p. 3.

The Kabbalists held that both God and the World are integral to the absolute totality, which is *Ein-Sof*, and that it is somewhat arbitrary as to which point in that totality we take as the beginning. According to the Zohar: "Just as the Supernal Wisdom is a starting point of the whole, so is the lower world also a manifestation of Wisdom, and a starting point of the whole."[63] According to Rabbi Schneur Zalman of Lyadi, the first Lubavitcher rebbe, depending upon our perspective either the finite world appears real and the divine realm is nothingness, or the divine realm is real and the finite and material are nothing:

> (Looking) upwards from below, as it appears to eyes of flesh, the tangible world seems to be Yesh and a thing, while spirituality, which is above, is an aspect of Ayin (nothingness). (But looking) downwards from above the world is an aspect of Ayin, and everything which is linked downwards and descends lower and lower is more and more Ayin and is considered as naught truly as nothing and null.[64]

For the Kabbalists, any worthwhile conception of *Ein-Sof* must include both God and the world. Indeed it must include all perspectives, and ultimately all things. In fact, although the Lurianists, for example, begin their exposition with *Ein-Sof* and then go on to describe cosmic entities and events (e.g., the *Sefirot*, the Foundational Letters, the Breaking of the Vessels, the evil realm of the *Kellipot*, *Partzufim*, humankind, and *Tikkun*), their conception of *Ein-Sof* is not complete until each of these entities and moments have been fully described and understood. For the Kabbalists, particularly the followers of Isaac Luria, *Ein-Sof* is not just the hidden, supernal beginning of all things, it is also the end and every point along the way. As *Sefer Yetzirah* and numerous Kabbalists since have affirmed, the essence of God's attributes, the *Sefirot*, is that "their end is imbedded in their beginning and their beginning in their end."[65]

The Lurianic Kabbalists took this idea to mean that the very origin of the cosmos, *Ein-Sof*, is dependent upon the so-called endpoint of the deity's development in *Tikkun ha-Olam*, and conversely that *Ein-Sof* contains within its original ineffability the entire progression from *Tzimtzum* to *Sefirot*, to

---

63. Zohar I, 153a; Sperling and Simon, *The Zohar*, Vol. 2, pp. 89–90.
64. Likutei Torah, *Devarim*, fol. 83a. Translated and quoted in Elior, *The Paradoxical Ascent to God*, p. 137–138.
65. *Sefer Yetzirah* 1:7, Kaplan, *Sefer Yetzirah*, p. 57.

the Breaking of the Vessels, etc., which leads to that endpoint in *Tikkun ha-Olam* (the redemption of the world). The entire system of creation, exile, and alienation, restoration and redemption, both in the abstract and as it is enacted in history, is, for Luria and his followers, the fullest expression of *Ein-Sof*. Indeed, it is only through the world's creation and redemption that *Ein-Sof* is transformed from a hidden and abstract being into a personal God.[66]

THE NECESSITY OF THE WORLD

I will now explore these ideas in more detail. For the Kabbalists, the creation of a finite world is both the will of God and an event that is part of God's very being and essence. The world is both independent of and fully contained within the godhead. The world's unique character actually results from two "crises," or negations within the godhead. The first results in *Ein-Sof*'s concealment and contraction (*Tzimtzum*), and creates a metaphysical space within which the finite universe can subsist. The second crisis brings about the world's "deconstruction" (*Shevirah*, the "Breaking of the Vessels") resulting in the imperfect, material, and corruptible nature of all finite existence. The *Shevirah* is a logically necessary event, the function of which is to splinter the cosmos into an infinite array of independent fragments that must ultimately be reunited through the process of *Tikkun*.[67] In the Lurianic Kabbalah, the fullest expression of divinity requires that *Ein-Sof* enter into a circular dynamic in which it becomes finite and particular only to have this finitude and particularity reunited with its infinite source. As Rabbi Aaron Ha Levi puts it:

> . . . the essence of His intention is that his *coincidentia* be manifested in concrete reality, that is, that all realities and their levels be revealed in actuality, each detail in itself, and that they nevertheless be unified and joined in their value, that is, that they be revealed as separated essences, and that they nevertheless be unified and joined in their value.[68]

We will see that the kabbalistic ideas regarding the mutual interdependence between the finite and the infinite, between God and man, are

---

66. Scholem, *Major Trends*, p. 215.
67. Elior, "Chabad," p. 165.
68. Ibid., p. 167.

paralleled in the philosophy of Hegel. Hegel, like the Kabbalists, held that the Absolute must alienate itself in finitude only to return to itself in a higher level of perfection. For Hegel, as for the Kabbalists, this self-alienation has several functions. First, it enables the Infinite to come to know itself through the confrontation with and gaze of an "other." As Vital puts it: "if there was no one in the world who could receive [God's] mercy how could He be called merciful?"[69] Second it allows the Infinite to actualize its full potential through the proliferation of an infinite array of finite particulars. Finally, in creating man in an "evil" world, an aspect of *Ein-Sof* (i.e., humankind) is faced with the material, intellectual, spiritual, and moral adversity that enables it to make those choices that fully actualize the values (the *Sefirot*) that lie at its very core.[70]

MAN MAKES "THE ONE ABOVE"

The Zohar affirms that man is not only a partner with God in creation, but that he also has the opportunity to actually *make* his creator. Adapting the wording of a rabbinic text,[71] the Zohar affirms: "He who 'keeps' the precepts of the Law and 'walks' in God's ways, if one may say so, 'makes' Him who is above."[72]

Further, we read in the kabbalistic text *Sefer ha Yichud*: "each and every one [of the people of Israel] ought to write a scroll of Torah for himself, and the occult secret [of this matter] is that he made God Himself."[73] It is in forming a relationship with the Absolute through deeds and prayer, that humanity creates God as a personal Being and also completes God by enabling God to become Himself. The Hasidim saw in the "nothingness" of *Ein-Sof* an infinite potential to be shaped by man. According to R. Levi Yitzhak:

---

69. *Sefer Etz Chayyim* 1:2, p. 24. Menzi and Padeh, *The Tree of Life*, p. 24.

70. See M. C. Luzzatto, *General Principles of the Kabbalah*, trans. Phillip Berg (Jerusalem: Research Centre of Kabbalah, 1970, pp. 247–249.

71. *Midrash Levitticus Rabbah*, 35:6.

72. Zohar III, 113a; Sperling and Simon, *The Zohar*, Vol. 5, p. 153. Idel translates this passage as follows: "Whoever performs the commandments of the Torah and walks in its ways is regarded as if he made the one above." Idel, *Kabbalah: New Perspectives*, p. 187.

73. Idel, *Kabbalah: New Perspectives*, p. 188.

The Nought is the most general category of all the wisdoms because it is a potential power that may receive [every] form. And when man wants to cause the descent of wisdom from there, as well as anything else, it depends only on the will of man, because if he wants to worship God he can draw down [Him] upon himself.[74]

THE WORLD IS AN ILLUSION

As we have seen, from one perspective the world and humanity is fully actual and real, while God is a mere abstraction until He is actualized in the world. However, the predominant emphasis in the Kabbalah is on the precise opposite perspective. In this view God is the one true substance and the world is relatively insubstantial or, more radically, a mere epiphenomena or illusion. Again, this latter view is given its clearest expression in the writings of the Chabad Hasidim. For example, according to R. Aaron Ha-Levi:

> For there exists in the world no entity other than Him . . . for there is no true substance other than Him. For if because of the vessels and conceal-ments, other entities appear to be substantial, in reality they are not substantial at all, for He, may He be blessed, is the substance of all substances, and there exists in reality, no other substance but Him.[75]

While the Lurianic Kabbalists held that finite things participate *peripherally* in the substance of *Ein-Sof*,[76] the Chabad Hasidim, by denying any substanti-ality to the created world, carried the Lurianic position to its logical conclusion. While at times these Hasidim distinguished between substance (*yeshut*) and existence (*qiyyum*), (holding that finite things have "existence" but no "substance") they generally denied even "existence" to the created world:

> Even though it appears to us that the worlds exist, this is a total lie.[77]

---

74. R. Levi Yitzchak, *Kedushat Levi*, fol. 6a–6b, quoted in Idel, *Hasidism*, p. 141.
75. R. Aaron Ha-Levi, *Sha'arey ha-Yihud veha-Emunah*, 1:2, Elior, "Chabad," p. 161.
76. Scholem, *Kabbalah*, p. 149.
77. Schneur Zalman, *Torah Or* 86b, see Elior, *The Paradoxical Ascent to God*, p. 55.

Everything is absolutely as nothing and nought.[78]

He is One Alone and there is no reality whatsoever apart from Him.[79]

QUIETISM AND ACTIVISM

One might suppose the idea that the world (or at least our world) is an illusion would nurture "escapist" trends within the Kabbalah that might be regarded as "Gnostic" or otherwordly. Indeed, there were such "quietist" elements within the Kabbalah, and certain Hasidim spoke of dissolving one's attachments to the worldly ego and cleaving only to an otherworldly God on high. However, these trends were more than balanced by a more typical Jewish embrace of the natural, experiential realm. Rather than escape this world, the Kabbalists and Hasidim *sought to spiritualize it*, by drawing down energy from on high. Indeed, as elsewhere there is a *coincidentia oppositorum* in their views on "quietism" and "activism" in religion. The Chabad Hasidim, for example, sought to repair this world by transcending it and to transcend this world by being wholly immersed in its restoration. The founder of Chabad, Schneur Zalman of Lyadi, describes such a twofold divine service as follows: "Just as one annihilates oneself from Being to Nothingness, so too (divine light) is drawn down from above from Nothingness to Being, so that the light of the infinite may emanate truly below as it does above."[80]

INFINITE INTERPRETABILITY

A corollary to the kabbalistic view that *Ein-Sof* (and hence the *Sefirot* and the world) unites within itself all opposing perspectives, is a view of the world's infinite interpretability. According to the Kabbalists, the Kabbalah is itself in constant flux along with the cosmos, and cannot be subject to a definitive

---

78. Schneur Zalman, *Igeret Ha Kodesh*, Ch. 6; Zalman, *Likutei-Amarim Tanya*, p. 421.

79. Zalman, *Likutei-Amarim Tanya*, p. 159. This is why, talmudic tradition has it, that not even Moses could see the full countenance of God and survive.

80. Schneur Zalman, *Torah Or*, p. 58; quoted in Elior, *The Paradoxical Ascent to God*, p. 150.

interpretation. As Vital puts it: "The worlds change each and every hour, and there is no hour which is similar to another . . . and in accordance with these changes are the aspects of the sayings of the book of the Zohar changing, and all are the words of the living God."[81] Moshe Idel aptly interprets this passage to imply that "even theoretically, the possibility of attaining its (*the* Zohar's) ultimate significance is nil: each moment brings its own novel understanding."[82]

THE KABBALISTIC DOCTRINES OF CREATION

A linguistic theory of creation is set forth in *Sefer Yetzirah*. This view accords well with the biblical account in which the world is created by God's word. In *Sefer Yetzirah* we read: "Twenty-two foundation letters: He engraved them, He carved them, He permuted them, He weighed them, He transformed them, And with them, He depicted all that was formed and all that would be formed."[83] According to *Sefer Yetzirah*, the world was created through these letters and the ten *Sefirot*, which at this stage were themselves conceptualized as mystical numbers (from the Hebrew *Sephar*) or as mystical text (from the Hebrew *Sepher*). Together the twenty-two letters and ten *Sefirot* comprise the "thirty-two mystical paths of wisdom" through which God "engraved" the finite world. *Sefer Yetzirah* adds, "It comes out that all that is formed and all that is spoken emanates from one Name."[84] Further, through the foundational letters, "He formed substance out of chaos and made nonexistence into existence."[85]

As we will see later in our discussion of the "foundational letters," the linguistic theory continued to play an important role in the Kabbalah and Hasidism. The Zohar, for example, combined a linguistic view of creation with one that likened creation to the emanation of light. This view is described in several places in the Zohar,[86] each of which are remarkable mystical meditations on the first chapter of Genesis. I will quote from one example:

---

81. Vital, *Sefer Etz Chayyim* 1:5, p. 29. As translated by Idel in *Kabbalah: New Perspectives*, p. 248. See Menzi and Padeh, *The Tree of Life*, pp. 63–64.
82. Idel, *Kabbalah: New Perspectives*, p. 248.
83. *Sefer Yetzirah* 2:2; Kaplan, *Sefer Yetzirah*, p. 100.
84. *Sefer Yetzirah*, 2:5; Kaplan, *Sefer Yetzirah*, p. 124.
85. *Sefer Yetzirah* 2:6; Kaplan, *Sefer Yetzirah*, p. 131.
86. Zohar 1:2a, Sperling and Simon, *The Zohar*, Vol. 1, p. 6; Zohar 1:15a,

When the most Mysterious wished to reveal Himself, He first produced a single point which was transmuted into a thought, and in this He executed innumerable designs, and engraved innumerable gravings. He further graved within the sacred and mystic lamp a mystic and holy design, which was a wonderful edifice issuing from the midst of thought. This is called MI (who), and was the beginning of the edifice, existent and non-existent, deep-buried, unknowable by name. It therefore clothed itself in a refulgent and precious garment and created ELeH (these), and ELeH acquired a name. The letters of the two words intermingled, forming the complete name ELoHIM (God).[87]

THE DOCTRINE OF *TZIMTZUM*

It is in Isaac Luria that we find the most distinctive kabbalistic theory of creation; a theory that enabled *Ein-Sof* to remain perfect and whole despite its emanation of a created, finite world. According to Luria, the fundamental act of creation was a negative one, a *Tzimtzum* or withdrawal, contraction, and concealment of the divine presence.

The doctrine of *Tzimtzum* has two major connotations, an ontological one connoting "contraction," "withdrawal," or "condensation," and an epistemological one that connotes "concealment" or "occultation." Both senses of the term are necessary to a full understanding of the Lurianic theory of creation.

ORIGIN OF THE DOCTRINE

While the concept of *Tzimtzum* is most clearly set forth in the writings of the disciples of Isaac Luria, earlier Kabbalists had anticipated its basic idea. For example, several Kabbalists understood an early midrash to the effect that God "restricted his *Shekhinah* [the divine 'presence'] to the square of an ell,"[88] as providing profound insight into the nature of creation. A very early kabbalistic source from Iyyun, which is quoted by the fourteenth-century Kabbalist Shemtov ben Shemtov, reads: "How did he produce and create

---

Sperling and Simon, *The Zohar*, Vol. 1, p. 63; Zohar 1:29a. Sperling and Simon, *The Zohar*, Vol. 1, pp. 110–111.

87. Zohar I:2a, Sperling and Simon, *The Zohar*, Vol. 1, p. 6.

88. Midrash *Shemoth Rabbah* 34:1.

His world? Like a man who holds his breath and contracts (*mezamzem*) himself in order that the little may contain the many. So He contracted His light into a hand's breadth, according to His own measure, and the world was left in darkness, and in that darkness He cut boulders and hewed rocks."[89] According to the Ramban (Rabbi Moses Ben Nachman, Nachmanides; 1194–1270) the divine wisdom (*Chochmah*) was created as a result of a *Tzimtzum* or contraction of the divine light or will in the highest *Sefirah*. As a result of this *Tzimtzum* a region of darkness was produced that serves as a medium for the clear light of *Chochmah* (Wisdom).[90]

The Zohar refers to the original light of Genesis I: 3 ("let there be light . . .") as a "hidden light" on the grounds that the world could not have endured unless this light were concealed.[91] Further, the Zohar also refers to the light of *Ein-Sof* as *manifest only when it is concealed*.[92] Moses Cordovero (b. 1522), an older contemporary and teacher of Isaac Luria, actually developed a theory of *Tzimtzum* that fully paralleled and informed Luria's later views. Cordovero held that the *Sefirot* were created via the concealment of the infinite God. Creation is simply our perspective on this concealment. For Cordovero, "revealing is the cause of concealment and concealment is the cause of revealing."[93]

TZIMTZUM IN LURIA AND VITAL

In Isaac Luria and his disciples (most notably Joseph Ibn Tabul and Chayyim Vital) *Tzimtzum* clearly becomes the first act of creation. Luria followed Cordovero in seeking out a principle that would allow God to create a finite world without, in effect, adding anything to His substance. Moses Chayyim Luzzatto explains Luria's notion as follows:

> Beware of thinking even for a moment that there is any change in the Creator Himself. Such an idea is unthinkable, for changes pertain only to the recipients of Light, according to their distance or proximity to the

---

89. See Scholem, *Origins of the Kabbalah*, p. 449, and Scholem, *Kabbalah*, p. 129.

90. Scholem, *Origins of the Kabbalah*, pp. 449–450.

91. Zohar 2:148b. Tishby and Lachower, *The Wisdom of the Zohar*, p. 441.

92. We learn that this light "was concealed and sown, like the seed that produces offspring, seeds and fruit."

93. See Scholem, *Kabbalah*, p. 402.

Source, the Creator. Think, for example, of a lighted candle that is placed before a person. If many veils were interposed, so that the person could enjoy but very little of the candle light, this would not mean a change took place in the light itself, but rather in the person, who could not see the candle light because of the intervening veils.[94]

According to Luria, in *Tzimtzum*, *Ein-Sof* contracts to "make room" for a world,[95] and it is, in effect, the diminution of the divine light, rather than the creation of any additional (non-divine) substance that brings about the finite world.

CONTRACTION AND EMANATION

While the logic of *Tzimtzum* would suggest that *Tzimtzum* is the only principle necessary to explain creation, the Lurianists held that creation is actually the result of an interplay between contraction and emanation, concealment and revelation. In Vital, we find the doctrine that *Ein-Sof* contracted itself to form a hollow metaphysical void, and then emanated weaker lights back into that void in order to produce the worlds.[96]

For Luria, the act of *Tzimtzum* is necessary in order to create the "vessels" (*Kelim*) that serve as the basic structures of the created world. These vessels are comprised of remnants of divine light that remain in the primordial void (*chalal*). Only after the *Tzimtzum* can there be an emanation of divine "light" into these vessels, as any emanation prior to the *Tzimtzum* would result in "uncondensed" light that would cause the disappearance of worlds.[97] *Ein-Sof* thus emanates a form of filtered or condensed light into the void or hollow (*chalal* or *tehiru*). According to Vital, myriads of worlds are emanated into the void: "many different kinds of worlds were emanated, created, formed, and made—thousands upon thousands and myriads upon myriads. Every single one of them is inside the empty space [the primordial void] . . . and nothing is outside of it."[98]

---

94. Luzzatto, *General Principles of the Kabbalah*, pp. 42–43.
95. Ibid., p. 42, 51.
96. Chayyim Vital, *Sefer Ez Chayyim*, 1:1. See also Menzi and Padeh, *The Tree of Life*, p. 13.
97. Luzzatto, *General Principles of the Kabbalah*, p. 42.
98. *Sefer Etz Chayyim* 1:1; p. 22; Menzi and Padeh, *The Tree of Life*, p. 19.

For Luria, creation is a dialectical process in which a series of negations or concealments alternate with a complementary series of positive acts, emanations, or divine revelations.[99] These negative and positive acts can actually be understood as complementary descriptions of the same event. For example, *Tzimtzum* is both a *negation* of God's light and the *positing* of the vessels (the *Kelim*) that ultimately serve as the structures of the world.

Vital describes the line or ray (*kav*) of divine light that enters the void subsequent to the *Tzimtzum*. This line circles along the outside perimeter of the circular hollow, thereby creating the first *Sefirah* (dimension or archetype of creation). The ray, which the Lurianists sometimes conceived of as a holy letter (the letter *yud*) orders the inchoate mixture of divine energy that had remained in the void after the initial *Tzimtzum*,[100] and the *Sefirah Keter* (Crown) is formed. Afterward the remaining nine *Sefirot* are formed by the ray spiraling inward toward the center of the void. As it moves toward the center, the ray becomes weaker, or, what amounts to the same thing, "denser" and more material in nature. It is the final *Sefirah*, *Malchut*, which channels what remains of the infinite light into the very center of the hollow, creating the material world, at the farthest remove from *Ein-Sof*, which surrounds it from all sides.

According to Vital, it is the narrow ray of divine light that both connects the *Sefirot* to the surrounding divine light, and with each other. He is emphatic, however, that a barrier, i.e., an element of void, must remain between the light of *Ein-Sof* and the first *Sefirah*, for if the latter were fully connected to the light it would return to its original state and be nullified. The *Tzimtzum*, by introducing an aspect of void or emptiness, brings limitation into the cosmos, and by creating a place that is void of the divine presence, sets up the possibilities of distinction within that presence, which are necessary for the existence of finitude and multiplicity.

"VESSELS"

For Luria the "possibilities of distinction" within the universe are referred to as *Kelim*, or vessels. Indeed, for Vital the entire purpose of the divine

---

99. Typically contraction is associated with the divine attribute of Judgment (*Din*) and emanation with the attribute of Kindness (*Chesed*). See Luzzatto, *General Principles of the Kabbalah*, p. 102.

100. Scholem, *Kabbalah*, p. 130.

contraction is the creation of such vessels. The vessels are linked to the light that is emanated into them to form the archetypes of creation, the *Sefirot*. The vessels are compared to curtains that filter and conceal the emanated light in varying degrees. Moses Cordovero had likened them to colored glass vessels that alter the appearance of water that is poured into them but that do not change the water itself.[101]

THE MEANING OF *TZIMTZUM*

The Kabbalists, for the most part, regarded the *Tzimtzum* and each of their other theosophical symbols to be purely metaphorical concepts that are simple "appeasements to the ear" and "aids to the understanding." According to Vital: "As for all the images and pictures that we use, it is not because it is actually so, God forbid, but only to appease the ear so that one can understand the higher spiritual things that cannot be grasped or comprehended at all by the understanding . . ."[102] Actually, a physical interpretation of the "contraction" involved in *Tzimtzum* is impossible. Since God or "*Ein-Sof*" does not originally exist within space and time, He cannot contract himself physically or temporally. Indeed, it is through God's metaphysical contraction in *Tzimtzum* that space, time, and matter come into being at all. We can understand this by observing that the distances of space and time, along with the opacities of material bodies are the fundamental limitations on human knowledge and endeavor. In contracting Himself via the *Tzimtzum*, *Ein-Sof* limits his knowledge and power, creating a perspective on being that has its locus in the finite situation of humankind. This perspective is the very spatio-temporal and material framework within which we reside. It is noteworthy that, according to Luria, the first being to emerge with the *Tzimtzum* is the Primordial Man. We might go so far as to say by contracting Himself in *Tzimtzum*, God becomes humanity.

The *Tzimtzum* therefore cannot itself occur in a spatio-temporal frame. It is simply a self-limitation within the totality of absolute being. The purpose of *Tzimtzum* is thus to create a metaphysical void in which finite beings are

101. Moses Cordovero, *Pardes Rimonim* IV:4, as discussed by Schochet in "Mystical Concepts" p. 868.
102. *Sefer Etz Chayyim* 1:1; p. 28, Menzi and Padeh, *The Tree of Life*, pp. 53–54.

able to exist without being dissolved in God.[103] As put by Moses Chayyim Luzzatto: "If not for the contraction, the overwhelming abundance of Light would cause the disappearance of all the worlds, for existence is nothing but a succession of condensations of Light essence."[104]

HASIDIC CONCEPTIONS OF *TZIMTZUM*

The Hasidim psychologized the doctrine of *Tzimtzum*, holding, for example, that it is through the divine contraction that God's thought becomes fully realized in the mind of man.[105] *Tzimtzum* also became the foundation of a Hasidic ethic, in which the individual is encouraged to imitate God, and in humility, "contract" his ego to make room for the thoughts and desires of the other. The first Lubavitcher rebbe, Schneur Zalman of Lyadi, provided a linguistic interpretation of *Tzimtzum* in which *Ein-Sof* is said to contract and invest its life force in the holy letters that comprise the so-called "ten utterances of creation," those passages in the book of Genesis in which God is described as creating the world through speech.[106] According to Schneur Zalman, the world in all of its manifestations is created through the combination of letters "by substitutions and transpositions of the letters themselves and their numerical values and equivalents."[107] This combination of letters, and the variations achieved via Gematria,[108] results in not only the linguistic expression for all things but their very existence as well.

According to Schneur Zalman God's revelation through divine speech is an act of *Tzimtzum*, a limitation of the divine essence. *Ein-Sof* is said to contract itself into the words and letters, which, for Schneur Zalman, are the "vessels" that contain the divine emanations. Letters and words function to

---

103. Schochet, "Mystical Concepts," p. 828.

104. Luzzatto, *General Principles of the Kabbalah*, p. 42.

105. Rabbi Dov Baer, the Maggid of Mezrich (1704–1772), cited in Rifka Schatz-Uffenheimer, *Hasidism as Mysticism: Quietistic Elements In Eighteenth-Century Hasidic Thought* (Jerusalem: Hebrew University, 1993), p. 207.

106. Zalman, *Likutei Amarim-Tanya*, p. 319 (*Shaar ha Yichud VehaEmunah* 7).

107. Ibid.

108. Gematria is the hermeneutic method whereby the meaning of a word or scriptural passage is derived (and hence altered) by considering the numerical value of the Hebrew letters in that word or passage and then either interpreting that number or finding other linguistic expressions that have the same numerical value and substituting them for the word or passage in question.

limit divine thought to some specific content and are therefore held to be equivalent to the vessels that structure the *Sefirot*.

TZIMTZUM AND THE PROBLEM OF EVIL

There is an inherent connection between *Tzimtzum* and the existence of evil. The Kabbalists regarded evil to be a necessary by-product of the created world, and linked it to the *negation* and *limitation* of the divine essence that was necessary in order to bring about the existence of a finite creation. The Lurianists further held that the act of *Tzimtzum* involves a catharsis of *din* (judgment), the negative, potentially evil element within the godhead. Another way of saying that *Ein-Sof* contracted and thereby created a region alienated from God's infinite Goodness, is to say that *Ein-Sof* expelled the roots of or potential for evil into a region that lies beyond the divine essence. This idea is put in graphic terms by Schneur Zalman, who says: "Indeed so great and powerful are the contractions and concealment of the (divine) countenance that even unclean things, the *Kelippot* (the 'Evil Husks') and the *Sitra Achra* (the 'Other Side') can come into being."[109] Evil, according to the Lurianists, is not only a necessary by-product of *Tzimtzum*, but part of the logical structure of creation itself.

Jewish theologians have appealed to *Tzimtzum* in their theodicies, i.e., their attempts to justify faith in God in the face of an obviously evil world. Such thinkers as Martin Buber,[110] Joseph Soloveitchik,[111] Adin Steinsaltz,[112] and Eliezer Berkowitz[113] have each in their own fashion turned to *Tzimtzum* (or the related notion of *hester panim*, the hiding of the divine countenance) to explain and justify evil in a world created and governed by God.[114] More

---

109. Zalman, *Likutei Amarim-Tanya*, p. 91.

110. See Martin Buber, "God and the World's Evil," in *Contemporary Jewish Thought* ed. Simon Noveck (New York: B'nai Brith, 1963), Vol. 4, p. 256.

111. See Joseph Soloveitchik, *Halakhic Man*, trans. Lawrence Kaplan (Philadelphia: Jewish Publication Society, 1983) p. 108; also compare Joseph Soloveitchik, "The Lonely Man of Faith," *Tradition* 7:2 (Summer 1965).

112. Adin Steinsaltz, *The Thirteen Petalled Rose*, trans. Yehuda Hanegbi (New York: Basic Books, 1980), p. 37.

113. Eliezer Berkowitz, *God, Man, and History* (Middle Village, NY: Jonathan David, 1959), p. 145–146.

114. See David Birnbaum, *God and Evil* (Hoboken, NJ: Ktav, 1989), pp.

recently, David Birnbaum has made creative use of *Tzimtzum* in arguing (along the lines we have been discussing) that in order to provide man with the freedom, independence, and creative potential to realize his spiritual destiny, God must *of necessity* conceal himself via *Tzimtzum*, and retreat further and further into "eclipse."[115]

THE *SEFIROT*

The symbol of the *Sefirot* is the defining notion of kabbalistic theosophy. The *Sefirot*, which are almost always conceived to be ten in number, are the building blocks of creation, the archetypes of existence, the traits of God, and the primary values of the cosmos. The earliest reference to the *Sefirot* is in the proto-kabbalistic source, *Sefer Yetzirah* (The Book of Formation), where, as we have seen, the ten *Sefirot* are grouped together with the twenty-two letters of the Hebrew alphabet[116] to comprise the "thirty-two wondrous paths of wisdom" through which God "engraved and created the world."[117]

The word "*Sefirah*" literally means "counting," but a number of other etymological connections are evident in *Sefer Yetzirah* and in the early Kabbalah. These include the words *sepher* (text), *sepharim* (books), *sippur* (communication), *sappir* (sapphire, brilliance, luminary), *separ* (boundary), and *safra* (scribe), which considerably broaden the term's connotative significance.[118] The term is not originally connected to the Greek *sphaira* (sphere). However, since later Kabbalists conceptualized the *Sefirot* as circles

---

122–135. We should note that Schneur Zalman, in *Tanya*, relates the two notions of *Tzimtzum* and *hester panim*. He writes: "These *tzimtzumim* are all in the nature of a 'veiling of the countenance' (*hester panim*), to obscure and conceal the light and life-force . . . so that it shall not manifest itself in a greater radiance than the lower worlds are capable of receiving." (*Tanya* I, C. 48, as cited by Schochet, "Mystical Concepts," p. 829.) *Hester panim* is a rabbinic metaphor for those periods where God chooses to withdraw a portion of his providence from the world.

115. David Birnbaum, *God and Evil*. (See also Sanford Drob, "Foreword," in the fourth and subsequent editions of Birnbaum's work.) Zalman, *Likutei Amarim-Tanya*, p. 293.

116. Scholem, *Origins of the Kabbalah*, pp. 26–27, referring to *Sefer Yetzirah*, Chs. 1 and 2.

117. Sefer Yetzirah 1:1; Kaplan, *Sefer Yetzirah*, p. 5. Cf. Scholem, *Origins of the Kabbalah*, p. 26.

118. See Scholem, *Kabbalah*, p. 100.

encompassing the material world, an associative connection with the heavenly "spheres" in the Ptolmaic picture of the universe is, readily apparent. *Sefer Yetzirah* spoke of the *Sefirot* as the "Breath of the living God"[119] and as living numerical beings that are the hidden "depth" and "dimension" to all things.

By the time of *Sefer ha-Bahir* (late twelfth century), the *Sefirot* were no longer regarded as numbers, but were understood in Gnostic or Neoplatonic terms as aeons or *logoi*, which serve as the instruments of creation.[120] *Sefer ha-Bahir* identifies the *Sefirot* with the *ma'amoroth* (the ten words or sayings by which the world was created)[121] and with *middoth* (God's attributes or traits). In doing so the *Bahir* establishes a link between the *Sefirot* and certain talmudic ideas. For example, we read in the Talmud that the world was created through ten things: "by wisdom and by understanding, and by reason and by strength (*Gevurah*), by rebuke and by might, by righteousness and by judgment, by loving kindness and compassion."[122] The connection with this and other talmudic, aggadic, and even biblical passages[123] suggests that the *Sefirot* are a hypostatization of these earlier Jewish ideas.

The question of whether the *Sefirot* are one with *Ein-Sof* or are emanated as independent entities is left somewhat ambiguous in most of the kabbalistic sources. Azriel, and later the Zohar, speak of them as being one with *Ein-Sof*, in the sense that the flame, the sparks, and the aura are one with the fire.[124] As we have seen, according to Azriel, the *Sefirot*, like *Ein-Sof* itself, have the dialectical character of being "the synthesis of everything and its opposite,"[125] a synthesis that is the source of all energy in everything whatsoever.[126] Both the Zohar and Joseph Gikatilla[127] equate each *Sefirah* with a biblical name of God, suggesting that if they are not to be completely identified with the deity, they are, at the very least, His aspects or powers.

---

119. *Sefer Yetzirah* 1:14. Kaplan, *Sefer Yetzirah*, p. 88.

120. See Scholem, *Origins of the Kabbalah*, p. 82.

121. As found in the talmudic tractate *Pirke Avoth* 5:1. Philip Blackman, trans., *Tractate Avoth: The Ethics of the Fathers*, (Gateshead, England: Judaica Press, 1985).

122. Talmud: Tractate *Hagiga*, 12a.

123. Isaac the Blind, the first Kabbalist to consistently use the word "*Sefirot*," related them to the biblical enumeration of God's traits in Chronicles 29:11 (see below).

124. Ibid., p. 92.

125. Dan, *The Early Kabbalah*, p. 94.

126. Ibid., p. 95.

127. Joseph Gikatilla, *Sha'are Orah* (*The Gates of Light*) trans. Avi Weinstein (San Francisco: HarperCollins, 1994).

The Zohar uses a variety of terms[128] among which are "levels," "powers," "firmaments," "worlds," "pillars," "lights," "colors," "dates," "gates," "streams," "garments," and "crowns" to refer to the *Sefirot*. The Zohar conceptualizes the *Sefirot* as dimensions, archetypes, spiritual forces, activities within the Godhead, gates to the divine world, aspects of God, and ways in which God is manifest in creation. The *Sefirot* symbolism implies that God, the cosmos, the human soul, and the act of knowledge are all a single, unified essence or substance.

Among the Lurianists we find the idea that the initial result of *Ein-Sof*'s "turning inward" via the *Tzimtzum* is a differentiation of divine *middot* or traits within the godhead.[129] The progressive differentiation of divine traits gives rise to the ten *Sefirot*, which are ultimately emanated as receptacles (*Kelim*) for the divine light emanated into the lower worlds. Further, Luria postulated that the *Sefirot* undergo dynamic transformations as a result of dramatic events that occur both within the godhead and in the created worlds. Among these are the "Catharsis of *Din*" and the "Breaking of the Vessels," each of which will be discussed below.

THE ORDER OF THE *SEFIROT*

The *Sefirot* number ten, but they were subject to a variety of appellations.[130] Isaac the Blind named six of the *Sefirot* directly for the praises of God enumerated in Chronicles 29:11:[131] "Yours, O Lord, is the greatness (*gedullah*), power (*gevurah*), the beauty (*tiferet*), the victory (*netzach*), the majesty (*Hod*) . . . yours is the kingdom (*Malchut*)." These *Sefirot* were, however, renamed by later Kabbalists, resulting in a system in which there are often several names for each *Sefirah*. *Keter* (Crown), for example, is also referred to as *Ayin* (Nothingness), *Ratzon* (Will), *Atika Kaddisha* (the Holy Ancient One), and *Ehyeh* ("I will be"). However, a fairly uniform scheme was

---

128. See Tishby and Lachower, *The Wisdom of the Zohar*, Vol. 1, p. 269. Other terms used by the Kabbalists for the *Sefirot* are "mirrors," "names," "shoots," "qualities," "sources," "aspects" (*sitrin*), "supernal days," and "inner faces of God." See Scholem, *Kabbalah*, p. 21.

129. Though a number of Kabbalists and Hasidim, including the first Lubavitcher rebbe, Schneur Zalman of Lyadi, held that all of these changes occur in the *Or Ein-Sof* (the divine light) and none within *Ein-Sof* himself.

130. Tishby, *The Wisdom of the Zohar*, Vol. 1, p. 270.

131. See Dan, *The Early Kabbalah*, p. 94.

adopted in the later Kabbalah, one that accords with the order of the *Sefirot* as given by Moses Cordovero.[132] This scheme (along with the most common alternative appellations and the corresponding names of God) is outlined in Table 2

Table 1–2
Order of the *Sefirot*

Sefirah	Name of God
Keter Elyon (Supreme Crown) or *Ratzon* (Will)	Ehyeh
Chochmah (Wisdom)	Yah
Binah (Intelligence)	YHVH (Vocalized as *Elohim*)
Chesed (Love) or *Gedulah* (Greatness)	El
Din (Judgment) or *Gevurah* (Power)	Elohim
Tiferet (Beauty) or *Rachamim* (Compassion)	YHVH
Netzach (Lasting Endurance)	*El Hai* or *Shaddai*
Hod (Majesty)	Elohim Zeva'ot
Yesod Olam (Foundation of the World) or *Tzaddik* (Righteous One)	YHVH *Zeva'ot*
Malchut (Kingdom) or *Atarah* (Diadem), or *Shekhinah* (Feminine divine presence)	Adonai

The scheme is frequently altered, however, in the Lurianic Kabbalah, which eliminates *Keter*, and interposes the *Sefirah Da'at* (Knowledge) between *Binah* and *Chesed*.

---

132. The scheme I have outlined is the one that is found in Cordovero's *Pardes Rimonim* (3:1ff).

THE CREATION OF THE *SEFIROT*

The Lurianists understood the *Sefirot* to have originally been emanated according to two complementary schemes, that of *iggulim* (circles) and *yosher* (lines). According to the first model, the *Sefirot* were emanated as a series of concentric circles, with *Ein-Sof* on the outside, and the final *Sefirah*, *Malchut*, farthest from the divine light, in the center. On the second, linear, model, the *Sefirot* are emanated in "the form of a human being (*adam*) with a head, arms, thighs, body, and feet . . ."[133] The *Sefirot*, which are here organized in a sequence of three lines, ultimately take on the form of *Adam Kadmon*, the Primordial Man, with each *Sefirah* representing a different organ of the body: *Chochmah*, corresponding to the brain, *Binah* to the heart, *Gevurah* to the right arm, *Chesed* to the left arm, etc.[134]

According to Luria both schemes, the circular and the linear, are "the word of the living God"; each are different perspectives on the same metaphysical events and process. While the circular scheme emphasizes the cosmic aspects of the world-creative process, the linear model represents the cosmos as an organic unity with the brains or mind of the Primordial Man in the center. Theologically we might say that the circular model represents a traditional transcendent point of view, with God in the heavens at the farthest remove from humankind,[135] while the linear model represents a more humanistic or immanent point of view with the divine located in the depths of the mind of man.[136] According to Vital: "Each world, and every single

---

133. *Sefer Etz Chayyim* 1:1; p. 22, Menzi and Padeh, *The Tree of Life*, p. 11.

134. The scheme of *Yosher* also organizes the *Sefirot* according to three lines or triads: *Chochmah-Chesed-Netzach* on the right, *Binah-Gevurah-Hod* on the left, and *Keter-Tiferet (Rachamim)-Yesod-Malchut* in the center. This arrangement underscores the dynamic relationship among the *Sefirot*; for example, the mediating or harmonizing functions of the middle group, in which *Tiferet* or *Rachamim* is said to harmonize the bounty of *Chesed* (Kindness) with the severity of *Din* (Judgment), and where *Malchut* is said to channel or mediate all of the other sefirotic powers.

135. *Sefer Etz Chayyim* 1:2, p. 29; Menzi and Padeh, *The Tree of Life*, p. 73.

136. Vital is not consistent in this characterization of the linear and circular models. He does say that "from our perspective" the Infinite is in the inside of all the emanations (*Sefer Etz Chayyim* 1:2, p. 23; Menzi and Padeh, *The Tree of Life*, p. 22), which suggests that the "linear model" is from the perspective of humanity. He also, at times, states the opposite. For a more complete discussion, see my *Symbols of the Kabbalah*, Chapter 4, note 46.

detail of each world, has these two aspects—circular and linear."[137] The two perspectives, immanent and transcendent, complement one another, another example of the kabbalistic principle of *coincidentia oppositorum.*

THE PRIMORDIAL MAN (*ADAM KADMON*)

The notion of a primal anthropus has a long history in Jewish mysticism. As we have seen in the *Shi'ur Komah*[138] of the *Merkaveh* mystics, a gigantic primal human is said to occupy the "throne of glory," and its gigantic measure is an object of mystical contemplation. The early Kabbalah, beginning with *Sefer ha-Bahir*, depicted the *Sefirot* in terms of the bodily organs and appendages of a primal human.[139] In the Lurianic Kabbalah, the Primordial Man is referred to as *Adam Kadmon*, and becomes a pivotal symbol linking God, Man, and the World. According to Vital, *Adam Kadmon* is the precursor of all things,[140] the first being to emerge after the *Tzimtzum*, and the vehicle through which the *Sefirot* and all the worlds are emanated. Man, who is created in God's image, is comprised of the very same *Sefirot*, which comprise the "body" of *Adam Kadmon.*

Adam Kadmon is said to emanate the lights that become the *Sefirot* and the various Worlds through four of his organs, the eyes, the ears, the nose, and the mouth,[141] corresponding to to the senses of vision, hearing, smell, and speech (*Reiah, Shmecha, Re'cha,* and *Dibor*). In addition, after the Breaking of the Vessels, at the time of *Tikkun ha-Olam*, lights emanating from the forehead of *Adam Kadmon* help serve to restore the fragmented *Sefirot.*

According to Vital, the description of a divine primordial human is one of two basic metaphors, the other being the theory of "linguistic atomism" (see below), that are helpful in comprehending the nature of the divine

---

137. *Sefer Etz Chayyim* 1:1, p. 25; Menzi and Padeh, *The Tree of Life*, p. 33.

138. *Shi'ur Koma*, translated as "Shiur Qoma," in Meltzer, *The Secret Garden*, pp. 21–37.

139. *Sefer ha Bahir* 116, *Book Bahir*, p. 86. Cf. *Sefer ha Bahir* 55, *Book Bahir*, pp. 65–66.

140. *Sefer Etz Chayyim* 1:1, p. 21; Menzi and Padeh, *The Tree of Life*, p. 6.

141. *Sefer Etz Chayyim* 1:1, pp. 25–26; Menzi and Padeh, *The Tree of Life*, p. 40.

realms.[142] *Adam Kadmon* is a metaphor that suggests that the cosmos is very much akin to a living human organism, and that the world, as created by God, itself has interests and values that resonate with those of humankind.

PARTZUFIM

The Lurianists, adapting ideas and terminology that are already present in the Zohar, held that the *Sefirot* are organized into *Partzufim*, "visages" or personal aspects of the godhead. Chayyim Vital explains that a *Partzuf* is an aspect or "face" of the divinity, structured like a person with "248 limbs." While each *Partzuf* is dominated by one or several of the *Sefirot*, they are each also arranged in a pattern that integrates and embodies all ten. Vital explains that for each *Partzuf* the first *Sefirah*, *Keter* (Crown), is the skull, and the next three *Sefirot*, *Chochmah*, *Binah*, and *Da'at* (Wisdom, Understanding, and Knowledge) are the "three brains" inside the head. *Chesed* and *Gevurah* (Kindness and Judgment) are the right and left arms, while *Tiferet* (Beauty, Compassion) is the torso. *Netzach* and *Hod* are the two thighs and *Yesod* the phallus. The final *Sefirah*, *Malchut* is the *Partzuf*'s "female," reflecting the ancient and biblical notion that man is not complete until he is joined with his female counterpart.

There are six major *Partzufim*: *Attika Kaddisha* (the Holy Ancient One), *Arich Anpin* (the Long-Suffering One), *Abba* (the Supernal Father), *Imma* (the Supernal Mother), *Ze'ir Anipin* (the Short-Faced One) or *Ben* (the Son), and *Bat* (the Daughter) or *Nukvah* (the Female).[143] The *Partzufim* are integrally connected to the Lurianic doctrine of the Breaking of the Vessels. According to Luria and his disciples, the *Partzufim* only fully emerge as integrated structures after the vessels have been broken. It is in part, through the efforts of mankind that the shards of the shattered *Sefirot* are reorganized into these divine personalities, which, according to Scholem, are aspects of an evolving Primordial Man.

The *Partzufim* engage in regular sexual and procreative relations that have implications for the restoration and repair of the worlds. For example, *Abba* and *Imma*, the Celestial Mother and Father are mates who alternately engage in "face-to-face" relations or turn their backs upon one another. The

---

142. *Sefer Etz Chayyim* 1:1, p. 28; Menzi and Padeh, *The Tree of Life*, p. 54.
143. Ibid., p. 56

state of their relatedness, which is at least in part dependent upon the worship and ethical deeds of humankind, has a major impact on the flow of divine energy throughout all the worlds. *Abba* and *Imma* also produce *Ze'ir Anpin*, a *Partzuf* that is said to develop in the womb of the Celestial mother. The reorganization of the *Sefirot* into *Partzufim* places them into a dialectical and procreative frame in which the creation and renewal of the world is a function of the union of God's masculine and feminine aspects.

THE UNFOLDING OF INTELLECT AND EMOTION

The *Sefirot*, according to the Kabbalists, provide us with insight into the unfolding of God's creative process, which is said to be analagous to the development of thought, emotion, and action in man. The highest *Sefirah*, *Keter*, is the general creative urge of divine will. *Chochmah*, the second *Sefirah*, is the intuition of an intention or idea, and *Binah*, the fulfillment of the idea. Ideas become values and emotions via the *Sefirot* from *Chesed* to *Yesod*, and become action in the world via, the final *Sefirah, Malchut*.[144]

LEVELS OF THE SOUL

According to Luria the *Sefirot* are perfectly mirrored in the soul of man, and there is a specific relationship between the *Sefirot* and the five levels of the human soul: the *nefesh*, or bodily soul; the *ruach*, which corresponds to the heart and emotions; the *neshamah*, corresponding to the brain; the *Chaya* or "living soul"; and the *Yechida*, meaning "united," the Godly soul which is united with man. Each of these soul levels are active not only in man but in the cosmos as a whole. Their equivalences to specific *Sefirot* are detailed in Table 1–3 below.

THE *BEHINNOT*

According to Solomon Alkabez and Moses Cordovero, light from each of the *Sefirot* is reflected and channeled into each of the others. As a result, each of

---

144. Schochet, "Mystical Concepts," p. 835.

the *Sefirot* include elements of each of the others within themselves. For example, the *Sefirah Chesed* is comprised of the *Chesed* of *Chesed* (i.e., pure *Chesed*), the *Gevurah* of *Chesed*, the *Tiferet* of *Chesed*, the *Netzach* of *Chesed*, etc. In their ethical theories the Kabbalists placed special emphasis on the final seven *Sefirot* and their permutations, holding that man's character involves the development of each of the forty-nine possible combinations of the seven moral *Sefirot* (*Chesed* through *Malchut*).

Moses Cordovero developed the notion that each *Sefirah* contains within itself an infinite number of aspects (*behinnot*).[145] Cordovero held that these "aspects," while they are inherent to the *Sefirot* themselves, are also dependent upon the perspective of the viewer. Cordovero's theory antici-pates modern constructivism, the theory that reality is a function of the manner in which experience is constructed by a human subject.

THE DOCTRINE OF THE FIVE WORLDS

In addition to emanating the *Sefirot* themselves, *Adam Kadmon* emanates lights that are structured into a series of *Olamot* or "Worlds."[146] Kabbalists such as Gikatilla and Luria spoke of tens of thousands and even millions of worlds. In general, however, the Kabbalists speak of four or five major *Olamot*: the worlds of *Adam Kadmon* (Primordial Man), *Atzilut* ("Near-ness" or Emanation), *Beriah* (Creation), *Yetzirah* (Formation), and *Assiyah* ("Making" or Action). Frequently *Adam Kadmon* is considered too high and exalted to be regarded as a world apart from *Ein-Sof* and is eliminated from the scheme, and *Atzilut* is regarded as the highest of the worlds. Each world from *Atzilut* to *Assiyah* is understood as being progressively more distant from the light of *Ein-Sof*. Vital refers to our "lowly world Assiyah" as occupying the center of the cosmic scheme, like the inedible pit of a date, with the edible fruit, representing worlds closer to *Ein-Sof*, all around it. Like the *Sefirot*, the "Worlds" were regarded in allegorical terms and understood as having reality only relative to humanity but no substance independent from *Ein-Sof*. From our point of view, our world receives only enough divine radiance through the interposition of many "screens" or "garments" to

---

145. Scholem, *Kabbalah*, p. 114, referring to M. Cordovero, *Pardes Rimonim* 5:5.

146. See Schochet, "Mystical Concepts," pp. 806–866.

maintain its tenuous existence.[147] At the lowest of levels there is a crystallization of only corporeal, completely lifeless, things.

The world of *Adam Kadmon* is the highest of the kabbalistic realms. Its characteristics are derived from the biblical notion that Adam, the first man, was created *betzaltzel*, in God's "image." The characteristics of this world are identical to those of *Adam Kadmon* himself. Like the *Sefirah Keter*, which dominates this world, *Adam Kadmon* is often described as *Ayin*,[148] nothingness, and is regarded as being so sublime and close to the infinite God as to be identified with *Ein-Sof* itself.

As such *Atzilut*, the world of emanation, is frequently spoken of as the highest of the four worlds. The term *Atzilut* is derived from a biblical term (see Numbers 11:17, Ecclesiastes 2:10) that connotes "nearness," suggesting its proximity to God. It is here that the *Sefirot*, which are perfectly unified and commingled within the Godhead, begin to take on more distinct form.[149] *Chochmah* (Wisdom) is the dominant *Sefirah* in *Atzilut*, which is a world of pure thought, or conception.

The world of *Beriah* (creation) lies directly below *Atzilut*. It is here that distinct, finite creatures first appear, albeit in purely spiritual form. In *Beriah* the *Sefirot* are "garbed" and begin to be limited in their radiance.[150] Angels, and the souls of the righteous appear here, and *Beriah* is said to have been accessible to the meditations of Ezekiel and the other prophets. *Beriah* is dominated by the *Sefirah Binah* (intelligence), and it is the first realm of creation in which the effects of the *Tzimtzum* become noticeable.

Yetzirah (Formation), the next world, is dominated both by what the Kabbalist Azriel referred to as the three "Psychical" *Sefirot* (*Chesed, Gevurah, Tiferet*; Kindness, Strength, Beauty) and the three "natural" *Sefirot* (*Netzach, Hod, Yesod*: Endurance, Majesty, Foundation).[151] Here the archetypes for all existing things are created, making *Yetzirah* akin to the realm of Platonic "forms." *Yetzirah* is a world of both intellect and emotion, and it is in this

---

147. Ibid.

148. Zohar II, 239a. Tishby and Lachower, *The Wisdom of the Zohar*, Vol. 1, p. 257; cf. p. 280.

149. Moses Cordovero, *Or Ne'erav* VI:1; Ira Robinson, *Moses Cordovero's Introduction to Kabbalah: An Annotated Translation of His Or Ne'erav* (Hoboken, NJ: Ktav, 1994), p. 138.

150. Cordovero, *Or Ne'erav* VI:4, 42b; Robinson, *Moses Cordovero's Introduction to Kabbalah*, p. 138.

151. Scholem, *Kabbalah*, p. 107.

world that the spiritual entities (lower angels), which man creates through his *kavannot* (intentions of mind and heart), take form.

The world of *Assiyah* (action, making, enactment) is the world of physical, corporeal being.[152] Dominated by the *Sefirah Malchut* (Kingship), *Assiyah* is the realm over which the God of the Bible reigns as king. It is in *Assiyah* that space, time, and corporeality come into existence. There is also a spiritual aspect of *Assiyah*, which is the realm of human consciousness.

Originally *Assiyah* was meant to be a completely spiritual world,[153] but with the Breaking of the Vessels it became enmeshed in the broken and fallen shards of the shattered *Sefirot*, resulting in our own world's submergence in evil. As the lowest of the worlds *Assiyah* is furthest from God, and at the farthest remove from ultimate truth. The higher worlds, particularly *Beriah* and above, are largely hidden from man's view, like shadows in the cave of human experience. Yet even *Assiyah* is sustained by divine activity, and each of the higher worlds are represented in the human soul.

As with the *Partzufim*, each *Sefirah* is present in each of the worlds, and again, particular *Sefirot* are dominant in each.[154] Further, each world corresponds to a specific level of the human soul, a specific letter in the holy name of God (YHVH), a particular name of God that is derived from the numerical value of the letters used in spelling out the pronunciation of YHVH in different ways,[155] and a particular emanating orifice in the head of *Adam Kadmon*. Table 3 provides the correspondence among the Worlds, *Sefirot*, *Partzufim*, Divine names, and other aspects of the Lurianic universe.

---

152. Cordovero, *Or Ne'erav* VI:4, 42b; Robinson, *Moses Cordovero's Introduction to Kabbalah*, p. 138.

153. Scholem, "The Four Worlds," *Encyclopedia Judaica* (Jerusalem: Keter, 1972), 16:642.

154. S. Zalman, *Likutei Amarim-Tanya*, p. 187ff.

155. As can be seen in Table 1–3, each of these names of God corresponds to particular *Sefirot*. The names reflect the numerical values of the letters utilized in "spelling out" the letters YHVH in God's name (e.g., in Hebrew each letter has a numerical value), and a renaming via an expression of the obtained numerical value through the use of Hebrew letters that are standard expressions for the obtained numbers. This is explained in my *Symbols of the Kabbalah*, Chapter 4, note 111, and Chapter 5. See also Louis Jacobs, "The Uplifting of the Sparks in Later Jewish Mysticism," in *Jewish Spirituality: From the Sixteenth-Century Revival to the Present*, ed. Arthur Green (New York: Crossroads, 1987), p. 105. Also in the same volume, Lawrence Fine, "The Contemplative Practice of Yihudim in Lurianic Kabbalah," p. 85.

Table 1–3:
Celestial Equivalences

World	Sefirah	Partzuf	Level of the Soul	Letter of YHVH	Name of God	Orifice of *Adam Kadmon*
Adam Kadmon	*Keter*	*Atik Yomin (Kaddisha)*	*Yechidah*	Tittle of *Yud*		Skull
Atzilut	*Chochmah*	*Abba*	*Chaya*	*Yud*	*'av 72*	Eye (Vision)
Beriah	*Binah*	*Imma*	*Neshamah*	*Heh (1)*	*SaG 63*	Ear (Hearing)
Yetzirah	*Tiferet - Yesod*	*Ze'ir Anpin*	*Ruach*	*Vav*	*Mah 45*	Nose (Smell)
Assiyah	*Malchut*	*Nukva*	*Nefesh*	*Heh (2)*	*Bon 52*	Mouth (Speech)

THE *SEFIROT* AS STRUCTURAL ELEMENTS OF THE WORLD

According to the Kabbalists, the *Sefirot* are both divine traits and the structural elements of the created world. Moses Cordovero wrote that the essence of all created things is dependent upon the manner in which the *Sefirot* are combined as elements in its formation.[156] Vital held that the world's changes are a function of the permutations and positions of the *Partzufim*, themselves comprised of *Sefirot*. In explaining this idea Vital compared the *Partzufim* to both the infinite number of combinations of letters that produce meaningful language and the constantly changing positions of the constellations in the sky.[157]

Vital, who apparently had an acute interest in astrology, held that, the *Sefirot* are in a perpetual state of flux, altering as a result of the procession of the stars, other natural occurrences[158] and historical events. Further, the *Sefirot* correspond to different days of the week and times of the year (e.g., *Malchut* with the Sabbath, *Binah* with the festivals) and are thus influenced by changes in the calendar. According to Vital the nature of the cosmic influences is so complex as to defy human understanding.[159] As we have seen, the changes in the *Sefirot* not only impact on the world's structure, but have a "hermeneutic" significance as well. According to Vital the interpretation of such texts as the Zohar varies according to the sefirotic alignment at the time of the interpretation, and as such, the Zohar and other texts are replete with a nearly infinite variety of significances.

From a philosophical perspective, the notion that the *Sefirot* are the structural elements of the world, places the Kabbalah firmly within the idealist tradition. As will become clear in our discussion of Plato and Hegel in later chapters, these thinkers held that the basic substance of the world is not matter but ideas. By articulating a theory in which such ideas and values as Will, Wisdom, Intelligence, Love, Judgment, Beauty, etc., are the *elements* of creation, the Kabbalists have provided us with a theory that accords well

---

156. Scholem, *Kabbalah*, p. 115.
157. *Sefer Etz Chayyim* 1:2, p. 31; Menzi and Padeh, *The Tree of Life*, pp. 101–102.
158. E.g., the "diminishment" of the moon; see Talmud Tractate *Hullin* 60b.
159. *Sefer Etz Chayyim*, 29a; Menzi and Padeh, *The Tree of Life*, p. 63.

with the Platonic view that material things are mere "shadows on the wall of a cave," and that the ideas they instantiate are the true reality.[160]

SEFIROT: SOME BASIC SYMBOLS

It follows from the theory that the *Sefirot* are the traits of God and the structural elements of the world that they should be capable of providing us with insight into both God and the totality of the created world. In order to accomplish this task, the *Sefirot* can hardly have a static, fixed meaning and reference. The Kabbalists conceived of the *Sefirot* as dynamic, "iridescent" forces that change their aspects according to their context, and that can only be understood through a variety of metaphorical schemes. For the Kabbalists, no single perspective could be adequate to account for the whole of the created world, and, as we have seen, the *Sefirot* were understood to be equivalent not only to a series of values, but to a host of divine names, linguistic structures, cosmic personalities, and sensory modalities. In addition, the Kabbalists developed a wide variety of metaphors to shed light on the *Sefirot* doctrine. These metaphors cover a wide range of both natural and human phenomena. Among these metaphors are:

The Cosmic Tree: The *Sefirot* were frequently depicted as the limbs and branches of a cosmic tree that grows downward from its roots. The highest *Sefirah*, *Keter*, is represented in the roots, with the various other *Sefirot* spreading downward through the trunk, branches, and crown. The cosmic tree gives symbolic expression to the kabbalistic idea that the universe is itself a living organism that, unlike earthly trees, is rooted in heaven.

The Individuation of God: According to the Kabbalists, the progression of the *Sefirot* reveals the identity of God.[161] The first *Sefirah*, *Keter*, is considered "nothing," and God's full identity is only revealed with the emergence of the final *Sefirah*, *Malchut*, at which point, by a reversal in the order of the Hebrew letters, Nothing (AYN) becomes an individuated "I" (ANY).

Biblical Personalities: Major biblical personalities are said by the Kabbalists to represent or embody the *Sefirot* from *Chesed* to *Malchut*. For

---

160. I have provided a detailed explanation and philosophical grounding for the sefirotic elemental theory in Chapter Four of my *Symbols of the Kabbalah*.

161. Scholem, *Kabbalah*, p. 110.

example, Abraham, known for deeds of loving-kindness, is linked to *Chesed* (Kindness); and David, the paradigm of Jewish royalty, is paired with *Malchut* (Kingship). The intent of this scheme was not to divinify these personalities but to make clear that a spark of divine light inhabits the souls and *deeds* of the righteous, and that these deeds provide another key to understanding the structure and significance of the created world.

The Letters of Divine Speech: As early as *Sefer Yetzirah* we find the notion that the *Sefirot* are related and/or equivalent to the twenty-two letters of the Hebrew alphabet, which are themselves considered to be elements of creation.[162] At times the letters are seen as complementing the *Sefirot*; at other times they are the *Sefirot's* equivalent. The *Sefirot* are also said to be equivalent to specific letters or parts of letters in the divine name. This "linguistic mysticism" will be discussed in more detail below.

Light: The metaphor of light is perhaps the most pervasive metaphor for the *Sefirot*. The metaphor is prevalent in the Zohar, where, for example, *Ein-Sof* is understood as "the light that does not exist in light,"[163] and the *Sefirot* are considered a series of lights, only the last of which, *Malchut*, is revealed. Vital even goes so far as to imply that while all other descriptions of the *Sefirot* are metaphorical, descriptions in terms of light are real. The *Sefirot* are understood as a series of lights of descending intensity, radiating outward from the center in *Adam Kadmon* or *Ein-Sof.*

Colors: The *Sefirot* were metaphorically understood to embody certain colors. *Chesed* is said to be white for the purity embodied in its beneficence, *Gevurah* is red because it is the origin of passion, and *Tiferet* is the yellow of an egg yolk because it is the dialectical medium of the first two.[164] The color black represents both the "nothingness" and unknowability of the *Sefirah Keter*;[165] the dark judgments of the *Sefirah Din*; and the darkness of *Malchut*, the only *Sefirah* to have no light of its own.[166]

As we have seen, Cordovero and other Kabbalists likened the *Sefirot* to a series of colored glass filters that selectively transmit various aspects of the light of *Ein-Sof.* In this way the unity of *Ein-Sof* was preserved and the differences in the *Sefirot* attributed to epistemological as opposed to meta-

162. *Sefer Yetzirah* 1:1; Kaplan, *Sefer Yetzirah*, p. 5.
163. Tishby and Lachower, *The Wisdom of the Zohar*, Vol. 1, p. 290.
164. Moses Cordovero, *Or Ne'erav* VI:3, 38b; Robinson, *Moses Cordovero's Introduction to Kabbalah*, p. 127. Cf. Tishby and Lachower, *The Wisdom of the Zohar*, Vol. 1, p. 292.
165. Tishby and Lachower, *The Wisdom of the Zohar*, Vol. 1, p. 292.
166. Ibid., p. 291.

physical factors. The Zohar compares the final *Sefirah, Malchut*, to the colorful iridescence in a burning flame. The appearance, disappearance, and reappearance of these colors is said to reflect the transmission of the light from the upper *Sefirot* through *Malchut* into the lower worlds. As the various colors sparkle in and out of prominence within the flame, *Malchut*, like a "crystal ball against the sun,"[167] alternately reflects and transmits a variety of sefirotic traits into our finite realm. This dance of the sefirotic powers reflects the dynamic character of the universe, a universe the essence of which is not a static, clearly defined structure, but rather an ever changing play of processes and events. These kabbalistic images further suggest that our own understanding of the worlds must be dynamic as well, proceeding from a variety of "iridescent" perspectives and interpretations.

Garments: The *Sefirot* are frequently referred to as the "garments" (*levushim*). However, the *Sefirot* are no ordinary garments, as they are woven out of the fabric of the wearer's own being and are thus indistinguishable from *Ein-Sof*. In this image the Kabbalists place the *Sefirot* at the dialectical limit between the "essential" and the "accidental," implying both that they are and are not a part of *Ein-Sof*'s very essence.

Sexuality and the Family: The Kabbalists made prolific use of sexual and erotic imagery designed to express the notion that the *Sefirot* are dynamic, living forces through which divine procreative energy flows into the lower worlds.[168] The *Sefirah Yesod* is spoken of as the male genitalia; and the final *Sefirah, Malchut*, is the image of the female (the *Shekhinah*), which is the necessary complement and completion of the Primordial Man. Both humanity and the cosmos in general can only be considered whole when there is a direct and harmonious coupling of male and female. Without woman, the Zohar tells us, man is defective, a mere "half body."[169]

Each *Sefirah* is understood to be male to the *Sefirah* below it and female to the *Sefirah* above it, and the entire cosmic scheme is said to depend upon the proper channeling of the *Sefirot*'s erotic energy. The *Sefirah Chochmah* (Wisdom) is personified as the Celestial Father (*Abba*) whose mating with *Binah*, the Celestial Mother (*Imma*), gives rise to the lower *Sefirot*, which develop in *Binah*'s womb. Further couplings, e.g., between *Tiferet* ("The Holy One Blessed Be He") and *Malchut* (*Shekhinah*), as well as between

---

167. Zohar II, 23a–23b. Tishby and Lachower, *The Wisdom of the Zohar*, Vol. 1, p. 323.

168. Ibid., p. 288.

169. Ibid., p. 298.

several additional pairs of *Partzufim* are critical for the creation, harmony, and restoration of the universe. Sexual and erotic symbols pass over into a symbolism of birth and human development, and ultimately into a symbolism of the family.

Questions: The *Sefirot* were equated with certain "questions" that indicate the *Sefirah*'s nature and level. *Binah*, which is connected with the "beginning" of creation, is referred to with the question "Who?" (*Mi* in Hebrew). *Malchut*, at the end of the emanative process, prompts a contemplation of the cosmos as a whole, and is therefore called "What?" (*Mah*). According to the Zohar the "What?" of *Malchut* refers to "these" (*eleh*), i.e., "these *Sefirot*," and, as we have seen, when the letters comprising the question "What are these?" (*Mah Eleh*) are rearranged we arrive at *Elohim*, the biblically revealed God.[170] Philosophers normally hold that a full and proper account of the world must be couched in terms of propositions. By equating the *Sefirot* with questions, the Zohar suggests the intriguing possibility that the cosmos is essentially interrogative as opposed to propositional, and that the deepest wisdom is found in "profound questions" as opposed to "purported answers."

THE TEN *SEFIROT*

Having reviewed several characteristics that pertain to the *Sefirot* in general we are now in a position to provide a brief review of each of the ten individual *Sefirot*. It should be recalled, however, that for the Kabbalists the *Sefirot* were dynamic and dialectically evolving, containing within themselves their own opposites, as well as the characteristics of each of the other *Sefirot*.

Keter Elyon (The Supreme Crown): The Kabbalists regarded *Keter* to be qualitatively distinct from each of the other *Sefirot*, some holding that it is so high and exalted as to be completely identified with *Ein-Sof* itself. *Keter* is occasionally referred to as the Holy Ancient One, a term that is otherwise reserved for *Ein-Sof*.[171] Like *Ein-Sof*, *Keter* is so sublime and concealed that, according to the Kabbalists, nothing at all can be predicated of it,[172] and like

---

170. See Zohar I, 2a; Sperling and Simon, *The Zohar*, Vol. 1, p. 6; and discussion in Tishby and Lachower, *The Wisdom of the Zohar*, Vol. 1, pp. 294–295.

171. Schochet, "Mystical Concepts," p. 852, note 34.

172. Zohar II, 42b; Sperling and Simon, *The Zohar*, Vol. 2, p. 131. With regard to *Keter*, the Zohar applies the formula: "Search not the things that are too hard for

Ein-Sof, *Keter* is spoken of as *Ayin*, nothingness, a "darkness" that is at the same time the source of all light.[173]

More positively *Keter* is spoken of as the *will of all wills*,[174] and is frequently called *Ratzon* (Will, Desire).[175] The divine name associated with *Keter*, "*Ehyeh*" (I will be), also suggests that *Keter* is a "primal will"; as God declares to Moses, "*Ehyeh asher ehyeh*," "I will be who (or *that* which) I will be."[176] In addition, *Keter* is associated with *Tinug* (Delight), which can be understood as an emotional force that drives will. According to Schneur Zalman, the first Lubavitcher rebbe: "The Torah derives from *Chochmah* (Wisdom, Reason), but its source and root surpasses exceedingly the rank of *Chochmah* and is called the Supreme Will."[177]

Chochmah (Wisdom): The second *Sefirah* is regarded as the first creative act of *Ein-Sof* and is frequently spoken of as *reishit* (beginning). God's will, embodied in *Keter* is channeled via *Chochmah*,[178] and according to the Zohar it is in this *Sefirah* that all of the "engravings" or models upon which the world was created took form.[179] *Chochmah*, according to the Kabbalists, inhabits and activates all things. It is the "seed of all creation," "the potentiality of what is,"[180] "the original idea," and the "inner thought." In Neoplatonic terms it is equivalent to *Nous*, the realm of the "Forms" or "Ideas." *Chochmah* is substantial in comparison to *Keter*, but it remains *nothing* (*ayin*) in relation to the natural world, as the ideas that it embodies are purely abstract.

---

thee, and seek not the thing which is hidden from thee" (Ben Sira 320–324, cf. Talmud *Chagigah*, 13a). See discussion in Schochet, "Mystical Concepts," pp. 836–837.

173. Tishby and Lachower, *The Wisdom of the Zohar*, Vol. 1, p. 280.

174. Zohar III, 129a, 288b. See discussion in Tishby and Lachower, *The Wisdom of the Zohar*, Vol. 1, p. 270 and p. 302, note 4. Also Schochet, "Mystical Concepts," p. 837.

175. Tishby and Lachower, *The Wisdom of the Zohar*, p. 270.

176. Exodus 3:14. Tishby and Lachower, *The Wisdom of the Zohar*, Vol. 1, p. 270. Zohar III, 65a–b; Tishby and Lachower, *The Wisdom of the Zohar*, Vol. 1, p. 345.

177. S. Zalman, *Igeret HaKodesh*, sec. I, as cited in Schochet, "Mystical Concepts," p. 837.

178. See Zalman, *Likutei Amarim-Tanya*, Ch. 35, p. 155ff.

179. Ibid., p. 281, 331; Zohar 1, 2a; Sperling and Simon, *The Zohar*, Vol. 1, p. 6.

180. Zohar III, 235b; *Tanya* II, Ch. 3.

Binah (Understanding): It is in the *Sefirah Binah* that the concealed thought that comprises *Chochmah* begins to take substantial form.[181] According to the Zohar, it is in *Binah* that existence is separated and differentiated.[182] Compared to *Chochmah*, which is conceptualized as a single point, *Binah* is a circle or a "palace."[183] The third *Sefirah* is also equated with the reasoning process,[184] which articulates in detailed, substantive form the abstract, general notions or "engravings" contained in the divine wisdom.[185] *Binah* dominates the World of *Beriah* (Creation), the world in which finite, distinct entities first appear. *Binah* is also the *Partzuf Imma*, the Celestial Mother,[186] and as such the lower *Sefirot*, and, hence, all of creation, develop in her womb.[187]

Da'at (Knowledge) is regarded as the "son" of *Chochmah* and *Binah*,[188] and is therefore said to bring to fruition the intellective process that was begun in the Celestial Father and developed in *Binah*, the Celestial Mother. The idea, which is abstract and potential in *Chochmah*, is reasoned through and elaborated in *Binah*, but only becomes unified and practical in *Da'at*. *Da'at* has two aspects, a higher aspect that serves to unify the *Sefirot* above it, and a lower one that channels the intellectual activity of the higher *Sefirot* into the six "emotional" *Sefirot* from *Chesed* to *Yesod*, and ultimately into the World of Action, through the final *Sefirah*, *Malchut*.

Chesed is the first of the moral or emotional *middot* (traits). It connotes God's boundless love and kindness, the very principle through which God created and continuously renews the world.[189] According to Cordovero the function of *Chesed* is "to help and succor" and "to nullify the power of the Outside Ones who accuse and vex man."[190] *Chesed* is the *Sefirah* that is experienced by the mystics and prophets as divine grace and love, and it is the

---

181. *Tikkunei Zohar* 22, 63b.
182. Tishby and Lachower, *The Wisdom of the Zohar*, Vol. 1, p. 270.
183. Ibid., Vol. 1, p. 282.
184. Schochet, "Mystical Concepts," p. 838 and p. 853, note 59.
185. Zohar I, 90a, *Sitrei Torah*; Tishby and Lachower, *The Wisdom of the Zohar*, Vol. 2, p. 568, cf. discussion in Vol. 1, p. 270.
186. Zohar III, 290a ff.; *Pardes Rimonim* 8:17.
187. Tishby and Lachower, *The Wisdom of the Zohar*, Vol. 1, p. 282.
188. Schochet, "Mystical Concepts," p. 840.
189. Zohar II, 168b; Sperling and Simon, *The Zohar*, Vol. 4, p. 81. See Psalms 89:3: "The world was built by *Chesed*."
190. Moses Cordovero, *Or Ne'erav* VI:3, 37b; Robinson, *Moses Cordovero's Introduction to Kabbalah*, p. 124.

divine trait that informs all human acts of loving-kindness.[191] As *Gedullah* (Greatness), this *Sefirah* is God's awesome presence, what the theologian Rudolph Otto spoke of as the *mysterium tremendum*.[192] *Chesed*, however, would be overwhelming to humankind in pure form, and hence must be modified by its dialectical inverse, Judgment (*Din*).

Gevurah (Power) or *Din* (Judgment): *Gevurah* is the divine principle of judgment, measure, limit, and restraint. *Gevurah* limits God's boundless love (*Chesed*) and distributes it according to the merit and capacity of the receiver. According to Cordovero, *Gevurah* "is a lash to punish man."[193] Still, *Gevurah* is absolutely necessary, in part because it introduces a dimension of divine *justice* and *righteousness* into the world.[194] *Gevurah* is needed for the moral order. It is only in its negative aspect that it brings about *moral evil*. *Gevurah*, as limitation and judgment, is also the measured restraint of *Tzimtzum*, the contraction, withdrawal, and concealment of the divine effulgence that, according to Luria, is necessary for the creation of a finite world.[195] It is only as a result of the limitations imposed by this *Sefirah* that finite creatures can subsist without being reabsorbed into *Ein-Sof*. Further, it is only as a result of the tension and complementarity of *Chesed* and *Din*, Kindness and Judgment, that the world can be created and maintained.

Tiferet (Beauty) or *Rachamim* (Compassion) effects the dialectical integration of *Chesed* and *Gevurah*. According to the Zohar: "It is evident that there can be no perfection except that one aspect be joined to the other and a third hold them together to harmonize and complete them."[196] A balancing of Kindness and Judgment is necessary not only for the divine judge to have compassion but is also essential as the foundation for beauty.[197] Beautiful things, we might say, contain the spiritual (*Chesed*) in a way that is conditioned and limited through form (*Gevurah*). This balancing is symbol-

---

191. Cordovero, *Palm Tree of Deborah*, pp. 82, 90–91.

192. Rudolph Otto, *The Idea of the Holy* (London: Oxford University Press, 1970). (Originally published: 1923).

193. Moses Cordovero, *Or Ne'erav* VI:3, 37b; Robinson, *Moses Cordovero's Introduction to Kabbalah*, p. 126.

194. Zohar II, 175b; Sperling and Simon, *The Zohar*, Vol. 4, p. 108.

195. Schochet, "Mystical Concepts," p. 855, citing C. Vital, *Mevoh She'arim* I:1, 1.

196. Zohar 176a; Sperling and Simon, *The Zohar*, Vol. 4, p. 110.

197. *Tikkunei* Zohar 70, 133b. See Schochet, "Mystical Concepts," p. 842.

ized in the *Sefirah Tiferet*. *Tiferet* further symbolizes the dialectical truth that opposite ideas and forces reciprocally determine, balance, and in effect, create one another. Because of its dialectical nature, *Tiferet* is also identified with *Emet* or absolute Truth.[198]

Netzach (Endurance), *Hod* (Splendor), and *Yesod* (Foundation): *Netzach*, *Hod*, and *Yesod* are the branches or channels for the higher *Sefirot* of *Chesed*, *Gevurah*, and *Tiferet*, respectively.[199] They receive the energies transmitted by these upper *middot* and serve as instruments for the application of kindness, justice, and compassion in the world.[200] Unlike the *Sefirot* above them, which act through the stimulus of will and reason, *Netzach*, *Hod*, and *Yesod* act mechanically[201] and thus follow the *causal* order of the natural, spatio-temporal world. Indeed, according to the Kabbalist Azriel these *Sefirot* correspond to the natural order. We might consider them as paradigmatic of the three spatial dimensions of the finite world.[202]

In channeling the energies of the higher *Sefirot*, *Netzach* represents the "Endurance" of divine benevolence and the continual outpouring of *Chesed*, while *Hod* represents the preservation of the divine "Majesty and Splendor," in such a manner that it is not wantonly dissipated by *Chesed*. *Yesod*, which mediates between *Netzach* and *Hod*, represents the "Foundation" through which the world receives an appropriate mixture of emanations from the higher *Sefirot*. In the imagery of *Adam Kadmon*, *Yesod* represents the Phallus, which transmits the powers of the upper *Sefirot* into *Malchut/ Shekhinah*, the female, which represents the finite world.

Malchut (Kingship): *Malchut*, was understood by the Kabbalists as fulfilling the purpose of the entire emanative process. *Malchut* fully actualizes what was only potential in the upper *Sefirot*, and thus provides God an arena in which He can actualize and manifest His qualities of kindness, judgment, mercy, etc. Further, *Malchut* provides God with the finite subjects, over whom He can reign as "King" and as such, this *Sefirah* is the very fulfillment

---

198. Schochet, "Mystical Concepts," p. 855, note 103, citing Zohar *Chadash*, *Toldot* 26, *Yitro* 31b, *Sefer Etz Chayyim* 35:3.
199. Schochet, "Mystical Concepts," p. 843, citing to *Tikkunei* Zohar 19:45a, 22:68b, 30:74a, Zohar III, 236a.
200. Ibid.
201. Ibid.
202. As I have discussed in Chapter Four of my *Symbols of the Kabbalah*.

of the divine plan.[203] In *Malchut Ein-Sof* finally comes to know Himself in an "other." While *Malchut*, like the moon, has no light of its own, it succeeds in reflecting and transmitting the light of all the other *Sefirot* into the finite world.[204]

According to Cordovero *Malchut* is the architect of creation. Nothing reaches the world except via its portals.[205] *Malchut*, is identified with God's feminine aspect (the *Shekhinah*), and is referred to as the "Lower Mother" (*Imma Tataah*),[206] who receives the embryonic world that was initially implanted and concealed in the womb of *Binah*, the Celestial Mother. It is in *Malchut* that this "embryo" fully develops and is born, and, as such, *Malchut* is the true mother of the earth. *Malchut* is also linked to the dimension of *time*. Like time, *Malchut* has no true being of its own, but comes into existence as a result of the activities of the other entities.[207] *Sefer ha-Bahir* calls the lowest of the divine powers *nischono shel 'olam*, "the duration of the world"[208]; and the Zohar further links *Malchut* to the dimension of time by referring to it as "the tree of death" and "the destruction of all, the death of all."[209] The first Lubavitcher rebbe, Schneur Zalman, explicitly states that *Malchut* is the origin of both time and space.[210]

203. Schochet, "Mystical Concepts," p. 835, citing Zohar III:69b, 237b; *Pardes Rimonim* 2:6; *Sefer Etz Chayyim* 1:1.

204. Zohar II, 145b; Sperling and Simon, *The Zohar*, Vol. 4, p. 13; and as discussed metaphorically in Zohar I, 249b, 250a; Sperling and Simon, *The Zohar*, Vol. II, pp. 389–393. According to the Zohar (I, 23a) the *Sefirot* are "lights upon lights, one more clear than another, each one dark in comparison to the one above it from which it receives its light." Sperling and Simon, *The Zohar*, Vol. 1, p. 94.

205. Schochet, "Mystical Concepts," p. 846, citing Cordovero, *Pardes Rimmonim* 11:2 and *Tikkunei Zohar* 19, 40b.

206. Zohar I, 50a; Sperling and Simon, *The Zohar*, Vol. 2, p. 160; II, 22a, ibid., Vol. 2, p. 74 ("two transcendent mothers").

207. See Schneur Zalman, *Shaar Hayichud Vehaemunah* (*Tanya*, Part II), Chapter 7. Zalman, *Lukutel Amarim-Tanya*, p. 307ff. *Sefer Etz Chayyim* 6:5, 8:4, as cited in Schochet, "Mystical Concepts," p. 845. Compare Zohar II, 127a; Sperling and Simon, *The Zohar*, Vol. 3, p. 159.

208. Scholem, *Origins of the Kabbalah*, 160. Cf. *Sefer ha-Bahir*, sec. 115. *Book Bahir*, Neugroschel trans., p. 85.

209. Zohar I, 50b–51b. Tishby and Lachower, *The Wisdom of the Zohar*, Vol. 1, p. 320.

210. Schneur Zalman relates that it is "the attribute *Malchut* from which space and time are derived and come into existence." *Shaar Hayichud*, Chapter 7; Zalman, *Likutei Amarim-Tanya*, p. 309.

OTIYOT YESOD: THE FOUNDATIONAL LETTERS

Parallel to the theory of the *Sefirot*, the Kabbalists, as we have already seen, held a view in which the world is composed of the "letters of divine speech." As we have seen this theory is presented in the earliest proto-kabbalistic work, *Sefer Yetzirah* (The Book of Formation). In that work we find, alongside the theory that the cosmos is composed of ten *Sefirot*, a parallel symbolism in which the entire cosmos is said to be created from the twenty-two consonant/letters of the Hebrew alphabet, the so-called *Otiyot Yesod*, the foundational letters. In *Sefer Yetzirah*, the *Sefirot* and the letters together are referred to as "the thirty-two wondrous paths of creation."[211] We read in that work that out of the twenty-two letters God "formed substance out of chaos and made nonexistence into existence."[212]

Linguistic mysticism is present in the earliest kabbalistic source, *Sefer ha-Bahir*,[213] much of which is an inquiry into mystical significance of the Hebrew alphabet. Further, the anonymous "Source of Wisdom," which later influenced the founder of Hasidism, Israel Baal Shem Tov,[214] held that the world was created through the inscription of divine speech in the *Avir Kadmon* (Primoridial Ether).[215]

Later Kabbalists and Hasidim consistently put forth a linguistic theory of creation. The Zohar held that "the supernal letters . . . brought into being all the works of the lower world, literally after their own pattern."[216] As we have seen, according to the Lurianists, there are two basic metaphors that can be used to describe celestial events, the form of the human body, which encompasses *Adam Kadmon* and the *Sefirot*, and the shape of written letters. Regarding the latter, Vital states: "There is yet another way to describe by analogy, which is to depict these higher things through the shape of written letters, for every single letter points to a specific supernal light."[217]

The parallels between the *Sefirot* and various linguistic schemes used in

---

211. *Sefer Yetzirah* 1:1; Kaplan, *Sefer Yetzirah*, p. 5.

212. *Sefer Yetzirah* 2:6; ibid., p. 131.

213. See especially *Sefer ha-Bahir*, secs. 11a, 13, 18, 27, 48, and 54. *Book Bahir*, Neugroschel trans. pp. 53–65.

214. Ibid.

215. Scholem, *Kabbalah*, p. 332.

216. Zohar 1, 159a; Sperling and Simon, *The Zohar*, Vol. 2, p. 111.

217. *Sefer Etz Chayyim* 1:1, p. 28. Also see Menzi and Padeh, *The Tree of Life*, p. 54.

describing the upper worlds are summarized in Table 1–3, above. I have discussed the significance and rationale of the Kabbalist's linguistic mysticism in Chapter Five of my *Symbols of the Kabbalah*. Here it will suffice to point out that for the Kabbalists the doctrine of *Otiyot Yesod* gives expression to the view that creation is essentially *conceptual* rather than material. Letters are the fundamental units of language, and it is through language that concepts are born. For the Kabbalists, God creates with words because He is a creator of possibilities, of eternal forms, categories, and ideas. Indeed for the Kabbalists, it is only after the Breaking of the Vessels that finite, instantial, material entities come into existence. The world as it was originally created is a purely conceptual/spiritual realm. When this is made clear, several otherwise difficult and opaque kabbalistic doctrines can be understood. Among these are the doctrines that the name of an object is its soul, that the world is created and sustained by divine speech, and that the world's substance is composed of letters in the holy tongue.

THE BREAKING OF THE VESSELS

The Breaking of the Vessels (*Shevirat ha-Kelim*), creates a further dynamic and dialectical movement in the realms of the *Sefirot* and the Worlds. Luria held that ten vessels were originally meant to contain the emanation of God's light, but were unable to do so, and as a result they were either displaced or shattered. The vessels *Sefirot* from *Chesed* to *Yesod* shattered completely; while *Malchut*, the final vessel, was broken only in part. Had all of the vessels, including *Keter*, *Chochmah*, and *Binah*, shattered, the universe would have been returned to the utter chaos, the *toho* and *bohu* which according to the book of Genesis prevailed prior to creation. The *Sefirot* representing Will, Wisdom, and Understanding remained intact, although displaced from their proper positions. The six *Sefirot* from *Chesed* to *Yesod*, those representing spiritual, moral, aesthetic, and material values, were broken, and according to Luria, are in need of restoration and repair (*Tikkun*). As a result of the Breaking of the Vessels, shards from the broken vessels hurtled down through the metaphysical void, entrapping within themselves sparks (*netzot-zim*) of the divine light that they were originally meant to contain. These trapped sparks fall into the *Sitra Achra*, the "Other Side," an evil realm that has become enmeshed with our world, and await their extraction, liberation, and reascent into the upper realms.

The Breaking of the Vessels also impacts on the *Sefirot* as they are personified as "Visages" or *Partzufim*. As a result of the *Shevirah* the Celestial Father and Mother, and the other masculine and feminine aspects of the cosmos, which had hitherto been in a "face-to-face" sexual union, are forced to turn their backs upon one another and become completely disjoined. The Breaking of the Vessels thus also leads to a universal erotic alienation; one that can only be remedied via a dialectical blending of opposites embodied in a renewed *coniunctio* of the sexes. Finally, like the water that breaks signaling the birth of a child, the *Shevirah* signals a birth of a new personal and world order to be completed by man in the process of *Tikkun ha-Olam*.

By introducing the *Shevirah* into the theosophical Kabbalah, Luria gave expression to the view that God's original creation must be radically altered and even destroyed, before man and God can be completed and perfected. This idea is based on the biblical stories of the Fall of Adam and the flood,[218] and most directly on the biblical allusion to seven Kings who died in Edom (Genesis 35:31), which the Zohar interprets as a reference to the midrashic story that God created and destroyed many worlds before arriving at the one that now stands.

The symbol of the *Shevirah* gives expression to the Lurianic view that the *Sefirot* from which our world is comprised are not the pristine divine values of the original creation, but rather the broken and displaced shards of values that have been shattered and alienated from their original source. The Breaking of the Vessels thus introduces a "crisis" into all things, divine and human, great and small, even into the very "molecular" structure of the cosmos itself. However, it is a crisis, as symbolized in the dynamic of *Shevirah* (Breaking or Destruction) and *Tikkun* (Restoration or Repair) that is fundamentally a vehicle for change and progress in man and the world.

The Breaking of the Vessels operates in all spheres: in history and the immediate moment; in the life of nations; and in the rational, spiritual, and emotional life of man. The *Shevirah* occurs on material, psychological, intellectual, and erotic levels. It is a symbol that brings the most diverse genres of human experience under a single dynamic idea.

Scholem held that the "Breaking of the Vessels" was a metaphor for the historical Jewish experience of "exile" (*galut*) and the consequent hope for "redemption" (*ge'ulah*). The broken shards, Scholem tells us, are cut off

---

218. As we have seen the Breaking of the Vessels is also implicit in the conditions that prevailed at the time of creation: Genesis 1:2: "the earth was empty and void." See Luzzatto, *General Principles of the Kabbalah*, p. 69.

from their source in God, much as the Jewish people in the diaspora, were cut off from their spiritual source in the land of Israel. The gathering and reassembling of these broken and scattered shards, and the liberation of sparks of divine light that they contain, is a powerful symbol for the ingathering of the Jewish people and their ultimate restoration to Zion. While quite powerful from a historical (and Zionist) point of view, this analysis reduces the "Breaking of the Vessels" to a symptom of a particular historical experience and robs it of any claim to general, philosophical significance. The Kabbalists themselves understood the "exile and redemption" embodied in the Lurianic symbols of *Shevirah* (Breaking) and *Tikkun* (Restoration) to be one manifestation of an archetype that resonates throughout human life, the world, and the very structure of the godhead. The Kabbalists held that the Breaking of the Vessels provides a symbolic explanation of the origin of the material world as well as the division between good and evil. The *Shevirah* also provide the arena in which humankind can fulfill its ultimate redemptive purpose.

As a result of the Breaking of the Vessels the world is in a state of conflict, alienation, and imbalance. Spirit has been alienated in the matter formed by the "husks" that fell into the Other Side subsequent to the *Shevirat ha-Kelim*. The world must, according to Luria, be repaired and restored. This restoration process, known as *Tikkun ha-Olam* (the Mending of the World) began spontaneously with the shattering of the vessels and the return of a portion of the divine light to its source. Lights from the forehead of the Primordial Man assist in this process. However, the complete restoration and respiritualization of the world rests on the shoulders of humanity, and it is this that is the task of each individual man and woman on earth: to restore those sparks that pertain to his or her own soul and to help reclaim the sparks that he or she encounters in the world at large. The Jewish people, in particular, through their observance of Torah and *mitzvot* (the precepts of the Jewish religion) can release the "sparks" (*netzotzim*) of divine light trapped in the world of the *Kelippot*, and raise them to be reunited with the infinite light from which they came.

THE PROBLEM OF EVIL

The Kabbalists held that evil is *implicit* in *Ein-Sof*, but *explicit* only in creation. For them, evil is rooted in and an essential part of the very perfection and goodness of the godhead, particularly in God's beneficence as the creator of the universe.

As we have seen, the Kabbalists, who frequently regarded *Ein-Sof* as the "Infinite All," also held the dialectical opposite, that *Ein-Sof*, in and of itself, is a species of nothingness. "Nothingness" or *Ayin*, is thus fundamental to the divine essence, and as such nonbeing, negativity, and hence evil, is part of the very structure of divine reality. However, the divine *Ayin*, is manifest in three moments of negation, Judgment (*Din*), Contraction (*Tzimtzum*), and Breakage (*Shevirah*).

The first of these negative aspects, the divine trait of Judgment (*Din*), is, along with each of the other sefirotic traits, perfectly commingled within the Godhead prior to the advent of creation. "Judgment" is significant for both creation and evil, because judgment, in the sense of making *distinctions*, contains within itself the roots of *finitude*, and thus evil and death. In order to create a world God must contain within Himself the potential for distinctions, and this potential, the divine trait of *Din*, is one origin of evil.

The Kabbalists held that actual evil originates in a *cathartic* act in which *Ein-Sof* seeks to purge itself of the very roots of *Din* or Judgment that exist at its core. The Zohar understands evil as a process of excretion through which the divine organism maintains its pure essence as the good. The Zohar uses the metaphor of a divine furnace that melts and refines the roots of evil, or *Din*;[219] "dross" from this process results in the *Kelippot* ("husks") that form the substance of the *Sitra Achra*, the "Other Side." The cathartic externalization of "severe judgment" produces a negative counterworld ruled by Satan.[220] Luria apparently adopted a similar "cathartic view"; one of his followers, Ibn Tabul, held that the lights in the primordial void were arranged in such a manner that *Ein-Sof* could eject the latent evil within itself.[221]

The Zohar makes reference to the midrashic tale of earlier worlds that were created and destroyed.[222] According to the Zohar, these earlier worlds consisted of the dross or refuse from the original divine catharsis, and were destroyed because, unlike our own world, they contained harsh judgments unmitigated by the divine *middah* of *Chesed*, benevolence. As described by Scholem, fragments of these earlier worlds, remain, "floating about our

---

219. Tishby and Lachower, *The Wisdom of the Zohar*, Vol. 2, p. 460.
220. Gershom Scholem, "Sitra Achra: Good and Evil in the Kabbalah," in G. Scholem *The Mystical Shape of the Godhead* (New York: Schocken, 1991), p. 63.
221. For a discussion of the cathartic theory see Scholem, *Kabbalah*, p. 130.
222. *Genesis Rabbah* 3:7 and 9:2.

universe like debris from extinct volcanoes."[223] These fragments are, according to the Zohar, the origin of the *Kelippot* or "husks" that are the source of evil and negativity on earth.

The second Lurianic symbol of negation and evil is *Tzimtzum*, the divine contraction and concealment that gives rise to a created world. In *Tzimtzum* God's beneficence is restricted in order that finite creatures can subsist without being reabsorbed by the infinite divine light. Evil, according to this theory, is an absolutely necessary by-product of creation, as created things could not exist unless God's goodness was limited in *Tzimtzum*. As a result of *Din*, the world is filled with *distinctions* between good and evil, and as a result of *Tzimtzum* the world is *alienated* from the ultimate source of goodness and therefore embodies evil as a sort of "privation" of the Good. On the other hand, since creation is itself a "Good," the privation and hence evil, which is necessary for creation, is regarded by the Kabbalists as good as well.

The Kabbalists are thus in the paradoxical position of asserting that *Evil is necessary for good*. This is yet another example of the the kabbalistic view that both *Ein-Sof* and the world are a *coincidentia oppositorum*. We read in the Zohar: "For this reason it says 'And behold it was very good' (Genesis 1:31). This (refers to) the angel of death. He should not be banished from this world. The world needs him . . . It is all necessary, good and evil."[224] One reason for the necessity for evil is that it brings into the world the possibility of sin, and hence also (by way of choice and contrast) the possibility for virtue and redemption. It is also in this sense that *evil is* good, for it is the condition for good's realization. As the Zohar states: "There is no true worship except it issue forth from darkness, and no true good except it proceed from evil."[225] Good proceeds from evil, when man, by his good acts and intentions transforms it into good. According to the Zohar: "when man enters upon an evil way, and then forsakes it, the Holy One is exalted in His glory . . ."[226] Evil is a prerequisite for human freedom, which is itself a condition for the ultimate good.

The third Lurianic symbol of negation, *Shevirat Hakelim*, the Breaking of the Vessels, constitutes the most original kabbalistic contribution to the

---

223. Scholem, "Sitra Achra," p. 62.
224. Zohar II, 63a–63b, Raya Mehemna. Tishby and Lachower, *The Wisdom of the Zohar*, Vol. 2, pp. 510, 523.
225. Zohar II, 184a; Sperling and Simon, *The Zohar*, Vol. 4, p. 125.
226. Ibid.

theory of evil. According to Luria and his disciples, evil is the inevitable result of the shattering of the *Sefirot*, the value archetypes through which God creates and structures the world. The Breaking of the Vessels results not only in a shattering of divine values, but a further alienation of divine light from its essence in the absolute Good. As we have seen, as a result of the *Shevirah*, sparks of divine light become entrapped in the shards of the broken vessels, forming *Kelippot*, the "Husks," which fall into the metaphysical void and comprise the *Sitra Achra*, "the Other Side," the dark realm of unholiness and evil. It becomes incumbent upon man to gather the sparks (*netzotzim*) of divine light, extract (*birur*) them from the *Kelippot*, and restore them to their place in a newly perfected God and world. This, according to the Lurianists, is the essence of *Tikkun ha-Olam* (the Restoration of the World). According to the Chabad Hasidim, the formation of the *Kellipot* was a necessary event in order to provide the context for man's *Tikkun*, the world's redemption. For Luria, the entire process from *Tzimtzum* to *Shevirah* and *Tikkun* is part of the divine essence. The existence of evil is thus necessary for the completion and perfection of *Ein-Sof* itself.

TIKKUN HA-OLAM: THE RESTORATION OF THE WORLD

The concept of *Tikkun ha-Olam* may well be rooted in the biblical conviction that mankind's lost paradise would be restored in a future messianic age, and in the belief that the exile would be overcome and the Jewish people restored to Zion. However, the symbol of *Tikkun ha-Olam* as first fully articulated by Luria in sixteenth-century Safed, is a symbol with metaphysical and theological implications. Luria and his disciples understood *every event* in the created universe, indeed the very act of creation itself, to be a prelude to *Tikkun ha-Olam*. For them it is only as a result of the world's restoration that both cosmos and God can be said to be complete.

A wide array of kabbalistic symbols inform the Lurianic understanding of *Tikkun ha-Olam*. I will discuss several of these symbols, linking them to the other symbols, which, as we have seen, play a pivotal role in Lurianic thought.

THE SYMBOLS OF *TIKKUN*

The Unification of God and His Shekhinah: An erotic union between the masculine and feminine aspects of God is an important kabbalistic symbol that predates and was incorporated into the Lurianic symbol of *Tikkun*. The Zohar holds that God's feminine aspect is exiled on earth as the *Shekhinah* and that she must be reunited with "The Holy One Blessed Be He."[227] The unity between the masculine and feminine aspects of the godhead was broken by the sins of mankind and the exile of the Jewish people, and is maintained by the "Other Side." Through the observance of the *mitzvot* and divine worship, humankind is able to reestablish the union between God and His *Shekhinah*, symbolized as the union between the *Sefirot Tiferet* and *Malchut*.

These ideas were adopted and elaborated upon in the Lurianic theory of *Tikkun*. According to Luria, the *Shevirah* results in numerous erotic separations (between *Sefirot*, *Partzufim*, divine names, etc.), each of which require their own emendation or *Tikkun*. The entire cosmic order is interpreted in sexual/erotic terms, and the reestablishment of cosmic harmony is contingent upon various *coniunctios* in the upper worlds.

The unification of divine masculine and feminine aspects of the godhead can itself be understood as symbolic of the blending of the opposites, which, according to the Kabbalists, is part of the perfection and harmony of the universe. In psychological terms it can be understood as the reunification of the feminine and masculine aspects of a divided self.

The Trees of Life and Knowledge: According to *Midrash Ha Neelam* in the Zohar, the *Sefirot* were revealed to Adam in the form of the twin trees of Life and Knowledge. Through his sin, Adam separated these trees, thus placing a division between living and knowing.[228] This division resulted in a fissure within both God and the world, and prompted Adam to worship the tenth *Sefirah* (the *Shekhinah*, God's manifestation on earth) without recognizing its unity with higher, more spiritual forms. By worshipping the *Shekhinah*, Adam became attached to the temporal, material world, represented by the Tree of Knowledge (of good and evil), and ignored the "Tree of Life" (the sefirotic values embodied in the Torah).

The goal of *Tikkun ha-Olam* is to heal the fissure between life and knowledge. Through observance of divine commandments, the individual reattaches him or herself to the *Sefirot* (Godly values) and hence effects a reunification between "knowledge" and "life."

The Raising of the Sparks (*Netzotzim*): The symbol of a divine spark

---

227. Zohar II, 216b, Sperling and Simon, *The Zohar*, Vol. 4, p. 235; III, 74a, Sperling and Simon, *The Zohar*, Vol. 5, p. 75; III, 79a, Sperling and Simon, *The Zohar*, Vol. 5, pp. 87–88.

228. Scholem, *Major Trends*, p. 232.

encased in earthly matter is an ancient Gnostic symbol, which takes on new life in the Kabbalah of seventeenth-century Safed. In the Gnostic version, a spark of divinity is entrapped in an alien and evil world, and imprisoned in the soul of man. According to the Gnostics, the individual's knowledge (Gnosis) of this inner spark results in its being liberated from this world, and the Gnostic adherent abandons both body and self to join the infinite pleroma.

In contradistinction to the Gnostics, Luria held that when the spark of divine light is freed, the world is reintegrated and restored, rather than escaped and discarded. According to the Hasidim it is the individual's divinely appointed task to liberate not only those sparks that are entrapped in *Kelippot* within his own body and soul, but also those sparks in the world that he or she encounters along life's way. Through proper ethical and spiritual conduct the individual is able to free the holy sparks from the *Kelippot* that contain them, enabling the exiled divine light to return to its source, thus promoting the completion of *Tikkun ha-Olam*. The "raising of the sparks" implies that there is something of spiritual value in all things, and it is man's task to discover and bring out the value in the material world, thereby transforming that world into a spiritual realm.[229] *Tikkun ha-Olam* will only be complete when the last spark has been raised and the entire world informed with spiritual meaning and value. For the Hasidim, the individual's life is a providential journey that places him/her in contact with those sparks which his or her person is uniquely suited to "raise." Each occurrence, each interaction along life's way, serves as an opportunity to either raise a spark of divine light or to increase the power of the *Kelippot* and thereby plummet the spiritual world into further darkness. In the process of raising the sparks within his soul and the world, the adherent comes to "discover the roots" of his own soul,[230] complete his own life work, and assist in the process of *Tikkun ha-Olam*.

The Transition from Exile to Redemption is an important metaphor for *Tikkun ha-Olam*. The exile of Adam and Eve from the garden of Eden, the exile of the Jewish people in Egypt, Babylonia, and later throughout the

---

229. It is for this reason that so many of the *mitzvot* involve the material world. For example, in building a *sukkah* the Jew takes common natural materials, e.g., wood and leaves, and transforms them into objects of divine service, thereby spiritualizing them.

230. M. Zacuto, commentary on Zohar I, 78a in Shalom b. Moses Busalgo, *Mikdash Melech* (Amsterdam, 1750); see Gershom Scholem, *Sabbatai Sevi: The Mystical Messiah*, pp. 41–42.

world, were understood by Luria and his followers as manifestations of a cosmic process. At various points in history (the Sinaitic revelation being the most prominent among them) the Jewish people had an opportunity to complete *Tikkun ha-Olam*; however, on each of these occasions the Jewish people chose to align themselves with the Other Side and failed in their mission. Currently, the purpose of the Jewish diaspora is for Jews to collect sparks from all over the world.[231] When this occurs, both historical and cosmic exile will be overcome, Zion will be restored, and the evil *Kelippot* eliminated.

Development in the Womb of the Celestial Mother. The Lurianists teach that the *Partzufim* play a crucial role in the process of *Tikkun ha-Olam*. In the first place, the *Sefirot*, which were shattered because of their disunity, are spontaneously reassembled into integrated *Partzufim* in the early stages of the *Tikkun* process.[232] Each *Partzuf* is said to represent a specific stage in the process of world emendation and serves as an archetype for the reunification of the opposites, conceptualized as the masculine and feminine aspects of *Adam Kadmon* or God.[233] When the *Partzufim* are engaged "face-to-face" (*panim be fanim*), the process of *Tikkun* is well underway.

The *Partzufim*, however, must be completed by man. According to Luria, one *Partzuf, Zeir Anpin* (The "Short-Faced" or "Impatient" one) is integrally connected with the aspect of *Tikkun* that involves the efforts of mankind. *Zeir Anpin* organizes within itself the six *Sefirot* that were completely shattered in the Breaking of the Vessels. *Zeir Anpin* is described as developing within the womb of *Imma*, the Celestial Mother, creating, according to Scholem, what appears to be a myth of "God giving birth to Himself."[234] In its development, *Zeir Anpin* (and its celestial mate, *Nukva*) are said to progress through five distinct stages: *ibur* (conception), *lidah* (pregnancy), *yenikah* (birth), *katanot* (childhood), and *gadolot* (maturity). The final stage, *gadolot*, is reflective of mankind's own intellectual and moral maturity. This development serves as a basic metaphor for *Tikkun ha-Olam*.

The Mitigation of Judgment by Kindness. The development of the world is understood by the Lurianists and other Kabbalists as a dialectical blending

---

231. See J. Schochet, "Mystical Concepts," p. 892 citing, *Sefer Ez Chayyim*, 3:6, 19:3, 26:1; and S. Zalman, *Tanya* I, Chapter 49.

232. Scholem, *Kabbalah*, p. 140.

233. Ibid. Scholem says that together the *Partzufim* "constitute the final figure of *Adam Kadmon* as it evolves in the first stages of *tikkun*," ibid., p. 142.

234. Scholem, *Major Trends*, p. 271.

of opposites. One opposition, which plays a critical role in the Lurianic conception of *Tikkun ha-Olam*, the moral dichotomy between *Chesed* (Kindness) and *Din* (Judgment), was singled out by the Kabbalists for special consideration. We have already seen how, according to the Zohar, earlier worlds were destroyed because the aspect of severe judgment within them was not mitigated by kindness and beneficence. The temperance of judgment by kindness (and vice versa) is the foundation of the *Sefirah Rachamim* (Mercy, Compassion), which, as we have seen, the Kabbalists came to equate with *Emet*, Truth. The pursuit of a balance between Kindness and Judgment (a balance which, according to Cordovero, must be weighted slightly in the direction of kindness),[235] is a critical aspect of *Tikkun ha-Olam*.

Much more could be said regarding the Lurianic concept of *Tikkun ha-Olam*. The role of human freedom, the function of "evil," and the place of *Gilgul* (reincarnation) in the Lurianic conception of *Tikkun* are each topics worthy of our consideration. The Kabbalists, for example, held the intriguing view that all souls were one prior to their fragmentation after Adam's sin, and that since that time, individual souls are connected to one of 613 odd soul-roots. Individuals within a given soul-root have a natural affinity with one another, and through either *Gilgul* (reincarnation) or *Ibbur* (spiritual impregnation) a soul can come to the aid of those in its "root" and help in their individual *Tikkun*. I have discussed these issues in depth in my *Symbols of the Kabbalah*.

A VERBAL THEOSOPHICAL PICTURE

This concludes our summary of the basic doctrines of the theosophical Kabbalah. For those who are unfamiliar with these doctrines, it is hoped that this chapter has served as an aid to understanding the "basic metaphor" I have outlined in the Introduction, and that it will also be helpful in comprehending the comparative studies to come. I want to emphasize that a full appreciation of the Lurianic theosophy rests on the idea that each of the Lurianic symbols are elements in a dialectical process; and that it is the entire process, including the withdrawal of *Ein-Sof* in *Tzimtzum*, the emanation of the *Sefirot*, their destruction in the Breaking of the Vessels, and the

---

235. Schochet, "Mystical Concepts," p. 842; M. Cordovero, *Pardes Rimonim* 8:2, 9:3.

redemptive activities of mankind in *Tikkun*, that constitutes a single divine
reality that encompasses and defines *Ein-Sof*, the world, and humankind. This
divine reality is summarized and provided with a "verbal picture" in Table 4
below.[236]

Table 1–4:
The Lurianic Theosophy

Ein-Sof (The infinite godhead), of which nothing can be said . . .
is the Union of being and nothingness, of "everything and its opposite,"
in coincidentia oppositorum, the complementarity of opposing, even
contradictory, principles.
Ein-Sof weaves itself out of its own nothingness.
It is the foundation of, yet also completed by, the world;
the creator of, and yet created by, man.
Ein-Sof performs a **Tzimtzum**
(Divine Concealment, Contraction, Withdrawal), which
leads to a . . .
Metaphysical Void (*tehiru*), a circle surrounded by *Ein-Sof* on all sides . . .
containing a residue (*Reshimu*) of divine light.
The light of the Infinite (*Or Ein-Sof*) is emanated into the void.
It is a thin line (*kav*) through which . . .
Adam Kadmon (Primordial Man) spontaneously emerges.
Lights, also conceived as holy "letters," flashing and recoiling from
Adam Kadmon's eyes, nose, mouth, and ears form . . .
Vessels (*Kelim*) for containing further lights, thus forming the
"World of Points" comprised of . . .
the *Sefirot* (Archetypes of Value and Being; constituents of the body
of *Adam Kadmon*):
Keter (Crown, Will, Delight, the highest *Sefirah*),
Chochmah (Intellect, Wisdom, Paternal),   *Binah* (Understanding, Maternal),
Chesed (Loving-Kindness),   *Tiferet/Rachamim* (Beauty, Compassion),
Din/Gevurah (Judgment, Strength),
Netzach (Glory),   *Hod* (Splendor),
Yesod (Foundation), and
Malchut/Shekhinah (Kingship/ Feminine principle).

---

236. This is a modified version of a table that appears in my *Symbols of the
Kabbalah*.

The vessels are also composed of the *Otiyot Yesod*,
the 22 letters of divine speech,
and are organized into . . .
Worlds (*Olamot*):
Adam Kadmon (A'K, identified with *Ein-Sof and Keter*),
Atziluth (Nearness),
Beriah (Creation),
Yetzirah (Formation), and
Assiyah (Making, the lowest world, including our material earth).
The weakness and disunity of the *Sefirot* leads to their shattering and
displacement, known as . . .
The Breaking of The Vessels (*Shevirat Hakelim*), which produces . . .
a rupture in the conjugal flow between Masculine and Feminine
aspects of God, and
Netzotzim (Sparks), which fall and become entrapped in . . .
Kellipot (Husks), which comprise the . . .
Sitra Achra (The Other Side, a realm of darkness and evil).
Lights from the forehead of *Adam Kadmon*, also conceptualized as
mystical names, reconstitute the broken *Sefirot*/vessels as
Partzufim (Faces or Personalities of God):
Attika Kaddisha (The Holy Ancient One)/ *Keter*,
Abba (The Father)/ *Chochmah*,
Imma (The Mother)/ *Binah*,
Zeir Anpin (The Impatient One)/ *Chesed - Yesod*,
Nukvah (The Female)/ *Malchut/Shekhinah*. . . . *This begins*. . .
Tikkun ha-Olam (The Restoration of the World), which is completed
by man, who via the **"raising of the sparks,"** brings about the
Reunification of the *Partzufim*, the masculine and feminine
principles of God.
The dialectic of *Ein-Sof* is Mirrored in Man,
but, properly speaking, there is no man, no world, only God.
All of the above, however, is, paradoxically said from the point of view
of man who is himself both an illusory and necessary being.
Yet *Ein-Sof* is most closely identified with the redemptive activities
of humanity, as
Tikkun ha-Olam results in the completion and perfection of **Ein-Sof**
(return to beginning) . . .

2

Comparative Studies

SOME ROUTES OF INFLUENCE

In this book I discuss the relationship between the Kabbalah and six major forms of non-Jewish ancient and modern thought: Indian philosophy, Platonism, Gnosticism, and the thought of Hegel, Freud, and Jung. While these comparisons are each, on my view, critical to a contemporary interpretation and reformulation of the Kabbalah, they hardly exhaust the possibilities for fruitful comparative study. Several figures, to be discussed briefly below, including John Scotus Erigena, Ibn 'al-Arabi, Jakob Boehme, Nicholas of Cusa, and Friedrich Schelling, could well provide material for full-length comparisons.

Table 2–1 provides a general historical outline of the Kabbalah, along with an outline of related non-kabbalistic movements and figures.[1] The table should provide a ready reference to the major figures who are discussed in this chapter and throughout this book, as well as provide a matrix in which the *potential* lines of influence and cross-fertilization *may* have taken place. I say "may" because our understanding of the relationship between the Kabbalah and other trends in Western (as well as Eastern) philosophy and

---

1. On the wider influences of the Kabbalah, see Scholem, *Kabbalah*, pp. 190–203.

Table 2–1:
The Kabbalah and Its Influences

	Jewish Religion, Philosophy, and Mysticism	Eastern Philosophy	Western Philosophy	Gnosticism and Alchemy	Christian Kabbalists	Occultists	Psychology
1500 B.C.E.		Rig Veda 1500 B.C.E.					
1000 B.C.E.		Upanishads 800 B.C.E.					
600 B.C.E.							
500 B.C.E.	Prophet Ezekiel Active 592– 571 B.C.E.		Pythagoras, sixth cent. B.C.E.				
400 B.C.E.		Sutras 400 B.C.E.– 600 C.E.	Plato, 438–328/7 B.C.E. Aristotle 384–322 B.C.E.				
300 B.C.E.							

200 B.C.E.	Bhagavad Gita 200 B.C.E.					
100 B.C.E.						
B.C.E.						
C.E.	Philo of Alexandria 15–10 B.C.E.–?			Simon Magus first cent. C.E.		
100	Merkaveh Mysticism			Valentinus, second cent. C.E.		
200		Plotinus, third cent. C.E.		Maria the Jewess second or third cent. C.E. Zosismos third cent. C.E.		
300						

Table 2-1: (*continued*)
The Kabbalah and Its Influences

	Jewish Religion, Philosophy, and Mysticism	Eastern Philosophy	Western Philosophy	Gnosticism and Alchemy	Christian Kabbalists	Occultists	Psychology
400	Sefer Yetzirah third to the sixth cent. C.E.		Proclus, fourth cent. Pseudodionysis sixth cent.				
600	*Shi'ur Koma* Before sixth cent. C.E.						
800		Sankara 788–c. 820	Scotus Erigena c. 810–c. 877				
1000							

1100	*Sefer ha-Bahir*, School of Isaac the Blind c. 1175–1200	Suhrawardi Maqtul (d. 1191)		
1200	Azriel of Gerona. *Sefer ha-Zohar* distributed by Moses deLeon (c. 1286)	Ibn al-Arabi (late 1100s, early 1220s) Meister Eckhardt c. 1260–c. 1328		
1300				
1400		Nicholas of Cusa 1401–1464		Giovanni Pico della Mirandola (1463–1494)

Table 2–1: (*continued*)
The Kabbalah and Its Influences

	Jewish Religion, Philosophy, and Mysticism	Eastern Philosophy	Western Philosophy	Gnosticism and Alchemy	Christian Kabbalists	Occultists	Psychology
1500	Moses Cordovero (1522–1570) Isaac Luria (1534–1572) Chayyim Vital (1543–1620)		Giordano Bruno 1548–1600	Paracelsus 1493–1541 Blasius Vigenerus 1523–1596 Heinrich Khunrath 1560–1601	Johannes Reuchlin 1455–1522 Guillame Postel 1510–1581		
1600	Sabbatai Sevi (1626–1676)		Jakob Boehme 1575–1624 Benedikt de Spinoza 1632–1677 Gottfried Wilhelm Leibniz 1646–1716	Blaise de Vigenere Robert Fludd 1574–1637	Knorr von Rosenroth 1636–1689		

1700	Moses Chayyim Luzzatto (1707–1746) Baal Shem Tov (c. 1700–1760) Schneur Zalman of Lyadi 1745–1813				F.C. Oetinger (1702–1782)	Martines de Pasqually 1727–1774	
1800	Aharon Halevi Horowitz of Staroselye 1766–1828		Friedrich Schelling 1775–1854 G.W.F. Hegel 1770–1831		Franz Josef Molitor 1779–1861	Eliphas Levi 1810–1875 Helena Petrovna Blavatsky 1831–1891	
1900	Gershom Scholem (b. 1897) Isaiah Tishby (b. 1908) Moshe Idel (b. 1947)						Sigmund Freud 1856–1938 Carl Jung 1875–1960
2000							

religion is very far from complete. For example, while it is clear that the parallels between Neoplatonism and kabbalistic theosophy originate in an important and direct impact that the Neoplatonists had upon the early Kabbalists, equally notable parallels between Gnosticism and the Kabbalah may rather be explicable on grounds of convergent evolution.

SCOTUS ERIGENA

Neoplatonic ideas could very well have been infused into the Kabbalah through a variety of intermediaries. Scholem has argued that the earliest Kabbalists in Provence, during the period 1180–1220, may well have possessed indirect or even direct knowledge of the writings of the Christian philosopher/theologian, Scotus Erigena (c. 810–c. 877) whose thought had been influential during that period.[2] Erigena, who was himself greatly influenced by Neoplatonic thought, and in particular by the Christian Neoplatonist Pseudo-Dionysius, held that the primordial causes, though multiple, were nonetheless a unity of divine wisdom,[3] that God is a *coincidentia oppositorum*,[4] and that in creating the world God first must descend into the depths of his own nothingness.[5] Each of these doctrines make an appearance in the early Kabbalah.

SANKARA

The relationship between Indian philosophy and the Kabbalah is discussed in detail in Chapter Three. There we will see that various Hindu, Jainist, and Buddhist formulations bear remarkable resemblance to important kabbalistic symbols and themes, most significantly *Ein-Sof, Adam Kadmon* (the Primordial Man), and *Kellipot* (the evil "husks"). Among Indian metaphysicians special mention should be made of Sankara.

Sankara (788–820 C.E.), the founder of the *Advaita* (nondualistic) Vedanta school of Hindu thought, was the most influential metaphysician in

---

2. Scholem, *Origins of the Kabbalah*, pp. 314, 422, 440.
3. Ibid., p. 314.
4. Ibid., p. 440.
5. Ibid., p. 422.

the Indian philosophical tradition.[6] Sankara provided detailed speculation on the nature of *Brahman* that parallels the Kabbalists' speculations regarding the negative (*Ayin*) and positive characteristics of *Ein-Sof.* For Sankara *Brahman* is called "nonbeing" prior to the origination of the world, but in its positive mode "Brahman is eternal, all-knowing, absolutely self-sufficient, ever pure, intelligent and free, pure knowledge, absolute bliss."[7] It is to Sankara that we owe the clearest and most systematic expression of the identity between *Brahman* and *Atman*, i.e., between God and the Self, an idea that appears in the kabbalistic notions that the macrocosm perfectly reflected in the microcosm and that the *Sefirot* are the components of both God and man. For Sankara, the multiplicity of empirical selves is essentially an illusion; only Brahman, the power that lies at the foundation of the cosmos, is real; a view that is approached by the Kabbalists in their notions that finite souls represent a contraction and concealment of God's light and that individual souls are fragments of the original soul of *Adam Kadmon*. Like the Kabbalists, Sankara held that the origin of individual selves from the highest self is akin to "the issuing of sparks from the fire."[8] Like the Kabbalists, Sankara made use of the image of the reflection of light to account for the distinction between the one and the many: Brahman "appears one and many at the same time, just as the moon is multiplied by its reflections."[9]

Sankara was preoccupied with the question of how the Absolute could be one and yet reveal itself as a multitude of finite entities. He held that "the self, although eternally unchanging and uniform, reveals itself as a graduated series of beings, and so appears in the form of various dignities and powers,"[10] an idea that is quite close the the kabbalistic conception of the *Sefirot*. Both Sankara and the Kabbalists called upon the idea of "vessels" to resolve this metaphysical problem. Individual selves and finite entities are for Sankara like "space" contained in a jar. In general, all space remains "one," even though it is temporarily contained in various vessels. The Kabbalists made use of similar imagery in describing the nature of the *Sefirot*.

Like the Kabbalists, Sankara proposed a two-level theory of reality. The

---

6. See Ninian Smart, "Sankara," in *Encyclopedia of Philosophy* ed. Paul Edwards (New York: Macmillan, 1967), Vol. 7, pp. 280–282.

7. Sarvepalli Radhakrishnan and Charles A. Moore, *A Source Book of Indian Philosophy* (Princeton, NJ: Princeton University Press, 1957), p. 512.

8. Ibid., p. 518.

9. Ibid., p. 536.

10. Ibid., p. 514.

term "Maya" connotes the illusory nature of the empirical world. However, according to Sankara, from the point of view of everyday existence it is correct to say that individual egos and all finite things exist; but from the point of view of *Brahman-Atman*, both the ego and the world are a total illusion. This idea is present in the Kabbalah[11] and is given an explicit formulation among the Chabad Hasidim. Sankara spoke of *Moksa* as a realization of the world's illusion that leads to a release from this world and to the chain of reincarnation. Similarly, the Kabbalists spoke of release from the wheel of reincarnation; only for them such release required the reincarnated soul to complete its assigned *tikkun on earth*.

SUFISM

Sufism, which was originally a practical mystical tradition, became a theosophical system as a result of the impact of Neoplatonism, Gnosticism, and the spiritual currents prevalent in the eastern Mediterranean and Persia. Suhrawardi al Maqtul (who was executed in Aleppo in 1191) developed a theosophical system in which he claimed to unite traditions of Islam with those of Zoroastrianism and Egyptian Hermetism. His metaphysics of illumination posited the "east" as a world of angels and light; and the "west," in which mankind is currently exiled, as a realm of darkness, evil, and matter.

Ibn 'al-Arabi (1165–1240),[12] who was born in Murcia, Spain, carried on the traditions of theosophical Sufism after Suhrawardi's death. According to this tradition, the Absolute "I" desired to be known, and thus infused being into the heavenly archetypes and ultimately into the world. The world and God are joined like two mirrors that reflect one another, and the world is both destroyed and created in every moment. Muhammed is the universal, archetypal, man, the prototype of creation, and as the "perfect man," the goal of the spiritual adept. The individual perfectly reflects the world; as put by Ibn 'Arabi, "My heart becomes capable of every form."

The major lines of influence seem to be from Sufism to Judaism. Such Jewish thinkers as Bahya Ibn Paquda (late eleventh century) and Abraham Moses ben Maimon (1186–1237), were greatly influenced by Sufism. The

---

11. See Idel, *Kabbalah: New Perspectives*, p. 138.

12. On 'Arabi, see Henry Corbin, *Creative Imagination in the Sufism of Ibn 'Arabi*, trans. Ralph Manheim, Bollingen Series 91 (Princeton, NJ: Princeton University Press, 1969).

parallels to and impact of theosophical Sufism upon Jewish mysticism are topics worthy of fuller exploration.

MEISTER ECKHARDT

The thirteenth-century radical Christian theologian Meister Eckhardt (1260–1327/8)[13] developed a sensibility that was in many ways similar to that of the Zohar and earlier Kabbalah. Like the Kabbalists, Eckhardt distinguished between the infinite deity and the personal God. He spoke of the ground of the soul as a "scintilla" or "spark," and held that man, by making a contemplative connection with this spark, could achieve unity with the godhead. God, for Eckhardt, is incarnate in man. He held that "the eye with which God sees me, is the eye with which I see Him, my eye and His eye are one . . ." Without God man would not exist, but without man God would not exist as well. Eckhardt's view here is reminiscent of the Zohar's claim that man can be credited with the "creation of the one above," and anticipates the Hasidic view that God's *actual thinking* can only occur within the mind of man.[14]

NICHOLAS OF CUSA

The Kabbalists also had a kindred spirit in the Christian philosopher and theologian Nicholas of Cusa (1401–1464).[15] Like the early Kabbalists, Nicholas, who was influenced by Erigena, spoke of God as a coincidence of opposites, who synthesizes opposition and difference within Himself in a manner that is incomprehensible to the human mind. For Nicholas, God is both the "maximum" and the "minimum," the greatest and the smallest of all things. God, for Nicholas, is his own definition—He cannot be defined by anything else because it is He who defines and lends meaning to all things.

In common with several Kabbalists Nicholas held there to be something

---

13. Ninian Smart, "Eckhardt, Meister," in Edwards, ed., *Encyclopedia of Philosophy*, Vol. 2, pp. 449–451.

14. The view is that of the Maggid, Dov Baer of Mezrich. See Rifka Schatz-Uffenheimer, *Hasidism As Mysticism*, p. 207.

15. See Friedrich Copleston, *A History of Philosophy* (Garden City, NY: Image Books, 1962), Vol. 3, Part 2, pp. 37–54.

of an equivalence among God, man, and the world. For Nicholas man is God, "a human God"; man is also the world, "a human world." Nicholas, like the Kabbalists, held that man, having been created in God's image, is a microcosm reflecting both God and the macrocosm, the world. Man is a universe unto himself who mirrors the cosmos as a whole, and like God, man is a *coincidentia oppositorum*. As the Chabad Hasidim were later to proclaim, Nicholas held that apart from God, the world does not exist.

Nicholas propounded a theory of divine "contraction," which in some ways anticipates Luria's doctrine of *Tzimtzum*. According to Nicholas, in the act of creation God's unity is contracted into plurality, necessity into possibility, eternity into succession, and infinity into finitude. The universe is, according to Nicholas of Cusa, a contraction of God, and finite things are a contraction of the universe.

Nicholas was himself influenced by Pseudo-Dionysus, John Scotus Erigenus, and Meister Eckhardt. Most of his ideas were in a very broad sense a development of earlier Platonic and Neoplatonic notions that were developed independently by the early Kabbalists, but which may very well have been rooted in some of the same sources.

JAKOB BOEHME

The speculations of the seventeenth-century mystic Jakob Boehme (1575–1624)[16] show many parallels with certain kabbalistic themes. Boehme was also an important influence on the development of the Christian Kabbalah. Indeed, Knorr von Rosenroth (1636–1689), whose Latin *Kabbalah Denudata* was the largest compendium of Jewish Kabbalism to be made available to the non-Jewish world, came to the Kabbalah after being exposed to Boehme's ideas. While a direct kabbalistic influence on Boehme is difficult to trace, his ideas that God is both the "ungrund" (the foundation of all things) and the "abyss," that he is the eternal One, the incomprehensible Will, neither good nor evil, and the "nothing and the all," are readily assimilable to the kabbalistic worldview. Boehme further held that all things are a function of the alteration between "yes" and "no," that a process of "self-manifestation" characterizes the inner life of God, and that God is

---

16. Copleston, *A History of Philosophy*, Vol. 3, Part 2, pp. 80–83; Ninian Smart, "Boehme, Jakob," in Edwards, ed., *Encyclopedia of Philosophy*, Vol. 1, p. 328.

manifest in the world as a series of contraries. Finally, Boehme spoke of seven qualities or energies through which God is manifest in nature, one of which, "contraction," is the power by which finite substances are individuated. Boehme had a considerable influence upon the German Romantic philosophers Friedrich Schelling (1775–1854), and G.W.F. Hegel (1770–1831).

THE CHRISTIAN KABBALAH

From the beginning of the fifteenth century many Christians began to take a lively interest in the Kabbalah, and such Christian Kabbalists as Giovanni Pico della Mirandola (1463–1494) and Johannes Reuchlin (1455–1522) brought kabbalistic ideas close to the mainstream of Western philosophy.

Christian Knorr von Rosenroth's (1636–1689) *Kabbalah Denudata*, the *Kabbalah Unveiled*, which was published in Sulzbach in 1677–1684, provided essays on the Kabbalah by Knorr's Christian contemporaries as well as Latin translations of portions of major kabbalistic texts, including the Zohar and works by Cordovero and Luria. Knorr's compendium served as the basic Western text on the Kabbalah until the end of the nineteenth century. Leibniz is said to have visited Knorr in 1687, and the two discussed kabbalistic themes.[17] Knorr's work, along with the writings of the alchemists, was Carl Jung's (1875–1960) major source for the kabbalistic ideas described in his later writings.

FRIEDRICH SCHELLING

The influence of Kabbalah on modern philosophy has yet to be fully explored. The ideas of the Jewish philosopher, Benedikt de Spinoza (1632–1677), have been attributed to Kabbalism from a very early date.[18] Leibniz's conception of the "windowless monad" that both reflects and constitutes the world is strikingly analogous to Cordovero's conception of the *Sefirot*. However, it is among the eighteenth-century German Romantics, specifically Schelling and Hegel, that ideas compatible with the Kabbalah find a more definite place in Western philosophical thought.

---

17. Scholem, *Kabbalah*, p. 417.

18. See Richard Popkin, "Spinoza, Neoplatonic Kabbalist?" in *Neoplatonism*, Lenn E. Goodman, pp. 387–410.

Friedrich Schelling (1775–1854),[19] whose work was influenced by Boehme and the Christian Kabbalist F.C. Oetinger (1702–1782), developed a number of ideas that show a kinship to kabbalistic doctrine. Schelling was one of the first to stress openly the significance of mythology for the understanding of philosophical ideas, and held that pure philosophy, with its abstract categories, suffered from being overly formal and external. Schelling believed that the main goal of philosophy is to explain the existence of the world, to answer the question "Why is there something rather than nothing?" He early on adopted the view that the ground of the world is an "I" or ego, an "I am I" that is an "infinite freedom" that transcends conceptual thought, very much akin to the Kabbalist's *Ein-Sof*. For Schelling, the absolute transcends the distinction between subject and object, and the world of nature is a visible manifestation of "spirit" while spirit is "invisible nature." For Schelling the bridge between the finite and the infinite is found in the identity of the human "self" with the Absolute.

For Schelling "all ideas are one idea"; they are the external reflection of the Absolute, which is manifest like light emanated from the sun. Indeed, the manifestation we call the world is really a function of divine self-knowledge. While man and the world are created in the image of the Absolute, the transition from the Absolute to the finite "real" is not a continuous one. Schelling, like the Kabbalists, was conflicted over the question of whether creation was a necessary or free event. Schelling ultimately held that freedom and necessity were in dialectical relation, they are one reality that appears different depending upon one's point of view. For Schelling, God is indeed the identity between necessity and freedom.

Like the Kabbalists, Schelling held that evil existed in potential within the Absolute but became actual in man. For Schelling, if evil did not exist neither could God.[20] Because the Absolute is purely atemporal, its evil can never emerge and act independently from the good. These traits, as the Lurianists would say, are perfectly "commingled" within the deity. However, what is integrated in God, becomes differentiated in humanity. Because man is a temporal creature, the divine potencies can act independently and in succession through man's will.

Like certain Kabbalists (e.g., Cordovero) Schelling held that the origin

---

19. On Schelling, see Copleston, *A History of Philosophy*, Vol. 7, Part 1, pp. 121–182.

20. Ibid., Vol. 7, Part 1, p. 167.

of the finite, sensible world is to be found in a radical breaking away from the Absolute, in Schelling's terms by means of a "leap," resulting in the creation of "an image of an image." Also, like the Kabbalists Schelling held that the biblical Fall, which resulted in a breaking away from God, is also the ground of human freedom, and it is this freedom that explains the possibility of there being a world. The finite ego represents the point of furthest alienation from God, and the goal of both life and history is to overcome alienation and return to the infinite. The human self is fallen, entangled in particularity, alienated from its center, mired in the illusion of selfishness, and it is enjoined to overcome its alienated condition and return to God. A man's true personality is not a given. It must be won; "All birth is birth out of darkness into light." These are themes that are reminiscent of the Zohar, and particularly of Luria's conception of *Tikkun ha-Olam* as the "raising of the sparks" and a return of man's soul to the infinite, *Ein-Sof.*

Indeed, Schelling developed a view of history that in many ways summarizes the Lurianic *Tikkun* doctrine: "The good must be brought out of the darkness into actuality that it may live everlastingly with God; and evil must be separated from the good that it may be cast into not-being. For this is the final end of creation."[21] However, Schelling was not content (as Hegel was after him) with a purely abstract, rational conception of the Absolute. Philosophy, he held must take the positive step of positing a personal, creative, and redeeming God.

Friedrich Schelling's philosophy provides an important point of contact between the Kabbalah and the Western philosophical tradition. Further, Schelling's philosophy anticipates certain developments in twentieth-century philosophy (existentialism) and psychology (Jungian thought) that recommend it to those interested in creating a rapprochement between kabbalistic theosophy and modern thought. Schelling was, of course, highly influential on his colleague and contemporary, G. W. F. Hegel, and it is Hegel's thought that will become a major focus later in this book.

---

21. Ibid., p. 167.

3

Jewish Mysticism and the Philosophies of India

Philosophy in India, in contrast to philosophy in the West, has always focused upon what might be called the "basic questions": what is this world, from where does it come, what is its value, and what is man's place within it. These are the questions, as Heinrich Zimmer has pointed out, that philosophers ask before they become critical of their own methodology, sources of knowledge, and cognitive states.[1] It is precisely such questions that Indian philosophy shares with the Kabbalah.

One should therefore not be surprised to learn of a number of parallels between the traditions of India (Hindu, Jaina, and Buddhist) and the Kabbalah. What is surprising is the extent to which the Kabbalah shares with these traditions not only an extensive set of fundamental principles, but also a number of specific concepts and symbols. Traditional Judaism has assiduously avoided any dialogue with the religious traditions of India, since Jewish law, as codified, for example, by Maimonides, regards these traditions as prime exemplars of the polytheism that is expressly condemned in the Torah. However, a close and fair reading of Indian philosophy reveals that it embodies the same concept of unity in difference that is expressed in the kabbalistic concept of the *Sefirot*. Indian philosophy and all the higher

---

1. Heinrich Zimmer, *Philosophies of India* (Princeton, NJ: Princeton University Press, 1971), p. 226.

religious traditions of Asia, while not discarding their early polytheistic mythologies, reworked those mythologies into a monism in which a single energy or principle, usually spoken of as *"Brahman,"* is regarded (as the Kabbalists regarded *Ein-Sof*) as the sole underlying reality. Brahman, is the energy of all life and mind. It is, one might say, cosmic power per se.[2]

BRAHMAN AND *EIN-SOF*: THE INFINITE DIVINE PRINCIPLE

Like *Ein-Sof,* the principle called *Brahman* (or in its creative mode, *Atman*), is in effect, beyond any God who can be addressed, worshipped, or described. It is beyond all qualities and distinctions: it is infinite, boundless, pure, and totally real, and like *Ein-Sof* it transcends all oppositions in *coincidentia oppositorum*.[3] In the Indian (as in kabbalistic) cosmology, this infinite spiritual principle is identified with "nothingness," a "no-thingness" that mystically coincides with the "life energy" (*prana*) of the cosmos.[4] Each of the Hindu gods and goddesses are understood to be just another aspect or manifestation of this single unitary principle in *Brahman*, much as, for the Kabbalists, the *Sefirot* or *Partzufim* are understood as aspects of *Ein-Sof.*

The Absolute in Indian thought, like *Ein-Sof* in the Kabbalah is completely devoid of all attributes. Known simply as the "imperishable":

> It is not coarse nor fine; not short nor long; not red (like fire) nor adhesive (like water). It casts no shadow; it is not darkness. It is not wind nor is it space. It is not attached to anything. It is not taste or smell; it is not eye or ear; it is not voice or mind; it is not light, or life; it has no face or measure; it has no "within," no "without." Nothing does it consume nor is it consumed by anyone at all.[5]

The Upanishad is clear that this Absolute is impalpable, ungraspable, indestructible, and free of attachment.

However, like the Kabbalists, the ancient Hindus struggled between

---

2. Ibid., p. 59.
3. Ibid., p. 21.
4. Ibid., p. 248.
5. *Brihadaranyaka Upanishad* III, vii, 8, in R. C. Zaehner, ed., *Hindu Scriptures* (Rutland, VT: Charles E. Tuttle, 1966), p. 63.

denying that anything positive could be predicated of the Absolute and the desire to exalt Brahman with the noblest of attributes. The Absolute in both systems of thought is regarded as the hidden soul, and the essence of all things. It is an essence, however, that is exalted and impenetrable, but that can nevertheless be described in grandiloquent terms, as in this passage from the *Maitri Upanishad*:

> Unthinkable [is he], unformed, profound, concealed, faultless, compact, impenetrably deep, devoid of attributes and beyond the "constituents" of Nature, pure, resplendent, the experiencer of Nature's constituents, awe [-inspiring], immutable, Yoga's Lord, omniscient, most generous, incommensurable, beginningless and endless, beautiful, unborn, wise, indescribable, all things emanating, the Self of all, all things experiencing, Lord of all, more inward than what is (most) inward in all things . . .
>   Beginningless and endless [is He], uncircumscribed, unlimited, not to be used by others, dependent on himself [alone], sexless (or "without characteristics"), informed, endless in power, ordainer, resplendent . . .[6]

Here in Hindu writings, which date from as many as four centuries before the common era, we find a description of the Absolute that is very close to the (second century C.E.) Gnostic conception of the Pleroma and the kabbalistic conception of *Ein-Sof*. Like the Kabbalists, the author of this Upanishad mixes a set of positive attributes (e.g., most generous) together with an insistence that the ultimate godhead is beyond all description.

Such an ambivalence and alteration between complete silence about an unknowable Absolute and a pressing desire to attribute everything to it, especially all significance and value, is characteristic of many of the world's mystical traditions, and may provide us with something of a clue into the very nature of the Absolute itself. Once the unknowable, ineffable "nothingness" is referred to, provided with a name, it must, it seems, explode into an infinite array of possibilities, swallowing everything in its wake.[7]

NOTHINGNESS

The mystical understanding of "nothingness," which we have seen to be of such significance in kabbalistic thought, is developed deeply in the traditions

---

6. *Maitri Upanishad* VII, 1–2, Zaehner, ed., *Hindu Scriptures*, p. 271.
7. See my *Symbols of the Kabbalah*, Ch. 2.

of India. Already in the *Upanishads* we discover that the ultimate force in the universe is spoken of as "*neti, neti,*" "neither this nor that."[8] As we have seen, for the Kabbalists, *Ein-Sof* itself is equated with nothingness inasmuch as it is completely beyond description and appellation, and therefore outside the realm of linguistic significance. In addition, *Ein-Sof* is the *absolute void* from which creation proceeds; it is the "negation" that brings all distinction (and hence delimited forms) into the world; it is the complete "unknown" reflected in the core of man's own being; and it is the "nothingness" that is the foundation of faith.[9] Similar concepts are developed in Indian thought, most explicitly in Buddhism. We find, for example, in the Buddhist reflections of Nagarjuna (early second century C.E.) a very similar equation of negation and the Absolute: "It cannot be called void or not void, or both or neither, but in order to indicate it is call the Void . . . It is on account of *sunyata* (the Void) that everything became possible, without it nothing in the world is possible. It is the basis of all."[10] Nothing, according to Buddhist tradition, can be said of the infinite, and the term *sunyata* or void is simply a pedagogical instrument to bring the mind beyond its attachments to worldly things, interests, and ideas. This void, however, phenomenalizes (reveals) itself as the Buddha and empirical reality,[11] just as in the Kabbalah *Ein-Sof* manifests itself as the God of Israel and the world.

In less guarded moments, the Yogacara school of Mahayana Buddhism gives a more positive connotation to nothingness: identifying *sunyata* (the void) with pure consciousness, thought, and wisdom.[12] Indeed the Buddhists speak of *Alaya-vijnana*, a void that is beyond all conception and imagination but that is at the same time the potentiality of all possible thought.[13] We have seen a parallel development in the Zohar, which insists that *Ein-Sof* is both *Ayin* (nothingness) and the primal consciousness, thought, or will.

---

8. Zimmer, *Philosophies of India*, p. 393.

9. The identification of *Ein-Sof* with "nothingness" is present, for example, in the thought of the thirteenth-century Kabbalist, David Ben Abraham ha-Lavan (see Scholem, *Kabbalah*, p. 95). Azriel of Gerona identified the divine "unknown" that is the foundation of all things with "faith." See Scholem, *Origins of the Kabbalah*, p. 423.

10. Zimmer, *Philosophies of India*, p. 520.

11. Ninian Smart, "Nagarjuna," in Edwards, ed., *Encyclopedia of Philosophy*, Vol. 5, pp. 439–440.

12. Zimmer, *Philosophies of India*, p. 525.

13. Ibid., p. 526–527.

DESIRE AND WILL

In a section of the *Rig-Veda* known as "The Song of Creation" we read that at a time when there was neither nonbeing nor being, when darkness reigned in chaos and all that existed was "hidden in the void," the One "evolved [and] became desire." "Desire," the *Rig-Veda* affirms, is "the first seed of mind."[14]

In the history of both Eastern and Western thought there arose two distinct yet interwoven traditions: the traditions of *intellect* and *desire*. We have already seen how these traditions are both present in the Kabbalah. On the one hand the Kabbalist's *Ein-Sof* is equated with the lights of Thought and Wisdom, while on the other hand its highest manifestation is understood to be Desire (*Ratzon*) and Delight (*Tinug*).

In the Brihadaranyaka Upanishad we find the daring speculation that the entire world was brought forth through *death*. Prior to creation "nothing at all existed here" and all was enveloped by death. Out of death emerged desire, "for what is death but hunger?" and death discovered that he was desirous of a "self." Death roamed around offering praise, and from this praise there emerged water, and from his joy in offering praise, fire, and so the cosmos came into being.[15]

In this myth of creation we have a dialectical development that in many ways anticipates the kabbalistic movement from *Ayin* (nothingness) to *Keter* (desire and delight), in the creation of the world. Nothingness, here in its existential manifestation as death, is dialectically understood as implicitly containing desire within itself ("For what is death but hunger"). This notion comes close to ideas in recent existential philosophy to the effect that desire and creativity are a response to the specter of finitude in death (Heidegger's being-towards death).

What is most interesting from the perspective of the Kabbalah, is the fact that the world that, according to the Upanishad, emerges from death's desire takes the form of a cosmic, primordial man: "In the beginning this [universe] was the self alone, in the likeness of a man."[16] The Upanishad even describes the measure of this man, who "encompassed the sun, fire and wind, where

---

14. *Rig Veda* X, cxxix, Zaehner, ed., *Hindu Scriptures*, p. 13.
15. *Brihadaranyaka Upanishad*, Zaehner, ed., *Hindu Scriptures*, p. 37.
16. *Brihadaranyaka Upanishad* I, iv, Zaehner, ed., *Hindu Scriptures*, p. 39.

head is the east, where back is the sky, and where chest is the earth."[17] This cosmic self desired union with a sacred self and thus this self who is Hunger and Death "copulated with speech by means of mind" giving birth to time.

The parallels with kabbalistic thought are striking. In both Hindu and Jewish mystical accounts we are witness to the emergence of a cosmos out of *nothingness* and *will*. This results in the formation of a Primordial Man, who in turn enters into a cosmic erotic relationship representing the union of abstract entities (in the Kabbalah we have the union of Wisdom and Understanding; in the Hindu account the union of Death/desire with Speech). In both accounts this union results in the creation of a temporal, finite world.

THE WORLD AS A PRODUCT OF DIVINE FORGETFULNESS

Like the Kabbalah, several schools within the Hindu-Brahmanic tradition hold the world to be an illusion created through a limitation in the infinite "All." The nondualistic Vedanta, for example, particularly as it is expressed by its leading advocate, Sankara (c. 788–820), views the world as a total illusion.[18] The world's existence, according to this tradition, is completely a function of divine forgetfulness and ignorance. The concept of *Maya* refers to the purely phenomenal, insubstantial character of the everyday world; a world that results from a process through which Brahman conceals itself from itself.[19] This concealment results in both matter and mind, each of which are brought into existence by Atman's ignorance or self-forgetfulness.[20] Such ideas, of course, are very similar to Luria's conception of the phenomenal world as an illusion produced by *Tzimtzum*, the concealment and contraction of the light of the Infinite God (Or *Ein-Sof*). In the final analysis, for both traditions the "illusion" of a world is predicated on the ignorance of *man*. It is such *ignorance* that (both in the Kabbalah and the philosophies of India) is the root, cause, and substance of both space and time;[21] and it is the overcoming of this ignorance, which, according to both traditions, is the task of mankind.

---

17. *Brihadaranyaka Upanishad* I, ii, 3, Zaehner, ed., *Hindu Scriptures*, p. 37.
18. Ninian Smart, "Sankara," pp. 280–282.
19. Zimmer, *Philosophies of India*, p. 19.
20. Ibid., p. 5.
21. Ibid., p. 25.

The idea that the phenomenal world is an illusion is echoed throughout Indian thought. According to the entire Vedic tradition, even the gods themselves are mere reflections of the cosmic (and human) ignorance of *Maya*.[22] In Chapter Ten of the *Bhagavad Gita* we learn that no creature exists without *Brahman*, but that each is both permitted and encouraged to maintain its own *illusion of independence*,[23] an idea that is strongly echoed and further developed in the Kabbalah. For the Kabbalists this illusion of independence is, in effect, what enables the infinite cosmic principle, *Ein-Sof*, to complete itself, through the *Tikkun*, or world-restorative acts, of man on earth.

We shall return to the whole question of the value of the "illusion" in Indian philosophy and the Kabbalah. Here it should suffice to say that while the Kabbalah is essentially univocal in its affirmation of this value, Indian philosophy is ambivalent. While the early Vedic traditions and the original Buddhists showed nothing but contempt for the illusions of *Maya* (holding that *samsara*, our world of birth and death, is an immense dream, or nightmare from which we must awake), the *Bhagavad Gita* and the Vedanta viewed the process of *avidya* (nescience), which is equivalent in many respects to the Kabbalists' *Tzimtzum*, as having both a negative and positive function, the latter being the creation of the "wonderful mirage" that is our world.[24] For the Vedanta, we are illusions who believe in our own existence,[25] a curious state of affairs that is in some ways more mysterious than *Brahman* itself,[26] one that some Kabbalists, and certainly many Hasidim, held to be the case with respect to *Ein-Sof*.

THE ABSOLUTE AS THE SELF

Like the Kabbalists, the ancient philosophers of India held that the infinite divine principle is mirrored and actually contained in the human heart. The *Brihadaranyaka Upanishad* presents an idea that is repeated throughout the history of Indian thought, i.e., that the self of man reflects or even embodies the self of the cosmos: "Whoso thus knows that he is Brahman, becomes this

22. Ibid., p. 393.
23. Ibid., p. 398.
24. Ibid., pp. 415, 419.
25. Ibid., p. 428.
26. Ibid., p. 419.

whole [universe]. Even the gods have not the power to cause him to un-be, for he becomes their own self."[27] This idea, which is articulated clearly in the Vedanta of Sankara,[28] reappears in somewhat obscured form, in the Kabbalah, in the notions that the human soul is a perfect reflection of the divine cosmic order, that each soul has a spark of the divine at its core, and that man in his worship and study can actually be credited with creating the one above. The Kabbalists, in their doctrine that the soul of man contains, in microcosm, a spark or image of God, were in fact torn between this Eastern panentheistic view of God, and the more traditionally Jewish transcendent view, which places an insuperable gulf between God and man. However, this conflict was generally resolved by the Kabbalists in favor of a panenthesistic view in which God is said to adhere in all things but not to simply be equal to the world.

The Kabbalists, as we have seen, held that all things emerge out of and are ultimately contained within *Ein-Sof.* The *Upanishads* provide two metaphors for the unique relationship between the cosmic self (*Atman*) and the world, one of which (the sparks) is also found in the Zohar and the Lurianic Kabbalah: "As a spider emerges [from itself] by [spinning] threads [out of its own body], as small sparks rise up from a fire, so too from this self do all the life-breaths, all the worlds, all the gods, and all contingent beings rise up in all directions."[29] We can recall the Zohar's simile that the *Sefirot*, the instruments of divine creation, are, in relation to *Ein-Sof,* like a flame to the coal, or as a garment that is itself part of the wearer.

"The All," according to the *Brihadaranyaka Upanishad,* "forsakes the man who thinks of the All as other than the self."[30] We learn that "by seeing the Self and hearing It, by thinking of It and knowing It, this whole universe is known."[31] The *Upanishad,* sensing the problematic of the identity of the self with the absolute inquires: "But when all has become one's very self, then with what should one smell whom? With what should one see whom? . . ."[32] The German mystic, Meister Eckhardt, seems to answer this very question when he observes that "the eye with which I see God is the eye

27. *Brihadaranyaka Upanishad* I, iv, 9, Zaehner, ed., *Hindu Scriptures,* p. 41.
28. Ninian Smart, "Indian Philosophy," in Edwards, ed., *Encyclopedia of Philosophy,* Vol. 4, p. 159.
29. *Brihadaranyaka Upanishad* II, i, 20, Zaehner, ed., *Hindu Scriptures,* p. 49.
30. *Brihadaranyaka Upanishad* II, iv, 6, Zaehner, ed., *Hindu Scriptures,* p. 51.
31. *Brihadaranyaka Upanishad* II, iv, 5, Zaehner, ed., *Hindu Scriptures,* p. 51.
32. *Brihadaranyaka Upanishad* II, iv, 14, Zaehner, ed., *Hindu Scriptures,* p. 53.

with which God sees me." This is precisely the conclusion that certain Kabbalists and Hasidim arrived at, in their doctrine that man is the vehicle through which *Ein-Sof* gains self-awareness. For example, the Maggid of Mezrich (1704–1772) held that the very significance of divine thought is contingent upon this thought making its appearance in the mind of man.[33]

According to the *Brihadaranyaka Upanishad* all suffering is part of the illusory world of the not-self. "This self that indwells all things is within you . . . What is other than (this self) suffers."[34] Like the Kabbalists who saw evil as a result of the *Tzimtzum* or contraction of *Ein-Sof*, the author of this *Upanishad* understands suffering as that which is removed from, or "other than" Atman, the Absolute spirit or self.

In the Hindu-Brahmanic tradition the words for the infinite cosmic principle (*Brahman*) and the self of man (*Atman*) are frequently spoken of in one breath, *Brahman-Atman*, underscoring their essential reciprocity and equivalence. The emanation of dreams and the passage from sleep to wakefulness are analyzed in Brahmanic thought as varieties of a daily recurring microcosmogony. Just as the world evolves from a secret, ineffable source, so does the dream arise out of the mysterious, ineffable self. The dream state is understood in the *Upanishads* as a window into various higher and lower worlds of Gods and demons both within and beyond the self; and dreamless sleep, a state of blissful nothingness, is identified with the perfection of *Brahman*. The idea that the abode of the Gods is to be found in the unconscious of man, a basic tenet of Jungian psychology, hardly originates in modern thought. As we have seen, it is present in the kabbalistic notion of the soul mirroring the divine *Sefirot*, and was taken for granted in ancient Brahmanic philosophy.

THE COSMIC MAN

The idea of Primordial Man (*Adam Kadmon*), which is of such importance in the theosophical Kabbalah, is, as we have already seen, also present in ancient Indian thought. In the *Upanishads*, for example, we learn that the "gigantic divine Being" is infinitely far yet at the same time near in the

---

33. Schatz-Uffenheimer, *Hasidism As Mysticism*, p. 207. Also see Zalman, *Likutei Amarim-Tanya*, Chapter 36, p. 163.

34. *Brihadaranyaka Upanishad* III, iv, 2, Zaehner, ed., *Hindu Scriptures*, p. 57.

innermost recesses of the human heart.[35] According to Indian tradition the "divinities" required *Atman* to find an abode on earth. Eventually they were led to man, and at Atman's command: "Fire became speech and entered the mouth, Wind became breath, and entered the nostrils. The sun became sight, and entered the eyes . . . The moon became mind, and entered the heart. Death became out-breath and entered the navel."[36]

The *Mandoka Upanishad* describes the Primordial Man as follows:

Fire is his head, the sun and moon his eyes,
The points of the compass are his ears,
His voice the Vedic revelation;
Wind is his breath, the whole universe his heart;
From his feet the earth [arose],
For He is the Inmost self of all contingent beings.[37]

We find here that the Primal Man is identified not only with the Absolute (Self) but also with the soul or essence of all beings whatsoever. This infusion of the macrocosm into the microcosm is expressed well in a traditional Indian meditation: "Just as a jug dissolves into earth, a wave into water, or a bracelet into gold, even so the universe will dissolve in me."[38]

As in the Kabbalah, the first result of divine creation is conceived of as a cosmic, archetypical man or woman who comprises both the earth and the heavens.[39] While the kabbalistic Primordial Man (*Adam Kadmon*), is spiritual in its structure (being composed of ten *Sefirot*), the Cosmic Man of Jaina and Hindu thought, like the primal man in the Jewish *Shiur haKomah* literature, is conceived of in more material terms. The surface of the earth is his waist, hell is his pelvic cavity, and "heaven" is his cranium.

Certain Jainist notions regarding the Primordial Man[40] bear a striking resemblance to ideas about *Adam Kadmon* in the later Kabbalah. According to the Jainists the entire universe is in the shape of this cosmic man, whose measure, like the measure of the primal anthropos in *Shi'ur haKomah*, is

---

35. Zimmer, *Philosophies of India*, pp. 366–367.
36. Ibid., pp. 8–11.
37. *Mundaka Upanishad* II, i, 4, Zaehner, ed., *Hindu Scriptures*, p. 208.
38. Zimmer, *Philosophies of India*, p. 11.
39. Ibid., p. 254.
40. Ninian Smart, "Janinism," in Edwards, ed., *Encyclopedia of Philosophy*, Vol. 4, pp. 238–239.

given in numbers that are astonishingly large even to the modern mind. For the Jains, our world, which is located at the waist of this cosmic man, is arranged as a series of concentric discs. Below the waist are seven levels consisting of millions of purgatories, while above the waist are a set of heavens with the gods hierarchically arranged within them. At the crown of this cosmic man is the summit of the cosmos, the abode of those souls that have been liberated from the cycle of earthly transmigration. The parallels to the Kabbalah are clear: like the Jainists, the Zohar, and particularly the Lurianists, understand the world as *both* a primal anthropos *and as* a series of concentric circles. Further, in both the Kabbalah and Jainist thought, the "cranium" of the primal man is regarded as the summit of the cosmos, and levels of reality exist both above and below this world, those above corresponding to the heavens and those below to an evil counterrealm.

An interesting parallel to the kabbalistic notion of the unification of the *Sefirot* in *Adam Kadmon* is found in the Jaina myth of the "seven life energies." Speaking together these forces recited: "Truly, in the state in which we now find ourselves, we shall never be able to bring forth. Let us make, therefore, out of these seven 'men' (i.e., themselves) one man . . . He it was who became the Lord of Progeny."[41]

Like the Kabbalah, in its doctrine of the *Sefirot* and *Partzufim* (divine Personas), the *Upanishads* speak of a number of secondary manifestations of the Absolute that embody particular characteristics or traits. In one *Upanishad* these are eight in number, and are spoken of as deities and persons, corresponding to certain points on the compass: "These are the eight dwellings, the eight spheres, the eight gods, the eight persons."[42] The Absolute, Brahman, splits these "persons" apart, puts them together and "then passes behind them." The splitting apart of these divine aspects and their reassembly as divine personas has its parallel in the Lurianic dynamic of the Breaking of the Vessels and *Tikkun*.

PSYCHOLOGICAL SYMBOLS

The various symbols of Indian philosophy provide for a ready transition from metaphysics to psychology and vice versa. In the schools of Sankhya and

---

41. Zimmer, *Philosophies of India*, p. 243.
42. *Brihadaranyaka Upanishad* III, ix, 26, Zaehner, ed., *Hindu Scriptures*, p. 66.

Yoga, for example, the metaphysical symbol of the universe arising out of a colossal cosmic "egg" is reinterpreted in terms of stages in the development of human consciousness. The creation of the world is understood as the unfolding of the perceptual environment from the human mind.[43] In Yoga, it is this microcosmic mind that is the chief focus: the metaphysics of the macrocosm is for the most part ignored. This psychologization is even more prominent in Buddhism, which is strictly "therapeutic" in its original formulation. Interpreted metaphysically, the Buddha preached a doctrine in which all that is of significance occurs on the level of the microcosm, in the release or *buddhi* (enlightenment) of the individual.

As we have seen, a similar psychologization occurs among the Hasidim, who reinterpreted the cosmological categories of the Kabbalah, including *Tzimtzum*, *Sefirot*, and *Shevirah* as referring to events in the development of the individual's soul. Later, in Chapters Seven and Eight, I will argue that just such an interiorization of metaphysical ideas is present in contemporary depth psychology. Jung, of course, equated the gods with the "collective unconscious" and held that the psychologization of myth was a modern phenomenon, occurring only after (as a result of scientific discoveries) men could no longer believe in their mythological projections. We have seen, however, that such psychologization has appeared on the historical horizon a number of times in the past. The oscillation between macrocosmic and microcosmic worldviews, between metaphysics and psychology, appears to be a recurring theme in the history of religions.[44]

It is a fundamental ethical axiom of both Indian and kabbalistic thought that man must integrate into his life and consciousness an aspect of himself (*Atman* in Indian thought; the *Tzelem*, divine spark, or Godly soul in the Kabbalah) that normally remains hidden.[45] Everything about one's conscious personality is in flux, and in a profound sense an illusion, while the *Atman* or Godly soul (which in the Kabbalah mirrors *Ein-Sof* itself) is permanent and real. Both *Atman* and *Ein-Sof* are beyond space, time, and

---

43. Zimmer, *Philosophies of India*, p. 331.

44. We ourselves may be living in a moment where the focus upon the microcosmic view, which has been such a predominant force in twentieth-century thought, is shifting, and metaphysics, which has been on the defensive since Kant, is about to gain new life. See Robert Nozick, *Philosophical Explanations* (Cambridge, MA: Harvard University Press, 1981), for an example of what I would call the "new metaphysics."

45. Zimmer, *Philosophies of India*, p. 3.

the causal nexus of happenings in this world.[46] Indeed, the rediscovery and reassimilation of the true self, which is paramount throughout Indian philosophy, is paralleled in the Kabbalah by the overcoming of the alienation and exile of the self. This process is symbolized in the Kabbalah by the raising of the sparks, *birur* (extraction of the divine element), and *bittul* (dissipation of the personality into God). The overcoming of personal exile is expressed in Indian philosophy in the concepts of *Nirvrtti* (disappearance, tranquillity, destruction) and *Moksa* (liberation, release, deliverance), and in the Buddhist concept of *buddhi* (returning to consciousness).

The parallels between Indian and kabbalistic meditational techniques are almost too great to regard as coincidental. Idel, for example, after pointing out the similarities between certain kabbalistic practices (specifically, meditation upon a visualized circle representing divine forces and colors) and Hindu meditation upon the *mandala*, suggests the possibility that Hindu techniques and traditions infiltrated the Kabbalah, perhaps via the Kabbalists' contact with *Sufi* (Islamic) mystics. In addition, as Aryeh Kaplan points out in his volume, *Jewish Meditation*, the Kabbalah shares with Hinduism the practice of "*mantra*" meditation, the repetition of a syllable, word, or phrase as a means of focusing and altering one's state of spiritual consciousness.[47] Such *mantra* meditation is found in *Hekhalot Rabbatai*, the classic of Jewish *Merkaveh* mysticism.[48] The Safedian Kabbalists made use of the repetition of a biblical verse in order to achieve higher states of consciousness and deeper insight into the Bible.[49] The Hasidic master, Rabbi Nachman, recommended to the novice that he simply meditate upon the phrase *Ribbono Shel Olam* (Master of the Universe),[50] a meditation that is reminiscent of the Hindu meditation on the all-encompassing "*Om.*" Further parallels are found in the kabbalistic and Indian techniques of clearing the mind of all thoughts and meditating upon "nothingness."

Idel points to parallels in the metaphors representing *unio mystica* in

---

46. Ibid., p. 3.

47. Aryeh Kaplan, *Jewish Meditation: A Practical Guide*, (New York: Schocken Books, 1985).

48. Aryeh Kaplan, *Meditation and Kabbalah* (York Beach, ME: Samuel Weiser, 1982), pp. 41–54.

49. One of them, Joseph Karo (1488–1575), recommended meditation on a portion of the Mishnah, to induce a state of consciousness in which a "maggid," or spiritual mediator, would speak to the meditator. Kaplan, *Jewish Meditation*, p. 56.

50. Kaplan, *Jewish Meditation*, p. 57.

kabbalistic texts and in the Upanishads: he compares the Hindu dissolution of a drop of water into the infinite waters of the sea[51] with the Kabbalist pouring of a jug of water into a running well (R. Isaac of Acre).[52] This metaphor, which also appears in Muslim and Christian mystical texts, represents the individual soul's union with the infinite divine principle. Later Kabbalists and the Hasidim made more precise use of the Hindu simile: as Idel points out, one Hasidic contemporary of the Baal Shem Tov, for example, speaks of "the single drop which has fallen into the great sea" as a simile for man's union with *Ein-Sof.*

KARMA AND KELLIPOT

Among the most important images or metaphors of spiritual liberation, one that recurs in Jaina, Yoga, Sankhya, and later Indian thought, is the symbol of Karma, several aspects of which finds close parallels in the kabbalistic concept of *Kelippot.*

The doctrine of Karma gives expression to the view that the fruits of an individual's actions cleave to the self in such a manner as to determine his spiritual status in both this life and in each of his subsequent lives. According to Jaina doctrine, a person's *Atman* or "self" is covered and hence obscured by layers of darkness that are the accumulated effects of his karmic activity.[53] There are six colors (*lesyas*) of Karma: the darker colors corresponding to more contemptible acts or sins (and hence bringing a darker stain upon one's self) and the lighter colors corresponding to lesser, more venial sins, or to even virtuous acts. The life monad of one who commits a serious moral offense (such as killing) is so deeply obscured as to be almost completely invisible behind the *lesyas*; and even men, for example, who engage in killing as a profession (in Jaina thought this included butchers as well as hunters and warriors), have life monads that are almost completely without light.[54]

The parallel to the kabbalistic doctrine of the *Kelippot* is plain. The *Kelippot,* like the *lesyas,* are regarded as layers of darkness that surround a central divine light or spark (*netzotz*), and that correspond both to spiritual uncleanness (also derived in Judaism from contact with "death") and moral

---

51. *Katha Upanishad* IV 15, Zaehner, ed., *Hindu Scriptures,* p. 200.
52. Idel, *Kabbalah: New Perspectives,* p. 67.
53. Smart, "Jainism," p. 238.
54. Zimmer, *Philosophies of India,* p. 250.

transgression. The *Kelippot* are also graded in terms of their degree of uncleanness or sinfulness, with darker layers corresponding to more trenchant evils and lighter layers (represented in the *Kelippah nogah* or "brightness") corresponding to acts and behaviors that are "translucent" because they are considered partly divine.

In Indian thought an individual's spiritual progress involves a cleansing of the inner crystalline life monad of all karmic coloring and contamination, such that this monad or self literally shines with translucent lucidity. When so cleansed the monad *Atman*, or self, mirrors the highest truth of both man and the cosmos;[55] just as the removal of the layers of *Kelippot*, in the Kabbalah, reveals the inner spark of a man's soul, which is a perfect reflection or image of God. The removal of the *lesyas*, like the disencumbrance of the Kabbalists' *Kelippot*, reveals an inner spirituality, and thus a reversal of man's ignorance of the divine. Just as "the extraction of the kernel" or "the raising of the sparks" enables the Kabbalist's soul to rejoin its source in the Infinite (*Ein-Sof*), the Jaina or Hindu whose life monad has been cleansed of karmic matter becomes completely identified with the infinite world principle, *Brahman-Atman*.

The idea of man's true essence being hindered, shrouded, or obscured by a limiting or darkening agent reappears throughout Indian thought. Various terms are used to denote this limiting, darkening agent. The Yoga sutras, for example, use the word *klesa* to denote that which adheres to man's soul and restricts its full manifestation. More specifically, the Yoga tradition speaks of *tamas* (literally black, darkness, or dark blue) to refer to the spiritual blindness and lack of consciousness that dominates the mineral, vegetable, and animal kingdoms, but that is also evident in man. *Rojas*, literally menstrual impurity and more generally "dust," refers to the spiritual impurity that dims both the cosmos and man's outlook upon it. *Rojas* are the passions, desires, and motives for earthly gain that grip a man's soul and prevent him from realizing his inner, divine self. Finally, *Avidya* denotes the ignorance at the root of our conscious thought, which prevents the individual from knowing his or her true self as but a manifestation of *Brahman*.[56] Each of these darknesses or impairments can be summed up under the category of the "ego" or "personality," and it is the task of the Yogic adept to disable these *klesas* or impairments so that his being can reflect *Brahman* with the clarity

---

55. Ibid., p. 251.
56. Ibid., pp. 294–297.

of a still, undisturbed pool. Again, we have parallels to the concepts of *birur*, liberation of the divine kernel/self, and the *Tzelem*, the reflection of the divine image in the soul of man.

The *Upanishads* conceive of the self or *Atman* as completely brilliant like the sun. The Brihadaranyaka Upanishad equates man's self with an inner light of understanding that resides within the heart.[57] However, this self is surrounded by a personality of ignorance and darkness, which prevents its light from shining through.

In the *Vedanta*, a later school of Indian thought, which paralleled the development of Buddhism, the idea of the darkening, obscuring shell is developed further.[58] According to the *Vedentasara*, *Atman* is "beset by unpellucid untransparent, or dull and limiting adjuncts . . . not endowed with an utterly brilliant self-effulgence."[59] While there is indeed a sense in which, as the Yoga sutras proclaimed, this karmic darkness is a mere illusion (owing to its origin in ignorance); it is nevertheless true that consciousness cannot act like the sun and dispel the darkness at will, for some of the darkness is unremovable because its nature is "mixed" or "unclean."[60] Each of these ideas is paralleled in the Kabbalah. The *Kelippot*, according to the Lurianic Kabbalah, are ultimately illusory, for they are composed of the shards of the *Sefirot* or vessels, which themselves originated in a concealment (or contraction) of God's light. Yet, for the Lurianists, some of the *Kelippot*, those that are darker and totally "unclean," cannot be removed by the efforts of man but must await either a superhuman effort (what the Talmud speaks of as *Ahavah Rabbah*, a "great love") or the grace of God.

These images of "inner light" and "surrounding darkness" underscore the idea that in Indian philosophy, as well as in the Kabbalah, the metaphor for human perfection is not *growth* (as it is in the West) but recollection, purification, and cleansing.[61] The goal, common to the Kabbalah and all of the traditions of India from Jainism to Buddhism, is the cleansing, awakening, recollection, and shining forth of a brilliant, inner, divine light, which had been hitherto hindered, polluted, and obscured.[62] In Jainism, the goal is

---

57. *Brihadaranyaka Upanishad* IV, iii, 6, 7, Zaehner, ed., *Hindu Scriptures*, p. 73.
58. Zimmer, *Philosophies of India*, p. 430.
59. *Vedentasara*, 44; ibid., p. 429.
60. Ibid., p. 429.
61. Ibid., p. 546.
62. Ibid.

the escape from the wheel of Karma; in Vedenta it is the realization of *Atman-Brahman*, the transcendental self; and in Buddhism it is *bodhi* (enlightenment). Each of these ideas is echoed in the various kabbalistic ideas regarding *Tikkun* (the restoration of the self and world).

Many of the specific details of the kabbalistic theory of the *Kelippot* have parallels in Indian thought. The kabbalistic image of the *Kelippot* falling into the metaphysical void and settling in the depths of the lower worlds is paralleled in the Jaina account of karmic matter pulling the life monad down into one or another of the lower worlds or spheres of ignorant action. In Jainism, as in the Kabbalah, we find a stratified universe of higher and lower spiritual realms,[63] more or less concealed from the radiance of truth.

Even some of the specific imagery used to describe the plight of the Jaina monad is echoed in the Kabbalah. The Jainists compare the life monad to a gourd covered with clay that sinks to the bottom of a tank of water—but as the clay slowly dissolves, the gourd, being naturally light will rise. In the Kabbalah, the *Kelippot* are compared to nuts, the husks of which must be removed, so that the kernel can rise or bear fruit; or, again, they are compared to shards of earthenware that entrap or adhere to drops of precious oil contained in a clay jar that has since shattered. In another Jaina image, karmic matter adheres to the *jiva* (the sum aggregate of all life monads) like dust adhering to a body anointed with oil."[64]

At times the Jainas spoke of Karma as a cloth or veil over the image of the divinity, which comes between the mind and truth.[65] The Kabbalists speak of the divinity clothing himself in various garments that obscure his essence from man. These garments are a metaphor for the sefirotic material, which ultimately comes to comprise the *Kelippot*.

It should now be clear that the ancient Indian doctrine of Karma and the kabbalistic symbol of the *Kelippot* are remarkably similar from both theoretical and mythopoetical points of view. One might even go so far as to argue that the Jaina doctrine of Karma can actually deepen our understanding of parallel ideas in the Kabbalah. This, of course, is not to deny that there are differences, for example, between Karma and *Kelippot*. The Indian notion has a clear volitional component that is only implicit in the kabbalistic one. Yet this difference is itself instructive. It is true that an individual, on the

---

63. Ibid., p. 254.
64. Ibid., p. 271.
65. Ibid., p. 227.

Hindu-Jainist view, is fully responsible for his own Karma, whereas the Kabbalists often speak of the *Kelippot* as a necessary byproduct of creation. However, when we examine these doctrines more closely, we discover on a deeper level that Karma too is a necessary by-product of human action, and that an individual's *Kelippot* are the results of those freely chosen acts through which he alienates himself from God. This is because, according to the Kabbalah, every act a man does, either increases or decreases the powers of the "other side." By juxtaposing the Indian and kabbalistic metaphors we are perhaps in a better position to understand fully the implications of each.

VESSELS

The kabbalistic concept of a recurring *Shevirah* or Breaking of the Vessels echoes the Hindu (not Jaina) notion that the universe is subject to periodic dissolutions.[66] Indeed the kabbalistic preoccupation with "vessel" imagery in the description of the *Sefirot* is itself paralleled in the Sankhya (one of the six *Vedic* systems of Indian thought) concept of *Ajiva*, a cosmic vessel or container that both holds and diminishes the energy of *Jiva* (the cosmic aggregate of all life monads) and the cosmic man.[67]

A more striking parallel to the kabbalistic imagery of the Breaking of the Vessels is found in the *Upanishads* (which date back to the time of the early biblical prophets, c. 800 B.C.E.). The *Upanishads* relate that "space is enclosed by earthen jars . . ." yet the space itself is not carried along when the jar is moved nor is it affected when the jar is destroyed. Speaking of the transitory forms of worldly existence, the *Upanishads* continue: "The various forms, like earthen jars, going to pieces again and again. He (*Atman*) does not know them to be broken; and yet He knows eternally."[68] The image here is used to refer to the transcendental unity of the cosmic self in the face of the destruction of all temporary and physical forms. It is remarkable that the very same image would be used some 2,000 years later by the Kabbalists of Safed, in their doctrine of *Shevirat ha-Kelim*: the Breaking of the Vessels. Only for the Kabbalists, the divine self, *Ein-Sof*, is not so implacable in the face of vessels shattering: some of the infinite's light is entrapped and carried away by the broken shards.

---

66. Ibid., p. 271.
67. Ibid., p. 270.
68. Ibid., p. 359.

REINCARNATION

A fascinating parallel between kabbalistic and Hindu thought is found in their respective treatment of the transmigration of souls. Spoken of as *Gilgul* (the wheel) in Judaism, reincarnation is an idea that was rejected by Jewish philosophers (such as Saadya Gaon and Maimonides) but taken for granted among the early Kabbalists, beginning with the *Sefer Ha-Bahir*. Reincarnation, which eventually became a core kabbalistic doctrine, was prevalent among second-century Gnostic sects, Manicheans, and several circles in the early Christian church,[69] and, according to Scholem, its presence in the Kabbalah conceivably reflects the influence of Indian philosophy through Manicheistic sources.[70] The Kabbalists related *gilgul* to issues of divine reward and punishment; some emphasized reincarnation as a means for meting out justice to the wicked, while others saw it as a divine reward. A number of Kabbalists held that the most righteous souls are in a state of perpetual transmigration so that they can benefit the world in each succeeding generation, an idea that echoes the Mahayana Buddhist teaching that the "*bodhisattva*" is one who stops at the threshold of *nirvanna* and continues on a perpetual cycle of reincarnation for the benefit of the world.

While certain early Kabbalists limited the transmigration of souls to man alone, others, notably the early fourteenth-century Kabbalist Shalom Ashkenazi, held that transmigration occurs throughout all existence from the lowest forms of inorganic matter to the highest angels and *Sefirot*; a concept that was accepted by the Kabbalists of Safed, and that parallels the teachings of both the Hindus and Buddhists. Again, according to both the Kabbalah and later Indian philosophy, the souls of individual men (and things) are but reflections, roots, or sparks (in Hebrew *nitzozot ha-neshamot*) of the one world-soul, which is represented symbolically in the image of the Cosmic Man.

In this context it is of interest to explore the Indian concept of the "savior"; an incarnation of the Godhead who descends into our realm to counterbalance the forces of evil during periods of moral decline in the affairs of men. This descent is represented as the projection of a minute particle (*amsa*) of the Godhead into the world.[71] While the Hindu savior, unlike his

---

69. Scholem, *Kabbalah*, p. 344.

70. Ibid., p. 345.

71. Zimmer, *Philosophies of India*, p. 390.

Jewish or Christian counterpart, reappears on numerous occasions and does so serenely, the idea of a particle of God, descending into the world as the soul of the savior, is echoed in both Jewish and Christian mysticism. It is Gnosticism that introduces this theme to the West; in the symbol of a divine spark that is sent forth into humanity, descends into a world of evil and darkness, and eventually takes the form of (or on some accounts is reunited with) the Messiah. This idea, which returns with a vengeance in the Lurianic Kabbalah, may ultimately be traceable to India.

REGARDING THIS WORLD

We have already touched upon one crucial difference in outlook between the Kabbalah and Indian philosophy. This difference derives from the world-affirming outlook that is explicit throughout the Jewish tradition. In spite of a few dissenting voices (the most famous occurring in the Talmud's declaration that it would be better had man never been created), Judaism is quite clear in its celebration of the existence of the created world. The Kabbalah itself is consistent in its affirmation of creation.[72] Indeed, in view of Judaism's emphasis on *ha-olam haba* (this world), the Lurianic view that this world is itself an illusion was something of an embarrassment to both the Kabbalists and Hasidim. The Kabbalists managed, however, to overcome this difficulty by declaring that the illusion of a created world is a necessary, indeed critical, stage in the development of God. God, as it were, grants an illusion of independent existence to man in order that he, in his moral, intellectual, and spiritual acts, can instantiate and concretize the values that are mere abstractions in the infinite godhead.

Indian philosophy, by way of contrast, is, on the whole, quite antagonistic to this world. *Maya* and *Samsara* are snares that must be escaped; and the human personality, far from being heroic in its worldly efforts, is an illusion that must be "starved," cut off, and transcended. This negative, even contemptuous, attitude toward the world of "difference" is carried to its logical conclusion in Buddhism, which in its original, purest, form, held that the world is by definition a realm of suffering caused by ignorance. For Buddhism the "problem" rests in the entire human way of life, which is both

---

72. This affirmation is also a critical difference between the Kabbalah and Gnosticism. See Chapter Five.

illusory and devoid of value. Buddhism articulates a skepticism and nihilism that is already implicit in Hindu thought, in its utter denial of the force and validity of everything that can be known.[73] Even Buddhist doctrine itself is considered meaningless and empty, as is the whole karmic struggle through multiple incarnations toward enlightenment and nirvana. Such concepts are mere expedients for releasing the adherent from the grip of this world, and they themselves become void of significance for one who has actually achieved enlightenment. To the enlightened, all is a silence that cannot be spoken. A Mahayana text expresses this notion mythopoetically in what can best be described as an example of Buddhist *anti-metaphor* (self-negating metaphor):

> The enlightened one sets forth in the Great Ferry boat but there is nothing from which he sets forth. He starts from the universe; but in truth he starts from nowhere. His boat is manned with all the perfections; and is manned by no one. It will find its support on nothing whatsoever and will find its support in the state of all knowing, which will serve it as a non-support. Moreover, no one has ever set forth in the Great Ferry boat; no one ever will set forth in it, and no one is setting forth in it now. And why is this? Because neither the one setting forth nor the goal for which he sets forth is to be found; therefore, who should be setting forth, and whiter?[74]

One cannot fail to respect the consistency of a philosophy of illusion that applies the notion of illusoriness even to itself. Certain Kabbalists held a similar view, to the effect that one who came face to face with the unity of *Ein-Sof* would at the very least be struck with a "silence" and dissolve like one who awakens from a dream. Yet in contrast to the Buddhists who see no value in the dream (and only seek to escape it), the Kabbalists placed a great value on the worldly illusion. The Kabbalist would be inclined to ask the author of the Buddhist anti-metaphor, why the illusion at all? Why not a never-ending void and silence? Of what value is the illusory journey through this illusory world?

Not only the Buddhists, but also the ancient Hindus, held that when the inner divine self becomes man's only desire the world itself is nullified, and the individual reaches a place where: "a father is no longer a father, a mother no longer a mother; states of being are no longer states of being, gods are no

---

73. Zimmer, *Philosophies of India*, p. 471.
74. Ibid., p. 484.

longer gods, the Vedas are no longer the Vedas . . . He is not followed by good, not followed by evil; for then he will have passed all sorrow of the here."[75] The tradition is very strong in India that the purpose of man's sojourn on earth is in order that he might be liberated (*moksa*) from this world: that he might, indeed, escape the cycle of life and rebirth, and be liberated from a world that is essentially one of suffering. Gnosticism represents this point of view in the West, in its doctrine that the divine spark entrapped within the soul of man must be liberated in order for man to achieve *Gnosis* and, ultimately, liberation from this world.

The Kabbalist, too, strives to encounter the divine self within, to know the root of his own soul, and to release this divine root or spark from its imprisonment in the corporeal world, the realm of the *Kelippot*. But unlike the Hindu and Gnostic, he does not conceive of this liberation as an escape; but rather as an opportunity to correct, restore, and transform the entire cosmic order, including the corporeal world and the realms of the Other Side. We find in the Kabbalah an adoption of Gnostic, and ultimately, I believe, Hindu transcendental themes that are provided with a surprising immanent, *this-worldly* interpretation. The images of "raising the sparks" and of "extracting the kernel from the husk" are used by the Kabbalists not, as one might suppose, to express an escape or a separation from the world, but as metaphors for the world's repair and restoration. It is almost as if the Kabbalists found themselves within a (mystical) metaphoric tradition of escape and transcendence, and chose to reverse the meaning of their images rather than abandon them altogether. Or perhaps by maintaining the transcendent, other-worldly images of earlier mysticism they could provide these images with *this-worldly* interpretations and thereby maintain a dialectical tension between transcendence and immanence in their ideas. The Kabbalists become those who restore the world by transcending it, or who transcend the world by working on its immanent repair.

It is clear that a number of kabbalistic symbols for *Tikkun* have parallels in the mysticism of India. Indeed, the metaphor of *birur*, of extracting the kernel from the husk, is found in the Katha Upanishad: "The inmost self, in the heart of creations abiding ever. Stand firm! and from thy body wrench Him out like pith extracted from a reed."[76] While for the Kabbalists the

---

75. *Brihadaranyaka Upanishad* IV, iii, 22, Zaehner, ed., *Hindu Scriptures*, p. 76.

76. *Katha Upanishad* VI, 17, Zaehner, ed., *Hindu Scriptures*, p. 204.

"extraction of the seed from the husk" is a metaphor for the restoration of the world, the Hindu or Jaina mystic is mostly concerned with the improvement of his own spirit: "As a man acts (Karma), as he behaves, so does he become. Whoso does good, becomes good, whoso does evil, becomes evil. By good (*punya*) works (Karma) a man becomes holy (*punya*), by evil [works] he becomes evil."[77] For the Kabbalah a man's acts not only determine the destiny of his own soul but also impact upon history, the value of the world, and the balance between destructive and restorative forces in the cosmos.

To be sure, there are certain strains within Indian philosophy that come very close to the Kabbalists' affirmation of the "world-illusion." For example, there is a joyous affirmation of life in the ancient Vedic "Hymn of Food"[78] and later in the *Bhagavad Gita*. In general, the Brahmans held a jubilant view of life and we find in the so-called Yoga of "Selfless Action" a sort of middle ground where the adherent is enjoined to carry out his particular duties while uniting his will with the universal ground of all being.[79] Samkara, the most influential metaphysician in the Indian philosophical tradition, held a "two-level" theory of reality, in which the world is said to be an illusion from the point of view of Brahman, but existent and real from the point of view of man. A very similar theory appears among the Kabbalists who adopted the Neoplatonic formula that the world is only real from "the point of view of the recipient."[80] We should note that several modern Vedantists, such as Radhakrishnan, played down the "acosmic" aspects of Hindu thought, affirming the role of mankind in bettering the corporeal world.

It is in the Tantra (a late form of Hinduism originating c. 200 C.E.), however, that we are presented with a view that comes very close to the kabbalistic notion of the complementarity and reciprocity of this world and its ultimate foundation. In Tantra, *moksa* or release is no longer seen as the highest goal, and this world is understood, as it is in the Jewish tradition, as a manifestation of God's glory.[81] Thus the nineteenth-century Tantric master, Sri Ramakrishna (1836–1886), affirms that "one cannot think of Brahman, without Sakti or of Sakti without Brahman,"[82] which signifies that

77. *Brihadaranyaka Upanishad* IV, iv, 5, Zaehner, ed., *Hindu Scriptures*, pp. 79–80.

78. Zimmer, *Philosophies of India*, pp. 345–347.

79. Ibid., p. 380.

80. See Idel, *Kabbalah: New Perspectives*, p. 138.

81. Zimmer, *Philosophies of India*, p. 555.

82. Ibid., p. 564.

there is no Absolute without the relative just as there is no relative without the Absolute. Ramakrishna relates: "In the Vedas creation is likened to the spider and its web. The spider brings the web out of itself and then remains in it." Ramakrishna states, rather "kabbalistically," "God is the container of the universe and also what is contained within it."[83] For Tantra, the world is to be wholeheartedly embraced. The Tantric hero is one who, rather than escaping from the world, goes straight through it and finds holiness and purity in all things, even those things that are ordinarily thought of as forbidden.

This latter idea, which is found in the Kabbalah and Hasidism, and is spoken of as "the descent for the purpose of ascent," is one of the defining characteristics of Tantra. The five forbidden things of the Hindu tradition—wine, meat, fish, parched grain, and sexual intercourse—actually become sacraments for the Tantric devotee.[84] This is reminiscent not only of those Kabbalists and Hasidim who formulated such ideas *in theory* but even more so of the heretical Shabbateans, whose messianic pretender, Shabbatai Zevi, said benedictions over forbidden foods and acts, blessing a God who had "commanded" him to do what was "forbidden."[85]

LINGUISTIC MYSTICISM

The identification of the cosmos with language, and particularly with the names of God, is a major doctrine in the Kabbalah, and is also found in Indian thought. In the *Brihadaranyaka Upanishad* we find the doctrine that the world was originally undifferentiated and that the distinctions within it were created by language.[86] The world as it is commonly known and expressed, according to the *Chandogya Upanishad*, is "no more than a name."

> The Rig Veda . . . the funeral rites of the dead, arithmetic, divination, chronometry, logic, politics, the etymological and semantic interpretations of the scriptures, the way to approach disembodied spirits, archery,

83. Ibid., p. 566.
84. Ibid., p. 572.
85. See Scholem, *Sabbatai Sevi: The Mystical Messiah.*
86. *Brihadaranyaka Upanishad*I, iv, 7, Zaehner, ed., *Hindu Scriptures*, pp. 40–41.

astronomy, the art of dealing with snakes and the fine arts. All this is merely a name . . .[87]

Yet the *Upanishad* instructs us to "revere the name," informing us that whoever does so "gains freedom of movement in the whole sphere of the name."

Yet the ancient Hindus held that the name, meaning the system of linguistic differentia that constitute the world of men, is itself transcended by other cosmic entities and processes, which themselves must be revered, perhaps even more so than language. The order provided by the *Chandogya Upanishad* (in ascending order of greatness) is the name, speech, mind, will, thought, meditation, understanding, strength, food, water, heat, space, memory, hope, and the "breath of life."[88] It is interesting that this order essentially reverses the chain of being as described by the Kabbalists, who held that the movement from language, to will, thought, etc., is a *descent* from the Infinite God. For the *Upanishad* the superiority of each succeeding category in this *ascension* is due to the fact that the lower category is dependent upon or diminished by the higher one. For example, 100 men of understanding tremble before one who is strong, yet strength is dependent upon food, which is in turn dependent upon water, etc. Interestingly the dialectic in this *Upanishad* flows from abstract, mental concepts, to practical, natural ones and then back to the concepts of memory, hope, and the breath of life, which embody the abstract or ideal in the concrete world of human existence. We might say that for the Hindus the ideal world of the mind and the practical world of "food and water" come together in man's "living breath," his living existential situation; and it is this situation, not the ideal or natural worlds per se, which is to be revered above all else. We should note that this breath of life, in Hebrew the *ruach elohim*, with which God ensouled Adam, plays an important role in the kabbalistic account of the soul.

THE PERSONAL GOD

The concept of a personal deity is a problematic one for mystical thought. For the mystic, who experiences ultimate reality as a unity beyond all distinctions,

---

87. *Chandogya Upanishad* VII, i, 4, Zaehner, ed., *Hindu Scriptures*, p. 126.
88. *Chandogya Upanishad* VII, i–xiv, Zaehner, ed., *Hindu Scriptures*, pp. 126–133.

the idea of a separate deity who addresses man in dialogue appears as something less than spiritual perfection. We thus find in the mystical traditions of India a disavowal of a personal creator deity that parallels a disavowal of the personality of man and the entire created world. In Brahmanic thought, for example, we find the doctrine that when *Brahman* becomes a personal, creative, omniscient, and omnipotent Universal God, it is itself already subject to the illusion of *Avidya*.[89] Such a God who believes himself to be sovereign, omnipotent, etc., is, like the man he creates, already a victim of self-delusion. This is because the secret of creation (and hence the truth of God the creator) is that *Brahman*, estranged from itself, ignorant of itself, *is* creation. Such, a view, while it is nowhere, as far as I can tell, explicitly stated by the Kabbalists, is implicit in their theory of the deity: for the God of Israel, as they put it, is not equivalent to *Ein-Sof,* but is rather to be identified with the already partially concealed realm of the *Sefirot.* We will see that the view of the creator God or demiurge as ignorant, even arrogant in its feeling of omnipotence, is voiced unhesitatingly by the Gnostics. The Kabbalists, of course, had too much respect for the biblical tradition to articulate such a view.

Still a far cry from the Jewish tradition of a personal creator God is the Vedantic view that "God" as He is conceived of in the minds of most men is simply a useful means for focusing the mind and disciplining the soul, and that such a God is like a raft that, once one has completed his journey across the river, is a burden and must be discarded.[90] *Brahman,* on the other hand, is without any of the characteristics, desires, and personality traits that are evident in the God of popular religion. In the Kabbalah we find the view that *Ein-Sof,* as it were, descends, degree by degree, through multiple contractions in becoming the personal God. Indeed, as I have argued in Chapter Two, for the Kabbalists it is man who in addressing the infinite brings the personal God into existence. The same view was expressed by the Indian poet Tulsidas (d. 1623): "There is no difference between the Personal and the Impersonal . . . He who is Impersonal, without form and unborn becomes Personal for love of his devotees."[91] This descent by degrees to a personal God is expressed in the Hindu conception of Brahman-Atman incarnating itself first as Isvara, the Lord of the created Universe, and then as *avatara* or

---

89. Zimmer, *Philosophies of India*, p. 424.

90. Ibid., pp. 426–427.

91. Quoted in Louis Renou, ed., *Hinduism* (New York: Braziller, 1962), p. 220.

a series of historical divine personages. The latter conception is also found in the Kabbalah's equation of each of the various biblical personages from Abraham to King David with a unique *Sefirah*: such individual *tzaddikim* thereby becoming something like the "avatars" of the kabbalistic tradition.

However, as we have seen in regard to the instantial, material world, the Kabbalah's attitude toward "God" is far more favorable, on the whole, than that of Indian philosophy. In India, the pantheon of Gods were tolerated by the philosophers as necessary symbols for the masses, but for reasons we have already explained, the veneration of a unique, personal deity (as in Judaism and Islam) never took hold among the metaphysicians. Again, it is only in Tantra that Brahman as an infinite abstract principle is set aside in favor of a personal (in this case matriarchal) deity. Having affirmed the world, the Tantrists were wont to affirm its creator as well. Tantra thus has much to recommend itself as an object of comparative study for those interested in a renewed appreciation of the Kabbalah.

4

The Kabbalah and Platonism

T he influence of Greek philosophical thought, particularly that of Plato and Neoplatonism, upon the development in the Kabbalah has long been recognized. Scholem, for example, relates that Jewish thought in the East, and in Spain and Italy, in the centuries prior to the emergence of the Zohar, "can be described as the struggle between Plato and Aristotle for the Biblical and talmudic heritage of Judaism."[1] Platonic notions, which had exercised such a prominent influence on Philo of Alexandria in the first century C.E., were also highly influential, if albeit indirectly, on Gnostic sources, which interacted profoundly with traditions that later emerged as the Kabbalah. A more direct influence resulted from the translation of such Platonic dialogues as the *Republic*, *Timaeus*, and *Crito* into Arabic; quotations in Arabic from several others; and their synopses (again translated into Arabic) by Galen. An even more profound influence resulted from the quotations and interpretations of Plato in Aristotle, the interpretations of Plato in such Neoplatonists as Plotinus and Proclus, and the work of Avicena.[2] The combined effect of these and other varied sources was that Jews living in Arabic lands were able to share fully in general

---

1. Scholem, *Major Trends*, p. 80.
2. "Plato and Platonism," *Encyclopedia Judaica* (Jerusalem: Keter, 1972), Vol. 13, pp. 629–630.

humanistic culture, so much so that Plato and Aristotle became the main intellectual influences upon Jewish theology.

There can be little doubt that even the early Kabbalah shows definite signs of Platonic influence. Scholem points out that the notion of higher "worlds" (*Olamot*), which made its first appearance among the Kabbalists of the circle of Iyyun in Provence, is undoubtedly Neoplatonic in origin.[3] The Book of Unity, which also originates with the earliest Kabbalists in Provence, describes the *Sefirot* as "seals" that serve as the minting stamps of the world, an idea that had originally been used in reference to the Platonic *eide* or ideas.[4] Scholem further argues that the thirteenth-century Kabbalist, Azriel of Gerona, may very well have been influenced by the Christian Neoplatonist, Scotus Erigena, both in his "negative theology" and in the important doctrine that God is a *coincidentia oppositorum*, a unity of opposites.[5] According to Scholem, the advent of the Kabbalah involved the superimposition of Neoplatonic notions on earlier forms of Jewish (*Merkaveh*) mysticism.[6] While the earlier Kabbalists borrowed from the Neoplatonists without attribution, later Kabbalists, including Isaac ibn Latif, Israel Sarug, and Abraham Cohen Herrera, were avowed in their attempts to provide a Platonic interpretation of kabbalistic ideas.[7]

The impact of Platonic and especially Neoplatonic themes on kabbalistic theosophy has been the subject of recent scholarly interest. Moshe Idel, for example, has pointed out that in contrast to Maimonidean Aristotelianism, the nascent Kabbalah emphasized the Platonic elements in medieval philosophy.[8] Neoplatonic images, concepts, mysticism, and even myths surface among the early Kabbalists.[9] For example, in the fourteenth century the Kabbalist Menahem Recanti had begun to speak disparagingly of Aristotle; and in the early fifteenth century the Kabbalist R. Shem Tov Ben Shem Tov held that the views of Plato were close to those of the Torah.[10] Idel points out

---

3. Scholem, *Kabbalah*, p. 329.

4. Ibid., p. 329.

5. Ibid., p. 440.

6. Ibid., p. 319.

7. In the case of Herrera the match was with Neoplatonic philosophy particularly as interpreted by Marsilio Ficino; Herrera, Abraham Kohen De, *Encyclopedia Judaica* (Jerusalem: Keter, 1972), Vol. 8, pp. 391–392.

8. Idel, "Jewish Kabbalah and Platonism," p. 319.

9. Ibid., p. 320.

10. Ibid., p. 322, citing *Sefer ha-Emunot* (Ferrara, 1556), fol. 27a–b.

that by the close of the sixteenth and beginning of the seventeenth centuries Kabbalists were eager to quote from Platonic and Neoplatonic sources.[11]

I will begin my discussion of Plato and the Kabbalah by drawing the reader's attention to several basic issues on which Platonism and the Kabbalah converge. As will become clear, it is my view that the *philosophical* foundation of kabbalistic thought (as opposed to its mysticism, myth, and practice) is to be found in Plato and Neoplatonism; and that the fate of Kabbalah as philosophy turns, to a large extent, on the fate of corresponding Platonic ideas. Minimally, it is certain that anyone interested in explicating the Kabbalah in a philosophic idiom must take into account such doctrines as the reality and substantiality of values and the equation of Being and the Good, which have become part and parcel of the Platonic heritage. Platonism, is indeed the first portal through which the Kabbalah can enter into full dialogue with the *western* intellectual tradition.

Of even greater significance for the Kabbalah, as well as for our own philosophical understanding of the kabbalistic symbols, is the philosophy of Neoplatonism, particularly as expressed in the *Enneads* of Plotinus. While there are crucial differences between kabbalistic and Neoplatonic theology, their problematics are so much alike that a study of Neoplatonic philosophy cannot fail to provide us with deeper insight into the Kabbalah itself.

After a general introduction to the relevance of Platonic thought to Jewish mysticism I provide an outline of the philosophy of Plotinus. An understanding of Platonic and Neoplatonic philosophy helps us to comprehend the "metaphysics" that underlies the Kabbalist's symbols and ideas. After a discussion of the relationship between Neoplatonism and the Kabbalah, I will discuss the philosophy of the modern Neoplatonist J. N. Findlay, whose lectures on the Platonic cave and its transcendence, both on earth and in worlds on high, provides a fascinating attempt to restate the problematic of Neoplatonism, and, indirectly that of the Kabbalah, in contemporary terms. We will see that the contemporary Kabbalist Adin Steinsaltz adopts an approach the major thrust of which is very similar to Findlay's philosophy.

THE DOCTRINE OF FORMS

The most important Platonic notion to find its way into kabbalistic thought is the doctrine of forms or ideas. Even prior to the advent of the Kabbalah,

---

11. Ibid., p. 325.

Platonic Idealism had infiltrated Jewish speculation regarding the creation of the world. In the *Midrash Genesis Rabbah*, we find the declaration that God looked into the Torah and created the world, as if the language of the Torah consisted of a set of forms or templates for creation.[12] The Hellenistic Jewish philosopher, Philo, understood an isomorphism between the laws of the Torah and the structure of the natural world.[13]

Plato was perhaps the first to articulate the view that the finite, particular, objects of the everyday, natural world are decidedly less substantial and real than the genera that they exemplify. For Plato, particular triangles, men, or acts of justice are only pale reflections or *instantiations* of ideal archetypes of triangularity, humanity, or justice. Plato was led to this view by the observation that one cannot identify, conceptualize, or even refer to a particular horse, for example, without invoking a generic idea; and that when one speaks of, say, a triangle in mathematics, one does not refer to a particular triangular object with all of its accidental properties and imperfections, but to an ideal type that is perfect triangularity per se. Plato concluded that an individual horse is what it is because it reflects, or participates in, the ideal *form* of "horseness"; an individual triangle is so called because it participates in the *form* of triangularity. For Plato, forms and ideas are substantial and real instants and material objects have a substantiality that is derived and dependent.

For Plato, the world is composed of a hierarchical organization of ideal types. A given entity is what it is, because it participates in or reflects a particular combination of forms. Plato is not perfectly clear or consistent regarding what he includes in his formal taxonomy. In some places he suggests that not everything manmade or debased has a form unto itself, but he generally holds that even these things may be identified by the combination of natural forms that they reflect or participate in. One thing is clear: for Plato the most estimable forms, those to which he attributes the greatest substantiality or being, are values such as "love" or "justice," which are (imperfectly) reflected in man. And it is precisely through this conception that Platonism enters the very heart of the Kabbalah, the doctrine of the ten *Sefirot*.

---

12. Genesis Rabbah, 1, 1. See Gershom Scholem, "The Meaning of the Torah in Jewish Mysticism," in Gershom Scholem, *On the Kabbalah and Its Symbolism* trans. Ralph Manheim (New York: Schocken, 1969), p. 40.

13. Philo, *Vita Moses* II, 51; cited in Scholem, "The Meaning of the Torah," p. 40.

In *Sefer Yetzirah* the *Sefirot* are introduced as archetypal, numerical, or ideational elements, a kabbalistic translation of or equivalent to the Platonic ideas. *Sefer Yetzirah*, however, adds a new linguistic dimension to the Platonic paradigm. In addition to the *Sefirot* or elemental numbers (which in the Kabbalah become the archetypal qualities of Will, Wisdom, Understanding, etc.), *Sefer Yetzirah* speaks of twenty-two Foundational Letters (*Otiyyot Yesod*), which are also said to constitute the ideational structure of both God and the world. This "linguistic idealism" is found neither in Plato nor the Neoplatonists but is present in Greek syncretistic texts of the period during which *Sefer Yetzirah* was composed.[14]

The doctrine of the ten *Sefirot* is, in essence, a world of Platonic forms, understood by the Kabbalists to be the value archetypes of the cosmos. In holding that both God and creation are comprised of such values as "will," "wisdom," "understanding," "kindness," "justice," and "beauty" the Kabbalists placed the Platonic doctrine of ideas at the core of their own theosophy. Like the Platonists, the Kabbalists maintained that it was these ideal values that are most substantial and real. The objects of the material world are these ideas' and values' shadows or reflections. Further, by limiting the number of ideal types to ten, the Kabbalists combined two aspects of the Platonic (and earlier Pythagorean) program; the tendency to equate substance with values and the desire to reduce the cosmos to a mathematical function of the ten "basic numbers." (The kabbalistic preoccupation with Gematria, or number mysticism in which all things are reduced to numbers via a consideration of the numerical values of the letters in the words that name them, is itself a relic of this Pythagorean/Platonic program.)

FORMS AND THEIR INSTANCES

A question arises within Platonism regarding the precise relationship between the ideal forms and the objects that instantiate them in the sensible world. We have already alluded to Plato's own solutions to this question, which involved either the vague notion of particular things *participating* in their respective forms, or more specifically *mirroring* their likeness. These solutions have themselves been a problem for Platonism, as they raise a whole host of further questions, such as whether the forms exist independently of instants; how it

---

14. Scholem, *Kabbalah*, p. 27.

is that an example of something "participates" in the form of which it is an instance; and how it is possible for an instance to be like an idea without involving another idea representing the manner in which the first two are alike; and so on *ad infinitim*. If the Kabbalists' *Sefirot* are to be understood as anything other than a fanciful metaphor, similar questions must be raised and answered about them as well.

The Kabbalists themselves struggled with the question of the relationship between the *Sefirot* and the particular things of the natural world. Their solutions to this dilemma illustrate the extent to which the Kabbalists departed from a strictly Platonic framework and incorporated elements of both Aristotelian and dialectical thought. The relationship between the *Sefirot* and our world is understood by the later Kabbalists via several ideas: immanence, *Tzimtzum* (concealment, contraction), and *Shevirat ha-Kelim* (the Breaking of the Vessels).

The first of these ideas is that the *Sefirot* are *immanent* in the objects of sense. The immanence of a form in the objects it informs is actually an Aristotelian solution to the Platonic dilemma, and one that was implicitly adopted by the Kabbalist Moses Cordovero. Cordovero held that the objects of the sensible world are actually *comprised of the Sefirot*: that the *Sefirot* in various combinations and proportions are the atoms and molecules of the natural world. It is, of course, difficult to make sense of this view if one pictures the *Sefirot* in extensional, quasi-physical terms. However, if the *Sefirot* are interpreted strictly as phenomenolgical forms, as a descriptive matrix for locating a given object in its physical, temporal, and value-descriptive dimensions,[15] Cordovero's atomic solution to the Platonic dilemma becomes more comprehensible. The forms need not exist apart from the objects of this world; rather, they *comprise* them as ten phenomenological or experiential dimensions, which determine not only their spatial and temporal characteristics but their existential, intentional, cognitive, and axiological status as well.

One can also conceive of the *Sefirot* as a deep structure determining the observable "surface structure" of the phenomenal world in much the same manner as a digital algorithm on a compact disc determines the surface structure of a (phenomenal) visual or musical display. The twentieth-century philosopher Ludwig Wittgenstein, in the period of his *Tractatus Logico Philosophicus*, held such a Platonic/Cordoverian view of the world, arguing

---

15. See my *Symbols of the Kabbalah* for a full discussion of this dimensional theory of the *Sefirot*.

that the things we speak about in everyday discourse are comprised of "atomic facts," represented by elementary propositions and ultimately "names," which are the immutable (but not observable) constituents of all existence.[16] Indeed, we find a similar theory in the Kabbalah as well, in the view that the world is comprised of letters in the holy tongue, and that each sensible object is what it is by virtue of the particular combination of immutable letters that comprise its name.[17]

The kabbalistic doctrines of the *Sefirot*, Gematria, and linguistic atomism can each be understood as attempts to provide solutions to the basic Platonic dilemma of permanence and change. Plato had offered his theory of forms in an effort to overcome the skepticism of Heraclitus (who denied the possibility of knowledge on the grounds that all is "flux") and the absurdities of Parmenides (who preserved an epistemological absolute at the expense of denying the existence of change in the natural world). Plato's solution was to hold that the phenomenal world is indeed in flux, but that the archetypes on which that world is grounded are immutable and eternal. The Kabbalists faced the same issue transposed onto a theological plane. For them the dilemma centered on the permanence and immutability of an eternal God and the obvious flux and mutability of His creation. If God is complete, self-sufficient, and unalterable, how is it that He can come to create a world that is subject to flux, degeneration, and corruption? Further, how can such a corrupt world be said to add anything to an already whole, perfect, and complete God?

The Kabbalists, like Plato, resolved their dilemma by acknowledging the corruptible character of the phenomenal world, but at the same time, denying that this world has any genuine independent substance. Underlying the world of sense, and determining it in its course, are the *Sefirot*, the absolute values, letters, and numbers that are the true essence of creation. It is these underlying objects that are completely unalterable and absolute. Carried to its logical conclusion the kabbalistic view is that the natural world is, in essence, an epiphenomena or illusion (albeit a necessary one). As we have seen in Chapter One this is precisely the view adopted by the Chabad Hasidim.

---

16. Ludwig Wittgenstein, *Tractatus Logico-Philosophicus*, D. F. Pears and B. F. McGuinness, trans. (London: Routledge and Kegan Paul, 1961). Originally published in 1921.

17. As we have seen in Chapter One, this view was first expressed in the proto-kabbalistic work *Sefer Yetzirah*, and was taken up by nearly all later theosophical Kabbalists.

OBJECTS AS OBSCURED IDEAS

The Kabbalists actually went further than Plato in their understanding of the gulf that exists between the divine unchangeable realm of archetypes and the world of particulars within which we reside. Their doctrines of *Tzimtzum* and *Shevirat Hakelim* were designed both to widen this gulf and to explicate the precise relationship that exists between these two realms.

I have described each of these doctrines in Chapter One. Here it should suffice to say that with the doctrine of *Tzimtzum*, the Kabbalists expressed the view that even the "forms" themselves (i.e., the *Sefirot*) are the result of a concealment of the unitary essence of the infinite God, and that particular finite things are themselves the result of a further process of obstruction and concealment. Put in another way, a finite particular object is an imperfectly known perspective on the very archetype it instantiates. When we encounter a particular horse, for example, we see only some of its aspects (its surface features as opposed to its depth, its behavior in this moment as opposed to its whole life history, etc.). We might go so far as to say that space, time, and materiality are the obscuring mediums that prevent us from knowing a horse or any other object as it truly is, in all of its dimensions, history, etc. If we were to know the horse completely it would become, as it were, a pure and total conception, and cease to exist in space and time. The doctrine of *Tzimtzum* implies that particular things exist because a series of garments or curtains (to use a favorite metaphor of the Kabbalists) have been drawn across the world of ideas. These curtains (which are partly identified with the *Sefirot* themselves) prevent us from seeing the pure essence of things, and situate what we do see in a spatial, temporal, and material framework.

For the Kabbalists, the world of particulars is, in essence, an obstructed view of the world of forms. Plato's metaphor of the cave is particularly relevant here, and is indeed an important precursor to the Kabbalist's doctrine of *Tzimtzum*. Plato in *The Republic* had compared the epistemological state of all mankind to the situation of men who spend their whole lives in "a cavernous chamber underground with an entrance open to the light and a long passage all down the cave."[18] These men are chained in such a manner that they face a wall at the rear of the cave and can only see what is in front of them. Behind them, further up the caves, is a fire, and between the men and the fire are persons carrying artificial objects, including figures

---

18. Plato, *Republic*, F. M. Cornford trans. (New York: Oxford, 1945), p. 514.

of men and animals behind a parapet, so that just the shadows of these objects are projected onto the wall that the chained men face. Such men spend the whole of their lives seeing the mere shadows of these artificial objects. These obscured shadows, Plato implies, are like the objects we ourselves experience in the natural world. It is only through acts of intellectual and, further, mystical ascent, that an individual can come to see the true objects of knowledge and witness the light of the fire or, to use another Platonic metaphor, the sun itself.

The Kabbalists, like Plato, were fond of metaphors involving darkness and light. Each regarded the sun as a symbol of the Absolute, which was held to be the source of all knowledge and being. Plato, who identified the Absolute with the "Form of the Good" (a unitary, undifferentiated value that is the source of all the lower forms) compared the Absolute with the sun: "It was the sun, then, that I meant when I spoke of that offspring which the Good has created in the visible world, to stand there in the same relation to vision and visible things as that which the Good itself bears in the intelligible world to intelligence and intelligible objects."[19] Our world, according to Plato, is a world of shadows in which the "light" of the form of the Good is diminished and obscured. As we will see Plotinus held that the material world bordered on total darkness, the complete privation of intelligible light. It is not far from this Neoplatonic view to the kabbalistic theory of *Tzimtzum*. At any rate, it is clear that the Kabbalists, in their doctrines of *Ein-Sof* (the infinite God), *Or Ein-Sof* (the light of the infinite), and *Tzimtzum* (concealment and contraction), have expanded upon an essentially Platonic analogy regarding knowledge, being, and the sun.

EIN-SOF AND "THE FORM OF THE GOOD"

The kabbalistic conception of God or *Ein-Sof* in some respects coincides with the Platonic "Form of the Good." Plato held the Form of the Good to be transcendent beyond truth and knowledge, stating in the *Republic* that it is "even beyond being, surpassing it in dignity and power."[20] The Kabbalists, who regarded the *Sefirot* as traits or aspects of the infinite God, understood *Ein-Sof* as a power transcending truth, knowledge, being, and perhaps even

---

19. Ibid., p. 506ff.
20. Ibid., p. 507.

Goodness itself. Like the Neoplatonists they held that nothing positive can be stated about this God whatsoever, holding with both Plato and Plotinus (as well as the Gnostics) that God the creator (Plato's "demiurge") is already a lower manifestation of this infinite principle. Still, it is arguable that *Ein-Sof*, whose first emanations are the set of ten value archetypes (the *Sefirot*), is to be identified with Absolute Value itself, and that the kabbalistic deity is very close indeed to the Platonic "Form of the Good."

THE DIALECTIC OF ORDER AND CHAOS

The Kabbalists, however, did not rest with the view that the objects of sense are an obscured version of the ideas. They further held that many of the ideal archetypes themselves, at least in the form in which they are manifest in creation, have been corrupted and broken with the result that their identity is almost hopelessly obscured. The objects of the phenomenal world, according to Isaac Luria, are not simply imperfect copies or obscured versions of their ideal prototypes, but are in fact admixtures of broken values and ideals, which have fallen perilously through a metaphysical void. The result of the Breaking of the Vessels is that no act of pure intellection can proceed through the objects of sense to an ideal world of forms. Since the forms have shattered, they must themselves be *reconstructed* through the acts of man. For the Kabbalah, unlike for Plato, the value-archetypes are not so much there to be seen, as they are to be made. What's more, this reconstruction is in a pattern (not yet determined) that is different and (because it is accomplished via the ethical and spiritual acts of mankind) superior to the original unshattered ideals. For the Lurianic Kabbalah, man is truly a partner of God in completing creation.

It is instructive to compare the Lurianic "chaotic" myth of the Breaking of the Vessels with a parallel "orderly" account of creation in Plato's *Timaeus*. According to the Kabbalists the *Sefirot* were originally emanated as vessels that were to contain in ideal form the light (knowledge, being) of the infinite God. These vessels, however, were unable to contain the force of the divine light and shattered, breaking into an abundance of shards, each trapping a spark of divine light and falling chaotically through the metaphysical void to create our world. Plato too understands creation to have occurred in a vessel, the "receptacle of becoming." But the process of creation is precisely the reverse of that found in Luria:

the four kinds of elements were shaken by the receiving vessel, which moving like a winnowing machine, scattered far away from one another the elements most unlike, and forced the most similar elements in close contact. Wherefore all the various elements had different places before they were arranged so as to form the universe.[21]

The implications of this distinction (between Plato, whose creation moves from chaos to order; and Luria, for whom this process is reversed) are far ranging, not only for metaphysics and theology but for ethics and politics as well. The notion that an ideal world already exists for those who can intuit it (Plato) obviously leads to ethical and political theories that are far more conservative and absolutist than the notion that the ideal world is as-yet unknown and must be constructed through the cooperative ventures of humankind. I believe that in spite of the Kabbalists' own adherence to the framework of normative Judaism, it is clear that their theories were potentially revolutionary in their implications. *Tikkun ha-Olam* is not a simple restoration of a prior perfect (but lost) condition created by God, but is rather an *emendation* or *reconstruction* that also creates something new and *better* than the world initially emanated by the deity. The attraction of progressive Jewish intellectuals to the *Tikkun* concept in our own time is no accident,[22] for this kabbalistic idea is essentially progressive and humanistic in its orientation.

THE MYSTICAL ASCENT OF THE SOUL

While the basic thrust of the concept of *Tikkun ha-Olam* (the restoration of the world) is *this*-worldly, there are mystical *other*worldly strains in the Kabbalah as well. The concept of "higher worlds," each dominated by a particular *Sefirah* or archetype, became standard doctrine among the Kabbalists, and was closely related to various practices of meditation and mystical ascent. It is of interest that Plato himself, who seems to have regarded the forms as existing in, or comprising a "higher world" spoke of the ascent to these worlds in decidedly mystical terms: "The ascent to see the things in the

---

21. Plato, *The Timaeus*, trans. B. Jowett, *Great Books of the Western World* (Chicago: Encyclopedia Britannica, 1952), 6:458.

22. Witness the success of *Tikkun* magazine, which has become the most widely read voice of the new, progressive Jewish intellectual.

upper world you may take as standing for the upward journey of the soul into the region of the intelligible . . . the last thing to be perceived and only with great difficulty is the essential Form of Goodness."[23] Here, in *The Republic*, Plato paints the outlines of a view in which the soul ascends stepwise into higher regions, ultimately reaching an apex in the Absolute. That Plato regarded this ascent as (at least in part) mystical as opposed to intellective is evident from one of his letters, where he writes that he never put into writing his views "about the subjects which I seriously study . . ." for these "do not at all admit of verbal expression like other studies, but, as a result of continued application to the subject itself and communion therewith, it is brought to birth in the soul on a sudden, as light is kindled by a sleeping spark, and thereafter it nourishes itself."[24] This passage is of interest not only because it attests to Plato's mystical tendencies but for its use of the metaphor of the "sleeping spark," which was to become so important in Gnosticism and the Lurianic Kabbalah.

As we will see, Plato's mystical tendencies were to be taken up and amplified by the Neoplatonists. Proclus, for example, viewed the soul as capable of ascending through a series of upper realms that are progressively less corporeal and more conceptual and spiritual in nature; a view that was later to be echoed in the kabbalistic doctrine of the "four worlds."

The Platonic hierarchy of being is one in which particular things are regarded as obscured versions of the ideas they instantiate; and in which these ideas are ordered into generas that exemplify higher-order values, and so forth, until the apex of the Absolute or The Good itself is attained. This theory provides the framework for the "higher worlds" doctrine in both Neoplatonism and Kabbalah. We find, for example, in Plotinus a *hypostatization* of those values such as "love" into spiritual beings, which inhabit a supramundane cosmos, a viewpoint that finds its parallel in the angelology of the Kabbalah. Similarly, the kabbalistic concept of individual souls as sparks or portions of the original soul of Primordial Man, has its antecedent in the Plotinian view that the souls of man are each simply aspects of an overarching heavenly World-Soul. Like the Kabbalists, both Plato and Plotinus accepted the doctrine of reincarnation, holding that each individual soul passes

---

23. Plato, *Republic*, p. 515.
24. Plato, *Letters*, trans. R. G. Bury (Cambridge, MA: Harvard University Press, 1929), Letter VII, p. 341.

through a number of corporeal souls until, in Plotinus's phrase "it will rise outside of the realm of birth and dwell with the one soul of all."[25] Such "*unio-mystico*" became a very important part of the ecstatic Kabbalah.

THE PHILOSOPHY OF PLOTINUS

In the thought of Plotinus (205–270) we encounter a blend of philosophy and mysticism that contains direct parallels to many of the basic doctrines that were to become important for the Kabbalah. Plotinus was himself influenced by earlier Greek modes of thought, including the Neo-Pythagoreans, the Stoics, Plato (especially the Plato of the *Timaeus*), and in some places, Aristotle. Plotinus developed such Platonic notions as the "cave," the forms, and The Good into a metaphysical doctrine that posits levels of existence, realms, or hypostases, emanating from an Absolute, the Platonic Good or One. These realms, which Plotinus sometimes speaks of in grandiloquent terms, are accessible to humankind through dialectic philosophy and, moreover, through a suprarational mystical intuition.

PLOTINUS'S ONE AND THE "NEGATIVE THEOLOGY"

Even more clearly than Plato's "Form of the Good," Plotinus's theory of The One provides an important antecedent to the Kabbalist's *Ein-Sof*. As the principle of everything that there is, The One is absolutely transcendental, and Plotinus in his famous "negative theology" goes to great pains to assert that it is ineffable and devoid of all predication: "Thus the One is in truth beyond all statement . . . we can give it no name because that would imply predication . . . If we make it knowable, an object of affirmation, we make it manifold."[26] "We can and do state what it is not, while we are silent as to what it is."[27] "Its definition, in fact, could be only 'the indefinable' . . . We are in agony for a true expression: we are talking of the untellable . . ."[28]

---

25. Plotinus, Third Ennead, Tractate 2, paragraph 4. Plotinus, *The Six Enneads*, trans. Stephen Makenna *The Great Books of the Western World* (Chicago: Encyclopedia Britannica, 1952), 11:388.
26. Plotinus, Ennead, 5, 3, 13. Plotinus, *The Six Enneads*, p. 534.
27. Plotinus, Ennead 5, 3, 14. Ibid., p. 535.
28. Plotinus, Ennead 5, 5, 5. Ibid., p. 542.

For Plotinus, even "the phrase transcending Being assigns no character, makes no assertion, allots no name," but "carries only the denial of particular being; and in this there is no attempt to circumscribe it; to seek to throw a line about that illimitable Nature would be folly, and anyone thinking to do so cuts himself off from any slightest and most momentary approach to its least vestige."[29]

In a number of passages in the *Enneads*, Plotinus asserts that because of its complete unity and lack of differentiation, the One has no knowledge, even of itself. This is because knowledge requires a distinction between subject and object, and thus a multiple, differentiated state. As such the One transcends both knowledge and ignorance. According to Plotinus, "The Good therefore needs no consciousness."[30] There are passages in the Zohar that echo this idea, and later Kabbalists imply that a major reason for creation was so that God, through man, could come to know himself. However, in contrast to the Jewish tradition of the "living God," Plotinus goes so far as to opine that "The first cannot be said to live since it is the source of Life."[31]

"Negative Theology" has a long history in Jewish thought. Philo, the earliest Jewish Neoplatonist, held that the "Existent," i.e., God, must be dissociated from any and every quality. He is "unnameable and ineffable."[32] However, in contrast to the later Neoplatonists, Philo was unfortunately lost to Jewish scholars until relatively modern times.

Plotinus's views on the complete ineffability and unknowability of the "One" are perfectly paralleled in the Kabbalists' attitude toward their own absolute, *Ein-Sof*. As the One is the inscrutable emanative source of the hypostases Intelligence, Soul, and Nature in Plotinus, *Ein-Sof* (the Infinite) is the completely unknowable emanative source of *Sefirot*. As we have seen in Chapter One, the Kabbalists, like Plotinus, hold that the absolute is unnamable, beyond knowledge and even reference. Some, like the author of an anonymous fourteenth-century kabbalistic work, *Ma'arekhet ha-Elohut*, went so far as to hold that because *Ein-Sof* cannot even be hinted at in language, its presence is not even acknowledged in the Torah![33]

---

29. Plotinus, Ennead 5, 5, 6. Ibid., p. 542.
30. Plotinus, Ennead 3, 9, 3. Ibid., p. 445.
31. Plotinus, Ennead 2, 9, 3. Ibid., p. 445.
32. Katz, "Utterance and Ineffability," p. 279.
33. Scholem, *Kabbalah*, p. 89. Idel, p. 341.

SPEAKING THE UNSPEAKABLE

In spite of his insistence that The One cannot be defined, Plotinus attributes to the One several positive characteristics, equating it, for example, with the Platonic "Good," "God," and "the Infinite," and holding that it has the "power" to emanate being. Plotinus speaks of the one as the "Potentiality of the Universe," and describes its emanations, particularly the realm of intelligibles, as "a potentiality which has become effective."[34]

The Kabbalists are even more inclined than Plotinus to slip into a discourse that dares to "speak the unspeakable" and penetrate the inner mystery of the Absolute realm. Philo had spoken of the absolute existent as One, the "First Principle, immaterial, unchangable, universal intelligence, active, 'Maker and Father' who acts freely out of benevolence and goodness."[35] Steven Katz has argued that in comparison to Plotinus who maintained a comparatively strict adherence to "negative theology,"[36] Philo, and the Kabbalists, developed more positive characterizations of the Absolute to accommodate the personal God of biblical theology.[37] While the Kabbalists held with *Sefer Yetzirah* that on matters regarding *Ein-Sof* one should remain completely silent, there is a decided trend toward "speaking the unspeakable" in the Zohar and other kabbalistic texts. In these texts *Ein-Sof* is characterized as the Cause of all Causes, the Supernal Thought, the Supreme Will, etc.

Azriel of Gerona speaks of the manifestations of *Ein-Sof* as actually permitting contemplation of *Ein-Sof* itself,[38] and there are significant passages in the Zohar that appear to speak of the inner nature of *Ein-Sof* in decidedly positive, descriptive terms. Moses de Leon, the presumed author of the Zohar, states in his *Sefer Ha-Rimmon* that since all forms of existence are linked one to the other, God's true essence is above as well as below and therefore by knowing and naming the things of the lower world we indirectly comprehend *Ein-Sof* itself.[39] Other Kabbalists characterized *Ein-Sof* by speaking of *Tzatzahot*, or "super-*Sefirot*" within the core of *Ein-Sof*. According to Idel, Isaac Luria was influenced by this doctrine, which resulted in his

---

34. Plotinus, Ennead 2, 8, 10. Plotinus, *The Six Enneads*, p. 442.
35. Katz, "Utterance and Ineffability," pp. 285–286.
36. Though as we have seen even Plotinus characterizes the Good in more positive terms.
37. Katz, "Utterance and Ineffability," p. 288.
38. Idel, p. 339.
39. Katz, p. 291.

placing *Adam Kadmon* in a realm above the (lower) *Sefirot.*[40] Further, both *Tikkunei Zohar* and Luria at times appear to identify the highest *Sefirah* (Keter) and the *Partzuf* (*Attika Kaddisha*, the "Holy Ancient One") with *Ein-Sof.*[41] As is so often the case in the Kabbalah, there is a *coincidentia oppsitorum* between *Ein-Sof*'s total ineffability and its potential to be known and understood. Both trends are fully expressed in the kabbalistic sources.

EMANATION

For Plotinus the One, as the origin of being, is "above being" and "above even self-sufficing."[42] (By the thirteenth century, a similar idea, i.e., the idea that God transcends both existence and nonexistence, began to play an important role in the Kabbalah.[43]) The One, however, is the source and substance of everything, and it engenders a series of lower realms or hypostases through a process that Plotinus refers to as "emanation." Plotinus regarded the One as an absolute power or energy that overflows itself into the lower worlds. He analogizes this process to the emanation of light from the sun, which spreads its power throughout the cosmos without itself being altered or diminished in its essence. According to Plotinus: "The entire Intellectual Order may be figured as a kind of light with the One in repose at its summit as King . . . we may think, rather, of the One as a light before the light, an eternal irradiation . . ."[44] While emanation must be described in temporal terms, it is actually a timeless, *logical* process, akin to the development of mathematical truths. For Plotinus, that which is emanated from the One is both independent of and completely filled with its source. According to him, emanation is a necessary process; it is part of the essence or meaning of The One that it should become plural and finite. Plotinus holds that God wills but that since God is identical to his will, what He wills he does so necessarily.[45]

Novak has argued that although the Kabbalists accepted the Neopla-

---

40. Idel, *Kabbalah: New Perspectives*, p. 342.

41. Katz, Utterance and Ineffability," p. 288.

42. Plotinus, Ennead 5, 3, 16. Plotinus, *The Six Enneads*, p. 533.

43. Idel, *Kabbalah: New Perspectives*, p. 344. See Sarah Heller-Wilinsky, "Isaac ibn Latif—Philosopher or Kabbalist."

44. Plotinus, Ennead 5, 3, 13. Plotinus, *The Six Enneads*, p. 534.

45. Plotinus, Ennead 6, 8, 21, 5, 5. Ibid., p. 670.

tonic problematic of the "One and the Many," their solution to it, via the doctrines of the *Sefirot* and *Tzimtzum*, were unique, in that they involve a freely chosen, creative act on the part of the Absolute. According to Novak, such a freely chosen act is completely foreign to Neoplatonism.[46] Things are not quite so simple. As we have seen, Plotinus acknowledges that God's necessity is also his "will," and even in the Kabbalah we find an affirmation of both of what appear at first to be mutually exclusive ideas. Vital informs us that it is both "necessary" (*mukhrah*) for God to actualize Himself in a world, and that creation is a freely chosen act (*ke-she 'alah bi-rezeno*).[47]

At any rate, according to Plotinus, the necessary act of Divine will transforms the One into the many, potentiality into actuality, and the supreme Good into a multiplicity of values; and provides a revelation or spelling out of the riches of the intelligible realm. At the same time emanation is conceived of as an apostasy and a fall, which is motivated by a will to power, isolation, and independence, and which results in an exile of true being from itself. This ambivalence toward creation is also present in the Kabbalah, which regards creation as both a magnificent revelation of God's power and goodness, and an alienation resulting in degeneration and evil. There is, in both Plotinus and the Kabbalah, a *coincidentia oppositorum* between the ideas of creation as revelation and exile, progression and fall. The world can neither be created nor progress without alienation, exile, and the generation of evil.

Emanation becomes a core doctrine in the early theosophical Kabbalah.[48] Like Plotinus, the Kabbalists speak of a singular, unknowable "Absolute" giving rise to or emanating a series of realms that are both part of and yet distinct from itself. For Plotinus, the Platonic "One," ineffable and infinitely "Good," gives rise to *Nous*, the realm of mind and intelligence, which in turn emanates the realm of "Soul," which then gives rise to the lowest realm of "Nature." In the Kabbalah, the emanative process is expanded to include ten *Sefirot* and at least four "Worlds," but the basic emanational logic is the same.

Azriel of Gerona held there to be an essential equivalence between

46. David Novak, "Self-Contraction of the Godhead in Kabbalistic Theology," in *Neoplatonism, in Jewish Thought*, Lenn E. Goodman, ed., (Albany: State University of New York Press, 1992), p. 307ff.

47. Novak, "Self-Contraction," p. 311.

48. It is only later that the doctrine of *Tzimtzum*, contraction, is added as a second principle of creation.

kabbalistic theosophy and Neoplatonic philosophy. His emanatory scheme organizes the ten kabbalistic *Sefirot* into four Plotinian realms: *Olam ha-Ne'elam* (The Unseen World), *Olam ha-Muskal* (the Intellectual World), *Olam ha-Murgash* (the World of the Psyche), and *Olam ha-Mutba* (the World of Nature). The highest of these realms, equivalent to the Neoplatonic "One," is, the realm nearest *Ein-Sof.* Three *Sefirot* are assigned to each of the three Plotinian "hypostases," and the final *Sefirah*, *Malchut*, is understood as a principle that actualizes the *Sefirot* in the created world.[49]

NOUS: THE REALM OF INTELLIGIBLES

For Plotinus, the second hypostasis (after The One) is *Nous*, the realm of intelligible forms. This hypostasis contains the Platonic essences or ideas, and is thus a level of actual being. Unlike Plato, however, who held the ideas to be independent entities, Plotinus holds that their existence is dependent on their being thought by a divine mind.

Both Isaac the Blind and Ben Sheshet held that the *Sefirot* and foundational letters exist in an intellectual container analogous to Plotinus's *Nous*, the second *Sefirah*, *Chochmah*.[50] The Kabbalists quite self-consciously equated this *Sefirah* with the realm of Platonic forms.

The process by which the *Sefirot* are emanated from the divine Will parallels the Neoplatonic notion of the emanation of Nous (Intelligence, spirit, mind) from the One.[51] Idel points out that there were tendencies within Neoplatonism to place the "divine will" as a hypostasis intermediately between the One and Intelligence,[52] thus providing a perfect parallel to the kabbalistic scheme of *Ein-Sof* emanating Will (*Keter*) and then Wisdom (*Chochmah*).

According to Azriel, the *Sefirot*, and everything that is to be created out of them, is hidden in the divine Thought (*Mahashavah*), and this "Thought" is equivalent to the Primordial Torah.[53] The idea that God looked into a Primordial Torah that served as a blueprint for creation dates back to midrashic times. This notion paved the way for the view, found in *Sefer*

---

49. Scholem, *Kabbalah*, p. 107.
50. Ibid., p. 330.
51. Idel, *Kabbalah: New Perspectives*, p. 326.
52. Ibid., p. 327.
53. Ibid., p. 328.

Yetzirah, that the twenty-two letters of the Hebrew language, the elements of the Torah, are also the creative elements of the world.[54] Ben Sheshet sees these letters as deriving from the second *Sefirah*, *Chochmah*, the realm of intelligible forms: "And out of Chochmah the letters were emanated and engraved in the spirit of the Binah [the third Sefirah], and the essence of the letters is that they are the forms of all creatures, and there is no form which has not a likeness in the letters or in the combination of two or three of them or more."[55] Idel points out that for Ben Sheshet, the third *Sefirah*, *Binah*, is conceived of as the "World of the letters."[56] The entire scheme is based upon a Neoplatonic model.

PROCLUS'S PRINCIPLE

According to Plotinus, the ideas are all interrelated, to the point that each is contained in each of the others without, however, losing their separate identity as individuals. Plotinus holds such a view about each entity in the cosmos, including the various gods or powers of the single divinity:

> Where each is all, blending into unity, distinct in powers but all one god in virtue of that one divine power of many facets.[57]

> While some one manner of being is dominant in each, all are mirrored in every other.[58]

This idea that "all is in all," although originating in Plotinus, came to be known for the later Neoplatonic philosopher, Proclus. This principle was adopted by the Kabbalists, for example in Ben Sheshet's view that "each letter comprises all of the others."[59] The same principle emerges as an important theme in the doctrine of the *Sefirot* in the later Kabbalah. Already in Asher ben David, a nephew of Isaac the Blind, we find the view that each divine

---

54. Ibid., p. 330.
55. Ibid., p. 330.
56. Ibid., p. 349, note 46.
57. Plotinus, Ennead 5, 8, 8. Plotinus, *The Six Enneads*, p. 555.
58. Plotinus, Ennead 5, 8, 4. Ibid., p. 552.
59. Idel, *Kabbalah: New Perspectives*, p. 330; Proclus, *Elements of Theology*, Prop. 176.

middah or trait is contained in each of the others.[60] In the Zohar, and most clearly in the work of Cordovero and the Kabbalists of Safed, there emerged the view that each of the *Sefirot* interpenetrate and thereby contain aspects (*Behinnot*) of each of the others. Further, this doctrine penetrated Jewish spiritual practice. During the forty-nine days between Passover and Shavuot (the period of the "counting of the Omer") each Jew is enjoined to work on each of the seven "emotional" *Sefirot*, from *Chesed* to *Malchut*, within his own soul, and the "aspects" of each of the seven that are contained within each of them, resulting in specific work for each of the forty-nine days.

Later Kabbalists, e.g., Abravanel, held that not only the second *Sefirah*, *Chochmah*, but the entire sefirotic system corresponded to the realm of Platonic ideas.[61] They are, according to Abravanel, "the divine figurations with which the world was created."[62]

SOUL

Below the level of Nous is the third hypostasis, "Soul," which, according to Plotinus, consists of a "World-soul" and individual souls, some of which become incarnated in celestial or earthly bodies. The doctrine of the World-soul entails that the entire cosmos is a living organism, another Neoplatonic idea that finds expression in the Zohar. According to the Neoplatonists, when individual souls become embodied in earthly bodies, however, they sink into matter and become alienated from their true home in Intellect. The kabbalistic notion of a spark of divinity exiled in worldly matter is a parallel if not derivative idea, which, as we will see in Chapter Five, is also present among the Gnostics.[63]

According to Plotinus, the souls of individuals are all united in a single soul, permitting them to communicate without the mediation of the senses. In our highest selves we are all one, and this means that "My feelings [are]

---

60. Idel, *Kabbalah: New Perspectives*, p. 331.

61. Ibid., p. 338.

62. Ibid., p. 332.

63. Plotinus himself was actually highly critical of Gnosticism's pessimism regarding the created world. While Plotinus clearly regarded the material world to be an alienation from the One and the source of evil, it was also for him a magnificent reflection of the ideas, the contemplation of which is a vehicle to transcendence of the world, which, however, is not to be scorned or abandoned.

felt by someone else, my goodness another's too, my desire his desire, all our experience shared with each other and with the (one souled) universe, so that the very universe itself would feel whatever I felt."[64] Not only are individual souls connected with one another and the cosmos as a whole, but each thing in the entire universe (which for Plotinus is a single cosmic body) directly affects and is affected by each other thing, leading to the power and efficacy of prophecy, magic, astrology, and prayer. The interconnectedness of all souls and things is even evident in everyday affairs: "A quiet word induces changes in a remote object, and makes itself heard at vast distances—proof of the oneness of all things within one soul."[65] For Plotinus, such cosmic "sympathy," as opposed to efficient causality, is the major power in the universe.

The original unity of all souls in a single primordial soul is an idea that reappears in the Kabbalah. According to the Lurianists, all souls originate in *Adam Kadmon*, which was fragmented as a result of the Breaking of the Vessels. Still, each individual soul is derived from a given soul "root," and souls from the same root are in a state of sympathy with and capable of assisting one another in their *Tikkun* or emendation.

NATURE

According to Plotinus, soul, which is the origin of "time," emanates the lowest hypostasis, Nature or Matter. In and of itself, matter is completely indeterminate, but when it is informed and illuminated by soul it becomes the physical world, which is a reflection of the intelligible realm. Purely indeterminate matter is a complete privation of the One or Good and is thus the origin of evil. However, informed by soul matter has the potential for realizing the Good. Plotinus holds that all of "existence is a trace of The One,"[66] and, indeterminate matter, as such, has no existence. Echoes of these ideas can be heard among the Kabbalists and Hasidim.

MATTER AND EVIL

For Plotinus matter and the evil it engenders are absolutely necessary for the life of the world. In the first place "Evil is not alone . . . it appears,

---

64. Plotinus, Ennead 4, 9, 1. Plotinus, *The Six Enneads*, p. 515.
65. Plotinus, Ennead 4, 9, 3. Ibid., p. 516.
66. Plotinus, Ennead 5, 5, 5. Ibid., p. 542.

necessarily, bound around with bonds of beauty, like some captive bound in fetters of gold." Further, "to deny evil a place among realities is necessarily to do away with the Good as well."[67] This is because evil is the origin of desire and is necessary for intellect, which itself permits judgment to distinguish between evil and good. Each of these doctrines are taken up in the theosophical Kabbalah. The Zohar refers to the evil as having a "brightness around it," connecting it to the side of the holiness and faith.[68] Accordingly: "there is no sphere of the 'other side' that entirely lacks some streak of light from the side of holiness."[69] The necessity of evil and the role of the evil impulse (the *yetzer hara*) in the origins of human desire and productivity are major themes in the theosophical Kabbalah and Hasidism.

There are places in the *Enneads* where Plotinus speaks of Soul as an artisan or demiurge that forges matter according to the model of the ideas. Soul continues to inform and animate the bodies it emanates but in doing so it remains connected with the realm of the intelligibles. In this regard, each of us as an individual has an aspect of our own soul that remains connected to the celestial realm, although for the most part we remain unconscious of our divine nature. This idea reappears in Gnosticism and the Kabbalah as the doctrine of the divine spark encased in matter and the human body. At times, Plotinus himself speaks as if the soul must escape the body to actualize itself fully in Nous; at other times he has a far more optimistic view of incarnation, holding that the soul is able to actualize itself within the corporeal realm.

THE *SEFIROT* AND HUMAN ACTION

The Kabbalists went beyond the Platonic notion of a static realm of Ideas, in detailing a highly dynamic and interactive theory of the *Sefirot*.[70] While Plotinus clearly holds that The One is both the source and goal of all things, and some things are "not yet so, (but) will be"[71] united with it, there is a decidedly static tone to his philosophy. The Kabbalists held a view that is foreign to both Plato and the Neoplatonists, i.e., that man's activities, in particular human acts of worship, have a theurgic impact upon the sefirotic

67. Plotinus, Ennead 2, 8, 11. Ibid., p. 336.
68. Zohar II, 203b; Sperling and Simon, *The Zohar*, Vol. 4, p. 189.
69. Zohar II, 69a–69b. Ibid., Vol. 3, p. 216.
70. Idel, *Kabbalah: New Perspectives*, p. 334.
71. Plotinus, Ennead 5, 2, 1. Plotinus, *The Six Enneads*, p. 524.

realm. Plotinus had held that the intelligible world is mirrored in the structure of the human intellect, and his doctrine of cosmic sympathy would seem to invite a theory of theurgy. However, he failed to conclude that on account of such sympathy man can influence the divine realm through his deeds. The *Sefirot* (and hence the world), according to the Kabbalists, are structured in the form of a cosmic, Primordial Man (*Adam Kadmon*) that perfectly mirrors the human body and soul; and on their view the individual, earthly man, can, through his deeds, unify, repair, and restore the entire world.

KNOWLEDGE AND MYSTICISM

For Plotinus, the universe is a living organism characterized by a double movement, the first away from, and the second a return to, the absolute or God.[72] Humanity is a participant in the life of the universe, as an exile whose goal is a return, via *unia mystica*, to the infinite One. These views are each echoed in the ecstatic Kabbalah, as well as in the Zohar and later kabbalistic theosophy.

Knowledge of the upper realms, and particularly of the One, is at best incompletely attained through rational, discursive means. Wisdom, according to Plotinus is not "a mass of theorems and an accumulation of propositions."[73] He follows the hints (noted above) in Plato's letters that suggest a form of suprarational insight is available to those who strive for a mystical union with God. In moments of mystical ecstasy the soul reascends, and the individual becomes united with its source. In such moments one abandons everything in this world, becomes purely simple and achieves a self-surrender to and union with the One. Plotinus asks "how is this to be accomplished," and succinctly answers: "Cut away everything."[74] He adds that for such a reascent the individual must first prepare himself through perfecting his virtues and the practice of dialectics. Both a quiet contemplation of the beauty and order of the universe, and a meditation on the innermost self, are regarded by Plotinus to be the vehicles of man's ascent.

---

72. Jones, p. 16.
73. Plotinus, Ennead 5, 8, 4. Plotinus, *The Six Enneads*, p. 553.
74. Plotinus, Ennead 5, 3, 16. Ibid., p. 537.

HIGHER WORLDS

Plotinus describes a "higher Heaven," dwelled in by divine beings and accessible to man in acts of mystic contemplation. In this realm, the categories and distinctions of personal identity, time, space, and causality are attenuated or transcended, resulting in a world of perfect peace, truth, communication, and lucidity:

> To "live at ease" is There; and, to these divine beings, verity is mother and nurse, existence and sustenance; all that is not of process but of authentic being they see, and themselves in all: for all is transparent, nothing dark, nothing resistant; every being is lucid to every other, in breadth and depth; light runs through light. And each of them contains all within itself, and at the same time sees all in every other, so that everywhere there is all, and all is all and each all, and infinite the glory . . . Movement There is pure [as self-caused] for the moving principle is not a separate thing to complicate it as it speeds.
>
> So too, Repose is not troubled, for there is no admixture of the unstable; and the Beauty is all beauty since it is not merely resident [as an attribute or addition] in some beautiful object. Each There walks upon no alien soil; its place is essential to itself; and, as each moves, so to speak, towards what is Above, it is attended by the very ground from which it starts; there is no distinguishing between the Being and the Place; all is Intellect, the Principle and the ground on which it stands alike.[75]

Plotinus is careful to indicate that the "There" is a purely intellectual realm, one that will not provide us with a sensory experience analogous to (but higher than) the one we have on earth: "We are expecting some impression on sense, which has nothing to report since it has seen nothing and never could in that order see anything."[76] Plotinus's theory certainly impacted upon the kabbalistic doctrine of higher worlds. As will become clear, his poetic characterization of these worlds attenuated corporeality, space, time, and identity can provide us with important insights in the Kabbalist's higher realms.

---

75. Plotinus, Ennead 5, 8, 4. Ibid., pp. 552–553.
76. Plotinus, Ennead 5, 8, 10. Ibid., p. 557.

MODERN NEOPLATONISM

J. N. Findlay, in a series of little-known but profound works, presents a modern Neoplatonic philosophy that can help serve as a guide to a contemporary interpretation of several kabbalistic symbols and ideas.[77] Findlay, whose Neoplatonism is enhanced by his readings of Kant and Hegel, provides a view of the deep philosophical antinomies of earthly life and experience, which point to the existence of realms higher than our own. As we shall see, many of Findlay's views are echoed by the contemporary Kabbalist, Adin Steinsaltz. Steinsaltz, who is a rather unique representative of what I would call the "New Kabbalah," will command considerable attention in the pages that follow.

Findlay holds a view of the Absolute that is in many ways similar to the kabbalistic conceptions of *Ein-Sof* and the *Sefirot*. For Findlay, the Absolute embodies not only "the metaphysical values of simplicity, unity, self-existence and power" but also "the values . . . of justice, mercy, truth, beauty, etc." Like the Kabbalists he holds that "God or the religious absolute cannot fail to will these values because, in a manner which defies ordinary grammar, he not only has them, but is them."[78] Yet, like the Kabbalists, Findlay also holds that the "will in the religious absolute can and must determine itself quite freely."[79]

On Findlay's view, the various values of mind, reason, intelligence, and will, along with those of satisfaction, happiness, freedom, fairness, beauty, etc., "culminate in a single, unique intentional object to which devotion, worship, unconditional self-dedication are the only appropriate attitude."[80]

THE ANTINOMIES OF EXPERIENCE

To this point Findlay is strictly Neoplatonic, and his views scarcely depart from those contained, for example, in Plotinus's *Enneads*. However, like the

77. J. N. Findlay, *Values and Intentions* (London: Allen & Unwin, 1961); J. N. Findlay, *The Discipline of the Cave* (London: Allen & Unwin, 1966); J. N. Findlay, *The Transcendence of the Cave* (London: Allen & Unwin, 1966); J. N. Findlay, *Ascent to the Absolute* (London: Allen & Unwin, 1970).
78. Findlay, *The Transcendence of the Cave*, p. 112.
79. Ibid.
80. Ibid., p. 98.

Kabbalists, Findlay adapts this Neoplatonic view to a far more dynamic view of the cosmos and God. He does this through a careful phenomenological description of the paradoxes, absurdities, and antinomies that are endemic to earthly life.

According to Findlay, "antinomy . . . is an all-pervasive phenomenon in the experienced and interpreted world."[81] Findlay states that the antinomies of human experience lead us to "find the world a queer place" and led Plato and others to describe it as a "cave."[82] He argues that "the pervasive antinomy of the world is far too serious and too deep to count as a mere formal contradiction."[83] Findlay's worldview is quite close to that of the Lurianic Kabbalah. Gershom Scholem has a succinct phrase that summarizes the contradictory nature of the world after the Breaking of the Vessels: "Nothing remains in its proper place. Everything is somewhere else."[84] As will become clear, the contemporary Hasidic thinker Adin Steinsaltz holds a view of the contradictoriness of the world that is quite similar to Findlay's. According to Steinsaltz, the world of experience is riddled with so many contradictions that only the hypothesis of a "higher world" can provide it with any genuine sense.

Findlay holds that while the world's antinomies can be specified as formal contradictions, this provides us with little insight because formal contradictions can be readily dissolved through a specification of the "senses" in which each pole of the contradiction is true and false. For Findlay, the antinomies of human experience are more akin to "discrepancies in a person's character," and it does us no good to either define or argue away an "apparent contradiction." Rather than adjust our concepts to accommodate antinimous experience, Findlay calls upon us to extend our experience to accommodate our concepts. Findlay seeks an accommodation that will "explain rather than explain away such antinomies."

The absurdities and antinomies of the world are many, and included among them are such classical philosophical and theological problems as the opposition between the principles of morality and the rewards bestowed upon the wicked, the opposition between our experience of free will and the scientific assumption of determinism; the puzzles engendered by the obser-

---

81. Ibid., p. 20.
82. Ibid., p. 21.
83. Ibid., p. 21.
84. Gershom Scholem, "Kabbalah and Myth." In Scholem, *On The Kabbalah and Its Symbolism*, Ralph Manheim, trans. (New York: Schocken, 1965), p. 112.

vation that we all know is the data of our own senses and our certainty of the existence of an objective, external world; and the absurdities associated with the ideas that we only have direct awareness of our *own* minds but also feel certain of the existence of the minds and inner experiences of others.

Findlay focuses upon several antinomies connected with space and time; he points out, for example, that these great "media" of experience appear to be the "containers" within which all events occur, but are also defined by the very events that transpire within them. A second antinomy arises from our consideration of the temporal "now," the series of which seem to constitute the march of time, but none of which can be defined apart from reference to a past and a future. There are antinomies related to the opposition between efficient causality and teleology, and, according to Findlay, the consequent absurdities of bodies adjusting themselves to (future) happenings that never actually occur.[85] There are antinomies that derive from a consideration of the fact that while we can appeal to the experience of others as proof of an occurrence we ourselves have observed, the very experience and testimony of the other is ultimately only apprehended through our own. Findlay also points to the paradoxical interdependence between the private and public criteria we utilize to comprehend our own and others' mental states. On the one hand we can only come to label and describe ours and others' inner states through the publicly observable manifestations of them, e.g., through the behavioral expressions of anger, grief, thoughtfulness, etc. On the other hand, our understanding of such outward expressions is itself dependent upon private "inner" states; both the "inner" states that serve as fulfillment of and thus give sense to public behavior and the inner states through which we are aware of our own observations.[86]

Findlay explores a number of paradoxes that relate to material bodies, for example, pointing out that while such bodies are thought to be completely independent of any mind cognizing them, they cannot even be conceived except as in relation to a conscious perspective upon them[87] or under the aegis of some category or idea. Findlay also holds that there is something highly paradoxical regarding our attitude toward our own bodies; on the one hand they seem essential to our mental and interpersonal life,

---

85. Ibid., p. 27.
86. Findlay, *The Discipline of the Cave*, p. 204.
87. Ibid., p. 261.

while at the same time they seem alien to it,[88] so much so that theologians have long posited the mind or soul's independence from them.

THE IMMANENT SOLUTION

Findlay proffers two broad metaphysical responses to the existence of the antinomies that are endemic to experience. These are, as I will argue, two possible "solutions" to the Kabbalist's Breaking of the Vessels. The first, *immanent solution* is to hold with such philosophers as Fichte and Hegel that the difficulties and conundrums posed by the world's antinomies are goads toward the development and perfection of humankind. According to these thinkers the world's absurdities and contradictions give rise to the forms of artistic, scientific, and philosophical representation that constitute our historical, communal, and cultural life.[89] On this view our varied ways of seeing and interpreting things do not reflect the world's fixed nature, but rather permit and encourage the emergence of the inquiry, debate, cooperation, creativity, and self-consciousness of our rational, social selves. The problems of this world are neither open to simple solution nor hopelessly enigmatic. Though they may present themselves as conundrums for millennia, they are eventually accommodated by the human spirit, and remain enigmatic only to the degree as to force the fullest development of human values, imagination, culture, science and philosophy.[90] As Findlay puts it: "these oppositions and indifferences exist for the sake of the rational activities they render possible."[91] And: "The untoward, the irrational, the merely personal, have the teleological role of providing the necessary incitement and raw material for the rational, common, self-conscious result, and so all phenomenal existence can be brought under the sway of values, and something like the dominion of Good taught in the *Phaedo* proven true."[92]

Findlay's immanentist solution has clear parallels to and implications for the kabbalistic doctrine of *Tikkun*.[93] For example, we read in Moses de

---

88. Ibid., p. 206.

89. Findlay, *The Transcendence of the Cave*, pp. 31, 100ff.

90. Ibid., p. 34.

91. Ibid., p. 101.

92. Ibid., p. 76.

93. This perspective, which Findlay refers to as the "German theology," will be discussed in more detail in Chapter Six, "Hegel and the Kabbalah."

Leon's *Ha-Nefesh ha-Hakhamah* (1290): "The purpose of the soul in entering the body is to exhibit its powers and abilities in the world . . . And when it descends to this world it receives power and influx to guide this vile world and undergo a *tikkun* above and below . . ."[94]

Findlay's world of antinomies can readily be likened to Luria's "World of making," our actual world, in which divine sparks have mixed with shards of the broken vessels, thus yielding a distorted, conflicted world that is desperately in need of restoration and repair. For the Kabbalists, the purpose of our highly imperfect world is precisely to provide a context for the exercise of human worship and other values necessary for the achievement of *Tikkun ha-Olam* and, thus, the completion and perfection of creation. For the Kabbalists, the world is perfected through the exercise of human free will in choosing good over evil, in proper worship of God, and through a deep understanding of reality as described by kabbalistic theosophy. According to Moses Chayyim Luzzatto:

> The partnership that exists between Israel and the Creator is described as follows: The Creator devised the darkness inherent in man as a means for maintaining the evil which is to be transmuted into good. Because of this man must effect many emendations in this darkness.[95]

> Man's service is the result of his own choice. It is this factor of choice which brings greater advantage to creation, resulting in its perfection and completion. Consequently, Man is partner to the Creator in maintaining and perfecting His world.[96]

This kabbalistic conception is clearly articulated by Adin Steinsaltz. In an interview with the author Steinsaltz relates:

> There is a quotation from the kabbalistic work of Rabbi Chaim Vital, Sefer Ets Hayyim, that our world is one that in its majority is a world of evil. Evil is the ruler of the world and there is very little good in it.

> . . . When you speak about the world from this point of view, it is, so to speak, a *tour de force*, an experiment in existence, an experiment in what I might call "conquering the utmost case." So in a way, existence in any

---

94. Quoted in Scholem, *Kabbalah*, p. 159.
95. Luzzato, *General Principles of the Kabbalah*, p. 249.
96. Ibid., p. 247.

other world is not "proof." "Proof" in the "utmost case" occurs only when you can do things under the worst of circumstances. *L'havdil.* If I want to test a new car, the way that I test it is not on the smoothest of roads, under the best conditions. To have a real test to prove that a car really works, I have to put it under . . . *the worst conditions in which there is yet hope.* I cannot test it by driving off a cliff, but I can test it on the roughest terrain where I must come to the edge of a cliff and have to stop . . . The same with Creation. Creation would have been pointless unless it was Creation under precisely these difficult circumstances. So I am saying, theologically speaking, that the worst possible world in which there is yet hope is the only world in which creation makes sense.[97]

Steinsaltz, who is himself a follower of Chabad Hasidism, is here clearly influenced by the Chabad doctrine that all things are revealed through their opposite, and specifically that divinity is revealed through evil and its transformation into good. As put by Rabbi Aharon Halevi Horowitz of Staroselye:

> It is known that all the descents are for the purpose of ascent. For His main intention, blessed be He, is to have his Blessed divinity be revealed precisely through inversion, in darkness, and in concealment. This is also in order to coerce the *sitra achra* [the realm of evil] and transform darkness into light . . . and it is precisely in the revelation of evil that His blessed will be revealed.[98]

THE TRANSCENDENT SOLUTION

Findlay proposes a second solution, a transcendental one, to the presence of antinomies, conflicts, absurdities, and contradictions in this world. This second solution is necessitated because the first solution "remains a difficult unstable way of viewing things which like some strange effort at stereoscopy, is ready at any moment to switch back again to the deeply unsatisfying, but more stable ways of viewing things out of which it arose."[99] Part of our

97. Drob, "The Mystic as Philosopher: An Interview with Rabbi Adin Steinsaltz," p. 14.

98. Aharon Halevi Horowitz of Staroselye (Shklove 182), as quoted in Elior, *The Paradoxical Ascent to God,* pp. 206–7.

99. Findlay, *The Transcendence of the Cave,* p. 103.

dissatisfaction with the immanentist solution is that it places human life and endeavor at the center of the universe and relegates to insignificance much of the vast cosmos of stars and galaxies.

Findlay now suggests that behind the antinimous manifestations of our "cave" there is another world or series of worlds that both explain our current condition and, when properly understood, provide a metaphysical solution to our philosophical and moral dilemmas. He asks us to consider the possibility that "the solution of this world's absurdities lies in another dimension and another life altogether."[100] This dimension or life is actually a "higher world," or better put an upper half to our own world, "and the two halves only make fully rounded sense when seen in their mutual relevance and interconnection."[101] At another place Findlay hints at the possibility of a number of "higher worlds": "Where scientific tensions only lead us to postulate new types of particle or modifications of fundamental scientific formulae, philosophical tensions lead us to complete our world with a whole new type or set of types of worlds."[102]

Findlay's transcendental solution to the conundrums of the earthly cave rests on an analogy with earthly geometry. According to Findlay our "world" occupies a region of maximum differentiation close to the "equator" and God or the absolute occupies a region of maximal convergence at the "poles." As we pass our equatorial zone and advance toward the "higher latitudes" there is a

> steady vanishing of the harsh definiteness and distinctness of individuals, and a steady blurring or coming into coincidence of the divisions amongst kinds and categories, until in the end one approaches and perhaps at last reaches a paradoxical unitary point of convergence, where the objects of religion may be thought to have their habitat.[103]

According to Findlay, the progress toward higher worlds or latitudes involves a steady diminution of individuality, corporeality, and temporality, and the objects in these worlds will be governed by associations of meaning as opposed to causality.[104] Individuality will begin to vanish, as things become

---

100. Ibid., p. 105.
101. Ibid., p. 121.
102. Ibid., p. 122.
103. Ibid., pp. 123–124.
104. Ibid., p. 127.

more and more indistinguishable from their species and genera, resulting in a realm of values that exist generically apart from any instantiation.[105] As individuality diminishes, the obstacles that it and materiality place between communicating minds will vanish as well, as will the communicative gulfs that exist between persons in our own realm.[106] The attenuated matter of the upper realms, rather than being an obstacle to consciousness and reason, will simply serve as a context for communication and a vehicle for the expression of thought and will.[107] Simple location will vanish, and all things will be "predominantly somewhere, but more distantly present everywhere else."[108] Temporality will be altered, and prophecy made possible, as alternative futures are displayed, teaching us what will almost certainly happen or will happen unless we take countermeasures, etc.[109] Finally: "At the mystical pole of our whole geography we may place an object of infinite and no longer puzzling perfection, which we need no longer conceive as a mere supreme instance of incompatible values, but as the living principle of all those values themselves."[110] Thus, at the apex of all the worlds, Findlay places what Plotinus described as "The Good" and what the Kabbalists understood as the Infinite, *Ein-Sof.*

Adin Steinsaltz describes the gradual descent from higher to lower worlds in much the same manner as Findlay:

> The highest of the four worlds, the World of Emanation . . . is a mode of existence characterized by absolute clarity, no concealment, and no separate beings. There is no individuation, and no "screens" or filters separate God from that which is not God. In fact, the World of Emanation is not a world in the sense that the other three are: in a certain sense it is the Godhead itself.[111]

As one descends in the system of worlds, there is more and more matter. Another way of stating this is that the beings of the lower worlds have a greater awareness of their independent, progressively separate selves,

105. Ibid., p. 137.
106. Ibid., pp. 134–135.
107. Ibid., p. 128.
108. Ibid., p. 129.
109. Ibid., p. 131.
110. Ibid., p. 137.
111. Adin Steinsaltz, "Worlds, Angels and Men," in his *The Strife of the Spirit* (Northvale, NJ: Jason Aronson, 1988), p. 50.

of their private "I." This consciousness of self obscures the divine light, and dims the true, unchanging "I" that exists within each individual being . . .[112]

According to Steinsaltz the higher worlds do not manifest "space as we know it, but a framework of existence within which all forms and beings are related." Further, "Time, too, is manifest in a totally different fashion in the higher world . . . the system of time becomes increasingly abstract . . . It becomes no more than the essence of change or the potentiality of change."[113]

A RATIONAL MYSTICISM

One might think that Findlay would follow Plotinus in an appeal to a suprarational mystical vision to justify his assertions regarding the upper worlds. However, he holds his philosophy to be rationally derived, as following logically from the antinomies and conundrums of our earthly existence. His mysticism is a *rational mysticism*. According to Findlay, the world as we experience it is broken, disjoint, absurd, and incomprehensible, and only begins to make sense when we posit a higher realm as its complement and completion. The various puzzles and antinomies of our world find a solution and vanish in the higher realms. Findlay argues that the kind of world that would resolve our philosophical dilemmas is very similar to the higher world, the "There" described in Plotinus's Fifth *Ennead*. It is also similar to the higher "Worlds" described in the Kabbalah.

The world described by Plotinus resolves our earthly antinomies because it is a *unified*, purely spiritual and conceptual world that exists outside of space and time. It is a world governed by thought, rather than material necessity, and in contrast to our own contingent, chaotic realm it is ordered by connections of reason and significance. It is a world in which acts of thought and volition are neither mediated, hampered, nor contained by space and time, and hence are unconstrained by material causation. As Plotinus emphasizes it is a completely translucent realm in which "every being is lucid to every other," and where the objects of thought are known clearly and immediately. In such a world the philosophical problems of the nature of

---

112. Ibid., p. 49.
113. Ibid., p. 44.

time, space, and eternity, of the relationship between the mind and matter, and knowledge of "other minds" are completely resolved, or, better, do not even arise. It is a world devoid of gross matter, and as such a world in which to know a concept is to know its instance, and vice versa. Finally, it is a world in which there are no material rewards for one's thoughts and deeds, and hence a world where thoughts and deeds are their own reward.

Much the same, of course, can be said of the "higher worlds" of the Kabbalah, and moreover, regarding the Lurianic system as a whole. The symbols of *Tzimtzum, Sefirot, Shevirat Hakelim, Tikkun*, etc., which the Kabbalists utilized to resolve their own theological problems[114] are relevant to the philosophical conundrums of our own age.

To begin with, the *Tzimtzum*, and to even a greater extent, the Breaking of the Vessels, results in a confused and chaotic condition in which the primordial values and ideas (the *Sefirot*) become entangled in a realm of "matter." As a result of these events, our deepest spiritual values, e.g., morality, freedom, teleology, knowledge, communication, etc., have become highly problematic and even appear to be contradicted by experience. Morality has no hegemony in a world of random, natural disaster and material power; teleology (the progression of events toward a rational goal) is upstaged by material causality; freedom too is contradicted by the processes of determinate causation; knowledge is questionable because a gulf exists between matter and mind; and communication is barred because others' minds are "enclosed" in bodies that render their inner life opaque to our own. From a kabbalistic perspective we might say that each of our philosophical notions (morality, teleology, freedom, knowledge, communication, etc.) have shattered and become enmeshed in a material world, which renders them contradictory and opaque. Only through an act of *birur*, extraction, can these values be restored and understood in the light of a higher conceptual and spiritual realm.

STEINSALTZ'S KABBALAH

Again Steinsaltz provides a contemporary kabbalistic parallel to Findlay's transcendental solution to the antinomies of worldly experience. Steinsaltz

---

114. For example, the problems engendered by the doctrine of creation *ex nihilo* and the difficulty of conceiving of creation at all by an omnipresent and (already) perfect deity.

analogizes the problem of higher worlds to a problem in two-dimensional geometry that can only be solved by positing a point in a third dimension. He holds that with respect to the problems of our world we are looking for a solution in four dimensions (the three dimensions of space and the fourth of time) when what is needed is a solution in "five." According to Steinsaltz,

> without getting to the fifth dimension, you cannot solve any problem in this world. Now when I speak about problems of the world I am talking about *all* the basic questions, not just the theological and philosophical ones such as "What is the purpose of things?" "Why are we here?" or "What is the justification of things we undergo and experience?" But I am speaking of other more mundane questions as well. I don't believe, for example . . . that you can really resolve problems regarding economic justice or social equity from within any given "earthly" frame . . . This is because the world contains enough contradictions, enough destructive elements, so as to eliminate any possibilty of a solution. The only way you can solve these questions is through movement to a higher dimension or world.[115]

As an example, Steinsaltz argues that "you cannot have an egalitarian society in which justice prevails unless you have a belief in something higher." The reason for this is that a democracy in which all individuals are equally valued and where each is provided with one equal vote, cannot be justified on any empirical or rational view that all men are equal. This is because, from an empirical point of view the equality of man is "obviously untrue." According to Steinsaltz:

> People are not equal from any point of view. Therefore to create a society based on the notion that the vote of a wise and learned man has the same value as the vote of somebody who is unlearned and doesn't know what he is talking about, you must posit that they have equal souls. This is also true with respect to the rights of man as well. Why should a person who is the highest intellectual be regarded as equal to somebody who is ignorant or who is a criminal with respect, for example, to the right to be saved by a given medical procedure? So you see, this principle, this belief that people have souls and that souls are of inestimable, equal value, is the source of every social structure we hold dear.[116]

---

115. Drob, "The Mystic As Philosopher," p. 14.
116. Ibid., p. 17.

FURTHER DIALECTICS IN KABBALISTIC
AND HASIDIC THOUGHT

Findlay and Steinsaltz each propose two solutions to the surds and antinomies of our world, the first an immanent solution and the second transcendental. According to the immanent solution, our world is perplexing, absurd,
and contradictory in order to bring forth the highest aspirations and
accomplishments of humankind—in kabbalistic terms, in order to actualize
the *Sefirot*, or value archetypes in man. According to the second, transcendental solution, the world's antinomies point to their own resolution in a
higher, spiritual realm.

We might observe, however, that each of these solutions, the immanent
and the transcendent, are themselves poles of yet another philosophical
antinomy; on the one hand the contradictions in this world appear to have no
explanation other than the solutions we create for them in our earthly
endeavors (the immanentist solution), while on the other hand they must
have a cause and a resolution in something real that transcends human
experience and endeavor (the transcendent solution).

Findlay, at least in his lectures on the cave, has a decided preference for
the latter, transcendental solution. The Kabbalah, on the other hand, sees
them in *coincidentia oppositorum*, and is inclined to accept both as valid and
true. On the one hand the broken state of affairs, the antinomies, injustices
of our own world, represented in the symbols of the *Kelippot* and the *Sitra
Achra*, are only spiritualized, emended, and restored through the moral and
spiritual efforts of mankind in forging *Tikkun ha-Olam*, an emendation of
this world. On the other hand, the antinomies of earthly life receive their
resolution only when man is able to transcend the perplexities of this life and
glimpse *ha-Olam habah*, the "World to Come," through *devekut*, "cleaving"
to the upper *Sefirot* and the worship of God. Unlike the Gnostics who saw
the world and human body as thoroughly evil entities from which the divine
spark in man's soul must escape, the kabbalistic program is at once a
transcendence and emendation or repair of *ha-Olam hazeh*, the world of the
here and now. This double movement of transcendence and immanence is
most clearly evident among the later inheritors of the kabbalistic tradition,
the Hasidim. As stated by Schneur Zalman: "There are two aspects to the
service of the Lord. One is love in tongues of flame . . . and [the heart]
seeks to leave *its sheath of bodily material* . . . The second is the aspect of

fervor . . . of *the drawing down of the divinity from above.*"[117] According to Schneur Zalman, the first divine service, what we have spoken of as the "transcendent" solution, involves a "quietist" effort to leave the body and seek union with the one above; while the second divine service, our "immanent solution," involves an "activist" effort to bring divinity into the daily activities of life.

Rivka Schatz Uffenheimer has pointed to the tension and ultimate balance between activism and quietism within Hasidic thought. The activist tendency is rooted in the Lurianic concept of *Tikkun ha-Olam* and involves engagement in the corporeal world, precisely in order to "redeem the external world by its spiritualization."[118] The quietist tendency, which is rooted in the ecstatic Kabbalah, seeks a union with the divine through a negation of this world and an annihilation of the self. According to Schatz Uffenheimer, the quietist "elevates his own will to the Divine 'nothing,' to the world of reconciliation of opposites in which 'he and his opposite are one.'"[119]

Both activist and quietist tendencies are evident in the writings of the foremost theorist of Hasidism, Dov Baer (The Maggid) of Mezhirech. According to the Maggid the broken nature of the World of Action is a necessary, even deliberate, divine act, in order to provide an impetus to human activity: "It was therefore necessary that there should be a *shevirah* (Breaking of the Vessels), for by this means forgetfulness occurs in the Root, and each one can lift up his hand to perform an act . . . and they thereby elevate the sparks of the World of Action . . ."[120] Yet the Maggid also holds that the happenings of this world are nothing in comparison to the treasures of the world to come. Accordingly human beings "must abandon themselves and forget their troubles, so that they may come to the world of thought where everything is equal."[121]

It is not much of a step to hold that part of the dialectical equalization that occurs within the godhead is a reconciliation of activist and quietist

---

117. Schneur Zalman, *Torah Or*, p. 49. Translated and quoted in Elior, *The Paradoxical Ascent to God*, p. 134.

118. Rivka Schatz-Uffenheimer, *Hasidism as Mysticism*, p. 121.

119. Ibid., p. 69.

120. Dov Baer of Mezhirech, *Maggid Devarev le-Ya'aqov*, par. 73, pp. 126–127. Quoted in Schatz-Uffenheimer, *Hasidism as Mysticism*, p. 121.

121. Dov Baer of Mezhirech, *Maggid Devarev le-Ya'aqov*, par. 110, p. 186. Quoted in Schatz-Uffenheimer, *Hasidism as Mysticism*, pp. 81–82.

modes of theory and worship on earth. Through a "quietist" renunciation of personal desire, one becomes better equipped for the active task of "raising the sparks" and spiritualizing one's worldly encounters. Conversely through such active "spiritualization" one is brought into close contact with the holy *Sefirot*, which constitute the world of thought on high.

While the relative prevalence of transcendent and immanent solutions to the world's broken state waxed and waned in the history of Jewish mysticism, the general tenor of the Kabbalah and Hasidism was to accept both; and to hold that in repairing this world one could transcend it, and in transcending this world one could restore it. It is the very acts prompted by the world's antinomies that both constitute the activist "immanent solution" and provide humanity with an intuition of the value archetypes or *Sefirot*, which comprise the higher worlds (the transcendent solution). Indeed, the Kabbalists held that in performing *Tikkun ha-Olam*, the individual could not only make emendations in this world, but in all the worlds on high as well. Those who suggest that there is a choice between these two solutions to the problems of the world's absurdities and contradictions have failed to be sufficiently dialectical in their theology.

There is a further dialectic that is present in the symbols of the Lurianic Kabbalah. According to the Lurianists, just as the higher worlds resolve the contradictions and absurdities that exist in our own world, *our world was actually created to resolve the antinomies of heaven and God*. The reason for this is that it is only in a material world of chaos, toil, and trouble that the values, which are mere abstractions in the heavens, can become fully real. The vessels *must* break, spirit *must* become enmeshed in matter, if the *Sefirot* (and God Himself) are to become what they truly are. As put by Vital: "If the worlds had not been created, along with all that is in them, the true manifestation of His blessed, eternal existence—past, present, and future— could not have been seen, for He would not have been called by the Name, HVYH."[122]

The Kabbalah, like Plotinus and the philosophers of the East, posits a transcendence of this material world as a means for relieving the puzzles, contradictions, and sufferings of our own. The Kabbalah however, implies a transcendence in the other direction as well. In creating the material world,

---

122. *Sefer Etz Chayyim* 1:1, Menzi and Padeh, *The Tree of Life*, p. 4. The term HVYH represents a rearrangement of the letters in God's holiest name, the tetragrammaton, and has the meaning "existence." Vital implies that God's existence is dependent upon creation.

Ein-Sof, as it were, transcends and thereby completes itself, by actualizing and fulfilling the values that lie at its core. It is in this sense that the Zohar can assert that humankind creates and completes God.[123] Our world is the answer to the problems of the heavens just as the heavens are a solution to the antinomies on earth. On earth we have imperfect, chaotic and obscured actions that seek pure values to give them *meaning*. In heaven God has pure, abstract values, that must be instantiated in a chaotic, dangerous realm to make them *real*. As Findlay puts it: "The other world is, in fact, not so much another world as another half of one world, which two halves only make full rounded sense when seen in their mutual relevance and interconnection."[124]

The dual trends in which man yearns to transcend finitude and God seeks to become actual and real, constitute *Ein-Sof*, in the fullest sense of this term. It is only as a result of the differentiation, deconstruction, and later restoration and reunification of these two complementary realities (God and man) that the purpose of creation is ultimately realized and fulfilled.

---

123. Zohar III, 113a. Sperling and Simon, *The Zohar*, Vol. 5, p. 153; cf. Idel, *Kabbalah: New Perspectives*, p. 187.

124. Findlay, *The Transcendence of the Cave*, p. 121.

5

The Kabbalah and Gnosticism

W hen we turn to the religious movement known as Gnosticism, we are confronted with a syncretistic spiritual phenomenon that is morphologically so close to the Kabbalah as to make the question of an historical relationship hardly debatable. The question that has gripped Jewish and Christian scholars alike at least as far back as the fifteenth century[1] is not whether a historical nexus between Kabbalah and Gnosticism exists, but rather what is the primary direction of the apparent influence. This is certainly an emotionally charged and complex question. The question is emotionally charged, because the very nature of the Kabbalah as an authentically Jewish esoteric doctrine appears, at least to some, to hang in the balance.[2] The question is complex, for several reasons: (1) because obviously "Gnostic" themes seem to arise spontaneously in kabbalistic writings originating in France, Castile, Italy, and Safed in various centuries without any direct traceable connection to earlier kabbalistic sources, (2) because the dating of the key kabbalistic text, the Zohar, has been the subject of

1. Idel, *Kabbalah: New Perspectives*, p. 5. Idel cites Cornelius Agrippa of Nettesteim (1486–1535) and Elijah ben Moses Abba Del Medigo (1460–1497) as examples of a Christian and a Jewish scholar who were both gripped by the question of the direction of the nexus between Kabbalah and Gnosticism.
2. Idel, *Kabbalah: New Perspectives*, p. 34.

152

acrimonious debate between those contemporary scholars who believe they have demonstrated it to have originated in thirteenth-century Castile and traditionalists who hold that its themes, if not its specific content, date back to mishnaic times and, (3) because many (mainly Christian) scholars hold that Gnosticism itself is essentially Jewish in origins.[3]

I have little to contribute to the debates surrounding these questions and I intend to provide only the briefest of summaries of the historical issues regarding the relationship between Kabbalah and Gnosticism in these pages. My main concern is with the phenomenology of each and, particularly with the question of whether and how a study of Gnostic texts and ideas can shed light on a rational/mythical inquiry into the Kabbalah, and moreover, how such study, along with the comparative study of other religious and philosophical movements (i.e., Hinduism, Neoplatonism, Hegelianism, etc.) can help us along the way of reconstructing (or constructing) a new Kabbalah, one that is specifically relevant to our own age.[4]

GNOSTICISM: ITS NATURE AND ORIGINS

The identity of Gnosticism is itself open to considerable debate. Traditionally, viewed as a Christian heresy that developed alongside the early Catholic Church in the second and third centuries, the discovery in 1945 of a library of Gnostic texts at Nag Hammadi along the Nile River in Egypt[5] and their eventual publication has led to a view of Gnosticism as a multifaceted religious phenomenon independent of Christianity. Prior to the discovery of these texts, our knowledge of Gnosticism was gleaned almost exclusively from heresiological sources, i.e., Christian apologists (Justin, Irenaeus,

---

3. See R. M. Wilson, "Jewish 'Gnosis' and Gnostic Origins: A Survey," *Hebrew Union College Annual* 45 (1974): 179–189. Among Jewish scholars, the nineteenth-century historian H. Graetz held there to be a Jewish origin of Gnosticism.

4. On Gnosticism see Kurt Rudolph, *Gnosis: The Nature and History of Gnosticism*, trans. R. M. Wilson. (San Francisco: Harper & Row, 1987) [First published in German 1977, revised and expanded, 1980]; Giovanni Filoramo, *A History of Gnosticism*, trans. Anthony Alcock. (Cambridge: Basil Blackwell, 1990); Bentley Layton, *The Gnostic Scriptures* (New York: Doubleday, 1987); as well as the English translations of texts in J. M. Robinson, ed., *The Nag Hammadi Library*, 3rd ed. (San Francisco: Harper & Row, 1988).

5. For an account of the discovery of the Nag Hammadi documents see discussions in Filoramo, Rudolph, and Robinson.

Hippolytus, Origin) and others (e.g., Plotinus) who presented the views of the Gnostics with the sole purpose of attacking them. With the discovery of the Nag Hammadi Library, scholars are now able to distinguish more clearly between a Gnosis that established itself firmly upon the foundation of Christianity and another non-Christian Gnosis, which, however related to the Christian Gnosis, developed as an independent religious phenomenon.

The origins of Gnosticism are far from clear. What is clear is that Gnosis arose in late antiquity during a period of great religious ferment. The Hellenization of the Middle East (and, later, the influence of Rome) had created an environment in which a synthesis among Jewish, Greek, Iranian, and Christian elements had produced a wide range of syncrestic, esoteric, and, at times, mystical and/or apocalyptic religious movements. It is this environment that produced such widely divergent religious phenomena as Christianity, the Essene sects of Judaism, Philo of Alexandria, Jewish Apocalyptic esotericism (the *Merkaveh* and *Hekhalot* literature), and Gnosticism. It was also in this environment that Jewish monotheism, Greek philosophy, and pagan religion interacted to produce the prototypes for many of the symbols and ideas that were eventually to be adopted by both the Gnostics and Kabbalists. Untying the knots of historical influence in this period is extremely difficult.

Scholem, whose views are the starting point for any contemporary inquiry into the historical development of Jewish mysticism, pointed to a variety of links between Gnosticism and both early and later Jewish esoteric movements. In the first place, he held that early Jewish mysticism, represented in the *Hekhalot* ("Palaces") and *Merkaveh* ("Chariot") literature was a Jewish parallel to Gnosticism, arising out of the same spiritual needs and religious milieu.[6] While there were many differences between early Jewish mysticism and the Gnostic sects, (most notably the absence of any clear-cut dualism between good and evil among the Jewish mystics), Scholem drew parallels between the Gnostic concepts of the *pleroma* (the divine fullness and totality of divine forces) and aeons (emanations of the divinity) and, e.g., the Merkaveh descriptions of the "Throne of Glory" and the "seven palaces" leading up to and surrounding this throne. Each of these symbolic structures, Scholem argued, were designed to bridge the gulf between an implacable, infinite, unknowable divinity and the created, temporal world of the aspiring

---

6. Gershom Scholem, *Jewish Gnosticism.*

mystical devotee.[7] While Scholem referred to the *Merkaveh* and *Hekhalot* mysticisms as "Jewish Gnosticism," he did not claim (as some understood him) that such Jewish Gnosticism was at the root of the entire Gnostic phenomena. Other scholars, however, have hypothesized a Jewish form of Gnosticism (not necessarily identifiable with the Merkaveh or Hekhalot literature) as the source of Gnosticism in general.[8] It is interesting that this thesis, which has been held largely by Christian scholars, would, if verified, provide a Jewish pedigree to those aspects of the Kabbalah that clearly echo "Gnostic" themes.

Some scholars look to the Qumran texts of the Dead Sea Scrolls and other apocryphal texts of Judaism, e.g., *The Book of Wisdom* and *The Book of Enoch*, which date from just before and during the advent of the Christian era, for the origins of the Gnostic quest for ontological knowledge and personal illumination.[9] For example, we find in the Dead Sea Scrolls the idea that "all that is and ever was comes from a God of *knowledge*.[10] Further, the literature of the Qumran sect is replete with the distinctions between the powers of light (goodness) and darkness (evil) that later become so important for the Gnostics. We read in the *Qumran Manual of Discipline*:

> Now, this God [of knowledge] created man to rule the world, and appointed for him two spirits in which direction he was to walk until the final Inquisition. They are the spirits of truth and perversity. The origin of truth lies in the Fountain of Light, and that of perversity in the Wellspring of Darkness. All who practice righteousness are under the domination of the Prince of Lights, and walk in ways of light; whereas all who practice perversity are under the domination of the Angel of Darkness and walk in ways of darkness.

The identification of "light" with "truth," its opposition to a world of darkness, and an angelology representing the dual aspects of good and evil is

---

7. See Scholem, *Jewish Gnosticism*; Scholem, *Major Trends*, pp. 40–79; and Joseph Dan, *Gershom Scholem and the Mystical Dimension of Jewish History* (New York: New York University Press, 1987), pp. 41–46.

8. See, for example, Hans Jonas, "Response to G. Quispel's Gnosticism and the New Testament," in *The Bible and Modern Scholarship* ed. J. P. Hyatt (Nashville: 1965), pp. 279–293, cited in G. Filoramo, *A History of Gnosticism*, pp. 145 and 234, note 14.

9. See Filoramo, *A History of Gnosticism*, p. 43.

10. "The Manual of Discipline," in Theodore H. Gaster, trans. and ed., *The Dead Sea Scriptures*, (Garden City, NY: Doubleday, 1956), p. 50.

clearly premonitory of Gnostic and later kabbalistic ideas. The *Manual* equates a man's spiritual enlightenment with his "communion with the spirit of truth," a conception, that was to become fundamental for all the Gnostic sects. The Dead Sea Scrolls even describe psychological views that anticipate later Gnostic and kabbalistic ideas. In this regard, the *Manual of Discipline* speaks of

> the man who would bring others to the inner vision so that he may understand and teach to all the children of light the real nature of men, touching the different varieties of their temperaments with the distinguishing traits thereof, touching their actions throughout their generations, and touching the reasons why they are now visited with afflictions and now enjoy periods of well being.[11]

On the basis of similar passages in Gnostic texts, Jung called the Gnostics the first depth psychologists, and it is passages like this one that lead many scholars to see Gnosticism, in spite of its own anti-Jewish polemic, as a deviation from an earlier Jewish tradition.

In this context, it is interesting to examine the views of traditional Jewish scholars. Needless to say, the Kabbalists themselves were either unaware of or chose to ignore the issue of the parallels between their own and Gnostic ideas. Some Jewish thinkers who did note such parallels viewed them as proof that the Kabbalah was a heretical Judaism originating in foreign influence (del Medigo). Others, more sympathetic to the Kabbalah, held that Gnosticism was itself a heretical form of the Kabbalah (Simone Luzzatto). The latter thesis, by the way, is readily acceptable to those traditional Jews who attribute the Zohar (itself a very "Gnostical" work) to the second-century rabbinic sage, Simeon ben Yohai; for such an attribution places the Kabbalah in a place and time where it could have conceivably influenced the formation of Gnosticism.

One need not, however, accept an early date for the Zohar, in order to hold, as do Idel and Liebes, that an ancient Jewish oral tradition is the source of both the Kabbalah and Gnosticism. Idel, for example, appeals to the long list of contemporary scholars who have partly abandoned the once accepted Iranian-Egyptian-Greek explanation of Gnosticism in favor of a view that Jewish sources were influential on an emerging Gnostic religion and not the

---

11. Ibid., p. 50.

other way around.[12] Idel hypothesizes: "ancient Jewish motifs that penetrated Gnostic texts remained at the same time the patrimony of Jewish thought and continued to be transmitted in Jewish circles, ultimately providing the conceptual framework of the Kabbalah."[13] Idel acknowledges that a "long series of links cannot be proven by extant Jewish texts" but points out that neither can we trace non-Jewish links between second-century Gnosticism and the emergence, a millennium later, of the Kabbalah in Provence. Further, Idel argues, it is hard to imagine why the early Kabbalists, who numbered among themselves such textual experts as Nachmanides, would permit a non-Jewish tradition to be incorporated into mystical Judaism.

Yehuda Liebes has attempted to provide some substance to the notion of an intrinsically Jewish origin to the idea of the *Sefirot*, an idea that many have held to be the central concept of the Kabbalah, and one that clearly parallels the Gnostic notion of the aeons. Liebes adduces a variety of talmudic aggadic passages in which God's "attributes" appear to be quasi-independent entities.[14] For example, we read in the Talmud, *Berakhot* 7a: "May it be My will that My mercy may subdue My anger, and that My mercy may prevail over My [other] attributes so that I may deal with My children in the attributes of mercy and on their behalf, stop short of the limit of strict justice."[15] A more clear-cut tendency toward an hypostatization of God's attributes is to be found in such Apocryphal works as the *Wisdom of Solomon* and the *Slavonic Book of Enoch*, where God's "wisdom," which had simply been understood as one of his attributes in Proverbs and Job 28, is regarded as an emanation or effulgence, an intermediary force through which God creates the world. These works, originally written in Greek, show strong Platonic and, in the case of *Enoch*, Iranian/Zoroastrian influences.[16]

It is clear that once the Jewish mystics embarked upon the process of hypostasizing God's attributes into *Sefirot*, they naturally turned to the biblical and talmudic tradition for the names and characteristics of these

---

12. Idel, *Kabbalah: New Perspectives*, pp. 30–31.

13. Ibid., p. 31.

14. Yehuda Liebes, *Studies in Jewish Myth and Jewish Messianism*, trans. Batya Stein (Albany: State University of New York Press, 1993), p. 10.

15. Ibid., p. 10.

16. "Enoch, Slavonic Book of," *Encyclopedia Judaica* (Jerusalem: Keter, 1972), Vol. 6, p. 797; "Solomon, Wisdom of," *Encyclopedia Judaica* (Jerusalem: Keter, 1972), Vol. 15, p. 119; Scholem, *Kabbalah*, p. 6.

attributes. This is obvious, for example, from a comparison between the names of the *Sefirot* and the Godly attributes enumerated in Chronicles 28:11. What Liebes has failed to demonstrate is that the very project of hypostatization (and the theosophical views that follow from it) is present in the talmudic tradition. The passages he adduces in support of this appear to be mere figures of speech rather than philosophy or theosophy. What's more, even if one accepts the view that an hypostatization of God's attributes is present in the Talmud and other early Jewish sources, this can hardly account for the advent of kabbalistic (let alone Gnostic) theosophy. This is because the products of this hypostatization, the *Sefirot* (or aeons), are, for the Kabbalists and Gnostics, hardly ends unto themselves; but are rather vessels (to use a rather precise kabbalistic metaphor) for a whole host of *dialectical* ideas, which are hardly conceivable within a talmudic framework. Such dialectical ideas as the reciprocity between God and Man, the paradox of the world's illusion and reality, the power of "nothingness," and the "goodness" of evil, are fundamental to the Kabbalah but are completely absent from rabbinic Judaism.

At any rate, the whole program of hypostasizing divine attributes is a decidedly Greek (rather than Jewish) phenomenon. Hypostatization, "the turning of a mere aspect of something into a self-subsistent entity," is an essential, if not the defining, characteristic of Platonic and Neoplatonic philosophy,[17] and was only practiced by the Jews after they were exposed to Greek thought. The attempt to discover a purely Jewish pedigree for the Kabbalah may well be as chimerical as the attempt to "kosher" Greek philosophy itself, e.g., through the Philonic claim that Plato is simply "Moses speaking Attic." The strength of Judaism has been its ability to integrate the ideas of the world into its unique ethical and monotheistic vision, and not in its capacity to evolve only according to its own nisus.

Of course, the possibility exists, as Scholem suggests, that Kabbalah and Gnosticism are in many respects parallel but independent religious phenomena, each arising from the respective application of Platonic and Neoplatonic thought to Jewish and Christian scriptural and apocalyptic material. Scholem, for example, argues that the emergence of decidedly Gnostical and Manicheistic themes among the Kabbalists in sixteenth-century Safed is purely convergent and coincidental. He states: "there can be no doubt that this fact

---

17. J. N. Findlay, *Plato: The Written and Unwritten Doctrines* (London: Routledge and Kegan Paul, 1974), p. 3.

is due not to historical connections between the Manicheans and the new Kabbalists of Safed, but to a profound similarity in outlook and disposition which in its development produced similar results."[18] In spite of or rather because of this, Scholem argues that students of Gnosticism have much to learn from the Lurianic Kabbalah, which he nonetheless calls "a perfect example of Gnostical thought, both in principle and in detail."[19] Of course, the opposite can be said as well, that students of the Lurianic Kabbalah can learn much from the Gnostics, who are in many ways "kabbalistic."

My own view is that the similarities in symbols and outlook between Gnosticism and the Kabbalah are too great to be a mere case of a coincidence of like minds. It would seem that the origins of the theosophical views embodied in both Kabbalah and Gnosticism are to be found in the interaction amongst Jewish, Greek, Iranian (dualistic), and later Christian elements, which formed the religious and intellectual milieu in late antiquity. It was such a milieu that produced Christianity, the Essenes, Philo of Alexandria, Jewish Apocalyptic esotericism, and Gnosticism. It was also in this environment that varying proportions of Jewish monotheism, Greek thought, and pagan/oriental religion interacted to produce the prototypes for the symbols and ideas that later came to be embodied in *Sefer Yetzirah*, and much later in the writings of the first Kabbalists in Provence and Gerona. These prototypes were transmitted through written and oral traditions that are still obscure, and later reappeared in a new and more powerful form, in the Kabbalah of Isaac Luria and his followers.

This view, of course, has all the disadvantages of imprecision. However, it also has the advantage of being able to account, at least in part, for three characteristics of the Kabbalah in general and of the Lurianic Kabbalah in particular: its decidedly Jewish biblical/aggadic point of reference, its systematic application of hypostatization (which is Greek), and its clearly dialectical character. It is this latter, dialectical feature that provides the Kabbalah with its "dynamics," that characterizes the Kabbalah as "Gnostic," and that distinguishes the Kabbalah from the various fusions of Greek philosophy and Jewish thought from Philo to the present day, which fall under the rubric of "Jewish philosophy." It is the dialectical aspect of the Kabbalah that is its "mystical core" and that I would hypothesize links it to the traditions of the East (the dualism of Zoroastrianism, and ultimately the

---

18. Scholem, *Major Trends*, p. 280.
19. Ibid., p. 280.

traditions of India). That such traditions interacted with Jewish and Greek thought in late antiquity is certainly a hypothesis worthy of our consideration.

THE ESSENCE OF GNOSTICISM: THE DIVINE SPARK IN MAN

Scholars have differed regarding the identity and defining characteristics of Gnosticism, some pointing, for example, to its dualism of good and evil, others to its theories regarding the aeons, and the demiurge, etc. However, a congress of such scholars, organized in 1966, to consider the origins of Gnosticism (the Congress of Messina) distinguished between "gnosis" in general as "knowledge of the divine mysteries reserved for an elite" and "Gnosticism" proper, which it defined as follows:

> The Gnosticism of the second-century sects involves a coherent series of characteristics that can be summarized in the idea of a divine spark in man, deriving from the divine realm, fallen into this world of fate, birth, and death, and needing to be awakened by the divine counterpart of the self in order to be finally reintegrated.

The document continues that this idea is

> based ontologically on the conception of a downward movement in the divine whose periphery (often called Sophia or Ennoia) had to submit to the fate of entering into a crisis and producing, even if only indirectly, this world, upon which it cannot turn its back, since it is necessary for it to recover the pneuma, a dualistic conception on a monistic background, expressed in a double movement of devolution and reintegration.[20]

Even a brief examination of the Congress's definition reveals it to be also applicable to the Lurianic Kabbalah, and a more detailed inquiry reveals some of the most important points of contact (and divergence) between these two religious movements.

It is of note that the theory of the divine spark in man, which is never explicitly formulated in the literature of the early Kabbalah, becomes a central

---

20. As quoted in Filoramo, *A History of Gnosticism*, p. 143.

concept in the Kabbalah of Isaac Luria. In the Lurianic scheme the spark or "sparks" become enmeshed in the lower worlds as a result of the cosmic catastrophe known as the "Breaking of the Vessels." We shall see that this catastrophe itself has its analogy in the crisis of Sophia, which in Gnostic theosophy is the outermost aeon or emanation of the deity. Here, however, we should note that both in Gnosticism and Lurianic Kabbalah the resolution of the cosmic crisis only occurs with the return of the "sparks" to the infinite God.

For the Kabbalah, which is considerably less alienated from this world than Gnosticism, the raising of the sparks is at once an ethical, political, and psychological redemption that is deemed to be a joint venture between God and Man. The sparks, according to the Lurianists, will only be raised when humanity conforms its behavior to the divine commandments, when the Jewish exiles are returned to the land of Israel, and when individuals discover the "roots" of their own souls. For Gnosticism, redemption is almost wholly an inner, psychological process. A psychological theory of the sparks was adopted, but only in part, by the Lurianic Kabbalah and the Hasidim. However, an examination of the Gnostics' point of view can shed important light on the kabbalistic/Hasidic theory of the soul.

For the Gnostics, the divine spark present in man is entrapped in an evil realm of shadows, which is a close parallel to the Kabbalist's Sitra Achra (the "Other Side"). This spark, in the guise of individual men, is unaware of its true origins, but nevertheless possesses an unconscious desire to return to its divine home.[21] The divine spark thereby constitutes the individual's essential but forgotten reality.[22]

The Gnostics held that the material, empirical, human being is essentially an illusion that envelops, indeed imprisons, the inner, true self.[23] It is only by acquiring knowledge or "memory" (in the Platonic sense of *anamnesis*) of this inner self that the Gnostic devotee can free himself from this hostile world and achieve ultimate spiritual fulfillment.

This knowledge, or *gnosos*, however, is not achieved through a purely cognitive procedure.[24] Gnostic knowledge is first and foremost knowledge of the heart; it is an experience of spiritual regeneration, of immediate salvation. It is in essence, the awakening of the long-dormant inner, divine self. For

---

21. Ibid., p. 38.
22. Ibid., p. 41.
23. Ibid., p. 23.
24. Ibid., p. 41.

Hermes in the first treatise of *Corpus Hermeticum* (a Gnostical work also known as the *Poimandres*) it is a combination of will and grace, intellect and emotion, which is needed for gnosos. Meditation, dialectic, and reflection are all useful in preparing the intellect, but the intervention of a divine luminous power creating a profound emotional experience is necessary to create the image of the "essential man," which is consubstantial with the divine world.[25] Filoramo, in noting the emotional component of this gnosos, tells us that Gnostic knowledge is *erotic* knowledge that somehow rises above itself, a characterization that brings Gnosos very close to contemporary psychoanalysis.

All of these ideas are found in relatively unaltered form in the Lurianic Kabbalah and later in the writings of the Hasidim. The existence of an inner divine self (*Tzelem*, image, or "Godly soul" in the Kabbalah), which acts as a forgotten "celestial counterpart" to a man's empirical ego, is common to both Gnosticism and Lurianism, as is the idea of the necessary awakening of this inner self and its ultimate reunion with the infinite divine principle. This awakening occurs, according to the Kabbalists, only through a person's attaining a deep, abiding, emotional/spiritual knowledge of his true self, and is achievable only when an "arousal from above" complements man's own "arousal from below."

Similar ideas are also, as we have seen, present in the philosophies of India, which invariably regard the empirical ego as an illusion enveloping man's true, divine self (*Atman*). What differentiates the Indian tradition from Gnosticism and Kabbalah, however, is that only for the latter two is the journey of the divine spark, or inner self, placed in the context of a historical drama of apocalyptic proportions. In India, a particular Hindu or Jainist achieves enlightenment or he does not; either his soul has finished with its series of Karmic reincarnations or its travels continue. For Gnosos and the Kabbalah the redemption of a single soul is ultimately connected to the historical redemption of the Godhead and the entire world. The Gnostics and Kabbalists, we might say, are much more in a hurry than their Hindu or Buddhist counterparts, and as such, their theories take on a far more dynamic character than those of India. The Hindus narrate no cosmic drama of the fall of a divine spark into the world of men and have little to say about the need to redeem *Brahma* itself through the acts of mankind.

---

25. Ibid., pp. 45–46.

THE VALUE OF THE WORLD

While Kabbalah shares with Gnosticism a dramatic, historical point of view, it differs from it with regard to one crucial idea: the value that it places on the world of human fate and endeavor. The Gnostics, in common with most (but not all) of the traditions of India were decidedly *anticosmic*. This world, they held, was a horrific realm of shadow and evil, which at all costs must be escaped. Indeed the creation of the world is conceived in Gnosticism as resulting from the arrogance of an ignorant demiurge who himself is regarded as evil. It is in a polemic against the Gnostics that Plotinus writes: "Nor would it be sound to condemn this Kosmos as less than beautiful, as less than the noblest possible in the corporeal; and neither can any charge be laid against its source."[26]

From a Gnostic point of view, the material world might well disappear once the last holy spark has been raised and rejoins the divine pleroma. Needless to say, this is hardly the view of the Lurianic Kabbalists. For them, the extraction (*birur*) of the sparks (*netzotzim*) from the husks (*Kelippot*) results in the elevation and sanctification of this world and not, as in Gnosis, in its abandonment. For the Kabbalah, this world is indeed a mixture of good and evil. The evil in this world causes it to sink into the world of darkness (the "*Sitra Achra*") and the good in it can cause it to rise above that nether realm. The purpose of restoring the individual to his *Tzelem* or Godly self is not so that he can escape a vale of tears, but so that he can perform his role in the world's restoration and repair (*Tikkun ha-Olam*). This crucial difference between Gnosticism and the Kabbalah makes for an important difference in their view of man: with respect to this world, the Gnostic is completely hostile and alienated, a true stranger; the Kabbalist, on the other hand, is merely *estranged*; for him a rapprochement is both possible and desirable.

JUNG'S VIEWS ON GNOSOS AND THE KABBALAH

It is noteworthy that Carl Jung (who once described Freud's theories as being rooted in the Kabbalah) considered the Gnostics to be the first "depth psychologists." For Jung, the Gnostics' interest in a hidden, yet-to-be-discovered "self," and their quest for an emotional knowledge of this inner

---

26. Plotinus, Ennead 3, 2, 13; Plotinus, *The Six Enneads*, p. 388.

man, were important precursors to psychoanalysis. For example, among the Nag Hammadi texts, in the Book of *Thomas the Contender* we read:

> Examine yourself and learn who you are, in what way you exist, and how you will come to be . . . although you are uncomprehending you have (in fact) already come to know, and you will be called "the one who knows himself." For he who has not known himself has known nothing, but he who has known himself has at the same time already achieved knowledge about the depth of the all.[27]

The Gnostics, like the Kabbalists, held that knowledge of the microcosm, man, was tantamount to knowledge of the cosmos and the inner workings of God. Yet the process of knowing the divine can only proceed psychologically. The *Epistle to Theophrastus* admonishes the would be Gnostic adherent to:

> cease to seek after God and creation and things like these, and seek after yourself of yourself and learn who it is who appropriates all things within you without exception and says "My God, my mind, my thought, my soul, my body?" And learn whence comes grief, and rejoicing and love and hatred, and waking without intention, and sleeping without intention, and anger without intention, and love without intention. If you consider these things carefully, you will find yourself within yourself . . . and will find the outcome of yourself.[28]

The Kabbalists, particularly Isaac Luria and his disciples, held similar views regarding self-knowledge and one's *Tikkun* or redemption. According to the Italian Kabbalist Moses Zacuto, it is man's divinely appointed task "to inquire into the roots of his self and soul in order that he may thereby perfect himself."[29]

Gnosticism and Kabbalah can be distinguished from modern depth psychology on the grounds that the knowledge sought by the former is regarded as a supramundane "gift of the divine,"[30] whereas the knowledge of psychoanalysis is clearly limited to the empirical, worldly, ego. Jung, however, denies the validity of this distinction, arguing that the individual Gnostics'

---

27. "Book of Thomas the Contender," (NHC II 138, 8–18), *Nag Hammadi Library*, p. 201.

28. Cited in Filoramo, *A History of Gnosticism*, pp. 101–102.

29. Scholem, *Sabbatai Sevi: The Mystical Messiah*, pp. 41–42.

30. Filoramo, *A History of Gnosticism*, p. 38.

knowledge of the presumed divine mysteries can be understood as a thinly veiled insight into the machinations of his own subconscious mind. For Jung, the labyrinthian creation myths of Gnosticism are best understood as descriptions of the development of the human psyche projected onto the cosmos as a whole. The Gnostic godhead, according to Jung, is a symbol of the primal unconscious, and the various elements of creation, including the demiurge (creator-god), the world and man himself, are progressive aspects of a developing self or ego that emerges out of the unconscious mind.[31] The exile of sparks in a world of matter, and their desire for return to the Godhead, are, for Jung, symbols of split-off or repressed aspects of the mind that the individual vaguely senses must be reintegrated into the wellspring of desire, thought, and action.

A similar Jungian analysis can be applied to the theory of the sparks in the Lurianic Kabbalah, with one crucial difference. The difference, as we have already noted, is that the Lurianic Kabbalah, unlike Gnosticism, does not abjure the world. As such the Kabbalah is, in Jungian terms, far less hostile to the ego (which on Jung's interpretation is the world's equivalent) than is Gnosticism. Richard Segal has aptly distinguished Gnosticism from Jungian psychology on the grounds that the former, in Jungian terms, would advocate a complete abandonment of the ego (represented by the world) in favor of a "reversion to sheer unconsciousness."[32] Jung himself, however, hardly advocated the abandonment of the ego, but rather saw therapy as an effort to enlarge the personality to include ever-widening aspects of both the ego and the personal and collective unconscious.

As I will detail in Chapters 7 and 8, psychoanalysis, and particularly Jungian analysis, is far closer to the Kabbalah than to Gnosticism. As we have seen, the Kabbalah does not renounce the world but rather seeks to discover the core of divinity that resides within it, and to thereby sanctify and raise this world to a higher level closer to God. By extension, the discovery of the Godly Soul within the Kabbalist or Hasid hardly results in the abandonment of the ego and rational mind. As I have discussed in detail in my *Symbols of The Kabbalah*, the Lurianic concept of *Tikkun* involves far more than simply discovering the roots of one's own soul. The kabbalistic "raising of the

---

31. Carl Gustav Jung, "Gnostic Symbols of the Self," in *Aion, Researches Into the Phenomenology of the Self*, Bollingen Series XX (Princeton, NJ: Princeton University Press, 1969), pp. 184–221.

32. Robert A. Segal, ed. *The Gnostic Jung* (Princeton, NJ: Princeton University Press, 1992), p. 30.

sparks" requires proper spiritual, ethical, and intellectual conduct, and (as expressed in such metaphors as the "development in the womb of the celestial mother") *Tikkun* involves a maturing of the ego's moral and intellective powers. The Chabad Hasidim, who developed their psychology on the basis of the Lurianic Kabbalah, are so named because of their view that man's emotional powers (the seven lower *Sefirot*) must be put to the service of knowledge, wisdom, and understanding (in Hebrew *Chochmah, Binah* and *Da'at*, the first letters of which form the acronym Cha B a D). The supreme goal of their Kabbalah is neither the complete immersion of man in God (*unio-mystico*) or the dissolution of the ego in the unconscious or "id." For Chabad, as for the Lurianists humanity's goals must be an integration of thought and emotion, a dialectical resolution of conflicting values and ideas, the "taming of the evil impulse," and the mitigation of judgment by kindness, all so that individuals might be better able to restore and perfect *this* world.

We can appreciate the value of applying Jungian notions to both Gnosticism and the Kabbalah without necessarily endorsing the metaphysical point of view taken by Jung himself. Jung claimed to make no judgment whatsoever regarding the metaphysical claims of religion, and hence no judgment regarding the *truth* claims made by the Gnostics (and Kabbalists). Still, his working assumption that the Gnostics' statements about God were indeed accurate descriptions of the unconscious mind has the effect of reducing theology to psychology, and actually undermining the transcendental claims of religion. Jung early on theorized that primitive and ancient man made contact with his own collective unconscious by projecting it onto the cosmos in the form of mythology and theosophy.[33] According to Jung, modern man, no longer able to believe in the ancient myths, had become estranged from the wellspring of the collective unconscious by holding the view that reason, science, and technology were the only (and sufficient) means of relating to both himself and the world. Only "contemporary man" (and by this Jung means *his* contemporaries, i.e., mainly those who had undergone Jungian analysis) is capable of understanding the collective unconscious directly. Jung, in effect, advocated a spirituality of inwardness, believing that the great source of cosmic creativity lay neither in the heavens, nor in man's rational and technical facilities, but rather in the heritage of humanity's collective inner psyche. And while he did not explicitly deny the

---

33. Ibid., pp. 13–14.

metaphysical and theological validity of religious belief, his psychologistic approach had the effect of making such belief wholly irrelevant to human spirituality.

Jung, of course, is not the first to have psychologized religious experience. Indeed, as we have seen, Sankhya and Yoga, and later, Buddhism, held almost purely psychologistic theories of the divine. We might here add that Hasidism provides an almost purely psychologistic conception of the Kabbalah, in which such cosmic concepts as *Tzimtzum, Sefirot,* and *Shevirah* ("concealment," "archetype," and "breaking") are reinterpreted almost exclusively in psychological terms. Such psychologizations, however, are invariably followed by a metaphysical reaction. The human mind, it seems, is never satisfied in discovering the spirit within itself, and however important and true the insight that the divine lies within, the human spirit craves something transcendent as well.

The great mystical traditions of the world are all in accord in the view that the microcosm mirrors the macrocosm and vice versa. Ours is an age that has found spirit in the former without fully understanding the divinity of the latter. Rather than look to Gnosticism and Kabbalah simply as confirmations of our own interest in depth psychology, we ought to look also to these theosophical disciplines as examples of how we might utilize our contemporary insights into the microcosm (man) to illuminate the cosmos as a whole.

PRIMORDIAL MAN

How we might ask, is the *world as a whole* to be understood as a reflection of the inner psyche of man? To begin to understand this idea we must inquire into another Gnostic symbol that also came to be elaborated upon in the Kabbalah: the primal anthropos or "Primordial Man."

The concept of a primal anthropos, a divinely created archetypical man, who embraces within his being the whole of the cosmos, is found in a number of religious and philosophical traditions. We have seen this idea in Jaina and other traditions of Indian thought. Interestingly, the same image is found in Plutarch, who relates that the entirety of the heavens is arranged in the form of a *macroanthropos,* a colossal human being who is conceived as a model for the human world.[34] For Plutarch, the sun is at the heart of this being and the

---

34. Filoramo, *A History of Gnosticism,* p. 51.

moon, the sun's androgynous messenger, is located in between the heart and belly. The Gnostics developed the idea that individual human beings are descended from the cosmic anthropos as a result of fragmentation. They inferred from the verse in Genesis "Let us make man in our own image," that the first earthly man was created on the model of a cosmic Adam on high.[35] In the Nag Hammadi text the *Apocryphon of John*, we learn that this anthropos is the first creation of "knowledge and Perfect Intellect" and the first luminary of the heavens.[36] This Anthropos becomes the heavenly model through which the demiurge forges an earthly Adam. Other Gnostic sources relate how the "archons" (conceived of as female demigods corresponding to each of the seven planets) formed an earthly Adam to fulfill their sexual desire for the heavenly anthropos who was beyond their spiritual reach. Among the Mandeans (a Gnostic sect that today survives in Iraq) the primal Adam is coextensive with the cosmos, his body is the body of the world, and his soul the soul of all souls.[37]

The concept of Primordial Man (*Adam Kadmon*) reemerges in the theosophical Kabbalah, particularly in the Kabbalah of Isaac Luria. According to Luria and his followers, *Adam Kadmon* is the first being to emerge in the *tehiru* or metaphysical void created by the *Tzimtzum*. Whereas in the Zohar, *Adam Kadmon* is conceived of as containing the ten *Sefirot* within his celestial body, in Luria the *Sefirot* (or archetypical values of the cosmos) are only contained within him *in potentia*. Beams of light emerging from the ears, nostrils, and mouth of *Adam Kadmon*, and later from his eyes, give rise to the *Sefirot* and fill them with divine light. Finally, lights from the forehead of *Adam Kadmon* are instrumental in beginning the repair (*Tikkun*) of the *Sefirot* after they have been shattered as a result of the Breaking of the Vessels. As such, *Adam Kadmon*, who embodies the entire cosmos in the Zohar, comes to act in the Lurianic Kabbalah as its creator and redeemer as well.[38]

The significance of the symbol as *Adam Kadmon* goes beyond the notion that the image of Primordial Man belies an anthropomorphic vision of the deity and world. Rather, we might say that *Adam Kadmon* symbolizes, among other things, the idea that man, or human consciousness and

---

35. Gershom Scholem, "Adam Kadmon," *Encyclopedia Judaica* (Jerusalem: Keter, 1972), Vol. 2, p. 248.

36. Filoramo, *A History of Gnosticism*, p. 65.

37. Rudolph, *Gnosis*, p. 109.

38. Though only in the heretical Shabbatean School is *Adam Kadmon* equated with the messiah.

experience, is *equiprimordial* with both God and the world. God, man, and the world are as inseparable from each other as, for example, a sphere is to its circumference and diameter. The cosmos exists because man *intends* it as such; that is because man, through his desires, projects, and language, constitutes it as a world. It is for this reason that the Gnostics (and Kabbalists) can reasonably hold that the entire destiny of the world is embodied in the essence of the Primordial Man.[39] While, from another more objectifying perspective, it is the cosmos (or God) that gives rise to man, even this perspective is a project of mankind, for it is man's desire that gives rise to the very projects (e.g. of science and theology) through which an "objective" view of the world takes form. It is not any man in particular who is central to the existence of "the world" but man in his most general, abstract form. Yet this abstract, primal man, who constitutes the world through his projects and desires, is very concrete and instantial as well: for it is only the concrete acts of everyday life that bring man's world into actual being. The world, which in the Kabbalah is represented by the ten *Sefirot* contained in the body of the cosmic anthropos, is a world of intellectual, spiritual, aesthetic, and material values; in short, a world composed of human interest. If not for such interest, if not for human desire, the world itself would never be constituted as such. This, for example, is the upshot of Freud's early pronouncement that ideas, images, and even *things* are a secondary manifestation of human libido. Because man needs (desires) objects, an objective world exists.

These ideas are also expressed in a contemporary idiom in Martin Heidegger's concept of *Dasein* (being there), the term Heidegger uses to denote that fusion of human interest and otherness that he identifies with "being" itself.[40] For Heidegger, who has frequently been spoken of as a contemporary Gnostic,[41] *Dasein* is the existential equivalent of Primordial Man. *Dasein* is a concept that overcomes all subject–object distinctions and expresses the equiprimordiality of humanity and the world. Through the word *Dasein*, Heidegger expresses the conviction that a theory of being must necessarily also be a theory of humanity. This, I believe, is the most important idea implicit in the symbol of Primordial Man.

---

39. Rudolph, *Gnosis*, p. 67.

40. Martin Heidegger, *Being and Time* (New York: Harper & Row, 1962).

41. It is of significance that perhaps the greatest interpreter of Gnosticism in the twentieth century, Hans Jonas, was a pupil of Heidegger's. See Hans Jonas, *The Gnostic Religion* (Boston: Beacon Press, 1963) and "Gnosticism and Modern Nihillism," *Social Research* 19 (1952): 430–452.

THE EROTICIZATION OF THE COSMOS

The Primordial Man of Gnosos and the Kabbalah is highly sexual and erotic, and as such there is a certain eroticization of the cosmos that present in the Gnostic and kabbalistic myths. In reading about all of the erotic unifications and schisms that, according to the Gnostics and, particularly, the Lurianists, determine the fate of man and the world, one is drawn to the conclusion that the very cosmos is woven out of the fabric of sexual desire.

The Gnostics saw a deep cosmic mystery in the act of sexual intercourse. In the Hermetic text *Asclempius* we find:

> And if you wish to see the reality of this mystery, then you should see the wonderful representation of the intercourse which takes place between male and female. For when the semen reaches its climax, it leaps forth. In that moment the female receives the strength of the male; the male for his part receives the strength of the female, while the semen does this. Therefore the mystery of intercourse is performed in secret.[42]

The Gnostics, particularly those of the School of Valentinus, understood human intercourse to mirror the act of spiritual matrimony that restores an original androgynous unity to a schismatic world. This unity is said to occur in the heavenly Bridal Chamber of the Pleroma.[43] The Valentinians even went so far as to create a series of rituals in which sexual intercourse is performed in cultic fashion and the man's sperm is offered to the heavens in order to facilitate the raising of the earthbound spark back to its origin in God.[44] A similar view reappears in the Lurianic doctrine that in the raising of the sparks mankind provides the *mayim nukvim*, feminine waters, for the divine intercourse that restores the harmony of the worlds.

That the Kabbalists, like the Gnostics, viewed the entire cosmos in erotic terms is evident from their conceptualization of the dynamic relationships among the *Sefirot* as a series of *Yichudim*, or sexual unions between the various personas or *Partzufim* within the godhead. For Luria the Breaking of the Vessels, for example, is conceptualized as a disruption in these erotic unions, and *Tikkun ha-Olam* as their resumption. The Kabbalists views can

---

42. Filoramo, *A History of Gnosticism*, p. 180.
43. Ibid., p. 182.
44. Filoramo, *A History of Gnosticism*, pp. 184–185.

also be gleaned from what they say about the mental states that must accompany the performance of the commandments and prayer. For Luria, such states are achieved through the recitation and meditation upon various *kavvanot* (intentions) and *Yichudim* (unifications) whereby the adherent concentrates upon performing a particular *mitzvah* for the purpose of unifying divergent aspects of the deity and thereby healing the fault within both the world and man. Typical among these meditations is a prayer that seeks to unite God and His *Shekhinah* (God and His "Bride"), the masculine and feminine principles of the universe. Frequently the feminine principle or bride is thought of as the people of Israel.

These *Kavvanot* and *Yichudim* frequently utilize the symbolism of sexual intercourse. The unification of the *Sefirot* is spoken of as *zivvug*, coupling[45] between the Celestial Father and Mother or between *Zeir Anpin* (The "Impatient One") or *Tiferet* (which is given the rabbinic name for God, "The Holy One Blessed Be He") and the female principle, *Nukvah, Malchut,* or *Shekhinah*. In order for the appropriate unification to take place, mutual male and female orgasms are necessary. The Yichudim help to reunify a deity who embodies both male and female cosmic principles. Such bisexuality is for the Kabbalists (as it was for the Gnostics[46]) an expression of the supreme perfection, a theme that is particularly salient in the Zohar, where we learn that it is incumbent not only for God but also for man to become "male and female."[47]

The Kabbalists themselves issue stern warnings against interpreting these metaphors in a literal, corporeal, or sexual fashion. Jung understood the Gnostics' cosmic eroticism as a projection of the dynamics of the human unconscious. When we take this perspective with respect to the Lurianic Kabbalah we come to view the world's redemption as a sanctification of the erotic. Understood psychologically, the Gnostics and Kabbalists have, as it were, projected their recognition of the primary significance of sexuality in human affairs onto the cosmos as a whole. Understood kabbalistically, they have raised the holy sparks of human eros, and captured, in metaphor, the essence of man's task in repairing the cosmos itself. This task takes as its model the unification of man and woman in erotic love.

45. Louis Jacobs, "The Uplifting of the Sparks," p. 107.
46. Rudolph, *Gnosis*, p. 80.
47. Zohar I, 49b; Sperling and Simon, *The Zohar*, Vol. 1, p. 158.

GNOSOS AND MYTH

The "philosophical anthropology" that is symbolized in the notion of "Primordial Man" provides us with insight into the Gnostic and kabbalistic attitudes toward myth. According to Jung, myths are a projection onto the cosmos of the unconscious archetypes of the human mind. Myths, by revealing the "collective unconscious," are vehicles through which man comes to know himself in the deepest, most universal sense. Yet, if, as we have argued, the universe itself is logically inseparable from the interests of humanity, myth becomes *the* portal into truth about the world as well. What the Gnostics seemed to grasp, and the Kabbalists practiced in their theosophy, is the idea that *a depth psychology of man is the method par excellence of philosophy.* Jung, in his attempt to remain within the fold of "empirical science," failed to draw out the logical conclusions of his own method: viz. that psychoanalysis is metaphysics. By applying human reason to the depths of the human unconscious expressed in dreams and myth, the depth psychologist provides an analysis of the constituent elements of reality itself.[48]

It is the dialogue between myth and logos, characteristic of Gnosticism and especially the Kabbalah, which joins these religious phenomena with contemporary psychoanalytic thought. Filoramo, in commenting on the Gnostic notions of Primordial Man and the divine "spark," says: "Myth profoundly imbued with reflection and logos, now narrates the activities of the god-human and the divine principle exiled and longing for return to the heavenly home."[49]

In articulating the most basic "routes of interest" of the human psyche, the Gnostic and kabbalistic theosophies (which are "myths imbibed with logos") become, as Plato affirmed, the "bridge between being and becoming." The cosmogony of the Gnostic Pleroma, aeons, archons, and demiurge, or of the kabbalistic *Ein-Sof, Sefirot, Shevirah,* and *Tikkun* are precisely what they claim to be, ontological inquires, revelations regarding being itself. Again Filoramo puts this quite aptly when he tells us that Gnostic theosophy seeks access to "the mystery of the first throb of Being, that initial moment,

---

48. This, by the way, is why an instrument like the Rorschach Exam, which elicits projections of form and content of the test-taker's human interests, and thereby prompts him to unwittingly generate a series of personal symbols, metaphors, and myths, is not merely a psychological test, but a *window into Being itself.*

49. Filoramo, *A History of Gnosticism,* p. 51.

that original conflagration from which the pleromatic universe would emerge."[50] For the Gnostics, man is the means through which being or God becomes manifest to himself.[51] As in the Kabbalah, the human soul (the microcosm) mirrors the life of the divine.[52] And, as in the Kabbalah, the knowledge that the Gnostic seeks is one in which the knower becomes the very knowledge and reality that is known.[53] The distinctions between subject and object, and the knowledge relation between the two, so important in Western philosophy, is but an illusion to be overcome in Gnosos.

COINCIDENTIA OPPOSITORUM

The overcoming of distinctions and oppositions is a characteristic of both Gnostic and kabbalistic thought, a characteristic that can rightly be spoken of as "dialectical." Gnostic thought seeks not only to overcome epistemological distinctions, but also to overcome, for example, distinctions of time and gender. We are continually reminded, for example, that to know one's *arche* (beginning) is the equivalent of knowing one's *telos* or end[54] and that such knowledge is tantamount to actually becoming the knowledge that is known (the reunion with one's celestial counterpart or divine self). For the Gnostics, the ultimate God or reality is androgynous; it is both "Father" and "Mother," and this androgyny is itself another metaphor for a wider *coincidentia oppositorum*, the conquest of dualities through the joining of opposites.[55] In one Gnostic image, God is said to create the world through an act of copulation with him/herself,[56] an idea that is expressed in Orphic sources as the logos that impresses the seals of the father upon matter only to return them to the father. Similar images in the ancient world, e.g., the serpent biting its own tail (and the Nassene image of the ocean descending from the heavens to bring its currents back to its source[57]) reflect the basically Gnostic notion that the world in all its distinctions has its origins and

---

50. Ibid., p. 53.
51. Ibid., p. 53.
52. Ibid., p. 24.
53. Rudolph, *Gnosis*, p. 55.
54. Filoramo, *A History of Gnosticism*, p. 42.
55. Ibid., p. 61.
56. Ibid., p. 61.
57. Ibid., p. 84.

destiny in a dialectical process. As Filoramo has pointed out, the Gnostic doctrine of aeons (which has its kabbalistic equivalent in the *Sefirot*) expresses the view that cognitive, emotional, and volitional acts originate in the deity, come to fruition in man's overcoming obstacles on earth, and realize themselves most fully in their return to God.[58] This notion, which is developed more fully in the Kabbalah, also anticipates Hegel, who held that the Absolute becomes itself only by descending into a world of finitude; and then, after overcoming all finite obstacles, returns to itself in a renewed and greater infinity. This is the historical destiny of the Gnostic divine spark that falls into an alien world of men.

We have seen (in Chapter One) how for the Kabbalists, the Infinite God, *Ein-Sof*, is regarded as the union of all contradictions in *coincidentia oppositorum*. There is, in the Kabbalah, a dialectical union and equivalence between such opposites as being and nothingness, reality and illusion, knowledge and ignorance, male and female, God and creation, etc. A similar *coincidentia* is strongly suggested in the writings of the Gnostics, who, for example, express their conception of the *coincidentia* between God and man boldly in passages like the following: "God created men, and men created God. So is it also in the world, since men created gods and worship them as their creations it would be fitting that gods should worship men."[59]

We should note, however, that for the Gnostics, the coincidence of opposites is often understood to represent a corrupt union between two manners of existence; the perfect, divine redeeming power and a world of deficiency and evil. Because the world itself is despised, the insight expressed by the *coincidentia* is into a corrupt reality, and not, as it is in the Kabbalah, into the highest value expressed in the Absolute God. A remarkable Gnostic expression of the coincidence of opposites is found in the Nag Hammadi document, *Thunder, The Perfect Mind*, in which a female figure, presumably Sophia but also representing the duality of man's soul,[60] declares:

> I am the first and the last.
> I am the honored and the scorned one.
> I am the whore and the holy one . . .
> I am the bride and the bridegroom,
>   and it is my husband who begot me.

---

58. Ibid., p. 66.
59. Rudolph, *Gnosis*, p. 93.
60. Ibid., p. 81.

I am the mother of my father,
  and the sister of my husband
  and he is my offspring.
. . . I am the silence that is incomprehensible
  and the idea whose remembrance is frequent
Why, you who hate me, do you love me . . .
You, who tell the truth about me, lie about me,
  and you who,
have lied about me, tell the truth about me.
. . . For I am knowledge and ignorance
. . . I am the one whom they call Life,
  and you have called Death.
. . . I am a mute who does not speak
  and great is my multitude of words.[61]

This is a document that can and should be read not only as an expression of the inner nature of an aspect of the godhead (Sophia or wisdom), but as a description of the human psyche, as well. Its themes are clearly echoed in the Kabbalah; the sexual imagery and conflation of family figures finding a prominent place in the Zohar.[62]

GNOSTIC AND KABBALISTIC THEOSOPHY

The basic symbols of both Gnosos and the Kabbalah are, as the Gnostics themselves stated so clearly, designed to reveal "who we are, what we have been cast out of, where we are bound for, what we have been purified of, what generation and regeneration are."[63] As such, these symbols constitute what I have referred to as a *basic metaphor*, a series of symbols or myths designed to encompass the totality of being, to explain all things. There can be little doubt however that the Kabbalah, particularly in its Zoharic and Lurianic expressions, represents a more complex and detailed symbolic structure than that of Gnosticism. Whereas the Gnostics, for example, simply

---

61. "Thunder: The Perfect Mind," Robinson, ed., *The Nag Hammadi Library*, pp. 295–303. (Compare *Bhagavad Gita* iix, 16–19, Zaehner, ed., *Hindu Scriptures*, p. 320, where the "blessed lord" describes himself as father and mother, origin and dissolution, death and deathlessness.)

62. Tishby and Lachower, *The Wisdom of the Zohar*, vol. 1, p. 299.

63. *Theodoto* 78:2. Quoted in Filoramo, *A History of Gnosticism*, p. 39.

speak of a divine spark fallen into a material and evil world, which must be redeemed through the insight (Gnosos) of man, Luria erects an elaborate edifice regarding the origin of this spark in *Ein-Sof* (the infinite deity) *Tzimtzum* (God's concealment/contraction), emanation, *Adam Kadmon*, the *Sefirot*, and the sparks' fate in *Shevirah* (the Breaking of the Vessels) and *Tikkun* (Restoration). However, as we have seen in reference to the symbol of Primordial Man, a close examination of Gnostic writings reveals that Gnosticism anticipated many of the details of the Lurianic system.

THE DOCTRINE OF GOD

The similarities in specific doctrine are evident in the Gnostic conception of the infinite God, which is in nearly all respects indistinguishable from the Kabbalists' *Ein-Sof*. Like the Kabbalists, the Gnostics distinguished an infinite primordial deity from the "God" of religious worship and devotion. Basilides spoke of a primal "non-existent" God, and Valentinus of a pre-existent perfect aeon, a "Pre- Beginning."[64] According to the *Apocryphon of John*, the true infinite is:

> pure light into which no eye can look . . . He is the invisible spirit of whom it is not right to think of him as a god, or something similar, for he is more than a god, since there is nothing above him, for no one lords it over him, for he does not exist in something inferior to him, since everything exists in him. For it is he who establishes himself. He is eternal since he does not need anything, for he is total perfection. He did not lack anything that he might be completed by it; rather he is always completely perfect in light. He is illimitable since there is no one prior to him to set limits to him. He is unsearchable since there exists no one prior to him to examine him. He is immeasurable since there was no one prior to him to measure him. He is invisible since no one saw Him. He is eternal since he exists eternally. He is ineffable since no one was able to comprehend him to speak about him. He is unnamable since there is no one prior to him to give him a name.[65]

---

64. Rudolph, *Gnosis*, p. 62.
65. Robinson, *Nag Hammadi Library*, pp. 106–107; Nag Hammadi II, 3, 71, quoted in Rudolph, *Gnosis*, p. 93.

The Gnostic God is beyond all perfection, happiness, and even divinity.[66] He is neither corporeal nor incorporeal, large nor small, and is beyond all existence whatsoever. In the Nag Hammadi *Letter of Eugnostos* the Gnostic deity is spoken of as the "God of Truth," who is indescribable, has no dominion or name, and has never been known to any creature from the beginning of time.[67] However, like the Kabbalists, who also declare *Ein-Sof* to be completely unknowable (and the Hindus who, as we have seen, make a similar declaration about Brahman), the Gnostics have seemingly much to say about their unnamable God. The author of this *Letter* not only refers to him as the "God of Truth," but describes him as unchanging, good, perfect, and the "Father of the Universe." However, the transcendent deity is not, according to the Gnostics, the creator of our world. According to the Gnostics the "god" who created the world is an ignorant, even arrogant, demiurge who is many steps removed from the infinite, unknowable, illimitable being we have just described. The names given to the deity in this world, for example, "God," "Father," "Holy Spirit," etc., belong to the realm of error, or have been introduced by the "archons," the corrupt, semi-divine beings who rule this world and lead men astray.[68]

Again, according to the *Apocryphon of John*, the supreme deity emanates a series of "light beings," or aeons, akin to the Kabbalists' *Sefirot*. The lowest of these aeons, Sophia, desires to produce an offspring without the highest God's consent. The result of her desire is a monstrous demiurge, Yaldabaoth, who, while containing an element of his mother's divinity, is ignorant and arrogant in his belief that he is the true and only sovereign of the created world. The Gnostics frequently (and anti-Jewishly) identified this demiurge with the "jealous God" of the Old Testament. The Kabbalists, as we have seen, also distinguished between the Infinite God, "*Ein-Sof*," and the God of the Bible. According to at least sevrral Kabbalists, *Ein-Sof*, who serves as the metaphysical ground of the biblical God, is Himself never even alluded to in scripture, nor is He the object of man's thoughts and prayers. The Kabbalists, of course, refused to follow the Gnostics in their condemnation of the creator God, but did follow them in an emanatory scheme in which the personality of "God" crystallizes somewhere on the path between the infinite, unknowable divine principle and creation.

---

66. Filoramo, *A History of Gnosticism*, p. 40.
67. Robinson, *Nag Hammadi Library*, p. 224, *Eugnostos* (II, 3).
68. Rudolph, *Gnosis*, p. 62.

AEONS, EMANATION, *SEFIROT,* AND *TZIMTZUM*

As we have seen the concept of "emanation" is Neoplatonic in origin. The power of this idea lies in its ability to account for a creation that is epistemologically but not ontologically distinct from the Infinite One. Both the Gnostics' "aeons" and the Kabbalists' "*Sefirot*" are cognitive, volitional, spiritual, and emotional aspects of the Infinite God, which in their being are no more distinct from the deity than the sun is from its own light. We have seen that the Kabbalists' *Sefirot* include such divine attributes as knowledge, wisdom, understanding, kindness, judgment, and beauty. Among the Gnostic aeons are "grace," "insight," "perception," "prudence," "providence," "lordship," "kingdom," and "wisdom."[69] Both the aeons, which, in Gnosticism are indeterminate in number (the Valentinians count thirty) and the *Sefirot,* which for the Kabbalists always numbered ten, are, as we have seen, Platonic hypostasizations of ideas that in the bible and Talmud are simply referred to as the traits and characteristics of God. Both the Gnostics and the Kabbalists also understood these hypostasizations as archetypes for the psychic powers in man. By delimiting their number to ten and predicating both a cosmology and psychology on their basis, the Kabbalists developed their doctrine of the *Sefirot* in a direction that assured its centrality not only for the Kabbalah but for the whole future of occidental esotericism as well.[70]

The kabbalistic notion of *Tzimtzum* (contraction/concealment) is also anticipated in the Gnostic conception of emanation. *Tzimtzum,* which plays a pivotal role in the Lurianic system, represents the idea that creation is the result of a contraction or withdrawal of the light of the infinite God. The existence of finite material things is, on this view, dependent upon God's absence rather than His presence, and created things are in essence a species of nonsubstance or nothingness, like shadows that exist only as the result of the obscuring of light. While the full doctrine of *Tzimtzum* is an original contribution of the Lurianic Kabbalah, we find the principle that creation involves a darkening, or ignorance, of God's light in a number of Gnostic sources. For example, *The Gospel of Truth* puts forth the view that the world was produced through an anguished ignorance that "thickened like a mist so

---

69. "The Gospel of Truth" (NHC 13, 17, 6–18, 11), quoted in Rudolph, *Gnosis,* p. 83.

70. I am here referring especially to the impact of the concept of the ten *Sefirot* on the Christian Kabbalah, 19th century European esotericism, theosophy and the tarot.

that none could see."[71] Such ignorance exists not only in man, but also within the divinity itself, for it is only a foolish and ignorant demiurge who could have created the world. The view that God must become ignorant of a part of Himself in order to create a world, becomes an esoteric theme in the Lurianic Kabbalah.

According to the Gnostics, even the positive act of emanation is not simply a process of production and enrichment, but is one of impoverishment as well. In Neoplatonic fashion the Gnostics held that as God's light moves away from its center it loses its intensity and substance to the point where matter (and hence evil) emerges as a deficiency rather than fulfillment of God's being.[72] This world, and the demiurge who has created it, exist only because the true God is concealed. Indeed, the very purpose of Gnosos is to escape from this impoverished realm by achieving knowledge of the true light. The parallels to the Kabbalist's *Tzimtzum* should be quite plain.

THE SIN OF SOPHIA

In the symbol of the "Sin of Sophia" we have a Gnostic parallel to the kabbalistic notion of the Breaking of the Vessels. Sophia, as we have already seen, is the final aeon in the Gnostic system, one that serves (like *Malchut/Shekhinah* in the Kabbalah) as the mediator between God and the world. We have also seen that in one version of the Gnostic myth, Sophia creates the demiurge, Yaldobaoth, out of a desire to produce an offspring without divine consent. In another version of this myth, Sophia is unable to contain the light of the primal Anthropos whom she seduces and "she was overfull and bubbling over the left side . . . The power that bubbled over from the Woman, having a trace of light, fell downwards . . . from the Fathers, but by their will retained a trace of light."[73]

As a result of these events, as a result of this "divine tragedy,"[74] Sophia produces an aborted, formless entity, which is the material world. For her own arrogance she is castigated. According to the Sethian myth it is as a result of the catharsis of her own laughter, pain, and tears that the luminous,

---

71. Rudolph, *Gnosis*, p. 77.
72. Filoramo, *A History of Gnosticism*, p. 59, cf. p. 25.
73. Ibid., p. 69.
74. Rudolph, *Gnosis*, p. 66.

corporeal, and liquid substances of the world are created.[75] Sophia's "passion," like the Kabbalist's "Breaking of the Vessels," is repeated throughout the various levels of reality.

In the symbols of an aeon (here Sophia) being unable to contain the divine light of the Primal Man, and of this light bubbling over and falling downward (resulting in the formation of an aborted world), we have important parallels to the Lurianic view that our imperfect universe is the result of the shattering of the *Sefirot*, which occurred when these vessels could no longer contain the divine light of *Adam Kadmon* (Primordial Man).[76]

THE DOCTRINE OF EVIL

The Gnostic theodicy is in several respects quite similar to the theory of evil presented in the Lurianic Kabbalah. While Iranian dualistic tendencies (presumably derived from Zoroastrian sources) are far more prominent in Gnosos than in the Kabbalah,[77] for the Gnostics, as for the later Kabbalists, evil is generally understood as follows: (1) it originates in the very heart of divinity,[78] (2) it results from a cathartic expulsion of spiritual matter, which serves as a scapegoat for the negativity inherent in God,[79] (3) it is a function of the gradual diminishment of God's light that is inherent in the process of creation,[80] and (4) it results from a crisis in the capacity of the vessels of creation (aeons or *Sefirot*) to contain the fullness of the divine light.[81] Further, both Gnosticism and the Kabbalah are in accord that the full redemption of the world can only take place after the spiritual principle of the cosmos has passed through the shadow realm of evil,[82] which in the later Kabbalah Hasidism is known as "descent for the purpose of ascent."

The Gnostics, of course, are well known for their view that this world is

---

75. Filoramo, *A History of Gnosticism*, pp. 74–76.
76. See Chapter Two, and Jacobs, "The Uplifting of the Sparks," for a more detailed description of the Lurianic metaphors.
77. See Rudolph, *Gnosis*, p. 65.
78. Filoramo, *A History of Gnosticism*, p. 56.
79. Ibid., p. 59.
80. Ibid., p. 73.
81. Ibid., p. 89.
82. Ibid., p. 70.

a battleground between the forces of good and evil, represented by divine angelic beings and the evil archons of this world. This image of battleground against evil is repeated in the Zohar and the later Kabbalah in the symbols of the "forces of the other side," "the ten crowns of evil," the wicked Samael, etc.[83] For the Kabbalists, however, the forces of the dark side are ultimately instruments of the one true God, a position that is prompted by the Kabbalah's commitment to monism. Gnostic and kabbalistic theodicies also differ insofar as the Gnostics understood the entire cosmos to be evil. While the Kabbalists held the created world to be, from one perspective, an embodiment of evil (inasmuch as it results from the *Tzimtzum* or negation of God), they dialectically also conceived of creation as the ultimate Good. This is because in being an obstacle to Godliness the world provides an arena for the actualization of the values that exist only *in potentia* in the transcendent God. As we have seen, while the Gnostics yearned for a return of the divine spark to God and a consequent escape from this world, the Kabbalists saw the raising of the sparks as an opportunity to redeem the created world itself. In the Kabbalah the pessimistic symbols of Gnosticism are provided a profoundly optimistic interpretation.

GNOSTIC EXILE

One can hardly expect to discover a precursor to the kabbalistic symbol of *Tikkun ha-Olam*, (the restoration of the world) among the Gnostics. If the world is indeed totally evil, and the goal of mankind is to transcend the cosmos, then the very idea of repairing, restoring, or redeeming the world simply makes no sense. Still, there are certain Gnostic ideas that, when reinterpreted in a kabbalistic context, seem to anticipate the concept of *Tikkun*. In the first place the whole kabbalistic (particularly Lurianic) emphasis upon "redemption from exile" has important Gnostic antecedents. Scholem, of course, is quite correct in his assertion that the theme of exile and redemption is a fundamental Jewish archetype. He argues that the entire Lurianic system, in which holy sparks must be redeemed from a dark world of matter, reflects the Jewish experience of exile after the Inquisition in Spain. However, this view hardly accounts for the presence of an almost identical

---

83. See Tishby and Lachower, *The Wisdom of the Zohar*, Vol. 2, pp. 475–546.

doctrine of the "sparks" in Gnostic literature in the second century. The Gnostics also conceived of themselves as strangers, exiled in this world, and hoped to overcome their exile through a true knowledge of God. In this way, they affirmed, the lost spark would rediscover, and return to, its home. Such a return, such a redemption from exile became a key element in the (much more worldly) kabbalistic conception of *Tikkun*.

OTHER PARALLELS

There are many other points of connection between Gnosticism and the Kabbalah that I can only touch upon briefly here. Throughout the history of religion, for example, "light" has been equated with "good" and "darkness" with "evil," and knowledge of God is spoken of as illumination and enlightenment. The Gnostics, however, went beyond these axiological and epistemological views to create an actual metaphysics of light in which the being of the true God or "self" is equated with the purest of lights and the material world is understood as a degeneration or decay in the essentially luminous substance.[84] In speaking of the *Or Ein-Sof*, the light of the infinite God, the Kabbalists followed the Gnostics in the view that the one substance of the world is luminous. However, like Plato, they insisted that this metaphysical light is only metaphorically related to the light of the sun. The world, according to the Kabbalah, results from a series of curtains or impediments to the divine light's emanation or effulgence, a view that, as we have seen, is similar to the Gnostic view of creation as a degeneration of divine light.

Another important symbol found in both Gnosticism and the Kabbalah is the "celestial counterpart," a divine, true self, which has its roots in both the individual and God. This self, who in effect runs counter to the individual's conscious, empirical ego, is regarded as the individual's true spiritual guide. Often referred to simply as "the planter," or "helper," the spiritual guide addresses itself to man's inner spark or true soul in saying: "You are my counterpart. I shall cause you to ascend and keep you safe in my garment."[85] The Kabbalists refer to this guide as the individual's *Tzelem*, or image, connecting it with the "image" in Genesis I:26–7, through which man is said to resemble God. For both the Gnostics and the Kabbalists this divine self is

84. Filoramo, *A History of Gnosticism*, pp. 44–46.
85. Rudolph, *Gnosis*, p. 177.

equated with the heavenly "spark" and is said to descend from on high to raise the self from its preoccupation with false, mundane affairs.

There are a number of parallels between the Gnostic and kabbalistic views of the savior or Messiah. For example, they share the view that the savior does not come so much to unite man with God, as to reunify man with himself.[86] This conception of the savior in psychological terms is present in the Hasidic view that the rebbe or tzaddik understands the roots of each man's soul and can prescribe each man a particular *Tikkun* or restorative act that will reunite him with his true self.[87]

MODERN GNOSTICISM

Our own time has seen a considerable revival of interest in Gnosticism. Once thought to simply be a second-century heretical Christian sect, Gnosticism in this century has been transformed into a precursor not only of depth psychology but of the entire alienated condition of twentieth-century man.[88]

Apart from Jung, whose status as a "modern Gnostic" has been hotly debated, contemporary scholars have traced Gnostic influences in the philosophies of German Idealism and the existentialists, most notably Martin Heidegger. In literature, representatives of the romantic tradition, including Blake, Melville, and Yeats have been shown to exhibit Gnostic characteristics. Among modern authors, Kafka, Faulkner, and most profoundly Herman Hesse have either implicitly or explicitly explored Gnostic themes. Madame Blavatsky claimed a Gnostic pedigree for her "occult movement" and most esoteric movements have been influenced by this view (as well as by an interest in the "Kabbalah") since her time.

A number of contemporary authors have been quite explicit in their exploration of Gnostic themes. These include the literary critic Harold Bloom, the philosopher Hans Jonas, the political theorist Eric Voegelin, the novelists Lawrence Durrell and Jack Kerouac, and the poet Allen Ginsberg. Gnostic themes have also found their way into science fiction in recent years.

---

86. Filoramo, *A History of Gnosticism*, p. 166.

87. Perhaps such a psychological view of the savior can help us understand how some contemporary Hasidim view their own living (or in the case of Lubavitch, recently deceased) rebbe as the biblically prophesized messiah.

88. See Richard Smith, "The Modern Relevance of Gnosticism," Robinson, *The Nag Hammadi Library*, pp. 532–549, and Filoramo, *A History of Gnosticism*, xi–xix.

Nicholas Roeg's film *The Man Who Fell to Earth* and the *Star Wars* trilogy are but two of the more obvious examples.

Because of the close relationship between Gnosticism and the Kabbalah any attempt to envision a "modern Kabbalah" must, of course, take into account these and other contemporary Gnostic expressions. As this work is only propaedeutic for this task, a detailed exploration of such contemporary Gnostics and Kabbalists must await another day.

6

Hegel and The Kabbalah

The relationship between the Kabbalah and the philosophy of Hegel is more complex than one might imagine. The reason for this is that our own understanding of the Kabbalah is, for better or worse, unavoidably mediated through the categories of Hegel's philosophy. As Susan Handelman has pointed out, the very terms through which Scholem and subsequent writers on the Kabbalah have framed their discussions have their origins in German Idealism.[1] This is not only because Scholem himself was steeped in such an intellectual milieu but because *any* contemporary discussion of the "Absolute," the "spiritual and the material," the "infinite and finite," and man's relationship to "God" cannot help but be framed in terms that are heavily influenced by Hegel. This fact, I might add, is independent of the relative esteem that is accorded to Hegelian thought. As has often been observed, Kierkegaard despised Hegel, but in the end could not escape from the Hegelian dialectic. And so it is with us, having read the existentialists and Freud, Marx, the deconstructionists, and Scholem, each of whom are deeply influenced by Hegelian thought: we cannot help but approach our subject matter with Hegel somewhere in mind.

---

1. Susan Handelman, *Fragments of Redemption: Jewish Thought and Literary Theory in Benjamin, Scholem and Levinas* (Bloomington and Indianapolis: Indiana University Press, 1991), p. 93.

This being said, it remains that there is undoubtedly a close natural affinity between the Kabbalah and Hegelian philosophy. Hegel's whole theory of the Absolute and its realization in a finite world of conflict and contradiction, his views on negation, and the dialectic itself, are all anticipated in the kabbalistic, particularly the Lurianic, symbols. As will become plain in the following pages, much of Hegel's philosophy can be profitably understood as a rational articulation of the very immanent (this-worldly) mysticism that is given symbolic expression in the Kabbalah of Isaac Luria. Indeed, part of Hegel's perennial appeal stems from just this fact: that Hegel put into rational discourse a mystical vision of the world that had hitherto been expressed only in symbols. As such, he is the mystics' philosopher par excellence, and his rational mysticism will naturally have appeal to all those who by disposition incline toward a mystical view of the cosmos. That his philosophy is most closely related to the immanent mysticism of the Lurianic variety and its view that man completes God through *Tikkun ha-Olam*, the Restoration of *this World*, should become clear as we proceed.

That Hegel was himself influenced by kabbalistic ideas is somewhat harder to prove. Hegel uses the Hebrew term *Adam Kadmon* to refer to the "archetype of humanity,"[2] and at one point refers to the hypostasis of divine wisdom as "Chokma."[3] He also makes passing reference to the doctrine of the *Sefirot*, where in a discussion of the Gnostic doctrine of God, he states that nothing of the deity's essence can be imparted "except through the medium of the sephiroth."[4] However, while Hegel is clearly familiar with Gnosticism, there is little else to suggest direct knowledge of the Kabbalah. Instead, kabbalistic ideas seem to have reached him indirectly. For example, Hegel's predecessor and early *maestro*, Friedrich Schelling, was himself of a mystical bent and was influenced by the Christian Kabbalah, the Swabian pietists, and such thinkers as Jakob Boehme, each of whom had transmitted kabbalistic insights into the Christian intellectual world. Boehme (1575–1624), in particular, seems to have been influenced by zoharic and other kabbalistic sources in his doctrine of the hidden, ineffable Absolute, who contracts himself, calls forth finite beings, and thereby becomes self-conscious and complete. Hegel made numerous references to Boehme (in

---

2. G. W. F. Hegel, *Lectures on the Philosophy of Religion*, ed. Peter C. Hodgson. (Berkeley: University of California Press, 1985), pp. 99, 288.

3. Ibid., p. 84.

4. Ibid.

one he attributes the term *Adam Kadmon* to him[5]) and several recent commentators have argued that Boehme provides much of the foundation for Hegel's theology.[6] The influence of the Kabbalah on German Idealism is a fascinating topic that is beyond the scope of this work. Here I wish only to pursue a number of morphological parallels between these two great intellectual movements, again in the hope that such comparative study can shed further light on the Kabbalah itself. My purpose, in part, is to sow the seeds for future thought by stimulating dialogue between Jewish mysticism and the Western idealist tradition.

THE LOGICAL STRUCTURE OF
THE LURIANIC MYTHS

The Kabbalah, evolving as it did over several centuries, is not a single, unified body of theory and symbols. However, one can, as we will see, find anticipations of dialectical, Hegelian thinking in such early Kabbalists as Azriel of Gerona,[7] in the Zohar, and among the later interpreters of the Kabbalah, the Hasidim.[8] However, the most striking parallels are to be found in the late sixteenth-century Kabbalah of Isaac Luria and his disciples.

If we examine the "logical" structure of the Lurianic myth we discover that its essential elements are as follows:

(1) An original, all-inclusive source of being and energy (*Ein-Sof*)
(2) contracts and conceals itself from itself (*Tzimtzum*), and
(3) becomes alienated in a seemingly independent, yet illusory realm.
(4) The source of being thereby embodies itself in an abstract humanity (*Adam Kadmon*),
(5) who is composed of and himself emanates structures of ideas and values (the *Sefirot*).

---

5. Ibid.

6. See Cyril O'Regan, *The Heterodox Hegel* (Albany: State University of New York Press, 1994).

7. See Azriel of Gerona, "Explanation of the Ten *Sefirot*," in Dan, *The Early Kabbalah*, pp. 89–96. On Azriel see Scholem, *Origins of The Kabbalah* pp. 370–378.

8. An interesting description of the theory of the Absolute in Chabad Hasidism that shows many parallels to Hegelian thought can be found in Elior, *The Paradoxical Ascent to God*. See also, Elior, "Chabad: The Comtemplative Ascent to God."

(6) These structures are inherently unstable and break apart (*Shevirat ha Kelim*),

(7) causing a further alienation of the divine spirit in a negative "counterworld" (*Kelippot, Sitra Achra*)

(8) and a rending apart of opposites (symbolized by male and female) that had hitherto been joined.

(9) This divine light undergoes a conjugal and then developmental process (the *Partzufim*) and is ultimately returned to its source,

(10) where it is reorganized and restored, resulting in the fulfillment and actualization of the original, all-inclusive being (*Tikkun ha-Olam*).

As I will show in this chapter and the next, this structure is essentially repeated by Hegel in the nineteenth century (and again by Freud in the twentieth). It is a "basic" metaphor, not only in the sense that it purports to explain the entire cosmos and man's place within it, but because it serves as the basis for a number of important theories in recent Western intellectual history.

THE HEGELIAN PROJECT

While Hegelian ideas are woven into the very fabric of contemporary thought, it is paradoxically the case that specific familiarity with Hegel's system is almost completely lacking outside (and sometimes even within) university departments of philosophy. It is unfortunate that it is also seriously lacking among university-educated students of Jewish mysticism. As it is my conviction that any in-depth contemporary interpretation of the Kabbalah must involve a basic familiarity with the Hegelian system, I will attempt, in the span of the following pages, to provide the reader with the barest outline of the Hegelian project.[9]

---

9. Hegel's philosophy is difficult, complex, and subject to a variety of interpretations. Recent scholars (Dieter Henrich, Robert Solomon) have offered decidedly nonmetaphysical interpretations of Hegel that are somewhat less amenable to comparison with the mysticism of the Kabbalah. In what follows I provide a more traditional, metaphysical perspective on Hegel's philosophy. As an introduction to Hegel the reader is referred to J. N. Findlay, *Hegel: A Re-examination* (New York: Oxford University Press, 1958); Charles Taylor, *Hegel* (Cambridge: Cambridge

Hegel conceived philosophy as providing a *rational* explanation for the cosmos, as answering the question of "Why does the world exist?" Hegel's answer to this question (and his entire system is but the development of this answer) is that the world exists as an arena for the fullest possible realization of Reason, Mind, or Spirit. For Hegel, Reason, is the one self-sufficient, independent principle that can be posited as the foundation of the world. In short, it is the one principle that can serve as its own explanation. (If we ask for the reason for "reason" we can only answer reason itself, for the very question presumes a reasonable response.) Reason is both the beginning and end of the world's development. Philosophy is both a rational explanation of the development of the "World-Spirit," and, because philosophy is the supreme rational expression, it is at the same time the ultimate manifestation of the World-Spirit itself.

For Hegel, then, the entire purpose and direction of the universe is the realization of knowledge, consciousness, or mind. This realization is itself a self-realization. Like Aristotle's "self-thinking thought," Hegel's Absolute is conceived of as Reason, or the "Idea" coming to know itself. Indeed, according to Hegel, the natural world, and, ultimately, mankind, exists precisely in order that Reason can have a mirror through which it comes to know itself. By the "Idea," Hegel meant nothing less than the complete rational order of the cosmos, which "prior" to its self-realization in man simply informs objects without any self-awareness. The development of the natural world, the progress of human history, and, particularly, the history of philosophy, is nothing but the march of Reason toward its own self-realization.

The Absolute, according to Hegel, progresses through three distinct but ultimately interrelated stages, "Logic," "Nature," and "Spirit." In Logic, the rational order or Idea exists in the abstract, separate from any determinate content (like the abstract number "seven," not otherwise determined or specified). In Nature, the idea becomes instantiated in a material, natural world ("seven apples," for example). Finally, in the realm of Spirit, the Idea becomes known and understood (man's consciousness in contemplating, for example, the difference between an abstract number and its instantiation).

According to Hegel, the abstract Idea, which has become estranged from itself, "alienated" or "negated" in Nature, "returns" to itself in the realm of Spirit (where man contemplates it and knows it in its abstract purity once more). Upon its return, however, the Idea is more complete than it had been in the realm of Logic alone, for now it has become conscious of itself. This movement from Logic to Nature and finally to Spirit and self-awareness, is spoken of by Hegel as the "negation of the negation." The Idea alienates or negates itself in Nature, which is in turn negated by consciousness or Spirit, which returns to the Idea. This movement of double negation is, for Hegel, the Absolute itself, and, indeed, the purpose of the entire cosmos.

The parallels to the Kabbalah should already begin to be apparent, for the Kabbalist's *Ein-Sof*, itself frequently identified with *Chochmah* or Reason, is said to alienate itself in a world of nature, exile, and evil, only to return to itself, in a more complete, perfected, and self-aware state with the advent of *Tikkun*. What's more, as for Hegel, the very process through which this divine alienation is overcome essentially involves the agency of man. Hegel's negations, the first creating the transition from Logic to Nature and the second from Nature to Spirit, have their precursors and parallels in the kabbalistic notions of *Tzimtzum* and *Shevirah*, the first of which negates an abstract ("logical") *Ein-Sof* in order to create a ("natural") world; and the second of which negates that world in order to provide the arena for a ("spiritual") restoration and return to *Ein-Sof* through man.

For Hegel, the movement from Idea to Nature to self-conscious Spirit is in no ways an arbitrary or contingent matter. Rather, it is part of the very nature, essence, and meaning of the Idea that it should complete itself in the process Hegel describes. Nor does this process necessarily occur in time. While the development of the Absolute does indeed have temporal manifestations (and Hegel goes to great pains to reveal these both in his philosophy of history and history of philosophy) it is, like all "logical" or conceptual progressions, essentially atemporal. For Hegel, the triple movement from Logic to Nature to Spirit is present in any and every idea, proposition, natural event, and act of consciousness whatsoever. For whenever we consider any idea (for example, the number "three") it is rationally part of the idea's essence that it be instantiated in Nature (e.g., as three apples, three stones, three oceans, etc.) and further, that it be known to consciousness or Spirit (as, e.g., different from five, as applying to certain calculations, etc.). For Hegel, it is only in the abstract that we can consider the idea of three apart from any instantiation in the objects of nature, and only hypothetically that we can entertain this or any idea apart from its presentation to a mind. The idea of "three," as it were, "rationally" passes over from Logic to Nature, and then "returns to itself" through a process whereby the sensuous presentation of three apples, stones, etc., moves the mind to abstractly contemplate "threeness" in self-conscious knowledge. The "negation of the negation," the movement from Logic to Nature to Spirit, is present in any and all of our cognitive acts, and since these acts are, according to Hegel's Idealism, coextensive with the cosmos, such movement is written into the very nature of the world itself.

Where previous philosophers had been content simply to note the rational relationships among universals, particulars, and knowledge, Hegel had both the insight and audacity to posit these relationships as illustrative of the fundamental principle or dynamic of the universe. Hegel even goes so far as to reinterpret the particularization of a universal God in the Christian savior, and the consequent knowledge of God brought to mankind, as the supreme historical manifestation of this dynamic.[10] That Hegel could so readily posit such a theological relationship helps us to understand the Christian interest in the Kabbalah, for the Kabbalists also posit a three-phased dynamic process in which a highly abstract deity (*Ein-Sof*) becomes manifest in a divinely conceived man (*Adam Kadmon*) whose fall (the Breaking of the Vessels) provides humanity with an opportunity to draw near to God. Where Hegel differed from the Kabbalists, however, is in his radical insistence that the cosmological processes he described were the necessary manifestations and development of Reason, and not simply mystical insights into the theosophical realm.

For Hegel, the movement from universal to particular, to knowledge of the universal in the particular, is a fundamental process of reason, a process that is not only disclosed in our presumably static contemplation of an idea or object, but that is also present in the rhythms of the natural world, and throughout human history, literature, the arts, and philosophy. It is part of the very essence of the Absolute in its identity as Reason, to become ever more conceptually rich, ever more manifest in nature, and ever more self-aware, the latter through its being cognized by mankind. Man's consciousness is, for Hegel, the self-consciousness of Reason itself, a Reason that could neither be complete nor fully rational without such self-awareness. As we have seen, it is a very similar movement toward self-awareness and identity that drives the Kabbalist's *Ein-Sof* to manifest itself in man.

---

10. See O'Regan, *The Heterodox Hegel.*

According to Hegel, it is equally true to say that Logic, Nature, and Mind (or Spirit) is the Absolute: for each of these realms contains each of the others implicit within itself, and as such encompasses an integrated whole that is the sum total and purpose of all reality. Man, particularly in his aspect of mind, expressed in art, religion, politics, society, history, and philosophy, is himself the Absolute as well, as each of these cultural projects is the Idea developing and reaching for self-conscious expression. Hegel, therefore provides us with a philosophical interpretation of the kabbalistic dicta that man creates or completes God,[11] and that "the beginning" (*Ein-Sof*) "is wedged in the end" (mankind) and vice versa.

Hegel's dynamic understanding of the notions of universal, particular, and knowledge gives rise to his famous dialectic: a species of, or perspective upon, reasoning in which notions are discovered to pass over into other notions, particularly their opposites, which they (paradoxically) imply. In dialectic this "passing over" frequently gives rise to a third term, which then serves as a basis for a new dialectical movement, and so on. Thus, in philosophy, we may come to realize that the universal is implicit in the particular and vice versa. Another way of putting this is that the universal, when it is fully contemplated and understood, "passes over" into the particular (and vice versa). For Hegel, this movement from universal to particular and back again provides insight into both creation and knowledge. This is because creation is nothing but the particular *instantiation* of a (universal) idea, and knowledge the *comprehension* of a universal idea in a particular object or instance.

Similarly, according to Hegel, "non-being" is implicit in the notion of "being" and "being" in the notion of "nothingness"; the former because the notion of pure being, devoid of all determination, is empty and hence "nothing," and the latter because nothingness negates, limits, and defines some "thing," and this limitation is itself a positive, even "creative," force. The transition from nothingness to being and vice versa gives rise to a third notion, becoming, which in turn serves as a basic concept in the structure of a new dialectical process.

It is precisely in this manner that Hegel's dialectic proceeds within the realm of Logic: Hegel attempts to show that an entire inventory of ideas and

---

11. Zohar III, 113a. Sperling and Simon, *The Zohar*, Vol. 5, p. 153. For a discussion of this concept see Idel, *Kabbalah: New Perspectives*, pp. 187–188.

categories, large and rich enough to describe all possible worlds, can thus be derived from what is implicit in the simplest of notions. Though it is no longer fashionable among Hegel commentators to interpret Hegel in this way,[12] Hegel's project was, in effect, to achieve in the realm of philosophy something akin to what Bertrand Russell and Alfred North Whitehead were to attempt in the realm of mathematics, i.e., to derive all that is known from the simplest of logical principles. Hegel sought to rationally derive the entire ideational universe from any given single notion, holding that it was, in fact, irrelevant where he began, because the Idea, i.e., all ideas, are implicit in any given one. Further, as we have seen, Hegel endeavored to show that ideas, i.e., Logic, must out of rational necessity pass over into Nature and finally into Spirit, holding that the natural world, mankind, and human culture can, at least in a general way, be "deduced" (and by this Hegel means "dialectically inferred") from such abstract "logical" notions as being, non-being, and becoming, and, ultimately, from the very notion of Reason itself.

For Hegel, the order of *thought* is identical to the order of *things*, but also the order of thought is both the beginning of the cosmos and its end, such order achieving self-conscious perspicuity in Hegel's own philosophy. This last proposition leaves Hegel open to the charge that on his own view, the entire cosmos, with its countless spiral galaxies and nebula, exists for no other reason than to become self-aware through Hegelian philosophy, a charge, I suppose that can be levied against any philosophy that identifies the Absolute with Reason.

This, in short,[13] is the Hegelian project in philosophy. In the following pages I will explore the points of contact between this philosophy and the Kabbalah, and examine the extent to which the Kabbalah, particularly the Lurianic Kabbalah, can be profitably understood from a Hegelian point of view. In addition I will demonstrate how Hegelian modes of thought can assist us in clarifying certain key kabbalistic symbols and ideas, in particular,

---

12. Among the older commentators Stace (op. cit.) defends the view that Hegel indeed thought to deduce at least the basic structure of the world. Robert Solomon argues against this point of view. See Solomon, *In The Spirit of Hegel*.

13. Hegelian philosophy cannot, of course, be encapsulated in such a brief review. The account given here accords with Hegel's systematic presentation in his *Encyclopedia of the Philosophical Sciences*, but does not capture the epistemoplogical (and psychological) philosophy of *The Phenomenology of Spirit*. Here I have summarized only that aspect of Hegelian thought which is most readily assimilable to theology.

the kabbalistic notion that *Ein-Sof* and the *Sefirot* are *haachdut hashawah*, an indistinguishable unity of opposites. As we shall see, the similarities between the Kabbalah and Hegel run very deep. Yet we will also see that a full understanding of such Lurianic notions as *Ein-Sof, Tzimtzum, Shevirah, ha-Olamot, Partzufim,* and *Tikkun* will lead us dialectically, beyond Hegel, into those twentieth-century thinkers, like Freud and Jung, who moved the dialectic beyond conscious reason in the direction of an essential unconsciousness.

HEGEL AND LURIA

We can organize our thinking about Hegel and the Kabbalah in relation to the "logical structure" of the basic metaphor discussed above:

(1) Hegel, like the Kabbalists, begins with an infinite, all-inclusive, Absolute being. Hegel's "Absolute" is analogous to the Kabbalist's Infinite, *Ein-Sof.*

(2) The Absolute, which Hegel conceives of as "Reason" (in a manner that parallels the Kabbalist's identification of *Ein-Sof* with Thought or Wisdom), is logically compelled to contract or alienate itself into the concrete particulars of a created world. This "self-alienation of the Absolute Spirit" is a direct parallel to the Kabbalist's *Tzimtzum,* the concealment and contraction of *Ein-Sof.* According to Hegel this negation or alienation is a logically necessary event, for the Absolute Idea, indeed any idea, can only fulfill itself by becoming particular and concrete. (The concepts of "horse" or "kindness," for example, are empty and abstract without actual horses and real acts of kindness.)

(3) Thus, as for the Kabbalist's *Ein-Sof,* Hegel's Absolute only *becomes itself* by limiting, negating, and alienating itself in an independent, created world. However, according to both Hegel and Luria this world is an illusion, for while it appears to have an existence independent of the "All," it is in reality simply an aspect, indeed a concealed aspect, of the Absolute itself.

(4) For Hegel, the Absolute negates itself into a realm of Nature, but begins the return to itself through the formation, within nature, of the World-Spirit, which is embodied in the spirit of man. Hegel's World-Spirit is analogous to the Kabbalist's Primordial Man.

(5) Like the Kabbalist's Primordial Man (*Adam Kadmon*), Hegel's World-Spirit creates, and, is, in effect, "composed of," the sum total of ideas and values that define mankind. Indeed, for Hegel, mankind's progress in history, philosophy, religion, ethics, and the arts marks the development of the Absolute in history, much as the Kabbalist's *Sefirot*, embodied in Primordial Man (and which also manifest cognitive, spiritual, ethical, and aesthetic values) mark the development of *Ein-Sof* in the world.

(6) Man's original values, ideas, and institutions, however, are, according to Hegel, insufficient to contain the full breadth of the Absolute, and through a dialectical process these structures break down and must be reorganized into ever-widening schemas that transcend and yet incorporate the original broken ideas. Hegel's discussion of the dialectic as a "breaking asunder" of ideas and values parallels the Lurianic notion of the *Shevirah*, the Breaking of the Vessels.

(7) Hegel refers to the broken state as the "Understanding," but for Hegel, the Understanding is indeed alienated and limited in its comprehension of the world. This is the Hegelian equivalent to the Kabbalist's alienation and exile.

(8) In the Understanding, the oppositions of this world (e.g., between good and evil, truth and error, being and nonbeing, etc.) are rent apart and their mutual interdependence goes completely unrecognized. This is Hegel's rational equivalent to the Lurianic division within *Ein-Sof* after the Breaking of the Vessels.

(9) For Hegel, the dialectic proceeds through all forms of thought, life, and historical expression, expanding itself into greater and deeper possibilities and antinomies, even into realms (analogous to the Lurianic *Sitra Achra*) that are regarded as negative and evil.

(10) It is only through mankind's creative efforts in the arts, religion, and the institutions of culture and the state that the broken, alienated condition is overcome and the Absolute can finally realize its essence and be complete. It is most fully through "speculative reason," manifest in the philosophy of Hegel itself, that the Absolute Idea, having alienated itself into a realm of Nature, can now, through the vehicle of mankind, develop, return and perfect itself in the union of Logic, Nature, and Spirit. In "Speculative Reason" the oppositions that had been broken apart

by the Understanding are rejoined and are seen to be mutually dependent conceptions. This, of course, is Hegel's equivalent to the Kabbalist's *Tikkun*. The Absolute that, of necessity, was exiled and alienated has now been redeemed and fulfilled.

RATIONAL MYSTICISM

Hegel's thought, as we have seen, can be characterized as an attempt to apply philosophical reason to the ideas and symbols of mysticism. Hegel himself tells us, "Speculative truth (the truth Hegel holds in the highest regard) . . . means very much the same as what, in special connection with religious experience and doctrines, used to be called Mysticism." Further, he affirms that ". . . the reason-world may be equally styled mystical—not however because thought cannot both reach and comprehend it, but merely because it lies beyond the compass of (the one-sided, linear thinking of) the understanding."[14] For Hegel, mysticism involves a form of thought and experience that allows for the possibility of contradictory and paradoxical truths. Hegel conceives of his dialectical logic as a means of accommodating contradiction, antinomy and paradox within philosophy. Hegel contrasts the "Understanding," which adheres slavishly to the law of noncontradiction, with true Reason, which acknowledges that the truth of any given proposition is dependent upon its contrary being embedded within it. Indeed, Hegel tells us, "that the task of Reason is to transcend the rigidity of the Understanding."[15] Mysticism had hitherto been the one form of thought to recognize the principle of *coincidentia oppositorum*, complementarity and mutual dependence of opposites. Hegel envisions a new logic that will do on the level of reason what mysticism does on the level of experience.

Hegel's intent in rationalizing mysticism was by no means an effort at despiritualization. Indeed, in the *Phenomenology of Spirit*, Hegel bemoans the loss of spirituality among his contemporaries:

Time was when man had a heaven, decked and fitted out with endless wealth of thought and pictures . . . The mind's gaze had to be directed under compulsion to what is earthly . . . Now we have apparently the

---

14. William Wallace, trans., *Hegel's Logic*, (Oxford: Clarendon Press, 1975), *Zuzatz*, Par. 82, pp. 120–121.
15. William Wallace, trans., *Hegel's Logic*, *Zuzatz*, Par 32.

opposite of all this; man's mind and interest are so deeply rooted in the earthly that we require a like power to have them raised above that level. His spirit shows such poverty of nature that it seems to long for the mere pitiful feeling of the divine in the abstract, and to get refreshment from that, like a wanderer in the desert craving for the merest mouthful of water. By the little which can thus satisfy the needs of the human spirit we can measure the extent of its loss.[16]

Hegel's idealism is designed to provide a rational basis for the mystical insight that the entire cosmos is reflected in the mind and spirit of man. His "Logic" is designed to provide a rational route to such mystical insights as the equivalence of being and nothingness, and of the identity of God and the consciousness of humanity.

THE ABSOLUTE

Hegel shares with the mystical traditions of both the Orient and the West a starting (and end) point in an infinite, all-encompassing, and immanent "Absolute." Like the Hindu's Brahman-Atman, Hegel's Absolute is the substance of the cosmos; it inheres in and informs all things, from the movements of the stars to the hearts of men; and like the Kabbalist's *Ein-Sof*, the Hegelian Absolute is said to realize itself in the historical development of mankind. Like *Ein-Sof*, Hegel's Absolute is both the cause and significance of all things, and the answer to humanity's ultimate questions regarding the origins of the world and the meaning of human life. Also like *Ein-Sof*, the Hegelian Absolute is only imperfectly understood via the concept of a personal God.

Like the Kabbalists, Hegel understands the Absolute as evolving through distinct phases, which ultimately result in the creation of the world and man. Indeed, Hegel's description of at least the early stages of divine evolution closely echoes the views of the theosophical Kabbalah. In his *Lectures on the Philosophy of Religion*, Hegel recognizes a moment in the history of the deity in which it is completely unknown.[17] In this moment, the divine "is the abstract element that is expressed as the abyss, the depth (i.e.

---

16. Hegel, *Phenomenology of Spirit*, translated and quoted in frontispiece of Weiss, *Hegel: The Essential Writings*.
17. Hegel, *Lectures on the Philosophy of Religion*, p. 196.

precisely what is still empty), the inexpressible, the inconceivable, that which is beyond all concepts . . ."[18] Hegel tells that this idea is prominent in the history of religious speculation, noting that "Philo, a Jewish Platonist, defines God as the ov, as what has being, in other words the hidden God who is unknowable, uncommunicative, inconceivable."[19] Hegel informs us that this moment in divine evolution is also spoken of as "the eternal one whose dwelling is in the inexpressible heights, and who is exalted above all contact."

If Hegel's first moment or definition of God is very similar to the Kabbalists' first *Sefirah*, *Keter* or *Ayin* (Nothingness), his second definition echoes the Kabbalists' second *Sefirah*, *Chokhmah* (Wisdom). Here the deity, for Hegel, begins to take a form akin to the Kabbalists' *Adam Kadmon* (Primordial Man). Hegel affirms:

> The second definition of God, however, as "Logos" is "that which reveals itself, the [first] mover, which posits differentiation." It is called "the Son of God, Sophia, Wisdom, the archetype of humanity, the First Man, the eternal one, heavenly revelation of the godhead, thinking, effective power."[20]

Further:

> The second moment, other being, the action of determining . . . rationally determinative activity, or precisely the word . . . also defined as σοφια, wisdom, the original and wholly pure human being . . . For this reason it has been defined as the archetype of humanity, Adam Kadmon, the only-begotten. This is not something contingent but rather an eternal activity which does not happen only at one time.[21]

Hegel holds that the third moment or definition of the Absolute is "community," for it is only in the community, in the institutions of the State, art, religion, and philosophy, that the Absolute can be self-reflectively articulated and understood. Here again, his view parallels that of the Kabbalists, who hold that it is the community of Israel (*Knesseth Yisrael*)[22]

---

18. Ibid., p. 288.
19. Ibid., pp. 196–197.
20. Ibid., p. 197.
21. Ibid., p. 288.
22. Which they identify with the tenth *Sefirah*, the *Shekhinah*.

that is able to restore the broken vessels and thereby perfect both the world and God.

REASON AS THE WORLD'S FOUNDATION

In Hegel we see a tendency to identify the Absolute with the "second moment" in the development of the divine: Wisdom, "rationally determinative activity" or *reason* itself. For Hegel, Reason, is conceptualized as a primal force that creates and lends significance to all things:

> Reason appears here as the fluent universal substance, as unchangeable simple thinghood which yet breaks up into many entirely independent beings, just as light bursts asunder into stars as innumerable luminous points, each giving light on its own account, and whose absolute self-existence is dissolved . . . within the simple independent substance.[23]

Hegel's image here is reminiscent of the Kabbalist's notion of the light of the infinite God, the *Or Ein-Sof*, breaking asunder into the multifarious objects of our world. As we have seen, like Hegel, certain Kabbalists identified this light with Thought or Wisdom (*Chochmah*) and understood Reason as the motive force of God and the world.

It will be instructive to examine Hegel's claim to ground his notion of the Absolute as Reason in philosophical terms. Like the Greeks, Hegel conceived the foundation of the world as a universal idea; but unlike Plato, who identified this idea with the universal Good, or Aristotle, who identified God with the "Active Intellect," i.e., thought thinking itself, Hegel was intent to arrive at an absolute that is completely nonarbitrary, nondetermined, and independent. While a first principle like the Platonic Idea of the Good, is not, according to Hegel, arbitrary and dependent in the manner of ordinary things of sense, it is arbitrary and dependent in the sense that one

---

23. G. W. F. Hegel, *The Phenomenology of Mind*, trans. J. B. Baille (New York: Macmillan, 1931), p. 376; reprinted in Weiss, *Hegel: The Essential Writings*, p. 81. Hegel's analogy here recalls the kabbalistic (and alchemical) notion that *Adam Kadmon*, the Primordial Man or original soul, has been torn asunder into a number of luminous scintillae or sparks, each of which informs a particular human soul, yet each of which also strive to be reunited with each other in the great, divine light.

can ask "Why the good?" and to answer this question one must invoke something other than goodness itself.

The world, according to Hegel, is not explained when we attempt to demonstrate that it is an effect following from some cause. This is because for any causal entity we posit as the world's foundation we can ask for *its* cause and so on *ad infinitum*. The world is only explained when we show it to be a conclusion that follows from a special sort of premise. This premise cannot, as we have already indicated, be an arbitrary axiom, but must rather be a principle that is not only self-evident but also completely self-determined. Such a principle cannot be found in the Eleatics' "Being" or even in the Cartesian "cogito," but can only, according to Hegel, be found in Reason itself. Reason is indeed the only principle that, on Hegel's view, can *serve as its own foundation*. If we ask for the "reason" of any object, notion, or event (other than "reason") we will always be led to another thing or principle, but if we ask "What is the reason of reason?" we can only appeal to "reason itself," for any answer we give must assume the possibility of providing a rational explanation. Reason, according to Hegel, is not only the one self-determined first principle in philosophy, it is also the ultimate explanation from which all other philosophical explanations are derived.

In this light we should recall that the Kabbalists regarded the essence of the *Sefirot* to be "Questions." According to the Zohar, the *Sefirah Binah* represents the primal "Who?" (*Mi* in Hebrew). The *Sefirah Malchut*, which is at the end of the emanative process, and which can therefore prompt a contemplation of the cosmos as a whole, is called "What?" (*Mah*). The Zohar informs us that this "What?" pertains to "these" (*eleh*) *Sefirot*, and when the letters comprising the Hebrew terms for "What are these?" (*Mah Eleh*) are rearranged we arrive at "Elohim," the revealed God of the bible.[24] In short, without their ever having been answered, a set of questions leads us to the creator God.

Like the Kabbalists, Hegel, as it were, derives the being of the world from the very act of asking "Why?"[25] For Hegel, this is because the very asking of questions implies the possibility of a rational answer. According to Hegel, "Reason as a whole, the entire principle of rationality"[26] is the ultimate foundation of the world. The Hegelian system, in its most grandiose

---

24. Tishby and Lachower, *The Wisdom of the Zohar*, Vol. 1, p. 294–295.
25. Stace, *The Philosophy of Hegel*, pp. 55–58.
26. Ibid., p. 58.

pretensions, is designed to deduce the categories of being, and ultimately their instantiation in concrete existence, from this initial self-sufficient principle. In effect, Hegel seeks to deduce the world from a question, or more precisely, from the fact that we ask a question of it. In effect the dialectic is the such *questioning* operating both in the mind of man and in the development of the world. Again, like the Kabbalists, who held that each of the *Sefirot* are contained in and derivable from each other, Hegel held that each of the categories (being, nothingness, becoming, substance, cause, etc.) are derivable from each of the others in such a manner that the entire universe is a dialectically ordered and connected whole.

Commentators differ in their assessment of the degree to which Hegel held that the material world is deducible from the Absolute Idea, and as to what role matter, contingency, etc., have in the Hegelian system. For our purposes it is sufficient that for Hegel the universe is grounded in Reason, and that its basic structure in some sense follows "logically" from this principle. In a sense, it does not matter where in the cosmic order we begin, for wherever we begin, Reason, dialectically weaving its way into and beyond all notions and their contradictions, will be seen as the *principle of creation.* In the *Logic,* Hegel commences with Being, and, through his procedure of dialectical inference, proceeds, as we have already seen, to demonstrate that Being implies "Nothingness," that the two together imply "Becoming," that Becoming implies "Cause," which implies "Substance," etc. The entire deduction makes its way through "Nature," which itself culminates in Man as a rational creature. It then moves on to philosophy, and hence back to the point where it had commenced. The entire chain, including all of the phenomena of the natural world, is, according to Hegel, simply the logical spelling out of Absolute Reason as the foundation of all.

We have seen that a similar dialectic is at work in the Kabbalist's understanding of *Ein-Sof. Ein-Sof* is not simply the source of all being and emanation, but, properly speaking, is the beginning, middle, and end of the entire kabbalistic system, including *Adam Kadmon,* the *Sefirot,* the emanation of the worlds, their shattering in the *Shevirah,* and restoration in *Tikkun ha-Olam* through the ethical deeds of man. *Ein-Sof* encompasses this entire circular dynamic, which like the Hegelian dialectic involves an outward movement into an imperfect, contradictory world, and a return to back to the "Absolute Self." Indeed it is this very evolution and development that makes *Ein-Sof* precisely what it is: the infinite, complete, and perfect being, literally "without end." *Ein-Sof*'s development is not a causal one, but is, particularly for the Kabbalists of Safed, completely logical or dialectical in nature. *Ein-Sof* enters into a dynamic of divine catharsis, contraction, emanation, destruction, and restoration almost by definition, for such a sequence of events is logically necessary for it to realize the fullness of its own essence. For the Kabbalists as for Hegel it is a logical truth that "the end is wedged in the beginning and the beginning is wedged in the end."

THE SIGNIFICANCE OF NEGATION

For Hegel, the fundamental characteristic of Reason is the power of *negation*. This is because negation provides mind with the power to reject spurious reasoning and to discriminate among ideas. Like the Kabbalists, who understood negation to be a core characteristic of *Ein-Sof*, Hegel's Absolute is empowered by its capacity to negate itself and each of the positions it takes up in thought and the world. Indeed, Hegel understands the Absolute as continually negating itself and passing over into its opposite. However, in doing so the Absolute does not become different from itself but remains identical with and actualizes itself.[27]

For Hegel, negation is the motive force of the world. Hegel equates dialectic with negation and declares that "Wherever there is movement, wherever there is life, wherever anything is carried into effect in the actual world there is Dialectic at work."[28] Compare Hegel's statement to that of the Kabbalist R. Joseph Ben Scholem of Barcelona [c. 1300], whom we quoted in Chapter Two: "there is no change, alteration, or transformation, in short no creative act at all, in which the abyss of nothingness is not crossed and for a fleeting mystical moment becomes visible,"[29]

The Kabbalists recognized three species or moments of negation, each of which passes over into a complementary affirmation or creative act. The first of these three negations is *Ayin*, the primal nothingness or abyss, which stands as the background to our questions about the world's origins. The second kabbalistic negation is *Tzimtzum*, the contraction or concealment of the infinite God that makes room for a created world and allows for

27. See the discussion of Hegel's "Notion" in Stace, ibid., p. 222.
28. *Hegel's Logic*, Par. 81, *Zusatz* 1, p. 116 (cf. Weiss, *Essential Hegel*, pp. 95–96).
29. Scholem, *Major Trends*, p. 217.

distinctions among created things. The third negation is *Shevirat ha-Kelim*, the Breaking of the Vessels, an archetypal event that brings chaos, antinomy, destruction, and death into a finite universe.

Each of these negative moments finds its place in Hegel's philosophy. The first, "Nothing" per se. Hegel derives from his view that the most fundamental of all thoughts is that *something* exists.[30] Hegel argues that such acknowledgment of a primal indeterminate being immediately raises the specter of "nothing" for, as Hegel puts it "There is nothing to be envisaged in pure Being."[31] Hegel, like the Kabbalists, acknowledged that there are indeed ways of thinking in which the whole world, as it were, disappears, and there is literally "nothing" before us, and like the Kabbalists he held that this "nothingness" is, in effect no different from the Absolute, indeterminate All, of which, by virtue of its lack of specificity, we have nothing to say. This view is articulated, for example, in the writings of the late thirteenth-century Kabbalist David ben Abraham ha-Lavan, who relates that the highest deity (*Ein-Sof*) has "more being than any other being in the world, but since it is simple, and all other simple things are complex when compared with its simplicity, so in comparison it is called 'nothing.'"[32] Hegel's fundamental "Being," like the Kabbalist's *Ein-Sof*, is as much a "nothing" as it is a "something," and the mutual dependence of being and nothingness leads Hegel to posit a new reconciling notion, Becoming, which is tantamount to "Creation."

Creation, for Hegel, is, in effect, a logical event. According to Hegel, Spirit, which is originally being in its most indeterminate and abstract sense, *must* become concrete and create a world. As Findlay puts it, for Hegel, the word "creation" is "merely an imaginative symbol for the entailment holding between the being of an abstract notion and the being of cases in which it may be instantiated."[33] For Hegel, creation must occur because the notion of an indeterminate, abstract being entails that there be determinate, particular instances of itself. As the Kabbalists themselves recognized, there can be no abstract divine "good" without concrete, worldly, good acts. Though they themselves struggled with the question of whether or not creation was a

---

30. Findlay, *Hegel: A Re-examination*, p. 154.
31. G. W. F. Hegel, *Science of Logic* I, trans. A. V. Miller (New York: Humanities Press, 1968), p. 88.
32. Quoted in Scholem, *Kabbalah*, p. 95.
33. Findlay, *Hegel: A Re-examination*, p. 154.

necessary event or a free choice of God,[34] the entire thrust of the doctrine of the *Sefirot* is that creation is logically part of the essence of *Ein-Sof*.[35]

That "nothingness" or "negation" is essential to the creative process was clearly recognized by Spinoza, who held that *all determination is negation*. For Spinoza, to determine or specify something is clearly to set it apart from other things. Hegel both inverts and elevates this principle in holding that *all negation is determination*, and that, in effect, to negate is to posit or create. Indeed, for Hegel, the positive nature of a thing consists in all of its "negations."[36] It is for this reason that in order to fulfill itself in creation, the Absolute Spirit must, as it were, "participate in its own nothingness" and become operative as *negation*.

The process by which the infinite, indeterminate Absolute becomes finite and specific involves a second negation in both the Kabbalah and Hegel. This negation is symbolized in the kabbalistic notion of *Tzimtzum* (divine contraction and concealment). In *Tzimtzum* the Kabbalists express the notion that creation is essentially discrimination, limitation, and negation. A similar idea reappears in Hegel, in the notion of the alienation or *self-deception of Absolute spirit*. According to Hegel, it is through the very process of negating itself as the Infinite All that the Idea becomes finite and particular. Further, the Absolute Spirit, according to Hegel, must enter into a "game" in which it first "pretends" itself to be finite, in order that it might overcome this pretense and recognize, by contrasting itself with a finite world, its own infinity.[37] For Hegel, as for the Kabbalists, Absolute Spirit, is the only reality; yet, like a king in need of subjects in order to recognize himself as king, the Absolute must create the illusion of something separate from itself. It is through an act of self-deception in which it posits the existence of a seemingly independent finite world, that the Absolute recognizes itself, first as something apart from the world, and then ultimately as the

---

34. See Scholem, *Kabbalah*, p. 91. Scholem points out that according to Cordovero, for example, the process by which *Ein-Sof* emerges from concealment to revelation is a purely free decision in no way reducible to a necessary consequent of the essence of *Ein-Sof*. Hegel, of course, sees no contradiction between a free and necessary rational act.

35. I.e., in order for *Ein-Sof* to be truly infinite it must be actual and concrete as well as potential and abstract; therefore its essence as an infinite being necessarily propels it into creating a world.

36. Stace, *The Philosophy of Hegel*, pp. 32–34.

37. Findlay, *Hegel: A Re-examination*, p. 38.

one true reality. Like an artist who, having first received the adulation of others, ultimately comes to recognize that his greatness resides totally within himself, the Absolute Spirit must negate itself, become other to itself, in order to recognize that it itself has all along been the totality and the all. For Hegel, it is only by becoming finite that the Absolute Spirit can be truly infinite. Indeed, the very "game" in which spirit negates itself by becoming finite and then overcomes this negation and recognizes its own absolute infinitude, is, for Hegel, the essence of spirit itself. Absolute Spirit is nothing more or less than this game. It is the rhythm, as the Hasidim would put it, of *descent for the purpose of ascent.* It is the logical movement from abstract to finite particular back to an abstract that includes the particular.

Hegel's "game of self-deception" is clearly present in the Lurianic Kabbalah if not stated in such clear philosophical terms. The process of *Tzimtzum* by which the infinite God contracts and conceals himself to make room for a finite world and the subsequent processes of emanation (*Sefirot*), "breakage" (*Shevirat Hakelim*), and restoration (*Tikkun*) by which this finite world is returned to the infinitude of God is a perfect parallel to the Hegelian scheme. For Luria, God, as it were, plays a game of self-concealment in order that a finite world can exist and ultimately return itself to infinity in God. What's more, as for Hegel, this very "game" of concealment, finite creation, and return is itself ultimately, for the Kabbalists, constitutive of God Himself.

The third and final negation in the Kabbalah, the "Breaking of the Vessels" (*Shevirat Hakelim*), is paralleled by the role that the dialectic plays in the philosophy of Hegel. Hegel tells us: "All things, we say—that is the finite world as such—are doomed; and in saying so, we have a vision of Dialectic as the universal and irresistible power before which nothing can stay, however secure and stable it may deem itself."[38] For Hegel, the tearing asunder of all finite things and conceptions is, as it is for Luria, a necessary stage in the development of the Spirit. "Death, as we may call that unreality, is the most terrible thing . . . But the life of the Mind is not one that shuns death, and keeps clear of destruction; it endures death, and in death maintains its being. It only wins to its truth when it finds itself utterly torn asunder."[39]

---

38. *Hegel's Logic,* Par. 81, *Zusatz* 1, p. 118 (cf. Weiss, *Essential Hegel,* p. 97).
39. Hegel, *Phenomenology of Mind,* pp. 33–34. See Findlay, *Hegel: A Reexamination,* p. 61. Here, I follow Findlay's translation of *Geist* as "spirit" as opposed

Mind, for Hegel, can only progress when it continually breaks apart its own concepts and reorganizes itself in new forms of thought and experience. Further, Hegel holds that negation, manifest in antinomy, contradiction, and death, is the motive force of the world. Spirit can only develop in a world in which it is confronted with conflict, contradiction, and apparent chaos. By applying itself to resolve such conflicts, understand such contradictions, and create order out of chaos, the Absolute Spirit, embodied in man, realizes the values that exist only abstractly in the idea of God. Similarly, for Luria the "Breaking of the Vessels" is a negation that assures that *Ein-Sof*, mirrored and embodied in man, is confronted with a hostile environment in which it can exercise its greatest virtues. This, we might say, is the Kabbalist's explanation of the "fall" and provides a theological explanation for the existence of destruction, evil, and death.

THE COINCIDENCE OF OPPOSITES

An essential feature of Hegel's thought is the notion that all concepts and things have their contraries, as it were, hidden away within themselves[40] and that, in an important sense, apparent opposites are actually identical. To take one example, for Hegel the notion of "pure being," which is thought of as something opposed to and distinct from "knowing," actually contains knowledge as part of its essence. This is because in order for anything to be, it must at least potentially be known. The object (being) is for Hegel precisely what consciousness makes of it, and knowing is conversely nothing but the contents of such consciousness. As such, the two are in an important sense identical.

Hegel frequently uses the term "dialectical" to refer to that logical or conceptual process whereby a concept or thing passes into its opposite and the distinctions between opposing terms are broken down.[41] This process is, for Hegel, the essence of creativity. However, as a result of the dialectic the original distinctions are not lost completely, but are overcome in such a manner as to provide insight into the essence of the original terms. This

---

to "mind" in the Baille translation. For Hegel, "Geist" refers to both man's psyche and the universal mind or spirit.

40. Stace, *The Philosophy of Hegel*, p. 90.

41. Ibid., p. 104.

insight reveals the opposing or contradictory terms to be mutually dependent ideas.

A remarkable parallel to these Hegelian ideas is to be found among the Chabad Hasidim, whose philosophy was formulated in the years both immediately preceding and subsequent to Hegel's publication of the *Phenomenology of Spirit* (1806).[42] As Elior points out:

> amongst the Chabad Hasidim "Divinity is conceived as a dialectical process comprising an entity and its opposite simultaneously: "divine emanation" (shefa- ve-atsilut) and "contraction" (*Tzimtzum*); "ascending" (ratso) and "descending" (vashov); the expanded state (gadlut) and the ordinary state (katnut); infinity and finity; expanding vitality (hitpashtut) and limitation and envelopment (hitlabshut); annihilation and embodiment; concealment and revelation; "unity" and "plurality"; "being" (yesh) and "nothingness" (ayin).[43]

It will be worthwhile to elaborate upon the Chabad conception of *coincidentia oppositorum* that was briefly presented in Chapter One. In this way we will be able to see how these Hasidim, building on a Lurianic foundation, were able to create a thoroughly dialectic conception of God and the world.

According to Schneur Zalman of Lyadi (1745–1813), the first Lubavitcher rebbe and founder of the Chabad movement, the creation of the world involves a dialectical movement between being and nonbeing:

> For this is the purpose of the creation of the worlds from *Ayin* (Nothingness) to *Yesh* (Being), to overturn it from the aspect of *Yesh* into the aspect of *Ayin*.[44]

> The purpose of the creation of the worlds from nothingness to being was so that there should be a *Yesh* (Creation), and that the *Yesh* should be null.[45]

---

42. It is very hard to conceive of any direct influence of German Idealism on Chabad, who, like all Hasidic Jews of their time, were largely isolated from secular culture.

43. Elior, *The Paradoxical Ascent to God*, p. 25.

44. Schneur Zalman, *Torah Or, Va-Yetse*, p. 44. Quoted in Elior, *The Paradoxical Ascent to God*, p. 26.

45. Schneur Zalman, *Likkutei Torah*, Leviticus, p. 83; quoted in Elior, *The Paradoxical Ascent to God*, p. 137.

According to Elior, for Chabad "The meaning of the concepts *Yesh* [Being] and *Ayin* [Nothingness] alternate respectively depending on the point of view from which they are discussed."[46] As it is put by Schneur Zalman:

> (Looking) upwards from below, as it appears to eyes of flesh, the tangible world seems to be Yesh and a thing, while spirituality, which is above, is an aspect of Ayin (nothingness). (But looking) downwards from above the world is an aspect of Ayin, and everything which is linked downwards and descends lower and lower is more and more Ayin and is considered as naught truly as nothing and null.[47]

A perfectly "Hegelian" conception of dialectic is present in the second generation of Chabad thinkers who were Hegel's contemporaries. Rabbi Dov Baer (1773–1827), the son of Schneur Zalman, states:

> and within everything is its opposite and also it is truly revealed as its opposite.[48]

> For the principal point of divine completeness is that . . . in every thing is its opposite, and . . . that all its power truly comes from the opposing power, and, according to the strength of the opposing power, thus the power of its opposite will be found truly.[49]

According to the Rabbi Aharon Halevi Horowitz of Staroselye (1766–1828):

> The intention of creation was from Him, blessed be He, so as to incorporate upper and nether and all the opposites, that is, so there would be a revelation of His completeness, blessed be He, precisely through the Yesh (creation) and through inversion (to nothingness).[50]

46. Elior, *The Paradoxical Ascent to God*, p. 53.
47. Schneur Zalman, *Likutei Torah*, Devarim, fol. 83a; Elior, *The Paradoxical Ascent to God*, pp. 137–138.
48. Rabbi Dov Baer, *Ner Mitzvah ve-Torah-Or* [1820] II, fol. 8a; Elior, *The Paradoxical Ascent to God*, p. 64.
49. Ibid.
50. Sha'arei ha-Avodah, Petah [1821] Ha-Teshuvah, Ch. 9. Quoted in Elior, *The Paradoxical Ascent to God*, p. 62.

Elior points out that for Chabad, the deity "longs to become both Nothingness and Being at the same time."[51] It is only by being "nothing" that *Ein-Sof* can truly "be." According to Rabbi Aaron: "All created things in the world are hidden within His essence, be He blessed, in one potential, in *coincidentia oppositorum* . . .[52] In their state of *hashawah* within *Ein-Sof*, opposites become united in a single subject and their differences are, in effect nullified. Again, according to R. Aaron: "He is the perfection of all, for the essence of perfection is that even those opposites which are opposed to one another be made one."[53] Indeed, for R. Aaron, in *Ein-Sof*, there is such an interpenetration of opposing principles that "the revelation of anything is actually through its opposite."[54] We can compare Rabbi Aaron's pronouncements with the following dictum of Hegel: "every actual thing involves a coexistence of opposed elements. Consequently to know, or, in other words, to comprehend an object is equivalent to being conscious of it as a concrete unity of opposed determinations."[55]

As we have discussed in Chapter Four a *coincidentia oppositorum* is also evident in Schneur Zalman's conception of the twofold means toward the unification of the finite world with the infinite divine principle. On the one hand, Schneur Zalman speaks of a Gnostic-like annihilation of both this world and the personal ego and their eventual absorption within the Godhead; on the other hand he speaks of the infusion of the divine into the material world through mankind's religious service and worship:[56]

> Just as one annihilates oneself from Yesh (Being) to Ayin (Nothingness), so too it is drawn down from above from Ayin to Yesh, so that the light of the infinite may emanate truly below as it does above.[57]

For Chabad it is dialectically true that mankind's service to God results both in an annihilation of this world and a suffusion of God's light into, and

51. Elior, *The Paradoxical Ascent to God*, p. 30.

52. See Elior, *Chabad*, p. 163.

53. Elior, *Chabad*, p. 166.

54. R. Aharon, Sha'arei ha-'Avodah II, Ch. 10. Quoted in Elior, *The Paradoxical Ascent to God*, p. 64.

55. *Hegel's Logic*, Par. 48, *Zusatz*, p. 78 (cf. Weiss, *Essential Hegel*, p. 158).

56. Schneur Zalman, Torah Or, p. 49; quoted in Elior, *The Paradoxical Ascent to God*, p. 134.

57. Schneur Zalman, Torah Or, p. 58; quoted in Elior, *The Paradoxical Ascent to God*, p. 150.

consequent spiritualization of, this world. In this way Chabad is able to combine the two seemingly contradictory principles of mystical quietism and religious activism.[58]

EVIL AND ITS TRANSCENDENCE

For the Kabbalists there is also a dialectical relationship between Good and Evil. This is but one more aspect of the kabbalistic/Hasidic view that each spiritual element can only be revealed through its opposite. For the Kabbalists, God's goodness can only be revealed through the creation of a potentially evil world. For it is only in such a world that mankind can exercise the virtues that are symbolized in the *Sefirot*.

Many of Hegel's ideas regarding evil echo kabbalistic and Hasidic views. For Hegel, as for the Kabbalists, the story of Adam's fall symbolizes the idea that knowledge and freedom, the defining characteristics of humanity, are also the origin of evil.[59] With regard to the biblical story, Hegel tells us that "it is in fact cognition that is the source of all evil."[60] Echoing the kabbalistic notion that Adam's fall (and hence evil) results from a "Breaking of the Vessels," Hegel informs us that "evil first occurs within the sphere of rupture or cleavage."[61] This rupture, Hegel informs us, is the origin of knowledge and freedom; which, like the Kabbalists, Hegel holds to be both the sources of evil and the origins of its redemption. Hegel holds that the "point where humanity is firmly posited as evil is the point where reconciliation has its source."[62] For Hegel, knowledge and freedom are "what produces the disease and are at the same time the source of health."[63] This is because Adam's fall is not only the source of evil but is the divine spark within humankind. Hegel tells us that "the confirmation of the fact that the knowledge of good and evil belongs to the divinity of humanity is placed on the lips of God himself," when He says, "Behold, Adam has become like one

---

58. Elior, *The Paradoxical Ascent to God*, p. 31.
59. On the Kabbalists' view of evil, see my *Symbols of the Kabbalah*, Chapter Eight.
60. Hegel, *Lectures on the Philosophy of Religion*, p. 206.
61. Ibid.
62. Ibid.
63. Ibid.

of us."[64] For Hegel, as for the Kabbalists, evil is absolutely necessary in order to assure the existence of good. Hegel writes: "both good and evil, are posited, but essentially in contradiction, in such a way that each of them presupposes the other."[65]

According to Hegel, in order to overcome evil, an individual must transcend his or her natural, individualistic impulses and identify with those universal causes and conceptions that constitute his spiritual and rational nature. The same idea is expressed in the Hasidic dictum that one must identify with his "Godly" as opposed to his "Natural" soul. For Hegel, those who define their fulfillment in terms of their own achievements or pleasure will, in the end, be overcome by their own individuality in death. It is only those who identify themselves with a goal beyond the self who can achieve a lasting good, and the harmony with the world that they long for. For Hegel "evil is nothing else than mind which puts its separate individuality before all else."[66] While Hegel holds that the World-Spirit achieves its rational purposes even through the acts of selfish men who have no awareness of a higher purpose,[67] the goal of humanity is to become conscious of and align itself with Reason.

Hegel held that each individual has within him a *genius*, by which he understands "the particular nature of a man that, in every situation and circumstance, decides his action and destiny."[68] A man's genius exists as a quiet inner self, "a self-like other," who, in effect, acts as "the oracle on whose pronouncement depends every resolve of the individual." Hegel's ideas again echo the kabbalistic notion of a *Tzelem* (image, astral body, or celestial counterpart) who exists alongside the individual and with whom the individual can consult in determining his deepest and truest sentiments and goals. For Hegel, the individual's relationship to his or her genius is both a self-relation (as a person has to the content of his dreams) and the closest of relationships to an other (Hegel here compares this to the relationship

---

64. Ibid., p. 302.

65. Ibid., p. 300.

66. G. W. F. Hegel, *Philosophy of Mind* (Part Three of the Encyclopedia of the Philosophical Sciences [1830], trans. William Wallace, together with the *Zusätze* in Bouman's Text (1845), trans. A. V. Miller (Oxford: Clarendon Press, 1971), sec. 382, *Zusatze*, p. 15.

67. G. W. F. Hegel, *The Philosophy of History*, trans. J. Sibree (New York: Dover, 1956), Introduction, p. 38 ff.

68. G. W. F. Hegel, *Philosophy of Mind*.

between fetus and mother). Philosophically speaking, one's genius is one's personal *essence*, the truth of both one's life and the source of one's unique talents. It is only through an understanding of one's genius that the individual can arrive at his particular task in life, and act on the universal principles that constitute the good.

DIALECTICAL REASONING IN HEGEL AND LURIA

The Lurianic Kabbalah anticipates the very manner in which Hegel later reasoned about concepts and premises. In contrast to Aristotelian logic, where nothing can obtain in a conclusion that is not explicitly entailed by the premises, the dialectical *reasoning* of the Kabbalah (and Hegel) is a logic in which concepts are said to develop in the direction of the notions they imply and in which the results of one's reasoning are only indirectly implied by one's premises. It is the sort of reasoning used by Descartes when he argued from the premise that the world may or may not exist to the inference that there *are beliefs or doubts about its existence*;[69] and as this example shows, unlike the case of deductive logic, it is a form of reasoning through which we can be introduced to new entities and ideas.

The Kabbalists make use of dialectical reasoning when they, for example, implicitly infer from the notion of *Tzimtzum* (which is a concealment of knowledge) the existence of structures (vessels, the *Sefirot*) that *act to conceal*, or when they (again implicitly) infer from the traits of any given category (e.g., *Chesed*, loving-kindness) the existence of other categories (e.g., *Din*, judgment) that appear to oppose or contradict the first one. They make use of dialectical reasoning when they infer from the notion of an all-inclusive perfection (*Ein-Sof* or God) the existence, *as part of that perfection*, of that which is imperfect and finite, which is tantamount to the existence of mankind in a created world. Dialectical logic, is of course, also at work in Luria's implicit (and rather bold) inference that an *all-inclusive* perfection (*Ein-Sof*) would include within itself as part of its "all-inclusiveness" certain aspects that would tend toward imperfection (the forces of *Din*) and hence that the original perfection implies a tendency toward improving itself by eliminating those (potentially) negative strains.

It is dialectical reasoning, or better put, a *dialectical process* that begins with an all-inclusive Godhead and results in the existence of *Orot* (Lights),

---

69. J. N. Findlay, *The Logic of Dialectic* (unpublished manuscript).

Kelim, (vessels), *Partzufim* (visages), and *Olamot* (Worlds). These entities are not, as one might suppose, simply speculative inventions of the kabbalistic mind, or intuitions encountered in states of mystical meditation (although they may be these things as well). Rather the entities that populate the Lurianic universe are actually logically implied by the Kabbalist's notion of "being" (or "God") itself. "Being," which is perfect, infinite, and One, logically tends toward the creation of that which is other, finite, and many. Such creation proceeds through stages in which the created becomes increasingly differentiated, finite, and spatial, and culminates in the existence of a purely instantiated, material world, only to return in the end to a restored, infinite unity.

The Lurianic symbol of the Breaking of the Vessels, in particular, can be interpreted as reflecting a critical moment or aspect of the dialectical process. This symbol implies that finite, singular concepts are always insufficient to encompass the subject matter to which they are applied and are consequently always expanding into other concepts, passing over into ideas that they imply. As Hegel puts it: "Finite principles are the most that the understanding can pick out—and these being essentially unstable and tottering, the structure they supported must collapse with a crash."[70]

For both the Kabbalah and Hegel the original structures, values, and ideas of the world (what the Kabbalists referred to as *Kelim* or *Vessels*), must of necessity break down, become a plurality, pass over into their opposites, and otherwise (to use more contemporary parlance) deconstruct. These vessels are then considered and approached from a different point of view and are reconstructed into new concepts, values, etc., in which the contradictions inherent within the original "vessels," are understood as necessary conditions for each other and thereby harmonized. This movement from original unity to contradictory and disharmonious plurality and ultimately to a renewed and higher harmony is the essence of both the Hegelian dialectic and the Lurianic doctrines of the Breaking of the Vessels and *Tikkun* (Restoration).

Each of the major kabbalistic symbols performs a dialectical blending of opposites with respect to contradictory philosophical ideas. For example, the symbol of *Ein-Sof* expresses the blending of Being and Nothingness; *Tzimtzum*, the blending of the negative (contraction/ concealment) and positive (creation/revelation); the *Sefirot*, the confluence between the One and the Many; and *Tikkun* the mutual interdependence of God and man. It

---

70. Hegel, *Logic*, par. 38, Zuzatz, p. 62.

is precisely these sorts of "harmonies in opposition" that are later expressed in the Hegelian dialectic.

Hegel's distinctions between the linear thinking of the *Understanding*, the contradictions of the *dialectic*, and the harmonizing effects of *Speculative Reason* are philosophical parallels to the kabbalistic symbols of *Sefirot*, *Shevirah*, and *Tikkun*. The Understanding attempts to comprehend the world in terms of simple, logically distinct, finite concepts (the ideas of science, or those of a particular ethical system, for example). These concepts and the objects they refer to, like the Kabbalist's *Sefirot*, are originally whole, noncontradictory, and systematic. The dialectic (like Luria's *Shevirah*) causes finite objects and notions to "break down," pass over into their opposites, and appear contradictory and absurd. Hegel tells us: "The battle of reason is the struggle to break up the rigidity to which the understanding has reduced everything."[71] Speculative reason, like the Kabbalist's *Tikkun*, resolves the contradictions inherent in the concepts of the Understanding by comprehending them as necessary conditions for one another. Contrary to a common misunderstanding of Hegel, his philosophy does not resolve contradictions by overcoming or eliminating them, but rather by preserving them in a context where they are seen to be reciprocally necessary. The dialectic continuously moves to higher-order conceptions in which, for example, the contradictions between the universal and particular, God and man, and freedom and necessity, are understood as both logically and spiritually necessary. Contradiction, represented in the Kabbalah by the broken state of affairs resulting from the *Shevirah*, is for both Hegel and the Kabbalah the motive force of the world.

THE BEGINNING IS DETERMINED BY THE END

For the Kabbalah, the Infinite, *Ein-Sof*, is both epistemologically *unknown* and ontologically *nothing* "prior" to its manifestation in a finite world. As such *Ein-Sof*, who is the origin of the world is as dependent upon creation as creation is dependent upon *Ein-Sof*. Already in *Sefer Yetzirah* (1:7) we have the doctrine that the "end is embedded in the beginning and the beginning embedded in the end." Compare this to a passage in Hegel's *Phenomenology of Mind*: "The True is the Whole. The Whole, however, is merely the essential nature reaching its completeness through the process of its own

---

71. Hegel, *Logic*, par. 32, Zuzatz, p. 53 (cf. Weiss, *Essential Hegel*, p. 134).

development. Of the Absolute it must be said that it is essentially a result, that only at the end is it what it is in its very truth."[72] Hegel tells us that spirit "is the process of its own becoming, the circle that presupposes its end as its goal, having its end also as its beginning . . ."[73]

Again, in the *Logic*, Hegel informs us: "The essential requirement for the science of logic is not so much that the beginning be a pure immediacy, but rather that the whole of the science be within itself a circle in which the first is also the last and the last is also the first."[74] For Hegel "the Absolute . . . is essentially a *result*, that only in the *end* is it what it truly is."[75]

Both *Ein-Sof* and the Hegelian Absolute achieve their essence through a breaking asunder into an infinite variety of manifestations and an ultimate return to unity. According to Rabbi Aron Ha Levi it is the fundamental divine purpose that the world should be differentiated and revealed in each of its finite particulars and yet united in a single infinite source.[76] Rabbi Aaron states:

> . . . the essence of His intention is that his *coincidentia* be manifested in concrete reality, that is, that all realities and their levels be revealed in actuality, each detail in itself, and that they nevertheless be unified and joined in their value, that is, that they be revealed as separated essences, and that they nevertheless be unified and joined in their value.[77]

This view, which understands differentiation and opposition, and their higher-order integration, to be at the very heart of both the Absolute and the world creative process, is also essential to the philosophy of Hegel. Compare R. Aaron's statement to Hegel's dictim that: "The Absolute is the universal and one idea, which, by an act of 'judgment,' particularizes itself to the system of specific ideas; which after all are constrained by their nature to come back to the one idea where their truth lies."[78]

72. Hegel. *Phenomenology of Mind*, pp. 81–82, cf. Findlay, *Hegel: A Re-examination*, p. 36.
73. Hegel, *Phenomenology of Mind*, p. 81.
74. Hegel, *Science of Logic*, p. 71.
75. Hegel, *Phenomenology of Mind*, p. 81.
76. Elior, *Chabad*, p. 165.
77. Elior, *Chabad*, p. 167.
78. Hegel, *Logic*, par. 213, p. 352 (cf. Weiss, *Essential Hegel*, p. 170).

THE SELF-ALIENATION OF THE ABSOLUTE SPIRIT

We have compared Hegel's conception of the Absolute to Aristotle's characterization of God as "Thought thinking itself." What distinguishes both Hegel's Absolute and the Kabbalist's *Ein-Sof* from this Aristototelian conception of God is that for both Hegel and the Kabbalah the Absolute is dynamic rather than static; it is constantly and *necessarily* transcending itself in the formation of a world. For Hegel, it is part of the essence of the Absolute, as Stace phrases it, that it "expel part of itself,"[79] creating an opposition between subject and object (the world) that permits the development of self-consciousness. Consciousness, as Hegel recognized, must be consciousness of *something*, and the Absolute cannot even know itself unless it is, at least temporarily, divided into that, on the one hand, which knows, and that, on the other hand, which is known. As such, the world becomes a necessary condition for the realization of the Absolute as self-conscious objective mind.

Ein-Sof is also constantly endeavoring to alienate an aspect of itself in order to provide the basis for its own identity and self-awareness. Both the "divine catharsis" and the *Tzimtzum*, are according to the Lurianists, designed to achieve this end. In the former, *Ein-Sof* is conceived of as expelling the roots of finitude from its essence in order to preserve its pure infinitude; in the latter, *Ein-Sof* contracts its infinitude in order to make room for a finite world. It is only by contracting itself and thus alienating an aspect of itself from itself that *Ein-Sof* can become perfect and complete. The result of both the divine catharsis and *Tzimtzum* is the creation of a finite realm through which the infinite can realize itself, its values (via the *Sefirot*), and its reign (as the divine "king"). Indeed, the Kabbalists held that it is through the process in which the divine opposes itself to an "other," that the nothingness (AyIN) of the infinite *Ein-Sof*, becomes the "I" (ANI) of a personal and fully realized God.[80] A slight shift in the order of the Hebrew letters *Aleph, Yud,* and *Nun* reflects the profound transformation of the deity, who only becomes a fully realized Self or "I" with the creation of the final *Sefirah, Malchut* (expressing his relationship to the world). Again, until *Ein-Sof* relates to a world that opposes Him, he is not fully realized as a self-conscious God or "king."

79. Stace, *The Philosophy of Hegel*, p. 72.
80. Scholem, *Kabbalah*, p. 110.

As we have already seen, for both the Lurianists and Hegel, God's self-alienation is also a form of self-deception. Both the Kabbalists and Hegel conceive of their respective absolutes as concealing an aspect of their infinite totality from themselves in order to allow for the existence of a finite, created world.

THE RECIPROCAL DETERMINATION OF GOD AND MAN

As we have seen, the Kabbalists developed the view that just as creation (man) is dependent upon God, God is Himself dependent upon man for his very being. For the Kabbalists, God only realizes and completes Himself through the activities of man. Man is created in God's image, and it is in the image of man that God comes to know Himself. Hegel adopts the identical point of view, quoting with approval a passage from the German mystic Meister Eckhardt that sheds light on the creative reciprocity between God and Man that is so prominent in the Kabbalah. According to Eckhardt: "The eye with which God sees me, is the eye with which I see Him, my eye and His eye are one . . . If God were not I would not be, and if I were not, He too would not be."[81] Hegel himself tells us:

> To know what God as spirit is . . . requires careful and thorough specu-
> lation. It includes, in its forefront, the propositions: God is God only so
> far as he knows himself; his self-knowledge is, further, a self-consciousness
> in man and man's knowledge *of* God, which proceeds to man's self-
> knowledge *in* God.[82]

In this view, Hegel is not only in a league with Eckhardt, Angelus Selesius, and Jacob Boehme, but he and each of these thinkers echo the kabbalistic view that the creation of a finite, natural world and, in particular, man, is *necessary* for the Infinite to know and be Himself.[83]

For the Kabbalists the *Sefirot* define the divine essence only *in potentia*. For both Hegel and the Kabbalah, God is more than an ineffable ground to all being, and more than a timeless and comprehensive consciousness. The

---

81. Quoted in Findlay, *Hegel: A Re-examination*, p. 48.
82. Hegel, *Philosophy of Mind*, sec. 564, p. 298.
83. Findlay, *Hegel: A Re-examination*, p. 48.

Hegelian Absolute like the Kabbalists' *Ein-Sof* is fully realized only in the activities of man. Consider the following passage in which Hegel equates God with the form and spirit of humanity: ". . . God appears in sensible presence; he has no other figure or shape than that of the sensible mode of the spirit that is spirit in itself—the shape of the *singular human being* . . . divine and human nature are not intrinsically different—God [is] in human shape. The truth is that there is only one reason, only one spirit . . ."[84] At times Hegel implies that the divine spirit is identical with the spirit of man. At other times Hegel's Absolute Spirit is integrally related to and dependent upon mankind. Hegel affirms:

> the unity of divine and human nature is itself absolute spirit.

> Spirit, therefore, is the living process by which the *implicit* unity of divine and human nature becomes *explicit*, or is brought forth.[85]

Hegel holds that the unity of the divine and human spirit enables mankind to rise above his natural state of being:

> By consciousness of the unity of divine and human nature we mean that humanity implicitly bears within itself the *divine* idea . . . In this consciousness humanity knows the universal, and [knows] itself to be determined for the universal. i.e. elevated above all locality, nationality, condition, life-situation, etc. Human beings [are] equal; slavery [is] intolerable; [there is] worth and absolute validity only in this perspective.[86]

However, for Hegel, "the unity of divine and human nature has a significance not only for the definition of human nature but just as much for that of the divine."

As we have seen, the Zohar and other kabbalistic texts affirm that one who performs the commandments and walks in the ways of the Torah, or who personally writes a Torah scroll, is considered to have made God Himself.[87] Though the activities he regards as "God-making" are obviously quite different, Hegel is in complete accord with this basic point of view. In addition to the worship and faith of the religious man, Hegel regards the

---

84. Hegel, *Lectures on the Philosophy of Religion*, p. 214.
85. Ibid., pp. 66–76.
86. Ibid., p. 109.
87. See M. Idel, *Kabbalah: New Perspectives*, p. 188.

creative works of the artist, the systematic insights of the philosopher, and the discoveries of the scientist as activities that bring about the realization of the divine spirit in humanity or, to use the kabbalistic metaphor, "raise the sparks" inherent in man's soul. Through a reading of Hegel we can broaden our understanding of such kabbalistic notions as *Tikkun ha-Olam* and the raising of the sparks and take them beyond a narrowly *halakhic* Jewish context.

Hegel tells us that one form in which the insight that human nature is implicitly divine is expressed is the concept of the Primordial Man: "human being as such, as the Only-begotten, the Son of God . . . Adam Kadmon, the Logos, Primal Man."[88] This, Hegel tells us, "is the archetype of humanity, this man who is the impress of the heavenly and eternal revelation of the hidden Godhead."[89] For the Kabbalists, *Adam Kadmon* represents essentially this Hegelian idea, that the divine spirit is realized in humanity as a whole.

Hegel's identification of God with the Primal man or spirit of humanity has led some commentators to hold that for Hegel God is nothing more than "the human spirit writ large."[90] Others have held that for Hegel, humanity is a vehicle for something larger than itself.[91] This is a basic point of contention in Hegel scholarship. I would argue that there is a *coincidentia* here as well, a *coincidentia* of God and man. Hegel, like the Kabbalists, creates a metaphysical system that can be alternatively understood in immanent and transcendent terms. Hegel's humanism is dialectically equivalent to his religious transcendentalism, and vice versa. Any other position fails to understand the nature of dialectical thought. The dialectic does not stop at some arbitrary point, e.g., between humanism and theism, but must, like the Kabbalist's *Ein-Sof* or the Hindu *Brahman-Atman*, necessarily swallow up all distinctions in its wake. We must always remember that for Hegel: ". . . a so-called basic proposition or principle of philosophy, if true, is also false."[92]

---

88. Hegel, *Lectures on the Philosophy of Religion*, p. 99.
89. Ibid., p. 84.
90. See Robert Solomon, *In The Spirit of Hegel*, p. 6.
91. See, for example, Taylor, *Hegel*.
92. Hegel, *Phenomenology of Mind*, p. 85. Compare Neils Bohr's distinction between superficial and deep truths: superficial truths are characterized by the fact that their opposites are false, whereas the opposites or contradictories of deep truths are true as well.

THE ILLUSORY WORLD

For the Kabbalists, the very nature of appearance and reality is in conceptual flux. From one point of view, *Ein-Sof* is the only reality, and our world, as a diminishment or concealment of the divine light, is a mere appearance or illusion. In part this follows from the kabbalistic doctrine of panentheism, the view that the deity is all, and apart from God there is nothing whatsoever. As the Safedian Kabbalist, Moses Cordovero, asserts: "he is found in all things, and all things are found in Him, and there is nothing devoid of his divinity, heaven forfend. Everything is in Him, and He is in everything and beyond everything, and there is nothing beside Him."[93]

The Chabad Hasidim went so far as to assert boldly that the world as we know it is an illusion. According to Schneur Zalman: "Earth and heaven are like a curtain that separates, for they do not see His blessed unity, and in truth they are merely fantasies for it is imagined that there is a world, but in truth there is only simple unity . . . and our seeing the existence of the world is only imagination."[94] Put less radically, the Kabbalists held that the very being and existence of finite entities is completely dependent upon the deity's indwelling within them. According to Schneur Zalman it is the very letters of divine speech that support the existence of finite things: "For if the letters (which comprise divine speech) were to depart [even] for an instant, God forbid, and return to their source, all the heavens would become nought and absolute nothingness, and it would be as though they had never existed at all, exactly as before the utterance, 'Let there be a firmament.'"[95] Hegel holds a similar view to the effect that it is the Absolute's "Notion" or Idea that supports the existence of finite things: "It is by the notion alone that the things in the world have their subsistence; or, as it is expressed in the language of religious conception, things are what they are, only in virtue of the divine and thereby creative thought which dwells within them."[96]

From another point of view, however, *Ein-Sof* and Hegel's Absolute are empty abstractions (i.e., species of "nothingness") until they are actualized in

93. Moses Cordovero, *Elima Rabati*, fol. 25a, as quoted in Elior, *The Paradoxical Ascent to God*, p. 50.

94. Schneur Zalman, *Boneh Yerushalayim*, p. 54, sig. 50. As quoted in Elior, *The Paradoxical Ascent to God*, p. 108.

95. Schneur Zalman, *Shaar Hayichud Vehaemunah*, Chapter 1; Zalman, *Likutei Amarim-Tanya*, p. 287.

96. Hegel, *Logic*, Wallace, par. 213, Zuzatz, p. 276.

a concrete, existing world. As we have seen, for both the Kabbalists and Hegel, there is a sense in which God is real and the world an illusion and a sense in which the world is real and God "nothingness." Indeed, for the Kabbalists, the world is necessary in order to make God real. Elior points out that for Chabad, "just as there is no separate reality and no discriminate essence in the world without God, so also God has no revealed and discriminate existence without the world. That is, just as one cannot speak of the existence of the world without God, so too one cannot speak of the existence of God without the world." Creation completes and fulfills the divine essence."[97]

Hegel goes to the trouble of utilizing different terms for the being of the Absolute and the being of the world. For Hegel only the Absolute is "real," while only the concrete world "exists." It is a basic tenet of Hegelian thought that while the external world "exists," it is not true "being," and, as such, is not "real" and is thus "untrue": "God, who is the truth, is known by us in His truth, that is, as absolute spirit, only in so far as we at the same time recognize that the world which He created, nature and the infinite spirit, are, in their difference from God, untrue."[98] Only being, which is represented in the Absolute Idea, is true and *real*, but since such being is only apprehended by the eye of reason, it does not *exist* in the sense that objects of sense are said to exist.[99] In distinguishing between two terms that are generally taken to be synonymous, Hegel provides a means for articulating, and perhaps explicating, how the Kabbalists can hold that the world is both real and an illusion.

THE WORLD AS THE ARENA FOR THE DEVELOPMENT OF SPIRIT

The world, according to the German Idealists, exists simply as a condition for the development of "Spirit," and by this they mean that the environment in which man lives can only be understood as an arena for the development and realization of *man's* cognitive, spiritual, aesthetic, and practical virtues. Hegel's predecessor Fichte saw the all-encompassing "ego" as a source of

97. Elior, *The Paradoxical Ascent to God*, p. 62.
98. Hegel, *Logic*, trans. Wallace, par. 83, Zuzatz, p. 129.
99. Stace, *The Philosophy of Hegel*, p. 61 ff.

infinite energy, which posits a resistant environment precisely because such an environment is necessary to elicit its own activities.[100] Further, Fichte held that this environment, this world, must of necessity be the worst of all possible environments, thwarting the ego at every turn.[101] This idea was taken up by Hegel in his view that spirit itself is conditioned by death.[102]

As we have already outlined in Chapter Four, the view that mankind, and ultimately the World Spirit itself, achieves its essence through a struggle with a perilous environment and ultimately with death itself is implicit in the Lurianic notion of the "Breaking of the Vessels" (*Shevirat Hakelim*), which the Kabbalists equated with Adam's fall and man's consequent mortality. Because of the "breakage," because of Adam's fall, man must struggle against mortality in a world that brings forth thorns as well as fruit (Genesis 3:18), that engenders confusion as well as clarity; and where contradiction, corruption, and decay confront him in all of his endeavors. Only by struggling in the face of such a world can man come to actualize those intellectual, spiritual, moral, and aesthetic traits that were abstractly conceived in the *Sefirot*. In this way man actualizes and, as per the Zohar, actually comes to create God.

Again, the Chabad Hasidim come close to articulating a typically Hegelian point of view. According to them the Breaking of the Vessels and the existence of a broken, chaotic, and evil world is necessary in order to provide the opportunity for humanity to turn darkness into light. For example, Schneur Zalman holds that it is the divine intention "that He should be revealed particularly in the reversal which is the *Sitra Achra* (the other side, i.e. evil), so that His glory should be revealed . . . through the reversal of the *Sitra Achra* and actually in the changing of darkness into light."[103] It is through the transformation of evil to good by man via the restoration of *Tikkun ha-Olam*, that God becomes manifest and fully real. According to Rabbi Aharon:

> . . . His blessed divine Substance, which is His essence, is not at all manifestable. Therefore, so that His blessed divinity could be revealed,

100. Findlay, *Hegel: A Re-examination*, pp. 50–51.
101. Ibid., p. 54.
102. Hegel, *Phenomenology of Mind*, pp. 33–34.
103. Schneur Zalman, Sha'arei ha-Yichud ve-ha-Emunah, V. Ch. 15. As quoted and translated in Elior, *The Paradoxical Ascent to God*, p. 116.

there had to be breaking and a restoration so that the aspect of *Yesh* would
be revealed as a separate aspect and through "restoration" Divinity would
be manifest in the aspect of the Yesh.[104]

With the transformation of the darkness of this world into light through the
efforts of mankind, God will become fully restored and complete, peace will
reign, and the world as we know it will no longer exist. According to Schneur
Zalman:

> Therefore there will be no peace in the world until the time of the end,
> when the good shall be disencumbered from the evil to become attached to
> the root and source, the blessed Source of Life.[105]

> and this is a source of contentment for the Holy One, blessed be He, both
> that there would be a Yesh (creation) and that the Yesh should be
> annihilated. This is precisely what he wishes.[106]

In a statement that we have already quoted at some length and which is
highly reminiscent of Fichte and Hegel, the contemporary Kabbalist and sage
Rabbi Adin Steinsaltz relates that Jewish optimism dictates that we should
live "in the worst of all possible worlds in which there is yet hope,"[107] for it
is only precisely under such conditions that Godly values can be fully realized
on earth. According to Steinsaltz, such a nearly impossible world is paradoxically "the best of all possible worlds." Referring to a similar view in Hegel, J.
N. Findlay compares the development of the Hegelian "Spirit" to the growth
of "natural bonsai" whose aesthetic appeal is conditioned by the harsh clime
of rock and wind to which they must adapt on the sea coast. By analogy,
Findlay argues that it is obviously true

> that in the absence of an empirical situation which presents difficulties for
> understanding or for manipulative mastery, and in the absence of many
> deep conflicts within ourselves, or between ourselves and others, the

104. R. Aharon Sha Av. II, Ch. 7. R. Elior, *The Paradoxical Ascent to God*, p.
74.
105. Schneur Zalman, *Likutei Amarim-Tanya*, pp. 234–235.
106. Schneur Zalman, *Torah Or*, p. 9.
107. Drob, "The Mystic as Philosopher: An Interview with Rabbi Adin
Steinsaltz," p. 14.

supreme spiritual achievements of science, art, religion, politics and morality would be impossible.[108]

In kabbalistic terms, the Breaking of the Vessels is a necessary condition for the full actualization of man, and, ipso facto, God himself.

Hegel argues that any way of viewing the world other than as an arena for the development of Spirit is of necessity partial and unsatisfactory. We must (and we actually do) proceed as if the setbacks and resistances of this world are present in order to yield progressively to our cooperative enterprise and understanding. It is precisely this view that informs the doctrine of *Tikkun* and the "immanent mysticism" of the Kabbalah, and that distinguishes the Kabbalah (and Hegel) from such wholly transcendental forms of mysticism as Gnosticism, which view the world as completely wretched and irredeemable.

It should be remembered that Hegel's dialectic, like the parallel symbols of the Kabbalah, has an ontological as well as an epistemological dimension. It is not only our minds that work through the phases of the dialectic, but the world as well. History and culture evolve through a series of dialectical stages, and the world as a whole is, for Hegel, progressing, through these stages toward the realization of the Absolute in time. Hegel grafts this progressive, redemptive view of the world (as well as his triadic dialectical scheme) onto a Christian theology and messianism. However, his this-worldly emphasis is in many ways closer to Judaism, and, moreover, kabbalistic in its basic claims.

THE WORLD AS CONTRADICTION

As we have seen, for the Kabbalist Azriel, *Ein-Sof,* the infinite God, is literally understood to be the union of all opposites and contradictions.[109] Further, the Lurianic Kabbalists, and, particularly, the Chabad Hasidim who adapted their views, held that everything in the world secretly contains its opposite, that the motive force of the world is contradiction, and that the completion of God involves the unification even of those oppositions that are in complete contradiction with one another.[110]

---

108. Findlay, *Hegel: A Re-examination*, p. 55.
109. Azriel, "The Emanation of the Ten *Sefirot*, in Dan, *The Early Kabbalah*, p. 94.
110. See the section, "The Coincidence of Opposites," above.

The kabbalistic claim that *Ein-Sof*, the individual *Sefirot*, and indeed everything in the world contain their oppositions or contradictories within themselves raises the question of how anything, even God or the Absolute, can be both something and the contradictory of that thing at one and the same time. In short, how can anything be both x and not x without running afoul of the "law of contradiction," which holds that a proposition cannot be both true and false. A consideration of certain themes in Hegelian philosophy can aid us in answering this query, and, as such, provide us with yet another example in which such comparative study can deepen our insight into the Kabbalah.

Hegel held that it is only "when our thought never ranges beyond narrow and rigid terms, (that) we are forced to assume that of two opposite assertions . . . the one must be true and the other false."[111] According to Hegel, the dialectic frees us from the linear thinking of the "Understanding," and in "Speculative Reason" we enter the realm in which contradictories are understood to be simultaneously true.

It is important to point out from the start that the kabbalistic view that the deity and the world themselves involve contradictions is not merely a matter of "perspective" (e.g., that God creates man from one perspective and man creates God from another). Nor is it merely a matter of "linguistic context" (e.g., the difference between "theological" versus "natural scientific" vocabularies). It is rather the case that opposition and even contradiction is inherent in the nature of the things themselves and is part of the very essence of *Ein-Sof* to exist unmoved in contradiction with itself. It is, I believe, in the spirit of the Kabbalah to hold that even after all differences in perspective have been taken into account, and all linguistic (and other) contexts clarified, there will remain certain "truths" that can only be adequately expressed using a language of contradiction and paradox. Given, for example, our clearest and most significant use of the terms "God" and "being," the truth of things is that God is both Being and Nothing.

Ein-Sof, the Infinite, which in the Kabbalah is alternatively spoken of as Nothing and the All, itself encompasses both this existence and nonexistence of the deity, and is understood theistically and atheistically. (In this regard, we should again note that the Kabbalist Azriel defined *Ein-Sof* as "the union of both faith and disbelief."[112]). The same can be said with respect to other paradoxes expressed in the Kabbalah, including the view that creation is both

---

111. Hegel, *Logic*, Zuzatz, par. 32 (3), p. 52.
112. See above, note 41.

the ultimate good and the very definition of evil, etc. Each, according to the Kabbalists, is expressive of an inherent contradiction within reality, and none of these contradictions are completely resolvable through, for example, a closer attention to language or a clarification of "alternative perspectives."

How are these ideas to be understood? How are we to make sense of a philosophical position that holds that "contradiction" exists at, and is in fact definitive of, the very essence of the cosmos? Our discussion of this issue can be greatly aided not only by Hegel, but also by those commentators on Hegel who have attempted to make sense of what some would regard as an absurd philosophical position.[113]

The Kabbalists themselves provide us with some insight into the notion that *Ein-Sof* is a union of contradictions in their view that the infinite, if it is to be truly infinite, must also be "finite," or else there would be some thing, i.e., that which is indeed finite, which is not *Ein-Sof* and therefore, at least conceptually, beyond it. Azriel, in particular, holds that we must ascribe "finite" as well as "infinite" power to *Ein-Sof*, otherwise he would be limited by virtue of his inability to limit himself.[114] A similar argument is reiterated by Vital.[115]

It is important to repeat that *Ein-Sof* must not only contain the finite, in the sense that an infinite numerical series "contains" the numbers "5" and "13," but it must *be* finite as well; otherwise there would be certain essences, i.e., those things that are finite, that would transcend the being of *Ein-Sof*. A similar line of reasoning is also silently at work in the Hindu notion that the Absolute, *Brahman-Atman*, *is this* spider or *that* very grain of sand, or *this* particular moment in time. A deity that was not all things, but that, for

---

113. In the discussion that follows I make the Hegelian assumption that a deeper sense of the kabbalistic (and Hegelian) views on contradiction can be obtained through the process of reasoned inquiry. I realize that, in addition to those who hold that any violation of the law of contradiction is utter nonsense, there are those who hold that the view that the world itself is contradictory, and that God embodies or resolves its contradictions, can only be understood or "deepened" through experience (mystical or otherwise), and that any attempt to provide such notions with rational sense is doomed because reason itself can in no way be employed to account for a phenomenon that violates its own laws. [A similar view is taken by Jung; see Chapter 8.] Here, I can only plead that like so much else in our study of the Kabbalah, the attempt to understand the nature of *coincidentia oppositorum* must be one that pushes the limits of sense and reason, and what I say here may indeed lie somewhere on the border between logic and metaphor.

114. Azriel, "The Emanation of the Ten *Sefirot*," p. 90.

115. Vital, *Sefer Etz Chayyim* 1:1.

example, merely contained them as parts, would not be the infinite, unified "All" required by the Kabbalah or the *Upanishads*. *Ein-Sof* is therefore at once infinite and also finite (non-infinite), unifying this contradiction in its infinite essence.

Hegel suggests in *The Phenomenology of Spirit* that the necessity of ascribing finitude (non-infinity) to the infinite is built into the notion of infinity in an even more intimate fashion. It is, according to Hegel, not only the case that infinitude could not properly be infinite if it were not also finite, but it is also true that the infinite unity, in the very act of positing itself as infinite unity, brings finitude and plurality into being. Hegel speaks of an absolute simple unity when he says: "What becomes identical with itself thereby opposes itself to disruption . . . in other words it becomes really something sundered."[116] What Hegel means here is that an absolute notion like the "infinite," which conceives itself (or is conceived) as an absolute, simple unity, must, if it is to be conceptualized at all, "oppose" or distinguish itself from "disruption" or difference. It is as if the All must say "I am one, infinite and *non-distinct*." However, according to Hegel, this very assertion brings the notions of plurality, finitude, and distinctiveness into the cosmos. Hegel holds that initially the Absolute excludes such finitude from itself, but it must subsequently reinclude it if it is to remain the all-encompassing All.

For both Hegel and Luria, the entire history of the cosmos is a drama in which the Absolute proliferates into an antinimous and contradictory world and ultimately, returns to itself as the Infinite One. The Infinite, for both the Kabbalists and Hegel, can thus be said to logically or "naturally" pass over into (and then include) finitude, plurality, and distinctiveness as part of its very essence. Hegel tells us that such "dialectical diremptions," through which notions logically imply and hence include their opposites within themselves, are fundamental to all thought and existence, and are the source of a pluralistic world. The Kabbalists, in holding that *Ein-Sof* is the unity of everything and its opposite, have envisioned an "All" that is capable of encompassing each of the world's dialectical inversions, e.g., the necessity that implies freedom, the good that implies evil, etc. For both Hegel and the Kabbalists, the Absolute is such that *in being itself* it is also every distinction that arises, as well as the "medium" through which such distinctions are all dialectically resolved.[117]

The dialectical "resolution" of contradiction rests on the observation

116. Hegel, *Phenomenology of Mind*, p. 209.
117. Ibid., p. 210.

that all oppositions are reciprocally determinative of one another. All things are what they are precisely because they are not what they are not. Day is not night, Good is not evil, truth is not error, being is not nothingness, freedom is not determinism, etc. However, if we reflect a bit more deeply we discover that a notion's opposite or contradictory is even more profoundly written into its own essential nature. Hence, as we have seen, pure being that is absolutely simple, unified, and indeterminate, has, as a result of its complete lack of specificity, an element of nothingness in its own nature, inasmuch as "nothing" (i.e., no specifiable content) can be predicated of it. "Freedom," which is conceived of as the ability to transcend the causal nexus through an act of will, must embody an element of determinacy (causality) in bringing about the ends it desires. "Truth," which is understood as freedom from error, is, as we know from the empirical sciences, itself a species of "error" that can only approximate its own ideal. All so-called scientific "truths" of the past and present have been, or will be, revealed to be errors of one form or another.[118] When we recognize the interdependence of such oppositions, they do not simply dissolve. Rather we understand these oppositions as logically necessary and we are, hence, no longer disturbed by them. Our understanding of *Ein-Sof* as the "union of all contradictions" embodies the limit of this understanding.

The notion that the world itself is contradictory, usually taken to be a paradigm example of absurdity, can be understood as expressing the profound insight that the ultimate nature of reality, whatever it may be, is itself best approximated through a variety of descriptions or models, some of which explicitly or implicitly contradict one another. Philosophy, and to a certain degree, common sense, have long labored under the delusion that it is possible to provide a single, truthful description of anything whatsoever, including the world as a whole. It is thought that one "map," if it is sufficiently detailed and profound, will, at least theoretically, provide a complete account of the world. The Kabbalah, with its proliferation of symbols, models, worlds, names, etc., suggests that this assumption is radically false, and that the world can only be understood through a series of sometimes contradictory metaphors. An analogy to cartography is helpful here. The problem of representing a spherical globe on a flat plane (i.e., a

---

118. In this light it is interesting to note that the first kabbalistic text, *Sefer ha-Bahir*, refers to "things that are understood only by him who has erred in them." *Sefer ha-Bahir*, sec. 100. *Book Bahir*, Neugroschel trans., p. 78.

map) is one that cannot be completely resolved via a single representation. For example, some maps of the world maintain the continuity of the earth's surface only through distorting the size of land masses near the poles; others correct for this distortion only by breaking up the world's continuity (by depicting the world as a flattened, and hence broken, "orange peel") or by sacrificing the parallelism on the earth's surface. No single map can capture the three-dimensional surface of the globe in two dimensions. This is analogous to our predicament in both theology and philosophy. The world as a whole has properties that transcend our capacity to represent the cosmos in a single model. Our models of representation, our languages, operate, as it were, in "two dimensions," while the Absolute (the world) exists in "three" (or "four" or "five"). We are like people from a two-dimensional world who, upon being shown both Mercator and Polar projections of the globe, cannot understand how both (and neither) can be complete representations of the one (three-dimensional) world.

We can refer to the world in its totality via a single term, e.g., *Ein-Sof* or the Absolute. However, the Absolute can only be described using language that is paradoxical or contradictory, for it is a world in which God creates man, *and* in which man creates God, in which all events are causally determined *and* in which man's actions are free, in which "things" are both independent of man's consciousness *and* constituted by his mind. It is, in short, a world, that answers to all the contradictory descriptions of science and philosophy. To call these contrary descriptions different "perspectives" or "languages" does not in any way diminish the inherent "contradictoriness of the object." Indeed, the very fact that contradictory perspectives can be taken upon the Absolute tells us that the Absolute has qualities that lend themselves to such descriptions. It is the world itself that is contradictory, at least, inasmuch as it can be known by *our* descriptions. Perhaps *sub specie aeternae* it can be known in another way, but such knowledge is, by definition, not open to finite man.

It must be recognized that part of our problem in describing the world as it is understood by the Kabbalists (or Hegel) *is* linguistic, in the sense that our common language does not contain vocabulary sufficient for the purpose, say, of referring to the existent and nonexistent ultimate that the Kabbalists designate as *Ein-Sof.* It is for this reason that learning a system of thought like the Kabbalah involves the learning of a new vocabulary, a new "language."

A careful analysis of the word "existence," for example, reveals that existence, as it is commonly understood, involves two notions or conditions, "matter" and "form," which are distinguished in philosophy (and the Kabbalah), but which are obscured in ordinary English. Indeed, ordinary language has no capacity to articulate a situation in which one but not the other of these conditions is realized, and is pulled in opposite directions with respect to the existence, for example, of the idea of a horse. We find that we don't know what to say or that we wish to say "yes" and "no" ("Yes the *idea* exists, but it does not exist; it's only an idea").

The fact that one or a number of the contradictions that appear to exist in the world itself can be attributed to the limitations of our vocabulary or grammar should not, however, lull us into the belief that all such contradictions can be so attributed and, further, that they can be "resolved" if only we had the proper or "ideal" philosophical language. While the vocabulary of the Kabbalah, or Hegel, enables us to refer to and perhaps appreciate the profundity of the world's contradictions, it does not "resolve" them in the sense of making them disappear. For example, the kabbalistic concept of *Tzimtzum* embodies the notion that creation is at the same time a limitation, and that what is good (i.e., creation) is at the same time the origin of evil; and if we understand *Tzimtzum* properly we will grasp the logic, and even the necessity, of these paradoxes. However, *Tzimtzum* does not remove the distinction between creation and negation, nor between good and evil, but rather highlights their mutual reciprocity and interdependence. Further, while an apparent contradiction in the world may indeed appear under one description of an event and disappear under another (as for example, when Hegel defines "reality" as idea and reserves "existence" for nature) this simply succeeds in moving a paradox or opposition within a single description to a contradiction between descriptions. In cartography we can resolve the problem of oversized land masses at the poles by changing our "projection," but only at the expense of creating other distortions.

In the end it hardly matters whether we say there are contradictions in reality or contradictions in our perspectives upon it. To say, for example, that the problem of free will versus determinism is a matter of "perspective" is as much a revelation about ourselves as it is about our thinking about ourselves (which may, at any rate, ultimately amount to the same thing). To say that the problem of the existence versus the nonexistence of God is a contradiction between theological and natural scientific perspectives is as revealing about the ultimate nature of things as it is about a human point of view. There are a number of reasons for this, not the least of which is that since Kant it has become virtually impossible to genuinely distinguish between the "the things in themselves" and our "constructions" about them; and since Saussure and

Wittgenstein it has become equally impossible to distinguish among reality, God (or anything else for that matter), and the way the words "reality" and "God" are used in our language (a viewpoint that, as we have seen in Chapter One, is itself described in the Jewish mystical tradition).

However, even if we hold on to the notion of an extra-experiential or prelinguisticized reality, the fact that we can fruitfully take contradictory perspectives upon this reality must tell us something about its (pretheorized) nature.

Kant, of course, attempted to cope with such contradictory perspectives by distinguishing between two worlds: the *phenomenal* world, which operates according to causal laws; and the *noumenal* world, which operates according to the laws of freedom, reason, and God. Hegel preferred to hold that there is only one world, a world that itself sustains both poles of an indefinite variety of contradictions. Both possibilities are present in the Kabbalah, and are present there as yet another example of *coincidentia oppositorum*. On the one hand, there are higher worlds than our own, whose organization, structure, and properties differ radically from our own "lowly realm." On the other hand, each of these worlds, each of the *Sefirot*, each of the "names of God" etc., are said to be operative even in our own realm. In the end, all the worlds, *Sefirot*, *Partzufim*, and names are part of the single infinite All, *Ein-Sof*, who is, as we have seen, both being and nothing, the "union of everything and its opposite."

The question remains: if the world itself is contradictory, why is it so? In order to properly address this question we must first note that the contradictions posited by the Kabbalah and Hegel are not static oppositions but dynamic relationships. The paradox between creation and limitation embodied in the kabbalistic notion of *Tzimtzum*, or between progress and destruction embodied in "the Breaking of the Vessels," is never an end in and of itself, but is rather an impetus to new development, described in the Kabbalah as *Tikkun ha-Olam*, the restoration of the world. As we have seen, the German Idealists, from Fichte to Hegel, held that the antinomies and contradictions of this world have the purpose of providing the impetus to mankind's own growth and creativity, which, on their view, is itself tantamount to the development of the World-Spirit. As we have also seen, this is a view that is adopted by the contemporary Kabbalist Adin Steinsaltz,[119] and is completely consonant with the kabbalistic and particularly the Lurianic

---

119. Drob, "The Mystic as Philosopher," p. 14.

tradition. On this view, mankind, in struggling to resolve the antinomies, paradoxes, and hardships of earthly existence, comes to "raise the holy sparks," precisely by embodying those moral, intellectual, spiritual, and aesthetic values that constitute the fulfillment and completion of God.

Yet as we have also seen there is another, more transcendent, perspective that can be taken on this matter, a perspective that is more Plotinian than Hegelian, and that is also very much present in the Kabbalah. On this view the antinomies of this world themselves point to their own solution in a higher realm or in God. Thus, the contradiction between freedom and necessity in our world, for example, is resolved in a spiritual world where acts of will need not be mediated by material events, and hence are not subject to a causal nexus, etc.[120] Such a view is explicitly adopted by Adin Steinsaltz, who holds, among other things, that the hypothesis of the soul's connection to a higher world is necessary to resolve the antinomy of "equal souls yet unequal men."[121]

The Lurianic texts themselves embody both transcendent and immanent perspectives on *Tikkun*. As we have seen, the Chabad Hasidim held the dual perspective that *Tikkun* involves, on the one hand, an annihilation of the self and world and an absorption of the self into God; and, on the other hand, an infusion of divine light into and the spiritualization of earth.

Perhaps the transcendent (higher worlds) view of *Tikkun* is not as distinct from the immanent (this-world) view as one might initially believe. This is because the very *mitzvot*, the very acts of kindness, compassion, etc., represented by the *Sefirot* are both the vehicles for transcending the world and for bringing spirit down into it. We might say that the contradictions of this world point to a realm in which they are potentially resolved; and it becomes incumbent upon man to reach for that realm in his actions, mind, and heart, and, in the process, bring the divine into his everyday, worldly existence.

BEYOND HEGEL: MEANING AS THE ULTIMATE PRINCIPLE

We have already seen that two traditions evolved within the Kabbalah: one in which the *Sefirot* begin with *Chochmah* and are understood as actualizing the

---

120. See above, Chapter Four.
121. Drob, "The Mystic as Philosopher," p. 14.

development of divine thought and wisdom; the other in which the *Sefirot* begin with *Keter* and are understood as actualizing the divine will and desire. Indeed, we might understand the second tradition as a dialectical complement to the first. We might say that the "irrational" realm of sexuality, Eros, will, and desire is actually implicit within the very notions of logic and reason, providing meaning and content to the syllogism, for instance, in the same way that matter provides actuality or "content" to form; or, to use a later, Jungian, vocabulary, in the same manner that the "shadow" or unconscious provides an irrational, but life-sustaining, counterpoint to the psychological ego or consciousness.

The question "What is the explanation of the world?," as Hegel observed, would seem to call forth for a *reason*. However, the request for an *explanation* may not be the only *ultimate question* about the world. Might we not also ask, "What is the *meaning or significance* of the world?" To answer *this* question by invoking "Reason" is not satisfactory, because while we cannot ask if Reason is rational we can always ask whether Reason is meaningful or significant. Indeed this was Kierkegaard's very question for Hegel: what *existential meaning* lies in a completely rational world order? The question points to the fact that reason is not meaningful in and of itself, or is, at best, simply one significance amongst others. Hegel's philosophy, by virtue of the question it poses, i.e., by operating in a framework of explanation, begins with a prejudice in favor of the rational; and thereby excludes or demotes those meanings and values that are irrational or, at least, nonrational (e.g., love, beauty, sexuality, power, compassion, majesty, splendor, etc.), precisely those values that are instantiated in the Kabbalist's "lower" *Sefirot*, beginning with the fourth *Sefirah, Chesed*. Hegel's approach to these values, if not to ignore or exclude them, is to provide them with rationalistic explanations, or to see them as mythical approximations to rational ideas. The Kabbalists, however, are not so one-sided in their approach. On the one hand, they understand the nonrational (emotional) *Sefirot* as existing on a lower plane than, and derivative of, the upper "intellective" *Sefirot* (the *Chabad*, or *Sechel Sefirot*). On the other hand, higher than even the uppermost intellective Sefirah, is *Keter*, which is defined as "desire" and "will." Furthermore, as we have seen, even the highest intellectual *Sefirot* (*Chochmah* and *Binah*) are understood as engaging in a process of sexual union, providing an erotic, nonrational parallel to the cognitive dialectic.

Hegel, in his rationalism, had followed Kant in regarding the ultimate categories of the world as a system of "pure, a priori, non-sensuous" universals.[122] Such concepts as unity, plurality, totality, affirmation, negation, and existence are, according to these philosophers, necessary if we are to even conceive of a world. For Kant, such categories and regular principles are the logical conditions of the world, and Hegel went a step further in arguing that the world could actually, in effect, be deduced from them.

It is, however, instructive to compare the Kantian/Hegelian categories with the Kabbalist's *Sefirot*, which, as we have already seen, include irrational as well as rational elements and ideas. Not only are some of the *Sefirot* nonrational, but even those that are rational are complemented by an opposing series of "negative" or "counter" *Sefirot*, which exist among the "crowns of the other side." Irrationality is admitted into the Kabbalah at almost every turn, in the "emotional" *Sefirot*, in the delight and desire of *Keter*, in the various erotic *coniunctios* of the *Partzufim*, and in the acknowledgment of the reality of evil. By asking the question of *meaning* instead of requiring an "explanation," the Kabbalists filled their system with a host of living categories with far greater depth than the "unity," "plurality," "affirmation," and "negation" of rationalistic thought.

We should not forget that while Hegelian rationalism was perhaps the dominant force in Western thought throughout much of the nineteenth century, hermeneutic modes of thought, specifically concerned with the "irrational" have come to dominate the twentieth. As will become evident in Chapters Seven and Eight, the psychologies of both Freud and Jung transcended the rationalism of German Idealism, and did so precisely by hearkening back to Gnostic, Alchemical, and kabbalistic modes of thinking regarding the irrational side of man. As such, the Kabbalists not only anticipated the philosophy of Hegel, but also anticipated its transcendence in psychoanalysis and, in particular, Jungian psychology.

THE UNKNOWN: KANT, HEGEL, AND THE NOUMENAL WORLD

There is another, related, arena in which the philosophy of Hegel (and Hegel's polemic with Immanuel Kant) can shed light on the Lurianic Kabbalah. This regards the question of whether the Absolute is, in principle, "unknowable." The Kabbalists held that *Ein-Sof* is in its essence completely

---

122. Stace, *The Philosophy of Hegel*, p. 61.

unknowable and unknown. Hegel, on the other hand, held that the Absolute was fully knowable to speculative philosophy. The contrasts between these two positions, and an understanding of the "philosophy of the unknown" in modern thought, promises to shed further light upon the kabbalistic conception of God.

The modern philosophical notion of radical unknowability makes its first appearance in the thought of Immanuel Kant. Kant, in his *Critique of Pure Reason*, held that there is an impenetrable barrier beyond which no knowledge is possible. This barrier, he asserted, was a function of the structures and categories of the human mind. These categories, or what Kant referred to as "modes of apprehension" (among which are space, time, and causality) make knowledge of "appearances" possible, but at the same time limit our capacity to know the *thing-in-itself*, the world as it *really* is. The limitation in our knowledge results from the fact that all knowledge is necessarily conditioned by the *a priori* categories of the human mind, and, hence, in knowing what we experience we, of necessity, can only know what has been constructed by our own modes of apprehension. Kant called this realm of appearances, within which things appear in space and time and are causally related to one another, the *phenomenal* world. The world as it is in itself, outside of the categories and modes of apprehension, Kant called the *noumenal* world. However, because this world exists beyond the very conditions of sentience and knowledge, it is completely unknowable to the human mind. Because "ultimate reality" is completely unknowable, metaphysics as it is conceived by traditional philosophy is, according to Kant, impossible.

Kant nevertheless held that the existence of the noumenal realm is a necessary hypothesis, which serves as the substrate for the vast array of phenomenal appearances. He did not wish to deny that there was some contribution of the *object* to human perception, but beyond this, Kant, at least initially, held that nothing of substance can be said of noumenal reality. All that can be said lies in the world of appearances. Even the categories, which are the *a priori* forms that organize our perception of the world of appearances, are empty and void without reference to the phenomenal realm.

Despite his early disclaimers, Kant (in his later works on ethics, aesthetics, and religion) eventually had much to say regarding the noumenal world. Kant noted that while the phenomenal world necessarily follows the laws of causal, mechanical necessity, the moral law requires man to transcend the causal nexus, act on the basis of will, and conform his behavior to the rule of reason. He therefore concluded in *The Critique of Practical Reason*[123] that the demands of ethics and man's ability to act in accordance with the moral law were "windows," as it were, into a nonphenomenal, noumenal reality. God, freedom, and reason were each understood to be necessary hypotheses for morality, and Kant, finding no place for them in the phenomenal order, placed them in the noumenal realm. He continued to maintain that nothing "metaphysical" could be said about these noumenal hypotheses, but by placing them in the noumenal world, he had reopened the door to metaphysics, a door that the German Idealists were to march through within a few years of his death.

From the point of view of the present study it is important to note that the very notions that Kant attributed to the "unknowable" noumenal realm, i.e., God, will, reason, and ethical values, are the same notions that, for the Kabbalists, are most closely identified with the unknowable *Ein-Sof.*

Kant, in the *Critique of Pure Reason*, had set out to delimit knowledge to the world of appearances, but had ended, in his ethical works,[124] with a two-world doctrine reminiscent of the philosophy of Plato. Hegel, for his part, questioned the entire distinction between phenomena and noumena, arguing that Kant's basis for positing the thing-in-itself involved, on Kant's own theory, an illegitimate extension of the phenomenal category of causality (into the presumed noumenal realm).[125] Further, Hegel held that if we know that the noumenal realm exists and provides the foundation for ethics, then it is no longer unknowable, thus undermining Kant's rationale for restricting "knowledge" to phenomena.[126] Hegel's conclusion was that anything whatsoever that can be referred to must, at least in principle, be knowable, and, furthermore, since all that can be known is either a presentation to or category of the mind, all knowledge, and, hence, all existence, is essentially "idea." For Hegel, the distinctions between knowledge and being, as well as between the mind and its objects, collapse completely, and with this collapse our reason for speaking about an essential unknown dissolves.

There is a sense in which the Kabbalah remains closer to Kant than to

---

123. Immanuel Kant, *The Critique of Practical Reason*, trans. Lewis W. Beck. (Indianapolis: Bobbs-Merrill, 1956).

124. Immanuel Kant, *The Critique of Pure Reason*, trans. Norman Kemp Smith (New York: St. Martin's Press, 1965).

125. Hegel discusses his differences with Kant's "Critical Philosophy" in his greater logic. See Hegel, *Logic*, especially pars. 40–51.

126. Stace, *The Philosophy of Hegel*, p. 43.

Hegel. For the Kabbalists, the distinction between an unknown, unspeakable realm, and the world of sense and "action," is axiomatic. Yet the Kabbalists include much more than Kant in their realm of the "known." Indeed, as we have seen throughout this book, the Kabbalists, in their system of *Sefirot*, *Haolomot*, *Partzufim*, *Shevirah*, and *Tikkun*, appear to include everything recognized in the Hegelian dialectic, and more besides. While it is true that for the Kabbalists, as for Kant, the world's and man's higher nature (i.e., values) issue forth from an unknowable absolute, they are nonetheless present and very real in our world. For the Kabbalists, in contrast to Kant (especially Kant of the first *Critique*) metaphysical descriptions, even of the inner nature of the godhead are completely possible. What then remains in the realm of the necessarily unknown?

THE NECESSITY OF THE UNCONSCIOUS

I believe the answer to our question, or at least the direction where we must begin to search for one, requires us to move beyond Kant and Hegel to the intellectual world of twentieth century, to the psychological visions of Freud and Jung, and the possibility that the unknown, which Kant had posited as existing beyond the mind, actually exists "behind" it, or, better, at the core of the mind itself.

For Hegel, to say that something is real means that it is a possible object for consciousness. What, we might ask, is the nature of this possibility? For Hegel, writing at a time when no one thought to question the primacy of consciousness in human experience, there were effectively no limits to this possibility. Whatever the mind set itself upon was, for Hegel, a possible object of thought. That there might indeed be an unknowable realm within the mind itself, a primary and necessary unconsciousness, was something that neither Hegel nor his contemporaries seriously considered. Freud, of course, did not address himself directly to the philosophical tradition we are considering, but the concept of the unconscious, which he introduced in a presumably clinical and scientific context, has implications for philosophy, particularly Hegelian philosophy, that are not always fully appreciated.

The Hegelian dialectic, for which conflict and opposition is the motive force in the world, is interiorized within the human psyche in the work of Freud, and, especially, Carl Jung. Whereas Hegel regarded contradiction to be endemic to reality, the depth psychologists held that it was rather a characteristic of the human psyche. Jung even went so far as to hold that

Hegel had (on Jung's view mistakenly, on ours and Hegel's view legitimately) turned psychological insights into metaphysical principles. Hegel, according to Jung, had exteriorized psychology. However, since this "exteriorization" occurred at a time prior to the discovery of the dynamic unconscious, we can say with the benefit of hindsight that Hegel's projection of the human psyche onto the cosmos was incomplete. What might his philosophy look like if it included a metaphysical analogue to the psychoanalytic *unconscious*?[127] The answer to this question can provide us with an alternative to Kant's vision of the unknown, and provide us with an elucidation of the unknown in the Kabbalah, *Ein-Sof.*

Had Hegel applied his own method to consciousness or mind in general, he actually would have been led, dialectically, to the notion of the unconscious. For example, he might have reasoned that since consciousness is itself always limited by some specific content, there is always something, some potential mental content that exists beyond its reach; such content being notable for its "absence." While the content of consciousness changes from one moment to the next, the general dialectic between "presence" and "absence" always remains. It is thus part of the concept of consciousness or mind that there is something, not yet specified, that is unconscious, or absent. This view, it should be noted, is developed quite thoroughly in the psychoanalyst Lacan, who holds that the "absences" in human experience, and, particularly, language (i.e., that which is not felt, not said, etc.) are evidence of a "lack" of being, at the core of human reality. The unconscious, as we might understand it through Lacan's interpretation of Freud and Hegel, is part of the very notion of consciousness itself. This formulation finds its parallel in the Kabbalah, where it is held that the *Sitra Achra,* the "other side," is part of the very essence of the world.[128]

It is a fundamental conviction, almost a logical axiom, of psychoanalytic thought that there must always be an unconscious, i.e., an unfathomed, unknown ground, to thought, feeling, and behavior. While it may be the case that any given thought or affect can always, at least potentially, be brought

---

127. Efforts in this direction have been made by the neo-Jungian psychologist James Hillman. See especially the anthology of Hillman's writings, *A Blue Fire,* edited and introduced by Thomas Moore (New York: Harper & Row, 1989, paperback edition, 1991) and Hillman's *Revisioning Psychology* (New York: Harper & Row, 1976; paperback edition, with a new preface by the author, 1992).

128. On the "other side" see Tishby and Lachower, *The Wisdom of the Zohar,* Vol. 2, Part 2, "The Other Side."

into consciousness, the *place* of the unconscious must always be occupied by something, i.e., something that is unknown. Freud filled this place with mostly personal (and some "collective," e.g., the Oedipus Complex) contents, and Jung filled it with the archetypes and symbols of the collective unconscious.

The Kabbalists were perhaps the clearest of all in their view of the necessity of an unconscious as part of the essence of both God and man. This view is not only expressed in the Zoharic insistence that man must give a "portion of his faith" to the "other side,"[129] but also in the heart of the Lurianic theosophy. The doctrine of *Tzimtzum* makes clear that "unconsciousness" is the fundamental condition of the world's creation. In contracting himself in *Tzimtzum*, *Ein-Sof* creates a condition in which no creature (perhaps God included) can effectively know all. For in *Tzimtzum*, *Ein-Sof* removes himself from a region of being, which, precisely because he has removed or "concealed" himself, becomes a separate and distinct, "created" world. Indeed, the act of *Tzimtzum* is one in which God conceals an aspect of Himself from Himself, and thereby, paradoxically, finds Himself, through the eyes of an "other" (man) who is but a concealed aspect of God. Just as individual "repression" is central to the development of human personality, a cosmic "repression" is central to the origin of the world.

Could there be a consciousness that knows itself completely? Such a consciousness, the Kabbalists affirm, would cease to exist as a separate, individual, mind; it would, of necessity merge with the infinite mind of *Ein-Sof* itself (which, because it is completely undifferentiated, is effectively *no mind* at all). The unconscious is, in effect, the price we pay for individual, separate existence, and on the Kabbalist's view, the price even God must pay for a world. In a radical inversion of the Cartesian formula, the Kabbalists might well say, "I don't think (everything) therefore I am." According to the Kabbalists such a proposition would, of necessity, also be appropriate for God.

What we, as finite creatures, fail to think or know, according to the

---

129. Zohar II, 203b: "Here we learn that even though this side (*Sitra Achra*) is nothing but the side of uncleanness, there is a brightness around it, and man does not have to drive it away. Why is this? Because there is a brightness around it; the side of holiness of faith exists there; and there is no need to treat it with disdain. Therefore one must give it a portion on the side of the holiness of faith." Tishby and Lachower, *The Wisdom of the Zohar*, Vol. 2, p. 492. Cf. Sperling and Simon, *The Zohar*, Vol. IV, p. 189.

Kabbalah, is the divine core at the center of our own mind (what Jung would later equate with the Kabbalist's "sparks" and *Adam Kadmon*[130]). This unconsciousness of the divine is at the same time a divine *unconsciousness*. It is not an empirical unknown, or epistemological barrier separating our minds from the world; rather, it is the unknown that is at the center of all being. It is this unknown, this psychological and metaphysical unconscious, which moves our search for kabbalistic understanding beyond Hegel to the works of Freud and Jung.

---

130. See Carl Gustav Jung, *Mysterium Coniunctionis, The Collected Works of C. G. Jung*, Vol. 14. trans. R. F. C. Hull, (Princeton, NJ: Princeton University Press, 1963), esp. pp. 48–56 (The "Scintillae") and 382–456 (Adam and Eve).

7

Freud and Jewish Mysticism

The relationship between Judaism and psychoanalysis has long been a subject of passionate debate. The Nazis, of course, spoke disparagingly of psychoanalysis as "the Jewish science" and Anna Freud, reflecting upon this appellation after the war, referred to it proudly as a "badge of honor."[1] Freud viewed himself as an opponent of religion and made no secret of his view that "God" is nothing but a projection of man's superego, the father "writ" large as a symbol of the law proscribing man's Oedipal strivings. Freud regarded himself as an atheist, and hoped that psychoanalysis would one day produce a "secular priesthood" that would lead men and women to a state free of neurotic suffering and devoid of religious beliefs and demands. As such, Freud has either been ignored or regarded with disdain in orthodox Jewish thought.[2]

On the other hand, psychoanalysts, Freud included, have never tired of

---

1. Anna Freud, "Inaugural Lecture" (read in Jerusalem in 1977 by Arthur Vlanstein), *International Journal of Psychoanalysis* LIX (1978): 148.

2. Exceptions to this lack of attention to the parallels between Judaism and psychoanalysis among orthodox Jews, can be found in Adin Steinsaltz, "Hasidism and Psychoanalysis," *Judaism* 19(3) (1960): 222–228, and S. Applebaum and A. Metzger, "Hasidism and Psychotherapy: An overview," *Intercom* 16(2)(1976): 15–25.

speculating on the role that Judaism played in the development of psychoanalysis. As we shall see, Freud regarded his Jewishness as the single most important factor in his personal background, viewing it as a motivating factor in his life and work. Several full-length studies have been devoted to the impact of Judaism on Freud's life and career. However, none of them, with the exception of David Bakan's *Sigmund Freud and The Jewish Mystical Tradition*, have attempted to relate the content of psychoanalysis to the Kabbalah.

Bakan's book attempted to draw parallels between psychoanalysis and Jewish mysticism and purported to show that Freud was a "crypto-Sabbatean," a follower of the heretical Shabbatai Sevi (a would-be "messiah" in seventeenth-century Poland). Unfortunately, Bakan's work was outlandish in its claims and virtually devoid of any serious discussion of kabbalistic ideas. The result has been that this often-cited work has had very little actual impact on our subsequent understanding of Freud's relationship to Judaism. Indeed, after Bakan, nearly all studies on this subject have tended to ignore Jewish mysticism as a possible background to psychoanalytic ideas. This is most unfortunate as the Lurianic Kabbalah (which was scarcely even mentioned in Bakan's work) can provide us with a genuine and specific theoretical link between Judaism and psychoanalytic theory. This situation is particularly troubling because, as we shall see, Bakan himself adduced that when Freud was made aware of the Lurianic Kabbalah he was extremely impressed and queried why these ideas had never previously been brought to his attention.

In this chapter I will consider a series of parallels between psychoanalysis and basic kabbalistic and Hasidic ideas. It has long been my conviction that psychoanalytic concepts can be instrumental for our contemporary understanding of the Kabbalah.[3] Here I will argue that the converse is true as well, that the Kabbalah and Hasidism provide an essential key to understanding the often-discussed relationship between Judaism and psychoanalysis. That our understanding of psychoanalysis can itself be deepened by this approach will emerge in the discussion that follows.

I have briefly described the basic parallels between the Lurianic Kabbalah and psychoanalysis in Chapter One. We should recall that Luria's infinite light or energy, the expression of divine desire, has its psychoanalytic equivalent in the Freudian libido, an energy that expresses human desire; that

---

3. See Sanford Drob, "Freud and the Chasidim: Redeeming the Jewish Soul of Psychoanalysis," *Jewish Review* 3(1): 8–11.

Luria's description of the erotic nature of God is paralleled in Freud's affirmation of the sexual nature of man; that Luria's conception of *Tzimtzum* or concealment as the origin of the created world is paralleled by Freud's notion of repression as the origin of personality; that Luria's "Other Side" is comprised of alienated and constricted divine light much as the Freudian unconscious is comprised of alienated and constricted libido; that for Luria redemption involves the liberation of the entrapped light and its return to the service of God's eros, just as for Freud, therapy consists of the liberation of constricted sexual libido and its return to the service of the ego, etc. We will have occasion to explore these and many other parallels in greater detail in the pages that follow.

FREUD'S JEWISH BACKGROUND

The comparisons I am about to make will undoubtedly raise a series of questions concerning the direct or indirect influence of kabbalistic and Hasidic ideas on Freud's theories. Indeed, the facts of Freud's early life are themselves suggestive of this possibility.

Freud was born on May 6, 1856, in Freiberg, Moravia. He himself claimed that his father's family had originated in the German Rhineland but had been driven east as a result of anti-Semitism in the fourteenth or fifteenth century. In the course of the nineteenth century the family had "retraced their steps from Lithuania through Galicia to German Austria."[4]

Freud, in a personal letter to A. A. Roback,[5] described his father as coming from a Hasidic background. His great-grandfather, Rabbi Ephraim Freud, and grandfather, Rabbi Shlomo Freud (for whom Freud himself was named), if not actually rabbis,[6] were most certainly orthodox Jews. Indeed, the town of Tysmenitz in Galicia, where Freud's father was raised, was one full of Hasidic life and learning.[7] Freud's mother, Amalie, was from a center

---

4. Sigmund Freud, "An Autobiographical Study" (1925). In the *Standard Edition of the Complete Psychological Works of Sigmund Freud*, ed. James Strachey (London: Hogarth Press, 1955–1967), Vol. 20.

5. A. A. Roback, *Freudiana* (Cambridge, MA: Sci-Art Publishers, 1957), p. 27.

6. Ernest Jones, *The Life and Work of Sigmund Freud* (New York: Basic Books, 1953), Vol. 2, p. 1.

7. W. Aron, "Furzeichnugen Wegen Opshtam fun Sigmund Freud in wegan

244 KABBALISTIC METAPHORS

of Jewish thought, Brody, in Galicia, near Lvov,[8] and at least one scholar has traced her ancestry to an eighteenth-century talmudic scholar, Nathan Halevy Charmatz.[9]

According to his biographer, Ernest Jones, Freud's parents reckoned dates by the Hebrew calendar up until the time of their marriage.[10] They had each migrated west to Moravia in 1844[11] where they met and were married in 1855 by a rabbi associated with the German Reform Movement, Noah Mannheimer.[12] In Austria they had been exposed to *Haskalah* (liberal, "enlightened" Judaism) and it is clear that by the time of Freud's birth their observance of Jewish law and ritual had declined. Still, Freud grew up in an environment very rich in Jewish religion and culture. His father would frequently illustrate an idea or moral by quoting a Jewish anecdote,[13] a custom that Freud himself maintained throughout his own life. Freud tells us that the Jewish scriptures were his main instruments of education until he attended school at age nine, and he maintained in later years that he had been greatly influenced by them.[14]

While there is some question as to whether Freud ever learned or later retained much Hebrew,[15] it is clear that his father was very knowledgeable in both Hebrew and Yiddish and that his mother, who lived until the age of 95,

---

sien Yiddishkeit," [Notes concerning the genealogy of Sigmund Freud and concerning his Jewishness] *Yivo Bleter* 40: 169.

8. David Bakan, *Sigmund Freud and the Jewish Mystical Tradition*, p. 56.

9. H. W. Puner, *Freud: His Life and His Mind* (New York: Crown, 1949), p. 11; Jones says he was a merchant and patron of scholars. Jones *Life and Work*, Vol. 1, p. 3.

10. Jones, *Life and Work*, Vol. 1, p. 2.

11. Emmanuel Rice, "The Jewish Fathers of Psychoanalysis," *Judaism* 36(1) (1987): 109–115.

12. Aron, *Furzeichnugen*, p. 166; Bakan, *Sigmund Freud*, p. 64.

13. Jones, *Life and Work*, Vol. 1, p. 3.

14. Ibid., Vol. 1, p. 19.

15. Although Jones (*Life and Work*, Vol. 1, p. 21) assumes that Freud had a knowledge of Hebrew and notes that Freud's father presented him with a family bible bearing a personalized Hebrew inscription on the occasion of Freud's thirty-fifth birthday, there is much, according to Peter Gay, to suggest that Freud either never knew or forgot his Hebrew by the time he was an adult. Peter Gay, *Freud, A Life for Our Time* (New York: W. W. Norton, 1988), p. 600. Indeed, Freud himself, in a "Letter to the editor of the Jewish Press Centre in Zurich" (1925), expressed regret that his own education in Hebrew was lacking (*Standard Edition*, Vol. 19, p. 291).

spoke Galician Yiddish as her almost exclusive language, suggesting that this was Freud's own language until he began formal schooling.[16]

Freud's early exposure to Jewish studies was facilitated by his childhood tutor, a Professor Hammerschlag with whom Freud was on very intimate terms for many years.[17] While this teacher seems to have emphasized the ethical and historical aspects of Judaism, as opposed to the study of Hebrew texts, Freud's father presented Freud with a Hebrew bible on the occasion of his son's thirty-fifth birthday, which contained the following personal Hebrew inscription:

> My dear son Schlomo:
>   In the seventh [year?] of your life the spirit of the Lord began to move you [cf. Judges 13: 25] and said to you: Go, read in my Book that I have written, and there will be opened to you the sources of wisdom, knowledge, and understanding. See the Book of Books from which the wise men dug out their wisdom and the lawmakers learned law and justice [cf. Numbers 21:18]. You have looked upon the face of the Almighty [cf. Numbers 24:4, 16], have heard and striven to climb upwards, and you flew upon the wings of the Spirit [cf. Psalms 18:10]. For a long time the Book has been hidden [kept safe] for the day on which you have completed your 35th year. I have had it covered with a new leather binding and given it the name: "Spring up, O well." Sing ye unto it, (cf. Numbers 21:17) and offer it to you for a remembrance and a memorial of love.
>
> From your father, who loves you with unending love.
> Jacob, Son of Rabbi Shlomo Freud
> In the capital city of Vienna 29 Nissan 5651, May 8 1891.[18]

While Bergmann[19] has argued that this inscription reveals Jacob Freud's own Haskalah tendencies, the phrase "wisdom, knowledge and understanding" is

---

16. Rice, "The Jewish Fathers," 109–115.

17. Indeed, it is reported that Freud named one of his daughters after Hammerschlag's daughter and another after his niece and that Freud said of his relationship with Hammerschlag, "there is such a secret sympathy between us that we can talk intimately together." Jones, *Life and Work*, Vol. 1, p. 163.

18. Rice, "The Jewish Fathers," p. 115. Translation from E. Freud and L. Grinbrich Simitus, eds., *Sigmund Freud — His Life in Pictures and Words* (New York: Harcourt Brace Jovanovich, 1978).

19. Martin S. Bergmann, "Moses and the Evolution of Freud's Jewish Identity," *Israel Annal of Psychiatry Disciplines* XIV (March 1976): p. 4.

most often associated with the Chabad Hasidim, whose very name is an acronym for these words. That Jacob Freud kept the family bible hidden until his son's thirty-fifth year may be an allusion to the tradition of revealing the hidden aspects of Torah (i.e., the Kabbalah) only to those who have achieved the age of 35 or 40.[20]

Bakan points out that Freud could very well have been exposed to kabbalistic ideas as interpreted by the scholar Adolph Jellinek, who was the most popular Jewish preacher in Vienna during the period of Freud's youth,[21] and who provided an annotated German translation of Adolph Franck's *La Kabbale ou la Philosophie Religieuse des Hebreux* (1843), which was widely circulated for several decades.[22]

While Freud does not discuss Kabbalah or Hasidism in any of his published writings, he reports in a letter to Fliess in 1897 (during the period of composition of *The Interpretation of Dreams*) making a collection of wise Jewish anecdotes.[23] Later in life, Freud is reported to have conversed on the subject of Kabbalah and Hasidism with the Lithuanian rabbi Chayyim Bloch.[24] In the preface to the 1975 paperback edition to his *Sigmund Freud and the Jewish Mystical Tradition*, Bakan reports on an interview with Bloch, who says that many years earlier he had approached Freud about writing an introduction to a German translation of a work by Chayyim Vital, the most prominent student and expositor of the Lurianic Kabbalah. According to Bloch, Freud read the manuscript and was beside himself with excitement. Freud exclaimed "This is gold" and queried why Vital's work had never before been brought to his attention. In a meeting in Freud's home Bloch reports that Freud agreed to write the forward and even volunteered to assist Bloch in getting the manuscript published. The relationship came to an end, however, when Freud showed Bloch a manuscript of Freud's own *Moses and Monotheism*. Bloch was aghast, stating, "Anti-Semites accuse us of killing the

---

20. Bakan, *Sigmund Freud*, pp. 55, 200.
21. Ibid., p. 81.
22. Idel, *Kabbalah: New Perspectives*, p. 8.
23. Sigmund Freud, *The Origins of Psychoanalysis: Letters to Wilhelm Fliess, Drafts and Notes: 1887–1902*, ed. Marie Bonaparte and trans. Anna Freud and Ernest Kris. (New York: Basic Books, 1954), p. 211.
24. As reported by Aron in "Farzeichnugen," p. 169; as quoted in Bakan, p. 55. Aron writes: "What it was that moved Freud to interest himself in Kabbalah and Hasidism is not hard to understand. He must have felt himself to be spiritually at home in these worlds."

founder of Christianity. Now a Jew adds that we also killed the founder of Judaism." Bloch reports that Freud left the room in anger, leaving Bloch in the library. In that library, according to Bloch, was a large collection of Judaica, including a number of books on the Kabbalah in German and a French translation of the *Zohar*.[25]

It is certainly of psychoanalytic interest that in spite of Freud's claimed adherence to a purely scientific Weltanschauung, he himself was extremely superstitious. In a letter to Jung he explained that he had derived from his friend Fliess "the specifically mystic nature of my mysticism," which involved a belief in the significance and predictive quality of numbers;[26] a belief that he held in common with the kabbalistic tradition of *Gematria* (number mysticism). In particular, Freud suffered from overwhelming death anxiety[27] and developed the conviction that he was numerologically destined to die at a certain age and date.[28] Freud had a belief, to the point of dread, in such concepts as a Doppelganger (or double), which is an echo of the kabbalistic concept of the *Tzelem* (or celestial counterpart). Indeed he once wrote Arthur Schnitzler: "I think I have avoided you from a kind of reluctance to meet my double."[29] One can only guess that in Freud's personal superstitiousness and mysticism there is a sort of "return of the repressed" that served as a counterpoint to his naturalism and a vital impetus to his work.

Freud's associates were, with very few exceptions, Jews, many of whom had been raised in religious homes. Joseph Breuer, for example, who Freud originally credited with the discovery of psychoanalysis, was the son of Leopold Breuer, a well-known Jewish teacher and religious leader,[30] and was himself a lifelong member of the *chevrah kiddusha*, the Jewish burial society.

While none of Freud's biographers speak of a specific Jewish religious influence upon psychoanalysis, several of them, including Jones, Paul Roa-

---

25. David Bakan, *Sigmund Freud and the Jewish Mystical Tradition*, paperback edition (Boston: Beacon Press, 1975), pp. xvii–xviii.

26. *The Freud/Jung Letters*, trans. R. Manheim and R. F. C. Hull. William McGuire, ed., (Princeton, NJ: Princeton University Press, 1974), Letter 220.

27. Max Schur, *Freud: Living and Dying* (New York: International Universities Press, 1972), p. 337.

28. Jones, *Life and Work*, Vol. 2, p. 184.

29. Quoted in Paul Johnson, *A History of the Jews* (New York: Harper & Row, 1987), p. 415. Johnson gives no further reference and I have been unable to trace it myself.

30. Max Grunwald, *History of the Jews in Vienna* (Philadelphia: Jewish Publication Society of America, 1936), p. 521.

zan,[31] and most recently Gay,[32] acknowledge that Freud's Jewishness was the single most important part of his personal background. Freud himself often conceived of his Jewishness as a motivating factor in his life, propelling him and providing him with energy to overcome what he felt to be the ubiquitous forces of anti-Semitism.[33] In a 1926 address to the B'nai B'rith, however, he stated that he remained attracted to Judaism because of "many dark emotional powers that are all the mightier the less they let themselves be grasped in words."[34] Such a statement is, interestingly, completely consonant with the Hasidic concept of the subconscious effects of the "Jewish soul" even upon apostate or assimilated Jews. Perhaps it was such "subconscious forces" that led to Freud's lifelong struggle with (and ambivalence) toward Moses,[35] and that contributed, in the view of at least one author, to Freud's own messianic predilections.[36] Perhaps, too, such forces ultimately expressed themselves in Freud's thinking and, as we shall see, lent a particularly Jewish, Hasidic cast to much of his work.

In this context it is noteworthy that more than one of Freud's more important disciples understood psychoanalysis to be greatly indebted to Judaism. Freud's daughter, Anna, for example, argued that psychoanalysis is a Jewish creation. In 1977 she commented that psychoanalysis "has been criticized . . . even for being a 'Jewish science.' However the other derogatory remarks may be evaluated, it is, I believe, the last-mentioned connotation which, under the present circumstances, can serve as a title of honor."[37] While some have seen this statement as an affirmation of the specifically

---

31. Paul Roazan, *Freud and his Followers* (New York: Alfred A. Knopf, 1971).

32. Peter Gay, *Freud: A Life for Our Time.*

33. See Jones, *Life and Work*, Vol. 1, p. 22. Jones relates that Freud reacted against his own father's apparent submission to anti-Semitism by identifying with historical figures such as Hannibal and Napoleon's marshal, Massena (who was thought to be Jewish), whom Freud saw as Semitic heroes. Max Graf in his "Reminiscences of Professor Sigmund Freud" *Psychoanalytic Quarterly* 11 (1942), 465–476 relates that Freud strongly advised a friend against bringing up his son as a Christian, stating, "If you do not let your son grow up as a Jew you will deprive him of those sources of energy which cannot be replaced by anything else."

34. Sigmund Freud, Address to the Society of B'nai B'rith (1926), *Standard Edition*, Vol. 20, p. 271–276.

35. See Freud's "The Moses of Michelangelo," *Standard Edition*, Vol. 23, pp. 3–140.

36. Bakan, *Sigmund Freud*, p. 102 ff.

37. Anna Freud, "Inaugural Lecture," p. 148.

Jewish origins of the psychoanalytic movement,[38] others, notably Gay, have understood it simply as a piece of rhetoric to affirm Jewish pride in a post-holocaust world.[39]

Of much greater significance in the present context, however, is Carl Jung's intimation of an important connection between psychoanalysis and Jewish mystical thought. According to Jung, a full understanding of Freud: "would carry us beyond Jewish orthodoxy into the subterranean workings of Hassidism and then into the intricacies of the Kabbalah, which still remains unexplored psychologically."[40] That Jung himself was drawn to mystical, particularly Gnostic, ideas is indisputable. What is remarkable here however, is his assertion that Freudian psychoanalysis itself needs to be understood in a kabbalistic/Hasidic context.

On the whole, in spite of its suggestiveness, it is not clear what conclusions can be drawn from the biographical data. On the one hand it seems unlikely that Freud actually read extensively in kabbalistic and Hasidic texts or that he consciously converted Jewish mystical notions into secular, scientific form. The thesis that Freud was an avowed Kabbalist who intentionally disguised the kabbalistic sources of his ideas in order to avoid their being rejected by anti-Semites seems quite far-fetched.[41] On the other hand, it seems almost certain that Freud was exposed as a child and adolescent to Hasidic and other Jewish stories, folklore, and psychological insights, and that such ideas influenced him in the very profound but general way that anyone is influenced by the culture of their youth.

The whole question of the influence of the Jewish religion upon Freud's work is one that cries out for fuller study, particularly in light of the flaws and inadequacies of previous efforts in this area.[42] This chapter, however, will

---

38. See, for example, Paul Schwaaber, "Title of Honor: The Psychoanalytic Congress in Jerusalem," *Midstream* XXIV (March 1978): p. 32.

39. Peter Gay, *A Godless Jew: Freud, Atheism and the Making of Psychoanalysis* (New Haven: Yale University Press, 1987), p. 118.

40. Carl Gustav Jung, *Letters*, Vol. 2, p. 359. Jung made this comment long after any advantage would have accrued to him by identifying psychoanalysis with Judaism. Earlier, in the 1930s, he had rather disparagingly argued that, in contrast to Freudian psychoanalysis, which was limited in its application to Jews, his psychology was applicable to the aryan spirit.

41. Bakan, *Sigmund Freud*, p. 26.

42. The only major study in this area that seriously considers the impact of Jewish religious thought on Freud's work is David Bakan's *Sigmund Freud and the Jewish Mystical Tradition*, a work that in spite of certain merits is flawed by virtue of

focus on the parallels that exist between the kabbalistic and Hasidic traditions and psychoanalytic thought. It will assume, regardless of whether (and to what degree) Freud was actually influenced by Jewish and Hasidic ideas, that it is possible, and indeed profitable, to view some of the basic tenets of psychoanalysis as secularized versions of Hasidic themes and concepts, and that these concepts can in turn be illuminated by comparing them to parallel psychoanalytic ideas.

SOME GENERAL CONSIDERATIONS

An examination of the most general features of the Freudian enterprise reveals a series of striking similarities between psychoanalysis and Judaism, particularly mystical and Hasidic Judaism, on the theoretical, technical, and sociological levels. The similarities are made all the more significant by the fact that while psychoanalysis shares these features with Hasidic Judaism, it does not share them with the (mostly somatic) psychiatry that was practiced in Freud's own time.[43]

Hermeneutics. The first, and perhaps most significant of these general features, is the fact that psychoanalysis, like Judaism, is an *interpretive* or *hermeneutic* discipline.[44] Here we might note that, while Darwin had

---

the author's lack of familiarity with basic Jewish, kabbalistic, and Hasidic notions and that, much to its detriment, leaves out any consideration of either Lurianic Kabbalah or Chabad Hasidism. Other works such as Dennis Klein's *Jewish Origins of the Psychoanalytic Movement* (Chicago: University of Chicago Press, 1985) and Peter Gay's *A Godless Jew* either see the impact of Judaism on Freud in extremely general terms (Klein's thesis is that psychoanalysis, like Judaism, is a redemptive social movement) or deny any religious or spiritual impact of Judaism on Freud's work. As noted previously, the studies by Steinsaltz, and Applebaum and Metzger (see note 1 above), have pointed to important parallels between psychoanalysis and Hasidism in a general manner but have not explored these parallels in a historical context.

43. For example, Jones (*Life and Work*, Vol. 1, p. 226) reports that prior to Charcot (with whom Freud studied in the 1880s) hysterical neuroses were either considered a simulation or a disorder of the womb to be treated via excision of the clitoris. Freud himself relates how his first psychoanalytic patient, Frau Emmy Von N., had been treated prior to his encounter with her "by a course of massage combined with electric baths." Sigmund Freud, "Studies in Hysteria, case Histories: Frau Emmy Von N." (1895), *Standard Edition*, Vol. 2, pp. 44–59.

44. For a discussion of the hermeneutic nature of psychoanalysis see Paul Ricouer, *Freud and Philosophy.*

brought the methods of natural science to an area of inquiry (the origin and development of the species) that had hitherto been understood *interpretively* as the creation of God, Freud brought the methods of *biblical* and *talmudic interpretation* to an area of inquiry (human psychopathology and dreams) that in his own day had been understood causally as a function of biology. As such Freud was decidedly *unscientific* by the standards of his own time and was, indeed, accused by his critics of propagating "an evil method proceeding from mystical tendencies and full of dangers to the medical profession."[45] Freud's interpretive or hermeneutic method, as described in *The Interpretation of Dreams*, is in many ways remarkably similar to the method of biblical exegesis employed by the rabbis of the Talmud. For example, among the talmudic rules of biblical exegesis is the notion of *notarikon* ("shorthand") where the letters of a given work represent the initial letters of a complete thought (compare with the psychoanalytic concept of "condensation"); the concept of *Al tikrei* . . . (Do not read . . . but . . .) where the meaning of a word is understood to be a word that sounds like it; and *ein mukdam v-me'ohar ba-torah* (there is no "earlier" or "later" in the Torah) whereby a Torah passage is reinterpreted by rearranging the sequence of events in its plain meaning (compare to Freud's dictim that there is no before and after in the unconscious). Each of these talmudic methods of interpretation is echoed in Freud's *Interpretation of Dreams*.

Of particular interest is Freud's technique of breaking the dream into its component parts and commenting on these components in terms of the dreamer's past life, current fears, and desires. Anyone who carefully studies Freud's comments on the "Irma dream" in *The Interpretation of Dreams*,[46] the very dream that Freud explicitly states had unlocked for him the secret of dreaming, cannot fail to note their formal similarity to exegesis of biblical passages in the Talmud or with those in a book with which Freud must have himself been thoroughly familiar, the Passover Haggadah. Freud's method of reporting his interpretation of this dream is first to recite the whole dream and then to repeat each element or proposition of the dream, along with his personal associations and commentary, just as the Haggadah first repeats an entire biblical passage relevant to the Exodus from Egypt and then repeats each element of that passage with biblical associations and commentary. It is

45. Alfred E. Hoche, as reported by Jones, *Life and Work*, Vol. 2, p. 111.

46. Sigmund Freud, *The Interpretation of Dreams* (1990), *Standard Edition*, Vols. 4 and 5. See especially Chapter 2: "The Method of Interpreting Dreams," Vol. 4, pp. 106–122.

of interest that Freud should report upon the dream that led to "psychoana-lytic redemption" using the same literary device as the Haggadah makes use of in reporting the redemption from Egypt.[47]

Bakan argues that Freud himself recognized that he was applying methods in psychology that the rabbis had applied to the Torah, and it was for this reason that he chose the pseudonym "Dora" for one of his earliest and most important psychoanalytic case histories.[48] The Hasidim, Bakan argues, regarded their leader, the rebbe or *tzaddik*, as a "living Torah," and for Freud, growing up in a milieu inundated with Hasidic ideas, it was only a small step to regard all men from this perspective. The concept of a human life as a "text," one that has become increasingly popular in contemporary psychoanalytic thought, is thus seen to have specifically Jewish antecedents.

It should also be noted, at least in passing, that Freud's technique of "free association" as a method of dream interpretation has its antecedent in a kabbalistic method of biblical exegesis. Abraham Abulafia (1240–after 1291) developed a method of biblical interpretation that involved the interpreter's meditation upon and free association to the words and letters of the Torah, the ultimate purpose of which was "to unseal the soul, to untie the knots which bind it," knots that separate an individual's personal existence from its natural connection with divine life.[49]

We do not have to go beyond Freud's early inner circle to find an awareness that psychoanalysis has certain talmudic qualities. In 1908, Freud's disciple Karl Abraham wrote Freud of his fascination with a passage in *Jokes and Their Relation to the Unconscious* that Abraham found "wholly talmudic" in construction, style, and argument. In commenting on this similarity Abraham notes: "After all, the talmudic way of thinking cannot suddenly have disappeared from us."[50]

Others have observed that Freud's penchant for using "stories" to make

---

47. See Bakan, *Sigmund Freud*, p. 253.
48. See ibid., p. 246 ff.
49. See Scholem, *Major Trends*, p. 131. With respect to Abulafia's method of free association see Moshe Idel, *Language, Torah and Hermeneutics in Abraham Abulafia* (Albany: State University of New York Press, 1989), esp. pp. 97–109. Abulafia is an example of an early Kabbalist who combined a psychological method of "free association" with the biblical text to achieve a psychological end: liberation from elements that bind the psyche or soul.
50. Abraham, Hilda C. and Ernst L. Freud, *Sigmund Freud and Karl Abraham; a Psycho-analytic Dialogue: The Letters of Sigmund Freud and Karl Abraham*

a point or illustrate an idea is quintessentially Jewish. As Paul Johnson has observed: "Its (psychoanalysis') Torah, its essential documents were Freud's own writings and cases, and they, like the Bible, were the apotheosis of the short story. The skill in illustrating a thesis by a tale had been characteristic of the sages which had re-emerged in Hasidism. Freud gave it scientific and secular status."[51] Freud, we know, was a collector of wise Jewish anecdotes and stories. At one point in his career he himself reflected: "It still strikes myself as strange that the case histories I write should read like short stories, and that as one might say, they lack the serious stamp of science."[52]

The Secret and the Hidden: A second, very general feature that psycho-analysis shares with mystical Judaism is a concern with the *secret* and the *hidden*. Indeed, the entire *raison d'être* for psychoanalytic inquiry is the belief that the meaning or significance of an individual's dream or psychological symptom is *hidden* from both the doctor and the patient and must be uncovered.

According to Freud's "official" biographer, Ernest Jones, Freud's ultimate goal was "the secrets of man's inner nature,"[53] and Freud himself once said that a marble tablet ought to be erected by the house where he himself had an especially illuminating dream, one which would read: "In this house on 24 July 1895, the secret of dreams was revealed to Dr. Sigmund Freud."[54] The analogy with the Kabbalah is plain, for while Freud concerned himself with the hidden or secret aspects of man, the Kabbalah is concerned with the hidden or secret aspects of the Torah, the cosmos, and God.[55] Again, the Hasidim provide us with a "missing link" between the Kabbalah and Freud, for, as will be discussed shortly in greater detail, Hasidism placed less emphasis than Kabbalah upon the secrets of the Torah or cosmos, and proportionately greater emphasis on the secrets or "roots" of the individual's own soul.[56]

1907–1926 (London: The Hogarth Press and the Institute of Psychoanalysis, 1965), 56 (46). Abraham to Freud, May 11, 1908.

51. Paul Johnson, *A History of the Jews*, p. 416.

52. Ibid., p. 416. Johnson cites Steven Marcus's *Freud and The Culture of Psychoanalysis* (London: Allen and Unwin, 1984), p. 83.

53. Jones, *Life and Work*, Vol. 1, p. 35.

54. Johnson, *A History of the Jews*, p. 414.

55. See Bakan, *Sigmund Freud*, p. 71.

56. The notion of inquiring into the secrets or roots of one's soul is hardly unknown in the Kabbalah, and is found in both the ecstatic Kabbalah of Abulafia and

Oral Confession: Psychoanalysis and Hasidism share the view that self-knowledge and self-improvement can be achieved through a verbal confession and dialogue with an authoritative yet sympathetic listener. Freud was undoubtedly aware of the practice of a private therapeutic encounter between *rebbe* and *Hasid* and, as Zalman Schachter has observed, many features of this encounter are to be found in psychoanalytic treatment. The use of interpretation, confrontation, and suggestion (i.e., to relieve an overly guilt-ridden conscience), as well as the encouragement of identification, were all practiced by Hasidic rebbes long before Freud's initial collaboration with Breuer.[57] The concordance in technique between Hasidism and psychoanalysis is deserving of its own separate study. Suffice it to say that while there are critical differences, the basic similarities are almost too great to be regarded as mere coincidence. As Adin Steinsaltz has aptly put it, the encounter between Hasid and rebbe, unlike Catholic confession (for example) is not a confession of sins but a "very practical outpouring of the soul, a self-analysis of various problems of the soul in the presence of a rabbi, who guides and directs the self-analysis."[58]

Written and Oral Teachings: The teaching and transmission of psycho-analysis came to approximate certain important developments within Hasid-ism. For example, as Bakan has pointed out, the kabbalistic practice of orally transmitting a received teaching from master to pupil hears its echo in today's psychoanalytic institutes.[59] As with Judaism there is both a "written" and "oral" teaching in psychoanalysis. The written teaching, embodied in large measure in *The Standard Edition* (of Freud's works) is frequently studied with the same reverence and attention to detail as the Talmud is studied in yeshivas. Yet the essential teachings of psychoanalysis, like the essential teachings of Kabbalah and Hasidism, cannot be learned from books alone, but must be transmitted orally in one's "didactic analysis" and supervision,[60] with a "senior analyst" who ultimately comes to serve in a capacity that is

---

the theosophical Kabbalah of Isaac Luria and his followers. However, it was the Hasidim who reinterpreted the major categories of theosophical Kabbalah [e.g., *Tzimtzum* (contraction), *Tikkun* (restoration), and *Sefirot*] in essentially psychologi-cal terms.

57. See Zalman Schachter, "The Dynamics of the Yehidut Transaction," *Journal of Psychology and Judaism* 3 (1978) pp. 7–21.

58. Adin Steinsaltz, "Hasidism and Psychoanalysis," p. 228.

59. Bakan, *Sigmund Freud*, p. 35.

60. Ibid.

quite similar to a Hasidic "rebbe." In addition, as was traditionally the case with the Kabbalah, one cannot simply decide to become a student of the psychoanalytic oral tradition but must first show signs of character and maturity and make the proper application with the circle or school of analysts with whom one wishes to study.

The Proliferation of "Schools": In this connection it is worth noting, even if just in passing, that psychoanalysts, particularly since the death of Freud, have splintered into a number of different schools, each with its own "revered" leader, each appealing to Freud's writings as foundational, and each claiming to be the true heirs to the psychoanalytic tradition. This historical development is in many ways similar to the splintering that occurred within the Hasidic movement after the death of its founder, Israel Baal Shem Tov (the Besht).[61] With the death of the Besht, his followers ultimately split into a variety of Hasidic courts with centers in various towns throughout Lithuania, Galicia, and the Ukraine, each court revering its own rebbe (the Bratslaver, the Lubavitcher, etc.) and each with its own emphasis or point of view upon the Besht's teachings.

LURIANIC KABBALAH: THE BASIC METAPHOR

One such Hasidic court or dynasty, Chabad or Lubavitch, developed a system of Hasidism that bears remarkable resemblances to psychoanalytic theory and practice. Chabad evolved an intellectual version of Hasidism with a well-developed and sophisticated psychology of the soul. They based this psychology on the Lurianic theosophy, which they understood to be equally applicable to the nature of the universe and the dynamics of the human psyche. It will be worth our while to review the basic outline of this theosophy in order to facilitate a comparison with analogous psychoanalytic metaphors and ideas. As we have seen, the Lurianic metaphor is often quite intricate in its details. However, in simple outline we have understood it as follows:

The creation of the universe is the manifestation of a cosmic drama involving the channeling, structuring, and containment of the infinite divine energy or light. According to Luria, the original act of creation involves a

61. For a popular, lucid presentation on the Besht and his followers see Aryeh Kaplan, *Chasidic Masters* (New York: Maznaim, 1984).

contraction or concealment (*Tzimtzum*) of God's infinite presence, which results in a void (*chalal*) within which a finite world can emerge. Into this void God emanates ten *Sefirot*, cosmic structures that are the crystallized representations of God's intellectual and emotional traits. These structures were meant to become vessels for the further emanation of God's creative energy, but for reasons that the Kabbalists believed were inherent in the scheme of things (and which eventually led to the existence of evil and hence of free will), these vessels could not contain the energy that was poured into them. The majority of the vessels shattered, causing some of God's light to cling to and become entrapped within the broken shards, which were then dispersed throughout the world. The shattered pieces, known in Hebrew as *Kelippot* (shards, husks) become the source of all that is dark, negative, alienated, and evil. These *Kelippot* are said to exile a portion of God's infinite light from its source, and as such to give rise to an alien, evil realm, the *Sitra Achra*—the forces of the "other side." A further result of this "exile" is that the masculine and feminine aspects of the godhead (the *Partzufim*), which had hitherto been "face-to-face" in a state of erotic union, now turn their backs on one another. It is man's divinely appointed task, through proper ethical and spiritual conduct, to discover the *Kelippot* as they manifest themselves in our world and to free or "raise" the sparks (*netzotzim*) of divine light within them so these sparks can return to their proper place as forces serving God's purposes and plans. The act of liberating this divine light and restoring it to the infinite God reunites the masculine and feminine aspects of the deity. This erotic unification results in *Tikkun ha-Olam*, the restoration of the world.[62] On the personal level, each individual is enjoined to liberate the sparks within his own soul that he may ultimately achieve his personal restoration and divine destiny.

The Kabbalists themselves recognized this drama to be a metaphor for deeper theological and, in their view, psychological truths; and if we examine this metaphor from a contemporary psychological perspective we will discover it to be strikingly "psychoanalytic" in nature. Indeed the metaphors of psychoanalysis and Lurianic Kabbalah are so similar that were it not for the fact that Lurianic Kabbalah antedated Freud by nearly 300 years, one would be tempted to call Luria's scheme a "psychoanalysis of God."

Like Luria, Freud begins his account with an appeal to a universal erotic,

---

62. The concept of *Tikkun ha-Olam* and its relation to the erotic is discussed in Chapter Nine of my *Symbols of the Kabbalah*.

procreative energy, the "libido," which is subject to the viccisitudes of alienation and reintegration.

According to Freud the development of the individual involves the channeling of the procreative libidinous energy, which is modified into structures,[63] the ego, and superego, whose function it is to channel and modulate further emanations of the individual's libido, much as the *Sefirot* were designed as vessels for channeling the light and energy of God's will. For reasons that are inherent in the nature of the conflict between instinct and culture,[64] the Freudian structures are not consistently able to maintain and modulate the libidinous energy in ways that are most adaptive to the individual. There is, one might say, a partial "shattering" of each of these structures and a splitting off (exile) of ideas and emotions from the main fabric of the individual's personality, just as in Luria's system divine sparks are separated from the main source of energy in *Ein-Sof*. For Freud, "splitting off" occurs, for example, when an individual becomes aware of an impulse, thought, or desire that his conscious self finds unacceptable. The impulse or idea and its associated affect is *repressed* and subsequently exists in a nether psychological realm, the "unconscious," which is analogous to Luria's *Sitra Achra* or "other side." Once in the unconscious these "complexes" of thought and affect, which are akin to the kabbalistic *Kelippot*, are inaccessible to the individual. They become, in a sense, "exiled" and are the source of all manner and variety of psychological mischief, which the individual experiences as depression or other neurotic symptoms, in the same way as the *Kelippot* are the source of negativity and evil on the cosmic level. Furthermore, these repressed ideas and impulses disrupt the individual's erotic life in such a manner that he or she becomes incapable of unifying male and female in full genital sexuality. The job of the analyst is to make these unconscious complexes conscious,[65] and, more importantly, to free the libidinous energy attached to them so that it can be made available to the individual for his own

---

63. Indeed Freud regarded the id, ego, and superego to be structures resulting from the modification of libidinous energy just as the Kabbalists regarded the *Sefirot* as modification of God's energy and will. See Sigmund Freud, "The Ego and the Id," *Standard Edition*, Vol. 19, pp. 3–68.

64. As explored by Freud in *Civilization and Its Discontents, Standard Edition* Vol. 21, pp. 59–148.

65. This is how Freud understood the therapeutic action of psychoanalysis during the period of his collaboration with Breuer.

erotic and other life goals;[66] just as, in the Lurianic Kabbalah, the energy trapped in the *Kelippot* must be freed and made available for a "divine eros," the service of God. Thus from a kabbalistic perspective the psychoanalytic endeavor is itself a form of *Tikkun* (restoration), which brings an end to a *galut* ("exiled" aspects of the individual's personality) and ushers in a *geulah* or psychological redemption.

We are now in a position to understand why some have called psychoanalysis a redemptive movement in the Jewish tradition.[67] What our discussion makes clear, however, is that Lurianic Kabbalah and psychoanalysis share much more than a vague concern with exile and redemption; for within the Lurianic metaphors we see significant precursors of notions that were to take an important place in the Freudian metapsychology, particularly in its economic, dynamic, and structural points of view.

An example of such a precursor, and another remarkable parallel between psychoanalysis and Lurianic Kabbalah, is reflected in their respective views of the origin of the "repressed" and the *Sitra Achra* or "Other Side." According to Freud, the repressed or "dynamic unconscious" is a function of prohibitions originating in the superego.[68] These prohibitions are essentially stern judgments to the effect that a particular affect or idea is unacceptable to the ego or self. It is thus moral judgments, or to be more precise, overly rigid and harsh moral judgments, which give rise to the repressed and ultimately to the specific form of pathology that psychoanalysis promises to cure. Quite remarkably, the Kabbalists of Safed held a nearly identical theory of the origin of the "other side," which, as we have seen, is a theosophical parallel to the Freudian repressed. The Kabbalists held that the origin of the "other side" is to be found in the unrestrained growth and dominion of the power of *Gevurah* or *Din*, severe judgment, and as a result of the severing of this power from its natural union with loving-kindness.[69] As in Freud, it is severe and unrestrained moral judgment that gives rise to conflict and negativity. It is only, according to the Kabbalists, by reuniting the powers of judgment and loving-kindness that evil can be subdued and intrapsychic conflict can be resolved.

---

66. Sigmund Freud, "Introductory Lectures on Psychoanalysis" (1916–1917). Lecture 28: Analytic Therapy. *Standard Edition*, Vol. 16, pp. 448–477.

67. See Dennis Klein, *Jewish Origins of the Psychoanalytic Movement.*

68. Sigmund Freud, *The Ego and the Id.* Appendix A: The Descriptive and Dynamic Unconscious." *Standard Edition*, Vol. 19, p. 60 ff.

69. See Scholem, *Kabbalah*, p. 123.

THE SIGNIFICANCE OF SEXUALITY

One might speculate that the "gold," which, according to Bloch, Freud discovered in the work of Vital, related to the latter's profound descriptions of the sexual relations among the *Partzufim*. As we have seen in Chapter One, the Lurianists held that the balance of the entire cosmos rests upon the proper flow of sexual energy among the various "visages" that comprise the godhead. The world is well-structured and harmonious, for example, when the Celestial Father and Mother are in a state of sexual union, and the cosmos threatens to fall apart when they, or the "Celestial Lovers,"[70] turn their backs upon one another and fail to consummate their sexual union. In another, related metaphor, the world's fate is conditioned by the free flow of masculine waters from heaven to earth, or by the proper relationship between God and his earthly bride, the *Shekhinah*. According to Vital, the proper restoration of the world (*Tikkun*), subsequent to the breaking of the vessels, is contingent upon the renewed *coniunctio* between the masculine and feminine elements in God. In each of these metaphors we find a significant precursor to the psychoanalytic view that a disruption in sexual discharge results in neurosis and that a free flow of sexual energy is a condition for the restoration of psychological health. The Kabbalists' metaphors differ from the psychoanalysts' in the simple manner that instead of applying to the individual man or woman they refer to the cosmos as a whole.

A cornerstone of Freudian psychoanalysis is the view that individual human development results from the vicissitudes of sexuality as it is expressed in both the actual and fantasized relationships between parent and child. Freud's understanding of human dynamics as a function of the child's desire for the opposite-sex parent, and, particularly in the case of the male, the father's prohibition of that desire's fulfillment, is regarded as one of Freud's unique psychological discoveries. In this regard it is certainly of interest that key elements of the Oedipus and Elektra complexes are to be found in the classic kabbalistic text, the Zohar. There we learn that the Celestial Father's desire for the Daughter and the Celestial Mother's desire for the Son provokes cosmic jealousy and an impulse towards retribution.[71]

> The father's continual desire is solely for the daughter, because she is the
> only daughter among six sons, and he has shared out portions, gifts and

70. The *Partzufim Yisrael Sava* and *Tevunah*.
71. Zohar I, 156b (Sitrei Torah) as quoted in Tishby and Lachower, *The Wisdom of the Zohar*, Vol. 1, p. 299.

presents to the six sons, but to her he has apportioned nothing, and she has no inheritance at all. But despite this he watches over her with more love and longing than over anyone else. In his love he calls her "daughter"; this is not enough for him and he calls her "sister"; this is not enough for him, and he calls her "mother" . . . Therefore, the supernal world [mother] says to her [to the daughter]: "Is it a small matter that you have taken away my husband? [Gen 30:15] for all his love is centered on you."[72]

Similarly, the "Celestial Mother" is said, by the Zohar, to favor the son over her husband.[73] This completes a cosmic Oedipal triangle: a vision of the cosmos in which "the world" is conditioned by the same elements and dynamics that according to psychoanalysis are present in the psyche of man.

In this light it is important to reemphasize the roles that "desire" and "delight" (*Tinug*) play in the kabbalistic understanding of the *Sefirot*. While a number of Kabbalists regarded *Chochmah* (Wisdom or Reason) to be the highest *Sefirah* and the primal manifestation of the Godhead, the majority placed *Keter* (Crown), which they understood as *Ratzon* (Desire, Will), above *Chochmah* and nearly coequal with *Ein-Sof*. The highest aspect of *Keter* was frequently understood as *Tinug*, the "delight" that motivates desire, and which appears in the Kabbalah as a theosophical equivalent to the Freudian "pleasure principle." The view that such delight or pleasure is at the heart of the divine is found in the theory of *Tzimtzum* (divine contraction), set forth by one of Luria's earliest expositors, Israel Sarug. Sarug's theory should be of particular interest to those psychoanalysts interested in the dynamic of autoeroticism, pleasure, shame, language, and law. As Scholem points out, Sarug held that *Ein-Sof* initially took pleasure in its own self-sufficiency and this pleasure produced a "shaking" within *Ein-Sof* itself, which aroused the roots of "judgment" and the subsequent engraving of the primordial letters and the language of creation and law.[74]

None of this is to suggest that the Kabbalists held an unusually "enlightened" view of human sexuality. As David Biale has shown, early Kabbalists, such as the author of the thirteenth-century manuscript *Iggeret-*

---

72. Ibid.
73. Zohar II, 145b; III, 100b, 258a. Cited in Tishby and Lachower, *The Wisdom of the Zohar*, Vol. 1, p. 299.
74. Scholem, *Kabbalah*, p. 132.

ha-Kodesh, took a generally positive attitude toward human sexual relations, providing instruction on such topics as sexual technique, foreplay, and the timing and position of sexual intercourse. This approach, however, was simply consonant with Moslem and Christian writings of the same era. What is unique amongst the Kabbalists, and especially the author of the Zohar, is the view that those couples who engage in proper and meaningful sexual relations on earth not only become holy themselves but actually assist the divine powers to come together in sexual union on high. These authors held, for example, that such theurgic activity is most propitiously performed on the Sabbath, a day that is dominated by the *Sefirah Malchut*, the *Sefirah* that is said to mediate between the divine and lower realms.

The author of the kabbalistic work *Iggeret-ha-Kodesh* goes to great lengths to demonstrate, on the basis of the medical theories of Galen, that semen is the most rarefied substance in the body and as such is particularly susceptible to both influence, and be influenced by, the soul. It is for this reason that the thoughts and bodies of both partners must be in proper conjunction if intercourse is to have its theurgic effect.[75]

While the Zohar and the later Kabbalists (including the Kabbalists of Safed) continued to maintain similar notions regarding the significance of divine sexuality, and the power of human behavior to impact upon the heavenly Eros, their attitudes toward human sexuality became progressively more ascetic. The Zohar takes an especially harsh view toward forbidden sexual activity, particularly masturbation; and Vital forbade sexual relations between scholars and their wives on all days but the Sabbath, denying the truth of a story that held that Isaac Luria himself had intercourse with his wife every night of the week just after midnight as a prophylaxis against nocturnal emissions.[76] In either case a clearly ascetic sensibility is in evidence.

It is thus clear that the sexuality that played such an important role in the Kabbalists' theosophy did not always translate into an open and free sexual expression. What is important in this context is not so much the sexual permisiveness or restraint of the Kabbalists (or, for that matter, the psychoanalysts) but rather their recognition of the significance of sexuality, and for the Kabbalists its nearly all-embracing power in both the heavens and earth.

---

75. David Biale, *Eros and The Jews* (New York: Basic Books, 1992), pp. 105–6.
76. Ibid., p. 115ff.

HASIDIC PSYCHOLOGY: PSYCHOLOGICAL CONFLICT AND THE INTERMEDIATE MAN

The Hasidim established their views on the nature of man's soul on the foundations of the Lurianic metaphors.[77] The Hasidim, however placed a psychological interpretation upon the Lurianic ideas. Relying on the kabbalistic belief that the microcosm (man) reflects the macrocosm (God), the Hasidim developed relatively sophisticated theories of how the *Kelippot*, the forces of the "Other Side," and the alienated divine light manifest themselves in the individual human psyche or soul. In the process they set forth a series of conceptions, firmly rooted in Jewish tradition, on the nature of man's basic drives, his inner conflicts and their resolution, the balance of reason and emotion, the sublimation of instincts, and the nature of human character, each of which are premonitory of basic psychoanalytic ideas.

In contrast to some of the earlier Kabbalists, whose symbols and metaphors are suggestive of the Freudian psychology of instinct, the Hasidim developed notions that are in many ways closer to the "structural theory" and psychoanalytic ego psychology. Indeed, in Hasidism we find a progressive reorientation of basic kabbalistic insights toward a more ascetic, "adaptive," and community-based point of view. Rather than focusing upon union with, or among, the divine *Partzufim*, the Hasidim emphasized the control and sublimation of sexual instinct, and a recognition of the individual's place in the Hasidic communal order. Although originally a movement of spiritual passion and fervor, Hasidism abandoned the idea that a direct experience of the divine was available to the average adherent; eventually coming to the view that only the Rebbe or Tzaddik was afforded such a direct revelatory experience. It is through a distancing from the theosophical center, and the consequent emphasis upon rational control, that Hasidism developed something of an early parallel to psychoanalytic ego psychology. Both developments can be understood as examples of a progression whereby an original flash of insight into the "Absolute" (divinity/the unconscious) is ultimately structured into normative theory and practice. Such a pattern is actually implicit in the kabbalistic theory of the *Sefirot*, which recounts how the original divine emanation (the Or *Ein-Sof*) is progressively structured as

---

77. Indeed, Lurianic notions such as "the raising of the sparks" were part of the common vocabulary of Hasidim in Freud's time and probably too among many Jews with Hasidic backgrounds residing in Freud's Vienna.

Kelim or vessels, which ultimately break, causing the process to start over on a newer, presumably higher level.

With these ideas in mind we can now explore the theoretical congruence between Kabbalah and Hasidism (in particular the Hasidism of Schneur Zalman of Lyadi) and structural psychoanalytic theory.

The Psychology of Instinct: Rabbinic Judaism had early on developed a psychology of instinct that bears many similarities to the Freudian view. The biblical view that "the inclination of man's heart is evil from his youth" (Genesis 8:31) was transformed in the Talmud into the doctrine of the two instincts, the *yetzer hatov*, man's "good inclination" and the *yetzer hara*, man's "evil inclination," the latter of which was held to be equivalent to man's nature, particularly his sexual instincts and passions. Like the Freudian instincts, the "evil inclination" was thought to be the source both of destruction and, if properly directed, unqualified good, for according to the rabbis "were it not for the evil impulse no man would build a house, marry a wife and beget children."[78]

The Kabbalists adopted and placed considerable emphasis upon the rabbinic instinct theory. As we have seen, the early Kabbalists interpreted God's creative powers in decidedly sexual terms.[79] Among the Hasidim we find the views of R. Nachman of Bratzlav and his followers who referred to sex as the "all-embracing urge."[80] Schneur Zalman, the founder of Chabad Hasidism and the author of *Tanya*, developed a relatively complex view of man's basic instincts in which he contrasted man's "Godly" and "animal" souls.[81] In its simplest form the animal soul embodies all of the natural,

---

78. *Genesis Rabbah* 9:7; compare Talmud Tractate *Yoma* 696.

79. Interestingly, in several passages in the Zohar we find the remarkably "Freudian" view of the essential bisexuality of both God and man. In reference to the latter we read: "The first man consisted of man and female for it says, 'let us make man in our image after our likeness'" (Genesis 1:26) which indicates that male and female were originally created as one and separated afterward" (Zohar II, 55a, Sperling and Simon, *The Zohar*, Vol. 3, p. 170). Also: . . . "all spirits are compounded of male and female, and when they go forth into the world they go forth as both male and female, and afterwards the two elements are separated" (Zohar I, 85b; see Tishby and Lachower, *The Wisdom of the Zohar*, Vol. 3, p. 1382).

80. Steinsaltz, *Hasidism and Psychoanalysis*, p. 188.

81. This contrast had already been made by Vital in *Sefer Ez Hayyim* (50:2) and is based on Isaiah 57:16, "until the spirit of the *souls* which I have made, shall be humble before me."

biological drives of man.[82] It originates in two "general powers," *oneg* (delight), which is roughly equivalent to Freud's "pleasure principle," and *ratzon* (will), which can be related to the instincts of aggression.[83] Interestingly, Schneur Zalman also developed a conception of two primary emotions, love and fear, which he derives from the two primary emotional traits discussed in classical Kabbalah: *Chesed* (love or kindness) and *Gevurah* (severity or power) (*Tanya*, Chapter 3). The latter, unless it is mitigated by kindness, is a totally destructive force. Indeed, according to rabbinic tradition, earlier "worlds" that were created exclusively through the power of Gevurah were said to self-destruct. The parallel to Freud's later (*Beyond the Pleasure Principle*) conceptions of the two primary instincts, eros (love and life) and thanatos (destruction and death), is striking.

Psychological Conflict: It is in Schneur Zalman's *Tanya* that we encounter the most fully developed *psychology of conflict* in Hasidic thought, a psychology that anticipates basic psychoanalytic ideas. According to the *Tanya* man experiences conflict throughout his life between his *yetzer hara* (the evil inclination) and his *yetzer hatov* (the good inclination); or as Schneur Zalman generally puts it, between his animal and Godly souls. It is a conflict between "ought" and "desire" but not necessarily a conflict between "mind" and "body," for each soul, on Schneur Zalman's view, has a mind and will of its own.[84] The body is in essence, a neutral battle ground upon which these two souls compete like armies, each one seeking to subdue and conquer a "small city."[85] As such the average individual constantly experiences an inner tension or conflict, which is relieved only in moments of inner harmony, such as during sincere ecstatic prayer.[86] At other times this conflict can lead to depression[87] or disturbing intrusive thoughts,[88] the alleviation of which is to

---

82. Schneur Zalman, *Tanya*, Chapter 1; Zalman, *Likutei Amarim-Tanya*, pp. 3–5. See also Nissan Mindel, *The Philosophy of Chabad*, Vol. 2 (Brooklyn, NY: Kehot, 1973), pp. 13–14.

83. See Mindel, *Philosophy of Chabad*, pp. 32–33.

84. Mindel, *Philosophy of Chabad*, p. 28.

85. Zalman, *Likutei Amarim-Tanya*, Chapter 9.

86. Ibid., Chapter 13. See Mindel, *Philosophy of Chabad*, p. 54.

87. Zalman, *Likutei Amarim-Tanya*, Chapter 26. See Adin Steinsaltz, *The Long Shorter Way: Discourses on Chasidic Thought* (Northvale, NJ: Jason Aronson, 1988), Chapter 26.

88. Zalman, *Likutei Amarim-Tanya*, Chapter 28; Steinsaltz, *The Long Shorter Way*, Chapter 28.

be found in an appeal to the individual's intellectual and rational powers,[89] the very powers that Freud was to refer to the "ego."

The Modulation of Emotion by Intellect: Indeed, Schneur Zalman's theory of the development and "cure" of the soul sees its parallel in later psychoanalytic ideas. Recall that in the Lurianic account of creation, God is said to have emanated ten *Sefirot* (luminaries or spheres) into the primordial void. These *Sefirot*, which are representative of God's cognitive and emotional traits, come to be embodied in the soul of man; and consist of three "intellectual" traits (according to the Hasidic scheme: wisdom, understanding, and knowledge) and seven "emotional" traits.[90] The emotional traits, which include *Chesed* (loving-kindness), *Gevurah* (severity, power, judgment), and *Rachamim* (compassion), are themselves incapable of acting for the good of either the individual or the community unless they are modulated by the intellect. The process of personal development is one in which emotions come to be modulated and ultimately controlled by cognition.[91] It is for this reason that the school of Hasidism founded by Schneur Zalman of Lyadi is known as Chabad, after the first letters of the Hebrew names of each of the intellectual *Sefirot* (*Chochmah*, *Binah*, and *Da'at*). Freud's famous description of the psychoanalytic cure, "where id was, there ego shall be,"[92] which, according to most analysts, refers to the process by which instinct and emotion come to serve the goals of the rational self, has an important antecedent in these Chabad conceptions.[93]

The Elevation of Instinct: Closely related to the doctrine of modulation of emotion by the intellect is the Hasidic view of elevating one's basic instincts in the service of higher, Godly, ends. In contrast to Judaism's *Musar* movement, which advocated strict control and suppression of one's natural instincts, Hasidism placed a strong emphasis on the *sameach* or "joy" of its

---

89. Zalman, *Likutei Amarim-Tanya*, Chapter 9.

90. Zalman, *Likutei Amarim-Tanya*, Chapter 3; Mindel, *Philosophy of Chabad*, p. 33; see also Schochet, *Mystical Concepts*, pp. 834–859 for a discussion of the *Sefirot*.

91. Zalman, *Likutei Amarim-Tanya*, Chapter 9; Mindel, *Philosophy of Chabad*, pp. 17, 46–47.

92. Sigmund Freud, *New Introductory Lectures on Psychoanalysis* (New York: W. W. Norton, 1965), p. 80. (Originally published in 1933.)

93. It should be noted that the Chabad Hasidim, in contrast to other Hasidim who place a more exclusive emphasis upon joy and human emotion, have a highly intellectualistic system of thought, one in which reason is charged with dominion over even the religious emotions.

adherents. As Adin Steinsaltz has so aptly pointed out, Hasidism generally recognized that "the attempt to suppress drives does not result in their cessation, but leads to their taking root in deeper levels of the soul."[94] Man's task is to redirect his inclinations in the service of moral, cultural, and spiritual ends and, indeed, it is the need for assistance in achieving this redirection or sublimation that prompts the Hasid to make an oral confession to, and receive guidance from, his rebbe.[95]

The seriousness with which the Hasidim view the process of transforming one's impulses can be gleaned from the recently deceased Lubavitcher rebbe's (Menachem Mendel Schneerson, 1902–1994) gloss on a famous story in the Talmud. The story describes a man who resisted the desire to have illicit sexual relations with a beautiful temptress who lay on a tier of seven golden mattresses. When the temptress learned that this man resisted because he was a Jew, she studied Torah and converted to Judaism, after which the man and woman were married and consummated their relationship on the very same tier of mattresses. The Lubavitcher rebbe asks why these mattresses, which are, after all synonymous with illicit temptation, were not burned, and he answers that it is not our task in life to destroy our illicit impulses and passions, but rather to convert them into the service of God.[96]

Interestingly both Freud and the Hasidim recognized the limits of human capabilities in elevating or redirecting one's primordial passions and desires. For Freud, only a small portion of the "id" can ever be reclaimed for cultural work, and for Schneur Zalman only certain impulses and certain acts can be elevated in the service of God. For most purposes it is only those acts, impulses, and desires permitted by the Torah that can be so elevated. To elevate acts and impulses that by the Torah's standards are regarded as sins, requires an extraordinary, almost superhuman effort.[97]

The Intermediate Man: The author of the *Tanya* presents a personology that is quite interesting from a psychoanalytic perspective. Schneur Zalman follows the Talmud in distinguishing among three essential character types:

---

94. Steinsaltz, *Hasidism and Psychoanalysis*, p. 226.

95. Ibid., p. 227.

96. See Sanford Drob, "Hasidus and Contemporary Psychology: A Dialogue with Rabbi Alter Metzger," *New York Jewish Review* 2(2) (Nov. 1988): 10–11.

97. This requires an act of *ahavah rabbah* (a great love), of which man is only capable through divine grace. It is a rare act limited almost exclusively to the greatest *tzaddikim*. See Zalman, *Likutei Amarim-Tanya*, Chapter 43; Mindel, *Philosophy of Chabad*, p. 134.

the *tzaddik* (or saint), the *benoni* (the intermediate man), and the *rasha* (the wicked). However, while the Talmud interprets these categories strictly in terms of the relative balance of good and evil deeds with which each has been credited, Schneur Zalman interprets them in terms of the extent to which each is dominated by his Godly as opposed to his animal soul.[98] While the *tzaddik* is a completely sublimated individual who is permeated by the love of God and whose "small city" has been captured by his Godly soul, the *rasha* is completely absorbed in evil, is without conscience or guilt, and is dominated by his "animal" passions. Between these two extremes is the *benoni*, the man in conflict, whose animal soul is under control but not sublimated, who is subject both to temptation and guilt, and who suffers because of the contradictions within his psyche.

One should not be surprised to discover that the *benoni* the individual in conflict is the major focus of Schneur Zalman as he is in Freud, for the *benoni* is one whose conscience or superego holds (tenuous) sway over his animal instincts or id. This is the individual who will go to any length, including the development of a full-blown neurosis, to prevent himself from entertaining an "evil" thought or committing a forbidden act. Such an individual experiences anxiety precisely because he *controls* the forces of his id rather than sublimating or redirecting them. The *rasha* (in psychological terms, the *psychopath*) experiences little or no guilt or anxiety precisely because he has an ineffective conscience. The *tzaddik* (the completely sublimated individual) experiences little or no anxiety because his id has been completely sublimated in the service of his rational self. It is only the *benoni*, the battleground of conflicting forces, who appears for spiritual or psychotherapeutic help.[99] It is the reconciliation of conflicting trends within the *benoni*'s (and neurotic's) personality that becomes the subject both of Hasidic and psychoanalytic work.[100]

The Confrontation with Evil: Hasidism adopted from the Kabbalah both

---

98. Zalman, *Likutei Amarim-Tanya*, Chapter 1.

99. On the *benoni*, see Zalman, *Likutei Amarim-Tanya*, Chapters 23 and 16; Steinsaltz, *The Long Shorter Way*, Chapters 12 and 16; and Mindel, *Philosophy of Chabad*, pp. 44–57.

100. See Adin Steinsaltz, *The Strife of the Spirit*, Chapter 1 and Steinsaltz, *The Long Shorter Way*, Chapter 15 (commentary to *Tanya*, Chapter 15, entitled "The Need for Conflict"). The notion of reconciling conflicting trends in the personality has been foundational for psychoanalysis since its inception [see Josef Breuer's study of "Anna O" in "*Studies on Hysteria*" (1895), Sigmund Freud, *Standard Edition*, Vol. 2, pp. 21–47].

a concern for the forbidden and a charge to *confront evil on its own terms*, each of which ultimately became hallmarks of the Freudian endeavor. The concern with evil and the forbidden is evident in the Zohar, where, as we have seen, it is written that "there is no worship of God except when it issues forth from darkness, and no good except when it proceeds from evil."[101] The scriptural derivation of this remarkable passage is to be found in Proverbs (3.6), where man is enjoined "to know God in all thy ways," which the kabbalistic tradition interpreted to mean that one should know and serve God both with one's higher *and* baser instincts. According to Luria and his disciples, the extrication of divine light from the evil world of the *Kelippot* and *Sitra Achra* (the "Other Side") could by definition only be accomplished by confronting evil in its own realm. There thus developed in kabbalistic circles the doctrine of *yeredah le-zorekh alliyah*, "the descent on behalf of the ascent,"[102] which entailed that redemption could only be achieved by confronting one's base desires, particularly one's sexual instincts, and transforming them for God's service. While the doctrine of "the descent on behalf of the ascent" and the related theme of *avodah-be goshmiyyot*,[103] "worship through corporeality," had verged upon and then passed over into heresy in the Shabbatian movement during the seventeenth-century,[104] these were concepts that remained a part of the Jewish mystical ethos. The founder of Hasidism, Israel Baal Shem Tov, is said, for example, to have taught that "a man should desire a woman to so great an extent that he refines away his material existence in virtue of the strength of his desire."[105] It is possible that Freud would have been exposed to such ideas as a young Viennese Jew whose own parents were raised in a Hasidic milieu. Perhaps it is in light of the Jewish doctrine of "the descent on behalf of the ascent" that we can understand the following remarks that Freud is reported to have made in reference to his life's work: "Do you not know that I am the devil? All my life I have had to play the Devil, in order that others would be able to build the most beautiful cathedral with the materials I have produced."[106]

101. Zohar II, 184a; Sperling and Simon, *The Zohar*, Vol. 4, p. 125.
102. See Rifka Schatz-Uffenheimer, "Hasidism," *Encyclopedia Judaica* (Jerusalem: Keter, 1972), Vol. 7, p. 1410.
103. Ibid., 1408.
104. See Gershom Scholem, *Sabbatai Zevi: The Mystical Messiah*.
105. Schatz Uffenheimer, "Hasidism," p. 1410.
106. R. La forgue, "Personliche Erinnerungen an Freud" in *Lindauer Psychotherapiewoche* (1954), p. 49. Quoted in Bakan, *Sigmund Freud*, p. 181.

JEWISH THEMES IN PSYCHOANALYTIC THEORY

Psychoanalysis, as I will argue, can in at least some of its aspects, be profitably understood as an "exiled" or secularized version of Jewish mysticism, a Kabbalah or Hasidism that has been purged of its moral and spiritual elements. However, is spite of its secularism, certain religious and mystical themes make their appearance in Freud's writings, albeit in truncated and distorted fashion. We have already seen how the decidedly Jewish theme of exile (*galut*) and redemption (*ge'ulah*) makes its appearance in the psycho-analytic theory of the unconscious (Freud's theory of neurosis implies that elements of the individual's personality have been "exiled" into the uncon-scious and must be "redeemed" in the analysis). However, it will be worth our while to examine the theme of exile and redemption as it appears in psychoanalysis in more detail, for Freud and his followers not only adopted the view that the themes of exile and redemption were embodied in the individual psyche; but they also, to a greater or lesser extent, viewed psychoanalysis as a whole in redemptive terms.

According to Dennis Klein, the psychoanalytic movement became the expression of the humanitarian ideals that were to follow in the wake of political emancipation in nineteenth-century Europe.[107] By freeing individu-als from the restrictive fetters of a collective, repressive superego, Freud hoped to provide mankind with a hitherto-unknown degree of personal autonomy. Freud's ambivalent preoccupation with the figure of Moses reflects his own redemptive struggle. Moses is both the redeemer who leads the Jewish people to freedom from slavery in Egypt, and from Freud's point of view, the lawgiver/repressor who institutes a new form of (now internal-ized) repression embodied in the superego.

The source of Freud's ambivalence toward Moses is in his identification with him as liberator on the one hand and in his desire on the other, expressed quite clearly in works such as *Moses and Monothesism*[108] and *The Future of an Illusion*,[109] to free the world from the yoke of harsh repression imposed by religion, and by Mosaic religion in particular.[110] By overturning

---

107. Dennis Klein, *Jewish Origins of the Psychoanalytic Movement*, Chapter 1.

108. Sigmund Freud, *Moses and Monotheism, Standard Edition*, Vol. 23, pp. 3–140.

109. Sigmund Freud, *The Future of an Illusion*, p. 58.

110. Bakan, *Sigmund Freud*, p. 121. Bakan also notes Freud's penchant for collecting idols as a direct expression of this desire (p. 134).

the Mosaic order, psychoanalysis would finally provide the redemption long promised by Western religion. In this regard Freud was no different than other would-be Jewish redeemers (Marx among them) who adopted the Jewish categories of exile and redemption (barely disguised in Marx as "alienation" and "liberation") only to turn them on their heads by declaring the promised redeemer, religion, to be the very source of repression and enslavement. Interestingly, the theme of liberation through the negation of religion or "redemption through sin" is itself a Jewish category, albeit a heretical one, and its presence in Freud, and moreover in later analysts such as Otto Rank[111] and Wilhelm Reich[112] is the loose justification for Bakan's otherwise unsupported claim that psychoanalysis is a latter-day Shabbatean-ism.[113]

It is significant that Freud, especially in his later years, expressed a certain pessimism with regard to the redemptive potential of psychoanalysis,[114] declaring, for example, that psychoanalysis is only capable of achieving the transformation of neurotic misery into "ordinary human unhappiness" and that psychoanalysis holds more promise as a method of science than as a therapeutic procedure. In this light, it is of note that, according to Jones, Freud devoted *all* of his intellectual interest in the last five years of his life to questions of the nature, origins, and psychology of religion.[115] We can only speculate that his concern reflected his own (perhaps unconscious) sense that a purely naturalistic conception of psychoanalysis was perhaps incomplete.

A second mystical theme that appears in Freud's writings can best be described as "the return of all things to their source." It is a fundamental truth for Kabbalah and Hasidism that all things have their origin in, and a desire or tendency to return to, the infinite God. Indeed, the very existence

---

111. See Otto Rank, *The Myth of the Birth of the Hero* (New York: Brunner, 1952).

112. See Wilhelm Reich, *The Function of the Orgasm* (New York: Noonday Press, 1942).

113. Bakan, *Sigmund Freud*, p. 299. Sabbatai Sevi, a sixteenth-century would-be Messiah, held a marriage ceremony between himself and a Torah scroll and preceded his forbidden acts with a blessing of God "who has commanded the forbidden." He is, as Scholem points out, the most radical representative of the "redemption through sin" philosophy.

114. Sigmund Freud, "Analysis Terminable and Interminable," *Standard Edition*, Vol. 23, p. 160.

115. Jones, *Life and Work*, Vol. 3, p. 367.

of finite beings separate and distinct from the deity is something of an illusion, resulting from the *Tzimtzum*, "contraction" and (moreover) "concealment" of God's infinite presence. The human soul, in performing its work of "raising the sparks" not only redeems the world but expresses its tendency to merge with the infinite God, which is the true source of its own being.

In *Beyond the Pleasure Principle* Freud expresses the speculative view that man has a desire to return to the formless inorganic void from which he came. Indeed there is, according to Freud, "an urge inherent in all organic life to restore an earlier state of things."[116] This urge, expressed in the "repetition compulsion" and *thanatos*, the death instinct, compels Freud to conclude that "the aim of all life is death."[117] This aim, Freud tells us, would be fulfilled, were it not for pressure of "external disturbing and diverting influences"[118] and the countervailing tendencies of the sexual instincts, which are, in Freud's view, the true instincts of life.[119] Freud's pronouncements are strikingly reminiscent of the views of the Baal Shem Tov, who, according to his disciple Joseph Polonnoye, held that "the soul, having been hewn from its holy quarry, ever ought to long for its place of origin, and, lest its reality be extinguished as a result of its yearning, it has been surrounded with matter, so that it may also perform material acts such as eating, drinking . . ."[120] Freud himself acknowledged that his views on this matter might "give an impression of mysticism," but he believed himself "quite innocent of having had any such purpose in view."[121] However, even his most devoted disciples recognized that his views on the death instinct were highly speculative and without empirical warrant.[122] We may therefore be entitled to regard them as a secularized, negative mysticism in which intimacy with a blessed God is replaced by a yearning for dissolution in inorganic death.

---

116. Sigmund Freud, *Beyond the Pleasure Principle, Standard Edition*, Vol. 18, p. 36.

117. Ibid.

118. Ibid., p. 38.

119. Ibid., p. 40.

120. Joseph Polonneye, *Toledot Ya'akov*, portion Tazi'ah. Quoted in Schatz-Uffenheimer, "Hasidism," p. 1408.

121. Freud, *Beyond the Pleasure Principle*, p. 39.

122. Jones, *Life and Work*, Vol. 3, p. 367.

272 KABBALISTIC METAPHORS

FREUD AND MYSTICISM: THE CASE OF
DANIEL PAUL SCHREBER

It is noteworthy that Freud's most in-depth analysis of psychosis appears in his commentary on a paranoiac whose religious delusions showed remarkable parallels to Gnostic and kabbalistic symbols and ideas. Freud's analysis is of a patient he himself never treated or even met: Daniel Paul Schreber, a former presiding judge in Dresden whose *Memoirs of My Nervous Illness* had been published in 1903.[123] Writing in 1911, Freud analyzed Schreber's delusions that he must be transformed into a woman and become the wife to God, as resulting from an outbreak of homosexual libido toward Schreber's former physician.[124] According to Freud, what was thoroughly forbidden to the high-minded Schreber in actual life, became obligatory in his religious delusion; and by placing his homosexual libido in the service of a divine order, Schreber could discharge this libido and without guilt, luxuriate in the "voluptuousness" of feminininity.

While Freud is convincing in his analysis of the sexual dynamics underlying Schreber's delusion, he is less convincing in his analysis of the specifically religious and mystical sources of Schreber's ideas. For example, Freud interprets Schreber's equation of "voluptuousness" with the "state of bliss enjoyed by departed spirits" as "a condensation of the two principal meanings of the German word 'selig' [blest], namely "dead" and "sensually happy."[125] Freud does not pause to consider that sensuality is indeed a common mystical metaphor for eternal bliss and that the word "selig" itself might indeed embody an *experiential* equivalence among sensuality, death, and blessedness. In a postscript to his essay on Schreber, Freud acknowledges that he may have not fully appreciated the relationship between Schreber's delusions and mythology and he acknowledges that "Jung had excellent grounds for his assertion that the mythopoetic forces of mankind are not extinct, but that to this very day they give rise in the neuroses to the same psychological products as in remotest past ages."[126]

---

123. Daniel Paul Schreber, *Memoirs of My Nervous Illness*, trans. Ida Macalpine and Richard Hunter (Cambridge, MA: Harvard University Press, 1988).

124. Sigmund Freud, "Psychoanalytic Notes Upon An Autobiographical Account of A Case of Paranoia (Dementia Paranoides)," in Freud: *Three Case Histories* (New York: Collier Books, 1972).

125. Ibid., p. 127.

126. Ibid., p. 185.

In this light it is important to consider that in common with many psychotics, Schreber regarded himself as a messiah whose mission it was to redeem the world from its fall from bliss.[127] Moreover, in declaring that his messianic mission meant that he must undergo a transformation in gender and become the wife of God, Schreber was indeed echoing earlier kabbalistic themes that man provides the "feminine waters" for divine erotic unifications and that humanity, or the "community of Israel" is itself actually the *Shekhinah*, the bride of God.[128]

In common with the Kabbalists Schreber developed a dynamic view of divine energy and light, holding that both God and man are composed of "nerves," which in their creative capacity to turn themselves into every imaginable created thing, are known as rays.[129] According to Schreber, these rays are equivalent to a primordial language, the so-called "root language," echoing the kabbalistic equivalence between the light of the *Sefirot* and the twenty-two elemental letters that comprise the world.

Schreber also echoed the kabbalistic theme that a corporeal destruction is the precondition for redemption. For the Kabbalists this destruction, symbolized in the Breaking of the Vessels, refers to aspects of the body of the Primordial Man; for Schreber it refers to his own body, which he says suffered many destructive injuries but was always restored by divine rays.

Because man is composed of the same forces that comprise God (the *Sefirot* for the Kabbalists, "nerves" for Schreber), man is capable of having a theurgic impact upon the deity, and indeed God needs man in order to complete (Kabbalah) or extricate (Schreber) His own being.

Schreber, like the Kabbalists, held that the deity is a unity in diversity. For Schreber God is divided into an upper (Ahriman) and lower (Ormuzd) deity. Like the Gnostics, Schreber's lower God is ignorant and arrogant, "completely ignorant of living men."[130] The notion of an ignorant deity is also present in the Kabbalah, for *Ein-Sof* is said to have created the world through a necessary ignorance, by concealing an aspect of himself from himself.

For both the Kabbalists and Schreber human souls are organized into higher-order soul complexes based upon their affinities to one another. Schreber's identification of the divine, the blissful and the redemptive with

---

127. Ibid., p. 112.
128. Ibid., p. 112.
129. Ibid., p. 118.
130. Ibid., pp. 122–123.

the erotic and the sensual[131] echoes mystical ideas present in Indian religion, Gnosticism, and the Kabbalah. The Kabbalists, for example, held that *Ein-Sof* in its highest manifestation is *ratzon* (desire) and, more significantly, *tinug* (delight); and there are Kabbalists who apparently identified the divine with both autoerotic[132] and hetero-erotic activity.[133]

One is struck by the emergence of many of the elements of kabbalistic theosophy in the religious delusions of a late nineteenth-century German jurist. The mythopoetic forces of humankind are indeed powerful, either emerging spontaneously in the minds of mystics and psychotics, or (on the assumption that Schreber was somehow familiar with mystical ideas) providing a font of material to which the mind readily attaches itself in illness. In this regard we should note that psychoanalysis itself shares many of the elements of both the Kabbalah and Schreber's delusions: the notion of personal redemption, a metapsychology of energy or "nerves," a glorification of the erotic, a unity in diversity (and conflict) among elements in the human (as opposed to divine) self, "ignorance" as a basic characteristic of the self, etc. These parallels suggest that psychoanalytic theory itself participates in the same mythopoetic forces that give rise to both madness and religion. If these forces, as I have argued, constitute a basic metaphor for the human psyche, then we should not be surprised to find this metaphor reappearing in religious visions and delusions, as well as in the theoretical edifices we construct to understand them.

LACAN, BION, AND THE "MYSTICISM" OF PSYCHOANALYSIS

While it is clear that Freud himself consciously regarded "mysticism" to be an anathema to psychoanalysis, certain psychoanalytic theorists, most notably among them Jacques Lacan and Wilfred Bion, have embraced clearly mystical themes and even referred to their own work as "mystical." Lacan, in particular, has, in his so-called "return to Freud" adopted certain views that bring him close to the Kabbalist's esoteric understanding of *Ein-Sof*. Indeed, much of Lacan's theorizing about the development of the "I" and the "ego,"

---

131. Ibid., pp. 126–127.
132. Scholem, *Kabbalah*, p. 132.
133. This identification is abundantly clear in both the Zohar and the Lurianic corpus. See section entitled "The Significance of Sexuality" above.

desire, and language echoes basic kabbalistic theosophical themes.[134] Lacan's "Real," for example, which is the unknowable, the impossible, and the absolute truth, and forever beyond human awareness, closely approximates the kabbalistic notion of *Ein-Sof*.[135] For Lacan, the "Real" is an original full

---

134. In this, it is likely that we can detect the influence not only of Freud but of Hegel, and, especially, Heidegger, who has himself been described as a contemporary Gnostic.

135. It is difficult to fully comprehend, let alone briefly summarize, Lacan's psychoanalytic oeuvre, but for our purposes it is most important to note that Lacan makes a crucial distinction among what he refers to as the Real, the Imaginary, and the Symbolic registers in man. The Real, for Lacan, is that original full awareness of lived experience that is covered over by images and language. The Real is spoken of as the unknowable, the impossible, the absolute truth, which is forever beyond human awareness. It is not to be conceived of as a state of knowledge, but is rather in the order of Being; or more precisely, it is the "want" or "lack" of Being that is at the core of the human soul. In many ways a psychological parallel to the Kabbalist's *Ein-Sof*, the Real is also conceptualized as "Nothing," and is known in actual life only via the gaps and miscommunications that exist in the imaginary and, particularly, the symbolic orders. The inability of our language to precisely cover all possible meanings, to clearly delimit what we wish to say, as is evident in slips of the tongue, metaphor, miscommunication, reinterpretations, etc., lays witness to the Real's presence (by way of absence) as the unconscious aspect of all human activity.

Lacan views the Imaginary as the psyche's attempt to fill up the gaps of the Real with an illusory "being" that provides a temporary and inauthentic surcease to the "want of being" or "lack" that is the fountain of lived human experience. The individual fills himself with images of who and what he is, images that are reflected back to him in actual mirrors; and more significantly in the reflections of his identity provided by others, in an effort to know himself, which is tantamount to providing himself with identity/being. The Imaginary, while a necessary stage in human development, is ultimately, according to Lacan, a snare that provides us with a false self, a false sense of ego and subjectivity. It can, I believe, be readily likened to the realm of the *Sefirot*, as originally emanated in the order of *Iggulim*, a pristine but illusory world of unbroken vessels, the existence of which is only preparatory for the next (linguistic) emanatory phase of *Yosher*, ultimately leading to *Tikkun* and a return to the infinite *Ein-Sof*. For Lacan, this imaginary, pristine world is manifest in the pre-Oedipal union between mother and child, which must be "broken" by the father if the child is ever to realize its own desire, and become initiated into language, law, and culture, the so-called "symbolic Order" (see M. Guy Thompson, *The Death of Desire* [New York: New York University Press, 1985]). Paradoxically it is the breaking of structure and security that provides the opportunity for a measure of psychological redemption.

awareness of *desire* that is hopelessly shrouded in the imagistic and symbolic trappings of human life.

Bion, who makes use of the sign "O" to designate "ultimate reality," the "absolute truth," and the unknowable, infinite Godhead, also provides a basis for understanding the Kabbalist's *Ein-Sof* in noncognitive, emotional/ spiritual terms. Bion holds that it is the revelation of personal spontaneity and genuine emotion in the psychoanalytic situation, the so-called "emotional truth of the session," which enables us to approach "O" and maintain our concern with that aspect of the infinite within ourselves. According to Bion, the attitude that enables us to reach out to "O" is one of no knowledge, memory, or desire, for any attempt to control or encapsulate truth inevitably cuts off truth's own essential capacity to reorient us in accord with itself.[136] "Faith in 'O' " involves a willingness to hold our theories, formulations, and representations in abeyance as the emotional truth of the psychoanalytic session emerges. For Bion, such an emergence is akin to a spiritual experience, one in which, on Bion's view, the infinite, what the Kabbalists refer to as *Ein-Sof*, can, momentarily emerge. For Bion, as for Lacan, the infinite and the Real can never be grasped, but can only be approached asymptotically in our openness to the mystery, that lies at the core of our own being.

Although profoundly influenced by the German Idealists (in Lacan's case Hegel, in Bion's Kant) these psychoanalysts, in contrast to Hegel,

---

It is, according to Lacan, only when we reach the Symbolic Order, the realm of language, that we are able to catch a glimpse of the nothingness, "lack," or primal desire that is at the core of our "existence." By attending to the gaps, errors, multiple meanings, and failures of communication that pervade our speech, and by constantly pursuing an unconscious meaning that forever just exceeds our grasp, we attempt, in the symbolic order, to represent the state of affairs (our "lack" in the Real) rather than foreclose it (see Michael Eigen, "The Area of Faith in Winnicott, Lacan and Bion," *International Journal of Psychoanalysis* 62 [1981]: 413). It is in this manner that we can catch a glimpse of our own true desire in the forest of "desires" that have been foisted upon us by the ubiquitous order. In kabbalistic terms, the Symbolic Order is the World of *Tikkun*, a world that recognizes the "broken vessels" and that attempts through the medium of these "fragments" to catch a glimpse of the original divine light, which lays entrapped within them. Indeed, according to Lacan, the human "subject" is completed (or a new subject born) as a result of psychoanalysis, providing another parallel to the Kabbalist's *Tikkun*, which brings about the completion, and, according to the Zohar, the very creation, of God.

136. Eigen, "The Area of Faith," p. 425.

understand the "infinite" in terms of desire as opposed to reason, the unknown as opposed to the known, and the emotional as opposed to the cognitive. In short, they provide us with an entrée to the kabbalistic *Ein-Sof* through *Keter* as opposed to *Chochmah*, and, in effect, provide us with a dialectical complement to the Hegelian point of view. For Lacan and Bion, the infinite is real, immanent in man, yet ultimately unknowable, a position that, as we have seen, is very close to that of the Zohar. Like Jung[137] they collapse theosophy into psychology, but can be interpreted (as Bion suggests) as providing a human path to a transcendent God. Both Lacan, in his notion of the "real," and Bion, in his conception of "O," suggest that something of the Absolute lays buried in man's psyche, covered over by the machinations of fantasy and language, but potentially accessible, at least in part, in the psychoanalytic hour. In short, they each, in their own way provide us with a contemporary interpretation of the kabbalistic "raising of the sparks." In our quest for a new understanding of the Kabbalah it will be worth our while to consider these thinkers.

SOME SIGNIFICANT CONTRASTS

If it is true, as I have been arguing, that at least certain elements of psychoanalysis can be profitably understood as a secularized version of Jewish mysticism, the question remains as to whether or not this development has been, in the broadest sense of these terms, valuable and good. David Bakan, who over thirty years ago put forth a similar thesis (for reasons quite different from my own), concluded that Freud "by closing the gap between Jewish culture and Western enlightenment . . . acts as the Messiah not only for Jewish culture but for Western culture as well."[138] While we cannot pretend to arrive at such a sweeping, apocalyptic conclusion ourselves, it may nonetheless be worthwhile, by highlighting some important *differences* between Kabbalah/Hasidism and psychoanalysis, to arrive at some more tentative conclusions concerning this secularization process. The following will, of necessity, be quite general in its approach, at times blurring distinctions among the various interpretations of both Kabbalah and Freud, the full attention to which would require a volume in itself.

---

137. See below, Chapter Eight, "Jung and the Kabbalah."
138. Bakan, *Sigmund Freud*, p. 299.

Descriptive vs. Moral Categories: Probably the greatest contrast between Kabbalah/Hasidism and psychoanalysis, from a psychological point of view, is the fact that the moral categories of the former become descriptive categories in the latter. What for the Hasidim were essentially distinctions between the good and evil inclination or between a person's Godly and his animal soul are converted in psychoanalysis to neutral, quasi-scientific descriptions (a tendency that is even more exaggerated when Freud is read in English translation).[139] Thus Freud, in his famous analysis of the "Rat Man," reports telling his patient that the conflict which the patient believes he experiences between his "evil" and his "moral" self is in reality a conflict between his unconscious and conscious mind; or, more precisely, between his repressed infantile desires and his conscious prohibitions.[140] Indeed the whole task of psychoanalysis, and the development of what Freud referred to as its "secular priesthood," was to provide neurotic patients with the opportunity to discuss their conflicts openly with a sympathetic listener who *would not judge* them in moral terms.

The therapeutic nature of the Freudian, nonjudgmental posture is clear. The psychoanalytic patient's failure to resolve his or her inner conflicts frequently results from a strict conscience, which prevents him from recognizing his passions and desires and hence from channeling them or coping with them in conscious, rational terms. The psychoanalyst, by acting as a representative of a freer, more liberal point of view, creates a context in which these conflicts can be recognized and resolved. The danger in the moral approach of Hasidism, as in orthodox religion in general, is one of creating what in Freudian terms would be spoken of as a superego (obsessive-compulsive or depressive) neurosis in its adherents. Indeed the frequent Hasidic preoccupation with the "problem" of "extraneous thoughts" (thoughts of a distracting sexual and aggressive nature)[141] suggests the presence of such neurosis in some Hasidim. One who is plagued by "extraneous thoughts" experiences these thoughts as a compulsion precisely because they are "forbidden. That some Hasidic teachers advised their adherents to ignore, redirect attention, or suppress these thoughts only adds

---

139. See Bruno Bettelheim, *Freud and Man's Soul* (New York: Vintage Books, 1984).

140. Sigmund Freud, *Notes Upon a Case of Obsessional Neurosis, Standard Edition,* Vol. 10, pp. 158–259.

141. See, for example, Zalman, *Likutei Amarim-Tanya,* Chapter 28 and Steinsaltz, *The Long Shorter Way,* Chapter 28, "Extraneous Thoughts."

to the vision of orthodox religion as potentially productive of neurosis. In this light it is important to note that the earlier kabbalistic insistence regarding the "value" of evil, a viewpoint that in the main came to be regarded as heretical after the Shabbatean heresy, can be taken by us as a valuable counterpoint to Hasidic moralism.

All of this granted, however, there are still a number of criticisms that can be and have been leveled against the "value neutrality" of psychoanalysis by the partisans of religious and (particularly) Jewish orthodoxy. The most often repeated of these criticisms is that psychoanalysis, by the very act of rendering moral categories into mere descriptions, encourages a laissez-faire attitude toward morality in which all acts are either justified or, at minimum, excusable, because they were caused by psychical mechanisms beyond the actor's own volition or control.[142]

An even more trenchant criticism from a therapeutic perspective is also related to the psychoanalyst's claim to be value neutral or value free. In spite of Freud's protests that psychoanalysis does not provide its adherents with a worldview,[143] it eventually, as Hans Sachs put it, "grew into a fundamental concept of psychology, of human civilization, and lastly of all, organic development."[144] For many of its adherents, psychoanalysis has indeed become a *weltanschauung*, one that, as we have seen, has many of the elements of a religion. Nevertheless, it provides no specific values to live by.[145] By drawing a sharp and fundamentally artificial distinction between psychological processes and the values that these processes structure and represent, and further, by ignoring the latter (or, what amounts to the same thing, by presumably leaving values and meaning up to the individual) psychoanalysis if taken as a worldview would thereby undermine the idea of shared, communal meanings and values; and thereby ultimately threaten the indi-

142. See Drob, "Chasidus and Contemporary Psychology."
143. Freud to Pfister, February 16, 1929. *Freud-Pfister Correspondence*, 139, "Analysis provides no new world view. But it does not need one, for it rests on the general scientific world-view with which the religious ones remain incompatible."
144. Hans Sachs, *Freud, Master and Friend* (Cambridge, MA: Harvard University Press, 1944), pp. 99–100.
145. However, it should be noted that developments within psychoanalysis itself have in recent years led to the recognition of the fundamental significant of adopting, structuring, and acting on the basis of values as a condition for psychological health. Analysts such as Frankl, Kohut, Erikson, and George Klein have come to see that the adoption of values is critical both for individual psychological development as well as for effective psychotherapy.

vidual with alienation and despair. In *The Future of an Illusion*, Freud's most trenchant critique of religion, he tells us, No, our science is no illusion. But an illusion it would be to believe that we could get anywhere else what it cannot give us."[146] One wonders if Freud would have uttered such a statement outside of his polemic against religion. If science does not provide us with values, there must, it seems, be another source from which they do arise. Without such a source we might well be led to the *thanatic* view that the ultimate aim of life is to return to the meaningless, inanimate void from which it presumably arose.

Animal vs. Godly Souls: Freud's attempt to create a value-free, purely secular psychology has several implications for our comparison of psychoanalytic and Hasidic thought that are well worth exploring in some detail. The first of these is that when we compare psychoanalytic ideas with analogous concepts in Chabad Hasidism, we discover that the entire metapsychology of the former is, in Hasidic terms, conceived from the point of view of the "animal soul."

Recall that according to Schneur Zalman each of man's souls has a will and a reason of its own. While man's ultimate conflict is between his animal and his Godly souls, the animal soul is not simply the equivalent of the Freudian id. In fact, according to the *Tanya* the animal soul contains within it the very traits (*middot*) of wisdom, understanding, and knowledge, which, when recast on a holier level, are the province of the Godly soul. In addition to its animal, biological functions, the vital or animal soul contains within itself a full range of psychological capacities including emotion, intellectual activity, self-esteem, pride, modesty, and ambition,[147] the very range of activities that ordinary psychology regards as exhaustive of the human mind.

By way of contrast, man's Godly soul is transcendental in nature and aim, in its desire for an emotional cleaving with the deity; a quest for knowledge of the creative, the sublime, and the holy; and its desire for the obliteration of the self (*bitul*) in a unification with the infinite God. In kabbalistic terms man's divine soul is the holy spark that is imprisoned in a *Kelippah* or husk of materiality (the animal soul), a spark that must be raised to a level where it achieves unification with the infinite divine light. It is the

---

146. Freud, *The Future of an Illusion*, p. 58.
147. Mindel, *Philosophy of Chabad*, pp. 12, 26; Zalman, *Likutei Amarim-Tanya*, Chs. 2, 47.

very "instinct to perfection," the existence of which Freud took great pains to deny.[148]

In psychological terms, man's Godly soul, is that aspect of his self that is concerned with the development, structuring, and implementation of *values* that transcend the self and the individual's biological and personal needs. It is, according to the Hasidim (and also, according to such spiritually oriented post-Freudian analysts as Jung,[149] Frankl,[150] and Fromm[151]), equivalent to that aspect of the self that provides the individual with his deepest sense of existential meaning and fulfillment. According to Freud's critics, it is the failure of psychoanalysis to guide the individual in his quest for his Godly soul (for a sense of meaning that transcends the self) and indeed its failure to acknowledge that this aspect of the psyche even exists, that is its greatest failing.

In this context it is important to note that Freud attributed religious morality to the superego, particularly to those aspects of the superego that are unconscious and beyond the individual's volitional control. He believed that analysis could assist the individual's ego in appropriating many superego functions,[152] in much the same manner as analysis enables the ego to appropriate segments of the id. In this way the individual would be freed from a harsh, restrictive religious conscience and his morality would come under his own volitional, rational control. By way of contrast, Schneur Zalman sees *true* religious morality as stemming from the Godly soul, an aspect of the self that, because of its transcendence of bodily desire and material necessity, is the only part of the self that is truly free.[153] The Hasidic point of view is actually close (both in time and spirit) to that of Kant, who held that the only real freedom derives from acts that are *in accord with the moral law*, all other acts being a function of natural necessity.[154] While the

---

148. Freud, *Beyond the Pleasure Principle*, p. 36.

149. Carl Gustav Jung, *Modern Man In Search of a Soul* trans., W. S. Dell and Cary F. Baynes (New York: Harcourt, Brace & World, 1933).

150. Victor Frankl, *Man's Search For Meaning: An Introduction to Logotherapy* (New York: Washington Square Press, 1963).

151. Erich Fromm, *Psychoanalysis and Religion* (New Haven: Yale University Press, 1950).

152. Freud, "Analysis Terminable and Interminable," pp. 224–229.

153. Mindel, *Philosophy of Chabad*, pp. 28, 72; Zalman, *Likutei Amarim-Tanya*, Ch. 31.

154. See Immanuel Kant, *Religion Within the Limits of Reason Alone*, trans. T.

Tanya recognizes that much conventional religious morality stems from operations of self-control that are analogous to the Freudian superego, this is far from the Hasidic ideal. The morality of the *tzaddik* (the saintly individual) as well as the morality of the *benoni* (the intermediate man), when he operates from the standpoint of his Godly soul, is neither repressive nor constricting; but derives from a free, spontaneous, and all-consuming love of God and the values that God represents.[155]

Pessimism vs. Optimism: Unlike psychoanalysis, Hasidism maintains a basically optimistic view regarding the resolution of psychological conflict. According to Schneur Zalman, the conflict between the Godly and animal souls in man is *not* an essential one. There is an original harmony between them in which the divine soul is dominant and acts toward the animal soul as a rider upon a horse.[156] It is only when a "spirit of folly enters" the animal soul that the divine soul is temporarily eclipsed. Indeed, God Himself has provided the animal soul with the strength to challenge the divine soul, but only for the purpose of improving and refining the latter in its exercise of free will.[157] In fact, it is Schneur Zalman's view that the animal soul is an instrument for the divine soul, an instrument that, paradoxically, can only accomplish its task by opposing the very master it is meant to serve. The animal soul provides a dialectical contrast, challenge, and reservoir of emotional power for its counterpart. As such it is assumed that the greater one's "evil impulse," the greater one's potential for saintliness.[158] The task of the animal soul is only to tempt, not to seduce,[159] and complete resolution of an individual's psychological conflict is only possible on the side of man's Godly self.[160] The Hasidim held that the greatest of evildoers still retains an

---

M. Greene and H. H. Hudson, with introductory essays by T. M. Greene and J. R. Silber (New York: Harper & Brothers, 1960). The parallels between Schneur Zalman and Kant are fascinating and deserving of their own separate study.

155. Zalman, *Likutei Amarim-Tanya*, Chs. 44, 50.

156. Mindel, *Philosophy of Chabad*, p. 14.

157. Ibid., p. 14.

158. Talmud, Tractate *Sukka*, 52a.

159. Zalman, *Likutei Amarim-Tanya*, Chapter 9. Schneur Zalman refers to a parable in the Zohar (II, 163a) to illustrate the notion that the purpose of the animal soul is to challenge the divine soul in order to strengthen it. In the parable a king tests (and improves) the moral strength of his only son by sending a charming harlot to seduce him. The harlot, however, inwardly desires that the son will have the moral strength to resist her charms.

160. Mindel, *Philosophy of Chabad*, p. 47.

essential love or spark of goodness, while the greatest of the *tzaddikim* (saints) have *completely* converted their vital or libidinal impulses to the service of the good. While such a complete resolution may not be possible for the *benoni* or "intermediate" man, it is one that all men can at least strive toward achieving.

The Potential for Saintliness. The contrast between Hasidism and psychoanalysis with respect to such concepts as morality, the superego, and the "Godly soul" has very important practical or "clinical" implications. Throughout his career Freud modified and added to his conception of the goals and therapeutic action of psychoanalysis, expressing his ideas on this matter via a series of succinct metaphors such as "making the unconscious conscious,"[161] "where id was there ego shall be,"[162] the after education of the superego,"[163] etc. While his terminology and emphasis changed over time, the basic goal of psychoanalysis remained essentially the same: to enable the individual to integrate hitherto repressed or split-off aspects of the libidinous and aggressive impulses or sanctions against those impulses, and to place them under conscious, rational control. The psychoanalytic procedure is one in which the patient is encouraged, through the vehicle of the doctor–patient relationship, to overcome his resistance to acknowledging, understanding, and integrating the repressed aspects of his psyche.

Hasidism also seeks to overcome resistance and promote self-understanding in the context of the rebbe–Hasid relationship,[164] and it too has a conception of the unconscious,[165] but one that goes a step beyond the Freudian conception. As Alter Metzger has put it, in addition to the "basement" of personality, which psychoanalysis refers to as the id, there is in Hasidism, a "subbasement which contains the core identity of the Jewish soul, a soul which has the inherent capacity for goodness."[166] It is the uncovering of this subbasement, the revelation of the individual's Godly soul to himself, and not the mere uncovering of repressed "natural" thoughts and affects, that is the goal of Hasidic "psychotherapy." The task of the Hasidic

161. Freud, *Introductory Lectures on Psychoanalysis* (1915–1917), Lecture 28, *Standard Edition*, Vol. 16, pp. 448–477.

162. Freud, *New Introductory Lectures on Psychoanalysis*, p. 80.

163. Sigmund Freud, *An Outline of Psychoanalysis* (1940), *Standard Edition*, Vol. 23, pp. 141–208.

164. Steinsaltz, "Hasidism and Psychoanalysis."

165. Ibid., p. 226.

166. Sanford Drob, "Hasidus and Contemporary Psychology."

rebbe is to achieve, through an empathic understanding of his Hasid's subconscious self, an awareness of that Hasid's specific potential for "saintliness." The rebbe must appreciate that potential in a way that the Hasid himself does not yet understand, and must convey that appreciation through the assignment of a task, course of prayer, or study that is particularly suited to the Hasid's personality and life-stage. Unlike the psychoanalyst who presumably remains neutral with respect to the patient's life decisions, the rebbe actually recommends a course of action or assigns a specific task that is calculated to serve as a catalyst for profound psychological, moral, and spiritual change. In this way the rebbe acts in a manner that is similar to a *strategic* psychotherapist,[167] albeit one who has adopted a specific ethic.

The Nature of Theory. In common with psychoanalysis, the theosophical Kabbalists and Hasidim who followed them developed what can be called a "metapsychology," an overall theoretical perspective on the nature of the human mind. However, unlike theory in psychoanalysis, the "metapsychology" of the Kabbalists and Hasidim is integrally related to the practical discipline of the adherent. In Hasidism, in particular, concepts such as the "divine sparks," the good and evil inclination, and *Tikkun* or restoration of the world and the soul, serve not only as a theoretical structure for the "therapist" (*rebbe*), but also as a source of direct inspiration for the "patient" (*Hasid*). Indeed, an essential component of the development of the adherent of Kabbalah and Hasidism is meditation and study upon the theory of Jewish mysticism. This is hardly the case with psychoanalysis. Apart from psychoanalysts in training, undergoing so-called "didactic" analyses, psychoanalytic patients are rarely encouraged to make an intellectual study of psychoanalysis, and when they do so on their own it is an activity that is said to as likely get in the way of the analysis as it is to aid it. The reason for the difference between Hasidism and psychoanalysis on this account is plain. The metapsychology of psychoanalysis may be intellectually stimulating but it is essentially *value-neutral*. It does not engage the individual spiritually or emotionally. By way of contrast, the theoretical structure of Hasidism is *value-laden*: it is simultaneously a theory of the human mind and a theory about the ultimate goal and purpose of mankind and the universe as a whole. What's more, the theory of Hasidism interfaces with the entire religion, culture, civilization, laws, rituals, languages, and texts of Judaism. No comparable claim can be

---

167. On strategic therapy, see Jay Haley, *Problem-Solving Therapy* (New York: Harper & Row, 1976).

made for psychoanalysis. Despite all the formal similarities between psycho-analysis and Jewish mysticism, it is only the latter that provides the individual with an ethic, a culture, a virtual firmament of values, and a blueprint for meaningful human existence. By comparison, the "value-neutral" psycho-analytic enterprise is theory without ultimate meaning, mythos without God.

However, the value neutrality of psychoanalysis is also its greatest strength. For as psychoanalysts since Freud have pointed out, it is only through a suspension of our theories, structures, images, and beliefs that we can ever hope to approach the truth of our being. From this perspective, the assumptions and values of Judaism, or any religion for that matter, can serve as a hindrance to emotional and existential truth. Indeed, any discipline that claims an ultimate interpretation (certain versions of psychoanalysis included) removes us from the infinite play of meaning that is the unconscious, and provides us with nothing but a dead, finite facsimile of a living, infinite truth.

THE VALUE OF MUTUAL DIALOGUE

We thus see that the main contrast between psychoanalysis and Hasidism is rooted in the former's value-neutrality. While this neutrality, as manifest in the analyst's nonjudgmental stance, can be instrumental in reducing neurotic guilt, promoting self-acceptance, fostering the tolerance of conflicting personal desires and trends, and even providing us with a vehicle to emotional and spiritual "truth," it also has the tendency to promote a relativism in morals and values. While Judaism clearly promotes specific values, it runs the risk inherent in all moral absolutism, of harming the mental fabric of its adherents by fostering excessive conflict and guilt. Whether and how Jewish mysticism and psychoanalysis are able to address their potential dangers and/or deficiencies will be determinative of their respective value for future generations. One can already see the beginnings of a dialectic of self-correction within these distant yet related spheres of human endeavor. For example, one sees within those Hasidic thinkers and members of the Hasidic community who come into contact with secular society, a tendency to emphasize the elements within Hasidism that are comparatively tolerant and nonjudgmental. We have already observed, for example, that according to the Kabbalah, evil and psychological conflict result from the unbridled dominion of the power of judgment (*Din*), and that it is only by tempering moral judgment with loving-kindness that evil can be transcended and intrapsychic conflict resolved. While a fair reading of Schneur Zalman's

Tanya reveals its author to be at least as concerned with strict control and forbearance from evil thoughts and acts as he is with their sublimation,[168] M. Schneersohn, the recently deceased Lubavitcher rebbe, has stated that the distinguishing mark of Hasidism as compared to *Musar* and other manifestations of Torah Judaism is its (comparatively nonjudgmental) emphasis on *asay tov* (doing good) as opposed to *tur meira* (turning away from evil).[169] A similar point of view is expressed by Adin Steinsaltz, perhaps the most creative Hasidic scholar of the current generation and himself deeply influenced by the *Tanya*, when he writes of the fallacy of "all or nothing" with respect to Jewish observance. Each of these men has had significant exposure to secular ideas and philosophy; Rabbi Steinsaltz even suggesting that while Hasidism is opposed to the orientation of psychoanalysis, it could itself greatly benefit from its various techniques and discoveries.[170]

Among contemporary psychoanalytic thinkers there has been a growing tendency to be both more tolerant and respectful of the claims of religion and to recognize the significance of meaning, values, and spirituality within the psychotherapeutic process.[171] What's more, certain trends within contemporary psychoanalysis have become far more compatible with the Jewish and Hasidic point of view along a variety of dimensions, including the role of the individual within the community, the nature of human motivation, the role of rules and self-discipline, and the potential for self-transcendence. The work of analysts such as Frankl,[172] Fromm,[173] Erikson,[174] Kohut,[175] and George Klein,[176] each of whom has understood both that the development of a cohesive, personal identity is a primary motivating factor in human life and

168. See especially, Zalman, *Likutei Amarim-Tanya*, Chapters 8, 14, 24, and 28.

169. Drob, "Hasidus and Contemporary Psychology," p. 11.

170. Steinsaltz, "Hasidism and Psychoanalysis," p. 228.

171. I am thinking of such analysts as Victor Frankl, Erich Fromm, Rollo May, Abraham Maslow, and Heins Kohut.

172. Victor Frankl, *Man's Search For Meaning*.

173. Erich Fromm, *Man for Himself* (New York: Holt, Rinehart & Winston, 1947).

174. Erik Erikson, "Identity and the Life Cycle," *Psychological Issues*, Vol. 1 (1959), 171.

175. Heinz Kohut, *The Restoration of the Self* (New York: International Universities Press, 1977)

176. George S. Klein, *Psychoanalytic Theory: An Exploration of Essentials* (New York: International Universities Press, 1976).

that this identity is inextricably linked to the actualization of values, has created the potential for rapprochement between psychoanalysis and the Jewish spiritual tradition.

REDEEMING THE PSYCHOANALYTIC SPARKS

If we consider the relationship between Freud and Kabbalah/Hasidism from the spiritual point of view, psychoanalysis is in some measure, as Bakan has claimed, a secularization of Jewish mysticism,[177] or to put it in Jewish terms, it is a form of Kabbalah that has been *exiled* from its source. The goal of a kabbalistic or Hasidic critique of psychoanalysis would therefore be to free the "holy spark" of spirituality at its core, thus permitting what is truly valuable in the psychoanalytic endeavor to rejoin the tradition from which it sprang. Indeed, I have made some tentative efforts in this direction in both this volume, and my *Symbols of the Kabbalah*.[178]

However, if we are to understand the relationship between Judaism and psychoanalysis in terms of exile and redemption, if we are to even pretend to "raise the psychoanalytic sparks," and reunite them with the Jewish mystical tradition, we must first more fully comprehend the role of "exile" as it has been understood in the Jewish tradition; for exile, as painful and alienating as it is felt to be, is not altogether a bad thing. Indeed, the Talmud tells us that the exile of the Jews in the land of Egypt was the "crucible" that forged them into the Israelite nation; and that each subsequent exile has had its purpose

---

177. Bakan, *Sigmund Freud*, p. viii.

178. In this light it is certainly worth nothing the valuable exposition and critique of psychoanalytic concepts that can be found in Bruno Bettelheim's slim volume, *Freud and Man's Soul*. Bettelheim provides a clear and quite cogent argument for the proposition that Freud, albeit in a secular, philosophical sense, was a great humanist who was concerned with man's soul and who held that the highest fulfillment of man consisted of being able to truly love not oneself but others; and of being able to find meaning and satisfaction in work that has positive value beyond one's immediate sphere. Bettelheim argues that the scientific prejudice of those who adopted psychoanalysis, and an endless series of mistranslations of Freud's writings (into English), served to distort and disguise Freud's humanistic/spiritual concerns. Indeed, without intending to do so, Bettelheim's critique goes a long way in showing that psychoanalysis is compatible with some of the highest ideals of the Jewish tradition, and thus in redeeming the "real Freud" from the exile imposed by his English translators.

in preparing the Jewish nation for its mission of *Tikkun ha-Olam*, the restoration of the world.

One can only speculate on the full significance of the "exile of Hasidism in psychoanalysis," but one might well suspect that the growth of psychoanalysis within a secular environment promoted the values of tolerance and acceptance in a manner that would have been difficult if not impossible in an orthodox religious context. As a result of its nonjudgmental posture, psychoanalysis was able to gain access and insight into the nature of the unconscious and the dynamic of psychological conflict that had hitherto been unavailable to the Jewish or any other tradition.[179] The challenge to Hasidism in redeeming the holy sparks within psychoanalysis is to raise the Freudian enterprise into a realm of spiritual value and significance without abandoning the openness to psychological truth and the willingness to accept man wherever he is, in the darkest as well as the brightest aspects of his soul, which is the crowning achievement of Freud and his followers.

------

179. See Steinsaltz, "Hasidism and Psychoanalysis," p. 224. Steinsaltz writes: "The awareness of the unconscious is not limited in Hasidism (nor in Judaism in general) to a few chance or random remarks. However, the context in which these comments about the unconscious are made would not by themselves be very instructive, and were it not that psychoanalysis had defined and elucidated these terms, we might never have been able to ascertain them from our sources alone."

8

Jung and the Kabbalah

In a letter to the Reverend Erastus Evans, written on the 17th of February, 1954, Carl Jung described the excitement of his first encounter with the kabbalistic symbols of *Shevirat Hakelim* (the Breaking of the Vessels) and *Tikkun Haolam* (the Restoration of the World):

> In a tract of the Lurianic Kabbalah, the remarkable idea is developed that man is destined to become God's helper in the attempt to restore the vessels which were broken when God thought to create a world. Only a few weeks ago, I came across this impressive doctrine which gives meaning to man's status exalted by the incarnation. I am glad that I can quote at least one voice in favor of my rather involuntary manifesto.[1]

Several years later, in a letter to a Ms. Edith Schroeder who had inquired regarding "the significance of Freud's Jewish descent for the origin, content and acceptance of psychoanalysis," Jung replies:

> . . . one would have to take a deep plunge into the history of the Jewish mind. This would carry us beyond Jewish Orthodoxy into the subterranean

---

1. Carl Gustav Jung, *Letters*, Vol. 2, p. 175.

workings of Hasidism . . . and then into the intricacies of the Kabbalah, which still remains unexplored psychologically.[2]

Jung then informs Ms. Schroeder that he himself could not perform such a task because he has no knowledge of Hebrew and is not acquainted with all the relevant sources.

In point of fact, Jung, in the last decades of his life, had taken a deep interest in the psychological aspects of a number of kabbalistic symbols and ideas; ideas that he had been exposed to primarily through his reading of sixteenth- and seventeenth-century alchemical texts, and, especially, through the writings of the Christian Kabbalist and alchemist Christian Knorr Von Rosenroth (1636–1689). As a result, Jung's last great work, *Mysterium Coniunctionis*, completed in his eightieth year in 1954, though ostensibly a treatise on alchemy, is filled with discussions of such kabbalistic symbols as *Adam Kadmon* (Primordial Man), the *Sefirot*, and "the raising of the sparks." These symbols became important pivots around which Jung constructed his final interpretations of such notions as the archetypes and the collective unconscious, and his theory of the ultimate psychological purpose of man.

Yet as great as Jung's acknowledged affinity to the Kabbalah, his unacknowledged relationship was even greater. For every reference to the Kabbalah in Jung's writings there are several to Gnosticism, and perhaps dozens to alchemy: yet the interpretations that Jung places on Gnosticism (itself a close cousin to the Kabbalah), and the very texts to which Jung refers to on alchemy, were profoundly kabbalistic, so much so that one could call the Jung of the *Mysterium Coniunctionis* and other later works, a Kabbalist in contemporary guise.

Jung has frequently been called a "Gnostic,"[3] but for reasons which I will detail in this paper, Jung is far more kabbalistic than he is Gnostic, and

---

2. Ibid., Vol. 2, pp. 358–359.

3. Interestingly, Jung's main accuser in this regard was the Jewish philosopher Martin Buber, who is well-known for, among other things, his work on Hasidism. See Martin Buber, *Eclipse of God: Studies in the Relation Between Religion and Philosophy*, trans. Maurice Friedman et al. (New York: Harper & Row, 1952). Among Christian theologians who have hailed Jung's "Gnosticism" is the "death-of-God" theologian Thomas J. J. Altizer. See his "Science and Gnosis in Jung's Psychology," *Centennial Review* 3 (Summer 1959):304. For a discussion of the whole question of Jung and Gnosticism, along with a collection of Jung's writings relevant to the subject, see Robert A. Segal, *The Gnostic Jung*.

he is "alchemical" precisely to the extent that the alchemists borrowed from and relied upon kabbalistic ideas.

In this chapter I will argue that Jung read Gnosticism in such a manner as to transform a radical anti-cosmic, anti-individualistic doctrine into a world-affirming basis for an individual psychology. Further, he interpreted alchemy so as to extract its kabbalistic spiritual and psychological core. Had Jung been sufficiently familiar with the Kabbalists (and Hasidim), his method could have been readily short-circuited, for their writings provide a far richer and psychologically oriented imagery and symbolism than either the "other-worldly" theories of the Gnostics or the radically material practice of the alchemists. Indeed, in some instances the Gnostics, the alchemists and the Kabbalists share the same symbols and images (e.g., the "sparks," *Adam Kadmon*) but in each case the kabbalistic approach to these symbols is the closest to Jung's own. In short, by providing a "this-worldly" interpretation of Gnosticism, and a spiritual–psychological interpretation of alchemy, Jung arrived at a view that was essentially kabbalistic in spirit. Indeed, Jung, in his interpretation of alchemy, succeeded remarkably (to use an alchemical metaphor) in extracting the kabbalistic gold that lay buried in the alchemists' texts and methods.

Jung can be interpreted as a contemporary Kabbalist, yet one who provides the basis for a radical *psychological* interpretation of the Kabbalists' symbols and ideas. Such a psychological interpretation was not altogether foreign to the Kabbalists themselves, who, on the principle of the microcosm mirroring the macrocosm, held that their own descriptions of cosmic events were also, and equally profoundly, descriptions of the dynamics within men's souls. Indeed, such an interpretation of the Kabbalah provided the major impetus for the doctrines of the Hasidim. Still, Jung took this psychologization process further than either the Kabbalists or Hasidim, living in a prepsychoanalytic age, could ever hope to do themselves.

An important question that is raised by any characterization of Jung as "Gnostic" or "kabbalistic" is the extent to which Jung shared in the metaphysical as well as the psychological assumptions of these religious and theological movements. Jung himself denied any metaphysical aspirations, holding throughout that his discussions of "God" or "*Adam Kadmon*," to take two examples, were merely meant to illuminate aspects of the empirical psychology of the self and that any inquiry into the external "truth" of these archetypal images was beyond the scope of his own investigation. In spite of these disavowals, Jung has been adopted (and at times criticized) by the theologians, and his work can be taken to have important theological, axiological, and metaphysical implications. Philosophically, Jung can be understood as part of a tradition, beginning with the Kabbalah and early Christian mysticism, and achieving supreme rational expression in Hegel, which sees the Absolute and man as progressing through a series of contradictions or oppositions in a quest for unity and, as Jung put it, "individuation."

JUNG'S FAMILIARITY WITH THE KABBALAH

Jung does not appear to have had any in-depth familiarity with the original texts of the Kabbalah. While *Mysterium Coniunctionis* includes citations to the Sperling and Simon English translation of the Zohar (first published in 1931–1934) as well as to a German translation of the Zohar by Ernst Mueller (1932),[4] nearly all of Jung's specific citations to kabbalistic symbols and ideas are to the writings of Knorr Von Rosenroth, whose *Kabbalah Denudata* (1684) is a Latin translation of passages from the Zohar, other kabbalistic writings, and essays on the meaning of the Kabbalah.[5] Jung had "visions" inspired by the symbolism of the Kabbalist Moses Cordovero, and Cordovero's Pardes Rimonim is cited in the bibliography of *Mysterium Coniunctionis*, but the only actual reference is in a single footnote, and this is cited through Knorr.[6] While Jung was undoubtedly aware of the writings of Gershom Scholem (whose *Major Trends In Jewish Mysticism* first appeared in 1942), he is unlikely to have read them closely prior to 1954. Otherwise he would have undoubtedly been familiar with certain doctrines of the Lurianic Kabbalah such as the Breaking of the Vessels and *Tikkun* prior to

4. Carl Gustav Jung, *Mysterium Coniunctionis, The Collected Works of C. G. Jung*, Vol. 14, trans. R. F. C. Hull (Princeton, NJ: Princeton University Press, 1963), pp. 634, 647.

5. Christian Knorr von Rosenroth's *Kabbala Denudata*, "The Kabbalah Uncovered, or, The Transcendental, Metaphysical, and Theological Teachings of the Jews" (Sulzbach, Latin, 1677–1684) was the most important non-Hebrew work on the Kabbalah up until the close of the nineteenth century and was the major source on the Kabbalah for non-Jewish scholars at least until that time. Knorr, writing after the advent and dissemination of the Lurianic Kabbalah, includes (among many other things) Latin translations of portions of the Zohar, Cordovero's *Pardes Rimmonim*, a detailed explanation of the kabbalistic tree after Luria, and even some of the writings of Luria himself. See Scholem, *Kabbalah*, pp. 416–419.

6. Jung, *Mysterium Coniunctionis*, p. 22. On Jung's visions inspired by *Pardes Rimmonim* see Carl Gustav Jung, *Memories, Dreams, Reflections*, recorded and edited by Aniela Jaffe (New York: Random House, 1961), pp. 293–295.

the date he acknowledges in his letter to Evans in February of that year.[7] Jung carried on a correspondence with a number of students who had first-hand knowledge of kabbalistic texts and even acknowledges to R. J. Zwi Werblosky that he received a copy of the Kabbalist R. Gikatila's text on dreams,[8] but the overwhelming evidence in both the *Mysterium* and the *Letters* is that Jung derived his working knowledge of the Kabbalah from Knorr Von Rosenroth, references to the Kabbalah in the writings of such alchemists as Dorn, and an occasional perusal of the French and German literature on the Kabbalah extant before the field was thoroughly transformed by Scholem.

Jung's limited familiarity with kabbalistic texts and ideas in no way prevented him from commenting profoundly on certain kabbalistic symbols, such as *Adam Kadmon*, of which he was aware. It is important to remember, however, that Jung never undertook a study of the Kabbalah in its own right, and his interest in the subject was almost exclusively adjunctive to his work on alchemy, upon which he ultimately based the symbolic and historical foundations of his psychology.

The major kabbalistic ideas that concerned Jung were those that had clear parallel formations in Gnosticism and alchemy: the notion of a spark of divine light contained within man, the concept of Primordial Man who contains within himself in *coincidentia oppositorum* the various conflicting tendencies within the human spirit, the theory of the *Sefirot* and their unifications, particularly the unifications of good and evil and masculine and feminine, etc. In spite of an occasional reference to Luria, absent from any consideration in Jung's major works are the symbols of *Tzimtzum* (divine contraction), *Shevirah* (the "Breaking of the Vessels," and *Tikkun ha-Olam* (the "Restoration of the World), which are unique to the Lurianic Kabbalah. It is true, however, that just as these concepts were implicit in the Kabbalah that preceded Luria (e.g., the Zohar), they are, as we will see, also implicit in the alchemical writings, which borrowed so heavily from the earlier Kabbalah. Had Jung been aware of these symbols prior to 1954, they would have been of invaluable service to him, not only in his attempt to grasp the spiritual and psychological nature of alchemy, but also in the expression of his own psychology of the self.

---

7. Jung relates that Knorr Von Rosenroth's *Kabbalah Denudata* was influenced by Isaac Luria (*Mysterium Coniunctionis*, pp. 412, 198) but Jung's familiarity with Knorr's work did not make him aware of the fundamenttal Lurianic ideas of *Tikkun* or *Shivirah* prior to 1954.

8. Jung, *Letters*, Vol. 2, p. 122.

JUNG AND GNOSTICISM: THE SEVEN SERMONS
TO THE DEAD

Jung's interpretation of Gnosticism is critical to his understanding of the Kabbalah. This is because many of the major kabbalistic themes are anticipated in the Gnostic sources with which Jung was familiar.[9] His comments on Gnosticism are scattered throughout his writings;[10] his major statement on the subject is contained in his essay "Gnostic Symbols of the Self."[11] However, long before he had systematically considered Gnosticism from the point of view of his own analytical psychology, Jung had been familiar with Gnostic theology and even constructed, in 1916, his own "Gnostic Myth," which he had circulated privately among friends but which, at his own request, was excluded from his collected works. In this myth, entitled *Septem Sermones ad Mortuos* (*Seven Sermons to the Dead*),[12] Jung registers a number of "Gnostic" themes to which he was to return many times in his later writings.

Among these themes, perhaps the most significant and pervasive is a concern with the coincidence of opposites. "Harken," Jung writes, "I begin with nothingness. Nothingness is the same as fullness. In infinity full is no better than empty. Nothingness is both empty and full."[13] The "pleroma" (or fullness of being, which for the Gnostics is the equivalent of the kabbalistic *Ein-Sof*, the Infinite) is characterized, Jung tells us, by "pairs of

---

9. On Gnosticism see Chapter 5 above, and the following: Rudolph, *Gnosis: The Nature and History of Gnosticism*; Filoramo, *A History of Gnosticism*; Layton, *The Gnostic Scriptures*; and J. M. Robinson, ed., *The Nag Hammadi Library*. The Nag Hammadi texts, discovered in Jung's lifetime (but after his composition of the "Seven Sermons"—see below), greatly increased our knowledge of the Gnostics. For an account of their discovery see discussions in Filoramo, Rudolph, and Robinson. A number of scholars have posited a Jewish origin of Gnosticism, and hence a common Jewish origin for the ideas shared by Gnosticism and the Kabbalah. On the subject of Jewish Gnosticism see R. M. Wilson, "Jewish "Gnosis" and Gnostic Origins: A Survey." Also see Gershom Scholem, *Jewish Gnosticism: Merkabeh Mysticism and Talmudic Tradition*, and Scholem, *Major Trends*, pp. 40–79.

10. See Segal, *The Gnostic Jung*, ibid., for a collection of these writings.

11. Carl Gustav Jung, "Gnostic Symbols of the Self," in *Aion: Researches Into the Phenomenology of the Self, Collected Works*, Vol. 9 (Princeton, NJ: Princeton University Press, 1969), pp. 184–221.

12. Carl Gustav Jung, "Seven Sermons to the Dead," in Segal, *The Gnostic Jung*, pp. 181–193.

13. Ibid., p. 181.

opposites," such as "living and dead," "Good and Evil," "Beauty and Ugliness," "the one and the many." These opposites are equal and hence void in the pleroma but are "distinct and separate" in man. "Thus," Jung writes, "we are the victims of the pairs of opposites. The Pleroma is rent in us."[14] "Abraxas," the "forgotten god" who stands above the God who is worshipped, and who would be the first manifestation of the pleroma, if the pleroma indeed had "being," speaks "that hallowed and accursed word which is life and death . . . truth and lying, good and evil, light and darkness, in the same word and in the same act."[15]

A variety of other typically Gnostic themes make their appearance in "The Seven Sermons." Among them are the doctrine that "because we are parts of the pleroma, the pleroma is also in us." We are also, according to Jung, "the whole pleroma"[16] on the principle that each smallest point in the microcosm is a perfect mirror of the cosmos.[17] Man, as a finite creature, is characterized by "distinctiveness," and the natural striving of man is toward distinctiveness and individuation. However, this battle against sameness and consequent death is ultimately futile because as we are immersed in the pleroma our pursuit of various distinctions inevitably leads us to seize each of their opposites. In pursuing good and beauty we necessarily lay hold of evil and ugliness as well. Hence, man should not strive after difference, which is at any rate, illusory, but rather after his own Being, which leads him to an existential (rather than an epistemological) awareness of the pleromatic "star," which is his ultimate essence and goal.[18]

Jung's prescription for man in "The Seven Sermons" is significant because it appears to be so typically Gnostic. This world of distinctiveness and individuation offers man nothing. Man must turn his back on the world of "creatura" and follow his inner star beyond this cosmos, for, according to Jung: "Weakness and nothingness here, there eternally creative power. Here nothing but darkness and chilling moisture. There wholly sun."[19] We shall see that years later when Jung comes to take a second look at Gnosticism through the eyes of a more fully developed archetypal psychology he interprets it in a manner that is far more kabbalistic than Gnostic, i.e., far more friendly to the world and man's individual ego struggling within it.

---

14. Jung, "Seven Sermons," p. 184.
15. Ibid., p. 187.
16. Ibid., p. 184.
17. Ibid., p. 185.
18. Ibid., pp. 185, 193.
19. Ibid., p. 193.

One more point regarding "The Seven Sermons" bears mention: its view of sexuality. Jung adopts the Gnostic theme of sexuality pervading the cosmos. For Jung, as for the Gnostics sexuality is a numinous phenomenon and not simply a natural function of mankind:

> The world of the gods is made manifest in spirituality and in sexuality. . . . Spirituality and sexuality are not your qualities, not things which you possess and contain, but they possess and contain you; for they are powerful demons, manifestations of the gods, and are, therefore things which reach beyond you, existing in themselves. No man hath a spirituality unto himself, or a sexuality unto himself. But he standeth under the law of spirituality and of sexuality.[20]

This passage is of particular interest with respect to Jung's own polemic with Freud. Years later, Jung would relate how Freud appeared to take an almost religious, worshipful view of the sexual instincts in man, but was not himself able to acknowledge the true spirituality of eros.[21] Jung, of course, would later locate spirituality and sexuality among the archetypes of the collective unconscious, and in this sense they would remain for him a law that exists beyond any individual man. Here in this Gnostic flight of fancy he sees them, however, as manifestations of the gods, "Platonic forms," which have an existence independent of man's mind. We will see how the Kabbalists came to epitomize the divine nature of sexuality in their theosophical writings.

The themes expressed in the "Seven Sermons" are well-known both to those familiar with the Gnostic sources[22] and, as we shall see, the Kabbalah. We will now have occasion to turn to Jung's unique contribution in this area, the psychologistic interpretation of Gnosticism that crystallized in his essay "Gnostic Symbols of the Self."

JUNG'S INTERPRETIVE METHOD

Jung's interpretation of Gnosticism, indeed his interpretation of religious phenomena in general, rests upon his theory of the history of the psyche in

---

20. Ibid., pp. 190–191.

21. Jung, *Memories, Dreams, Reflections*, p. 152.

22. As a result of discoveries at Nag Hammadi, we are in possession of many more original Gnostic texts than was Jung. See Robinson, *The Nag Hammadi Library in English*.

man.[23] According to Jung, man has historically moved from a state in which he projects the contents of his unconscious onto the world and heavens to one in which, as a result of his total identification with the rational powers of the ego, he has withdrawn his projections from the world. In this state he fails completely to recognize the archetypes of his unconscious mind. The world's great religions, Christianity and Gnosticism among them, developed at a time when men projected their collective unconscious onto the world and then worshipped these contents as gods. In essence, the ancients understood these unconscious contents as events independent of their own psyches. Modern man, according to Jung, as a result of the development of a fully independent rational and conscious ego, has withdrawn his unconscious projections from the world and heavens, resulting in a loss of faith in the gods and a loss of interest in mythological language and symbols. In the twentieth century, Jung writes, "we lack all knowledge of the unconscious psyche and pursue the cult of consciousness to the exclusion of all else."[24] The unconscious, however, cannot be ignored or eliminated, and it forces itself on modern man in the form of ennui, superstitious fears and beliefs (e.g., "flying saucers,"[25] or in our time "New Age ideas"), and, most significantly, in neurosis and aggression. According to Jung: "The gods have become diseases; Zeus no longer rules Olympus but rather the solar plexus, and produces curious specimens for the doctor's consulting room, or disorders the brains of politicians and journalists who unwittingly let loose psychic epidemics on the world."[26]

Jung's prescription for contemporary man is a new, nonprojective awareness and experience of the collective unconscious to replace the dead projective metaphors of religion. Psychology, specifically Jungian psychology, is in a position to provide man with a direct awareness of the archetypes within his own psyche. This, Jung believes, can be accomplished through an interpretation of the spontaneous symbolic projections of the unconscious in fantasy, art, and dreams, guided by a new *psychological understanding* of the

---

23. Segal, *The Gnostic Jung*, pp. 11–13.

24. Carl Gustav Jung, Commentary on "The Secret of the Golden Flower," in *Alchemical Studies, Collected Works*, Vol. 13 (Princeton, NJ: Princeton University Press, 1967), pp. 1–56.

25. Carl Gustav Jung, "Flying Saucers: A Modern Myth," in *Civilization In Transition, Collected Works*, Vol. 10 (Princeton, NJ: Princeton University Press, 1970). Originally published in 1958.

26. Jung, Commentary on "The Secret of the Golden Flower," p. 37.

basic archetypal images that have presented themselves in the history of myth and religion. Jung turns to this history to provide him with a catalogue or map of the contents of the collective unconscious and he interprets his patients' (archetypal) dreams and images accordingly. His interest in the "dead" religion of Gnosticism, as well as in the forgotten science of alchemy, lies in the fact that their symbolisms presumably contain a more or less pristine crystallization of the collective unconscious, undisturbed by the ego oriented reinterpretations of reason and dogma. Indeed, the long incognizance of the Kabbalah in official Judaism suggests that it too preserves elements of the collective unconscious in a relatively pure form.

JUNG'S INTERPRETATION OF GNOSTICISM

Jung interpreted the Gnostic myths, including the origin of the cosmos in the pleroma, the emergence of an ignorant God or demiurge, the creation of a Primordial Man, and the placing of a spark of divinity within individual men, in completely psychological terms. The Gnostic myths do not, according to Jung, refer to cosmic or even external human events, but rather reflect the basic archetypal developments of the human psyche. The pleroma, within which is contained the undifferentiated unity of all opposites and contradictions, is, according to Jung, nothing but the primal unconscious from which the human personality will emerge.[27] The "demiurge," who the Gnostics disparaged as being ignorant of his pleromatic origins, represents the conscious, rational ego, which in its arrogance believes that it too is both the creator and master of the human personality. The spark, or scintilla, which is placed in the soul of man, represents the possibility of the psyche's reunification with the unconscious, and the primal anthropos (*Adam Kadmon* or Christ), which is related to this spark, is symbolic of the "Self," the achieved unification of a conscious, individuated personality with the full range of oppositions and archetypes in the unconscious mind. "Our aim," Jung tells us, "is to create a wider personality whose centre of gravity does not necessarily coincide with the ego,"[28] but rather "in the hypothetical point

---

27. A similar view, interestingly enough, had been hinted at by Freud. See Freud, *Shorter Works, Standard Edition*, Vol. 23, p. 300.

28. Jung, "Gnostic Symbols of the Self," p. 190.

between conscious and unconscious."[29] Jung sees in the Gnostic (and kabbalistic) image of Primordial Man a symbol of the goal of his own analytical psychology.

JUNG'S INTERPRETATION OF ALCHEMY

Jung provides a similar if more daring and far-reaching interpretation of alchemy, which is usually considered to be the unscientific and magico-religious forerunner of modern chemistry (much as astrology is understood as the prescientific antecedent to astronomy). As we have seen, for Jung, the Gnostics' speculations concerning the inner life of the godhead were better understood as projected insights into the inner workings of the Gnostics' own (unconscious) minds. According to Jung, what the alchemist sees in matter, and understands in his formulas for the transmutation of metals and the derivation of the *prima materia,* "is chiefly the data of his own unconscious which he is projecting into it."[30] For example, the alchemist's efforts to bring about a union of opposites in his laboratory and to perform what he speaks of as a "chymical wedding" are understood by Jung as attempts to forge a unity, e.g., between masculine and feminine, or good and evil aspects of his own psyche.[31] "The alchemical opus," Jung tells us, "deals in the main not just with chemical experiments as such, but with something resembling psychic processes expressed in pseudochemical language."[32] It is for this reason that the alchemists have occasion to equate their chemical procedures with a vast array of symbolical processes and figures; for example, equating the *prima materia* with the philosopher's stone (*lapis philosophorum*), a "panacea," the Spirit Mercurius, and a divine hermaphroditic original man.[33] Indeed, according to Jung, alchemy is of special interest to the psychologist because in projecting their unconscious onto their work, the alchemists laid bare their psyche without ever realizing that they were doing so.[34] As such, alchemy provides a pure crystallization of the collective unconscious unaltered by conscious censorship or obfuscation.

29. Jung, Commentary on "The Secret of the Golden Flower," p. 45.
30. Carl Gustav Jung, *Psychology and Alchemy, Collected Works,* Vol. 12 (Princeton, NJ: Princeton University Press, 1968), p. 228.
31. Ibid., p. 132.
32. Ibid., p. 242.
33. Ibid., p. 232.
34. Jung, *Mysterium Coniunctionis,* p. xvii.

In his *Mysterium Coniunctionis* Jung provides a catalog of alchemical symbols, interpreted in the context of the alchemists' principle of *solve et coagula* (separation and bringing together). According to Jung, "the alchemist saw the essence of his art in separation and analysis on the one hand and synthesis and coagulation on the other."[35] The process, ending in what the alchemists spoke of as the *coniunctio*, is personified as a "marriage" or union between sun and moon, *Rex* and *Regina* (King and Queen), or Adam and Eve. This union, according to Jung, reflects "the moral task of alchemy," which is "to bring the feminine, maternal background of the masculine psyche, seething with passions into harmony with the principle of the spirit."[36] In Jungian terms, this amounts to the unification of *animus* and *anima* or of the ego with the unconscious.

The *solve et coagula* (separation and unification) of the alchemist is, according to Jung, perfectly paralleled in the contemporary process of psychotherapy. Therapy, according to Jung, approaches a personality in conflict, separates out, i.e., analyzes, the conflict, and ultimately aims at uniting the dissociated or repressed elements with the ego. The alchemist, in striving for a permanent, incorruptible, androgynous, divine "unification," was himself unconsciously striving after a process of individuation, the forging of a unified self.[37] As we shall see, the alchemists borrowed such kabbalistic symbols as the "spiritual wedding," "the raising of the sparks," and *Adam Kadmon* (Primordial Man) to further articulate this unification process.

It is interesting to note, if just in passing, that Jung, without much elaboration, interprets astrology in a similar psychological manner. Indeed, he applauds alchemy and astrology for their ceaseless preservation of man's bridge to nature (i.e., the unconscious) at a time when the church's increasing differentiation of ritual and dogma alienated consciousness from its natural roots.[38] In regard to astrology Jung writes: "As we all know, science began with the stars, and mankind discovered in them the dominants of the unconscious, the 'gods,' as well as the curious psychological qualities of the zodiac: a complete projected theory of human character."[39] It is well

---

35. Ibid., p. xiv.
36. Ibid., p. 41.
37. Ibid., p. xv.
38. Jung, *Psychology and Alchemy*, p. 34.
39. Ibid., p. 24.

to remember that certain Kabbalists, such as Chayyim Vital were also prac-titioners of both alchemy and astrology.[40]

KABBALAH, GNOSIS, AND JUNGIAN PSYCHOLOGY

Regardless of the direction of influence it is clear that nearly all of the basic symbols and ideas of Gnosticism are to be found in one form or another in the Kabbalah and vice versa. As we have seen in Chapter Five, the notion of an unknowable Infinite godhead, which contains within itself a coincidence of metaphysical opposites, the gradual manifestation of the Infinite through an emanation of *logoi* or *Sefirot*, the notion of a cosmic "accident" giving birth to the manifest world, the distinction between the God of the Bible and the true Infinite, the estrangement of man from his true essence, and the entrapment of a divine spark within man's material nature—these are all themes that found their way into both Gnosticism and the Kabbalah. As we have also seen the question of origins is complicated by the fact that although the Kabbalah arrives on the scene centuries after the first manifestations of Gnosticism, many scholars hold that Gnosticism itself grew out of an even earlier Jewish mystical tradition that (centuries later) also gave rise to the Kabbalah.[41] There is also speculation to the effect that apparent Gnostic themes arose *de novo* among the Lurianic Kabbalists in sixteenth-century Safed.[42]

Yet for all the similarities between Gnostic and kabbalistic doctrine, certain essential differences emerge that are of ultimate significance for Jungian psychology. The major difference is that Gnosticism has no equiva-lent concept or symbol for the kabbalistic notion of *Tikkun ha-Olam*, the Restoration of the World. For the Gnostics, the goal of religious life is not a restoration, but an escape from what they regard to be a worthless, evil world. The Gnostic identifies with the divine spark within himself in order that he might transcend his physical self and the material world. The Kabbalist holds a radically different view. Although there are also escapist or

40. See Scholem, *Kabbalah*, p. 443.

41. Among these scholars are Gilles Quispel, George MacRae, B. Pearson, B. Stroumsa, and J. Fossum, as cited in Idel, *Kabbalah: New Perspectives*, ibid., p. 31.

42. See, for example, Scholem, *Major Trends*, p. 260. In this regard it is interesting to note that Jung believed that such themes also arose *de novo* among certain 16th-century alchemists (see Jung, *Mysterium Coniunctionis*, p. 563).

"Gnostic" trends within the Kabbalah, the majority of Kabbalists held that the realization of the divine spark both in man and the material world brings about an elevation, restoration, and spiritualization of man and his environment.[43] In Gnosticism the world is escaped; in the Kabbalah it is elevated and restored. The latter view is one that is much more congenial to Jungian psychology, not only on the obvious principle that for Jung life in this world, and the world itself, is worthwhile, but also with respect to the (less obvious) psychological interpretation that Jung places on the Gnostic myths. As Segal has pointed out, as interpreted by Jung the Gnostic ethic would, strictly speaking, lead to a complete identification of the ego with the unconscious mind. This is because the Gnostic attempts to escape from the world (which Jung equates with the ego) into a complete identification with the infinite pleroma, which, as we have seen, Jung identifies with the unconscious.

By way of contrast, for the Kabbalists and Jung (and the alchemists as interpreted by Jung) the godhead creates the world and mankind in order to fully realize itself. By analogy the unconscious mind manifests itself in a conscious, reflective ego in order to complete and know itself as a "Self." "The difference," Jung writes, "between the natural individuation process, which runs its course unconsciously, and the one which is consciously realized is tremendous, in the first case consciousness nowhere intervenes; the end remains as dark as the beginning."[44] For Jung and the alchemists, the world, and its psychological equivalent, the ego, far from being the superfluous, harmful, and lamentable conditions envisioned by the Gnostics, are necessary, beneficial, and laudable.[45] Both God and man must pass through the world and redeem it in order to realize their full essence. This is precisely the view of the Kabbalists, as expressed in their symbol of *Tikkun ha-Olam*. On the other hand, as Segal has pointed out, Gnosticism actually advocates the precise opposite of Jungian psychology.

---

43. This positive characterization of the world is present in the earliest kabbalistic source, *Sefer ha-Bahir*, which describes a "cosmic tree" that is the origin of both the "All" and all mundane things. Wolfson argues that this positive attitude toward the material world is evidence, contra the view of Scholem, that *Sefer ha-Bahir* is essentially non-Gnostic in character. See Elliot R. Wolfson, "The Tree that is All: Jewish Christian Roots of a Kabbalistic Symbol in *Sefer Ha-Bahir*," in his *Along the Path: Studies in Kabbalistic Myth, Symbolism and Hermeneutics* (Albany: State University of New York Press, 1995), pp. 63–88.

44. Carl Gustav Jung, *Answer to Job* (New York: Meridian, 1960), p. 198.

45. Segal, *The Gnostic Jung*, p. 32.

Interestingly, the alchemists are far more compatible with Jung (and the Kabbalah) on this crucial point than are the Gnostics. The *raison d'être* of alchemy is the transformation of worldly matter,[46] not the escape from it. For Gnosticism, the dissolution of the world is an end in itself, for the alchemists, it is a precondition for a new creation, just as in the Kabbalah the *Shevirat ha Kelim*, the Breaking of the Vessels and destruction of earlier worlds, sets the stage for the world's redemption in *Tikkun ha-Olam*.

Jung is more kabbalistic than Gnostic on a number of other crucial points as well. For example, according to the Gnostics, the demiurge or creator God, (the God archetype in Jung) is thoroughly evil, whereas for Jung (and the Kabbalah) it represents both good and evil, persona and shadow, a coincidence of opposites.[47] Indeed, Gnosticism holds a radical dualism of good immateriality and evil matter; while for Jung, as for the Kabbalah, good and evil originate (and end) in the same source, are mutually dependent upon one another, and are not simply to be identified with spirit and matter. Had Jung been more familiar with the Kabbalah, particularly in its Lurianic form, he would have found a system of mythical thought that was far more compatible with his own psychology than Gnosticism. In 1954, shortly after his discovery of the Lurianic Kabbalah and after essentially completing *Mysterium Coniunctionis*, Jung all but acknowledged this point of view. In a letter to James Kirsch (16 February 1954) he writes:

> The Jew has the advantage of having long since anticipated the develop-
> ment of consciousness in his own spiritual history. By this I mean the
> Lurianic stage of the Kabbalah, the Breaking of the Vessels and man's help
> in restoring them. Here the thought emerges for the first time that man
> must help God to repair the damage wrought by creation. For the first time
> man's cosmic responsibility is acknowledged.[48]

For Jung, in contrast to the Gnostics, man is not enjoined to escape the world, but is rather responsible for its repair and restoration. It is this notion

---

46. Ibid., p. 10.

47. See G. Quispel, "Jung and Gnosis," in Segal, *The Gnostic Jung*, pp. 219–238. Quispel writes that the "fundamentally Jungian interpretation, according to which the representation of God, and thus the godhead, encompasses both good and evil, has no analogy in the Gnostic sources. It is not Gnostic at all. One can call it magical, but only magic with a Jewish foundation."

48. Jung, *Letters* II, p. 155.

of "world restoration," what the Kabbalist's referred to as *Tikkun ha-Olom*, that most connects Jung to the Jewish mystical tradition.

JUNG'S GNOSTICISM

Before turning to our next major theme, the relationship between the Kabbalah and alchemy, I will comment briefly on a question that has been a subject of controversy over many years, the question of Jung's so-called "Gnosticism." The question takes on a certain moment in the present context for the fact that Jung's main "accuser" in this regard was the Jewish philosopher Martin Buber, himself an expositor of Hasidism and sometime interpreter of the Kabbalah. Buber castigates Jung for reducing God to an aspect of the self, and for failing to recognize that the primary experience of the deity is via a relationship to one who is wholly "other," an experience that Buber himself had articulated in his book *I and Thou.*[49] Jung's theology, according to Buber, is Gnostic in the disparaging sense that Jung reduces God to humanity.

Jung bitterly rejected the Gnostic epithet, not because he rejected any particular Gnostic symbol or theory, but because he viewed himself as an empirical scientist who was, in his work, completely *agnostic* with respect to any metaphysical or theological claims.[50] For Jung, God, the pleroma, the divine spark, etc., are real psychologically, but he insists that he can make no judgment regarding their metaphysical status. As for Buber's criticisms, Jung held that a genuine encounter with the self was a necessary prerequisite for an authentic and sustained "I-thou" encounter with God.[51]

Buber and others have not been willing to let Jung off the hook with

---

49. Buber, *Eclipse of God*, p. 84. Buber had articulated a dialogical philosophy in *I and Thou*, trans. R. G. Smith (New York: Charles Scribner's & Sons, 1937).

50. For example, Jung writes: "I do not go in for either metaphysics or theology, but am concerned with psychological facts on the borderline of the knowable. So if I make use of certain expressions that are reminiscent of the language of theology, this is due solely to the poverty of language, and not because I am of the opinion that the subject-matter of theology is the same as that of psychology. Psychology is very definitely not a theology; it is a natural science that seeks to describe experienceable psychic phenomena . . . But as empirical science it has neither the capacity nor the competence to decide on questions of truth and value, this being the prerogative of theology." C. G. Jung, *Mysterium Coniunctionis*, p. vii.

51. Jung, Commentary on "The Secret of the Golden Flower," ibid., p. 50.

such a general disclaimer. Maurice Friedman, a disciple and expositor of Buber, calls Jung a Gnostic because Jung offers the psychological equivalent of salvation, a salvation of turning inward into one's own psyche or soul.[52] Thomas J. J. Altizer, a theologian who himself proclaimed the "death of God" (and the deity's subsequent dispersal throughout humanity) writes: "Despite his frequently repeated and even compulsive scientific claims, Jung has found his spiritual home in what he himself identifies as the Gnostic tradition."[53]

One can hardly demur from Altizer's characterization, a characterization that is particularly apt given Jung's late-life confession that the fantasies and dreams that culminated in his Gnostic "Seven Sermons" prefigured and guided all of his later work. In *Memories, Dreams, Reflections* he writes: "All my works, all my creative activity, has come from these initial fantasies and dreams which began in 1912, almost 50 years ago. Everything that I accomplished in later life was already contained in them, although at first in the form of emotions and images."[54] Yet even with this confession, and even if we discount Jung's own professed agnosticism, Jung, as we have seen, makes a radical break from the Gnostics, both in his affirmation of the individual human ego, and, more importantly, the world. It is as a result of these affirmations that Jung can be described as more kabbalistic than Gnostic, and it is, in part, for this reason that Jung turned from Gnosticism to the more "worldly" (and kabbalistic) alchemy in his historical exploration of the symbols of the unconscious.

KABBALAH AND ALCHEMY

Jung was himself aware of the strong relationship between the Kabbalah and late alchemy, and frequently spoke of specific kabbalistic influences on the alchemists of the sixteenth century and later. "Directly or indirectly," Jung writes in the *Mysterium*, "the Cabala [Jung's spelling] was assimilated into

52. As cited in Segal, *The Gnostic Jung*, p. 45.
53. Altizer, "Science and Gnosis in Jung's Psychology," p. 304. Altizer himself was, in part, inspired by Jung's pronouncement that for contemporary Protestants "the person Jesus, now existing outside the realm of history, might become the higher man within himself" (C. G. Jung, Commentary on "The Secret of the Golden Flower," ibid., p. 54).
54. Jung, *Memories, Dreams, Reflections*, p. 192.

alchemy. Relationships must have existed between them at a very early date, though it is difficult to trace them in the sources."[55] Jung points out that by the end of the sixteenth century the alchemists began making direct quotations from the Zohar. For example, he provides a quotation from Blasius Vigenerus (1523–1596) that speaks of the feminine *Sefirah*, *Malchut*, as the moon turning its face from the intelligible things of heaven.[56] Jung points to a number of alchemists, including Khunrath and Dorn, who made extensive use of the kabbalistic notion of *Adam Kadmon* as early as the sixteenth century, and informs us that works by Reuchlin (*De Arte Kabalistica*, 1517) and Mirandola had made the Kabbalah accessible to non-Jews at that time.[57] Both Vigenerus and Knorr Von Rosenroth, Jung informs us, attempted to relate the alchemical notion of the *lapis* or philosopher's stone to passages in the Zohar that interpret biblical verses (*Job* 38:6, *Isaiah* 28:16, *Genesis* 28:22) as making reference to a stone with essential, divine, and transformative powers.[58] He also notes that Paracelsus had introduced the sapphire as an "arcanum" into alchemy from the Kabbalah. Two of the alchemists most frequently quoted by Jung (Knorr and Khunrath) wrote treatises on the Kabbalah, and others, e.g., Dorn and Lully, were heavily influenced by kabbalistic ideas. We shall see that the notion of the "sparks," which was to become a key element in the Lurianic Kabbalah is present, and provided with a kabbalistic (as opposed to Gnostic) interpretation in their work.

While Jung clearly recognizes the relationship between Kabbalah and alchemy he only provides us with part of the story. The spiritual aspects of alchemy, which interested Jung, were to a very large extent Jewish in origin. Even Jung's own view of alchemy appears to have its origins in Jewish sources. Maria the Prophetess, the Egyptian Hellenistic Jewess who is regarded by Zosimos (third century) to be the founder of alchemy (and by modern scholarship to be among its earliest practitioners), viewed the alchemical work as fundamentally a process through which the adept attains spiritual perfection.[59] Maria regarded the various metals in the alchemical work to be analogous to aspects of humanity; hence her famous maxim, "Join

---

55. Jung, *Mysterium Coniunctionis*, p. 24, cf. p. 384.

56. Ibid., p. 24.

57. Ibid., p. 410.

58. Jung, *Mysterium Coniunctionis*, pp. 394, 446.

59. Raphael Patai, *The Jewish Alchemists* (Princeton, NJ: Princeton University Press, 1994), p. 3.

the male and the female and you will find what is sought," an aphorism that could well serve as a motto for much of Jung's own interpretation of alchemy.

Centuries later Khunrath (1560–1601), another alchemist frequently quoted by Jung, was influenced deeply by the Kabbalah in his view that the alchemical opus reflects a mystical transformation within the adept's soul.[60] Raphael Patai notes, "under the impact of the Kabbalah and its gematria the medieval alchemical tradition underwent a noticeable change, and became during the Rennaissance a more mystically and religiously oriented discipline."[61] The Kabbalah and alchemy were indeed closely linked even in the middle ages and, indeed, Jewish mystical ideas are to be found in an alchemical manuscript dating from the eleventh century, *Solomon's Labyrinth*.[62]

Paracelsus (1493–1541), an alchemist to whom Jung devotes an entire work,[63] held that expert knowledge of the Kabbalah was *required* for the study of alchemy.[64] His teacher, Solomon Trismosin (six of whose alchemical illustrations adorn Jung's *Psychology and Alchemy*),[65] had boasted that he drew his teachings from kabbalistic sources that had been translated into Arabic, and that he had acquired during his travels to the south and east.[66]

By the end of the fifteenth century a number of Christian scholars had become attracted to the Kabbalah and through them the doctrines of this Jewish mystical tradition became accessible to the Christian alchemists.[67] Among these scholars were Johann Reuchlin (1455–1522), Pico della Mirandola (1463–1522),[68] and Pietro Galatinus (1460–1540). Cardinal Egidio da Viterbo (c. 1465–1532) composed his own work on the *Sefirot* and translated significant portions of the Zohar and other kabbalistic works into Latin. The alchemists, for their part, saw in the doctrine of the *Sefirot* a

---

60. Ibid., p. 3.

61. Ibid., p. 522.

62. See B. Suler, "Alchemy," *Encyclopedia Judaica* (Jerusalem: Keter, 1972), Vol. 2, p. 546. On the relationship between Kabbalah and alchemy in general, see Patai, *The Jewish Alchemists*, Chapter 12, "Kabbalah and Alchemy: A Reconsideration."

63. Carl Gustav Jung, "Paracelsus as a Spiritual Phenomenon," in *Alchemical Studies, Collected Works*, Vol. 13, pp. 109–208.

64. Suler, "Alchemy," p. 544.

65. *Psychology and Alchemy*, figures. 32, 95, 112, 134, 166, 219.

66. Suler, "Alchemy," p. 544; Patai, *The Jewish Alchemists*, p. 268.

67. Patai, *The Jewish Alchemists*, p. 154.

68. See Johann Reuchlin, *On The Art of the Kabbalah*.

theosophical justification for their belief in the infinite malleability and underlying unity of all things; and in the kabbalistic number mysticism, *gematria*, they saw a vehicle for explaining and rationalizing alchemical transformations. Thus a form of "kabbalistic alchemy" developed not among Jewish alchemists but among their Christian counterparts.[69] It became the practice of many Christian alchemists to learn Hebrew, seek out Jewish mentors, and learn the mysteries of Kabbalah and gematria as a means of attaining the highest alchemical art and knowledge.[70]

In the Kabbalah the alchemists found a spiritual justification for their view that the one basic substance of the universe, the *prima materia*, took on a multitude of manifestations and forms, and in joining itself to the Kabbalah, alchemy developed itself as a spiritual as well as a material discipline. Indeed, it is this spiritual aspect that is exploited by Jung in his psychological interpretation of alchemy.

Many of the alchemists discussed by Jung were either Jews, Christians posing as Jews in order to give their works "authenticity," or Christians who openly acknowledge their debt to Jewish, frequently kabbalistic, sources. For example, Gerhard Dorn wrote an alchemical commentary of the opening verses of the Book of Genesis,[71] spoke of Adam as the "invisibilus homo maximus"[72] (an allusion to the kabbalistic doctrine of Primordial Man), and held that the legendary patriarch of alchemy, Hermes Trismegistus, though Egyptian, was taught by the "Genesis of the Hebrews."[73]

Jung was aware of the correspondence between the alchemists' *chymical* marriage of sun and moon, gold and silver, spirit and body, king and queen; and the conjugal unifications of the various *Sefirot* and *Partzufim* that are central themes in the Kabbalah. As we shall see, Jung himself had kabbalistic dreams on these themes, which he interpreted as illustrating the coincidence of opposites—e.g., animus and anima—which is requisite for the unification of the self.

It is thus clear that by the time of Knorr von Rosenroth alchemy had taken a mystical turn. By the seventeenth century alchemy had actually become synonymous with the Kabbalah among many Christians. A number of alchemists adopted the kabbalistic theory of the *Sefirot*, *Gematria*

---

69. Patai, *The Jewish Alchemists*, p. 155.
70. Ibid., p. 519.
71. Ibid., p. 18.
72. Jung, *Mysterium Coniunctionis*, p. 383n.
73. Patai, *The Jewish Alchemists*, p. 18.

(numerology), and letter combinations, frequently inscribing Hebrew characters in their vessels on the theory that such letter combinations would facilitate the combining of metals.[74] In certain alchemical writings the *lapiz* is represented by a *Magen David* enclosed in a circle: the circle alluding to *Ein-sof* (the Infinite God) and the two triangles comprising the *Magen David* alluding to the primal elements of fire and water (*Esh* and *Mayim* in Hebrew), which when combined (and slightly altered) form the Hebrew word for heaven (*SheMayim*). The alchemists hoped that from this mixture of fire and water, they could extract Mercurius, which to them was an arcane, transformative substance equivalent to the *prima materia*, Adam and Christ.

While the main direction of influence was from the Kabbalah to alchemy, certain Kabbalists took a lively interest in, and were influenced by, alchemical ideas. Patai points to several passages in the Zohar and other writings of its supposed author, Moses de Leon, in which alchemical concepts are utilized to illustrate mystical, religious themes.[75] Certainly the presence of alchemical terminology in works of the Kabbalah further served to provide a Jewish mystical justification for alchemical beliefs and practices among Jewish and non-Jewish alchemists. Prescriptions for making gold are found in a number of works dealing with the practical Kabbalah, and the kabbalistic efforts to create a *Golem* (an artificial man) can be understood as a concretization of the alchemists' belief that in deriving Mercurius they were symbolically creating a Primordial Adam.[76] Interestingly, Paracelsus was himself concerned with the alchemical creation of a *Golem*.[77] The creation of an artificial man, perhaps even more so than the alchemists' efforts to create gold, can be understood in Jungian terms as an attempt to forge a Self. The fact that the Kabbalists conceived of the *Golem* as being created through the permutations and combinations of Hebrew letters, reinforces the parallels between the *Golem* and the Self. This is because the Self, too, is on many levels a construction of language.

It is of more than passing interest that Chayyim Vital (1542–1620), the foremost disciple of the Kabbalist Isaac Luria, and the man to whom much of our knowledge of the Lurianic system is due, should have also been

---

74. Suler, "Alchemy," p. 545.

75. Patai, *The Jewish Alchemists*, pp. 160–169.

76. On the idea of the *Golem* see Moshe Idel, *Golem: Jewish Magical and Mystical Traditions on the Artificial Anthropoid* (Albany: State University of New York Press, 1990).

77. Suler, "Alchemy," p. 543.

steeped in alchemy. Vital apparently desisted from alchemy during the two years that he had contact with Luria, but returned to it after Luria's death.[78] His interest in alchemy, however, appears to have been purely technical. According to Patai he somehow managed to compartmentalize his activities, writing about alchemy without the least reference to his mystical writings and ideas. It is striking that Vital could somehow ignore or remain unconscious of the parallels between alchemy and the Lurianic system, with its abundant unifications and transformations among the *Sefirot* and worlds. It is as if in his alchemical work Vital had an opportunity to act out unconsciously the very transformative forms of thought that occupied him theoretically in his Kabbalah.

In the main, however, the direction of influence was from the Kabbalah to alchemy, and this influence increased in proportion as alchemy progressively moved from being a protoscience to a mystical (and psychological) discipline. Jung's interest in alchemy is, of course, in its mystical and psychological aspects, and as such we would expect him to focus on those elements in alchemy that were most compatible and assimilable to kabbalistic ideas. Among these elements are the alchemical doctrines of the unification of opposites, the divine wedding, Primordial Man (*Adam Kadmon*), the scintillae (or sparks), and *solve et coagula*. As we examine Jung's treatment of these (and other) themes we will see how close indeed he is to developing a kabbalistic view of the cosmos and man.

PSYCHOLOGICAL HERMENEUTICS IN THE KABBALAH

Jung held that the religious symbols of God, the heavens, cosmic happenings, and higher worlds could be empirically understood as projections of the archetypes of the collective unconscious; that is, as reflections of the deepest, most universal structures of the human mind.[79] This is the simple basis of his entire interpretation of Gnosticism and alchemy and it can, I believe, provide

---

78. Patai, *The Jewish Alchemists*, p. 341.

79. See Carl Gustav Jung, "Archaic Man," in *Civilization in Transition, Collected Works*, Vol. 10, pp. 50–73; Carl Gustav Jung, "Psychology and Religion," in *Psychology and Religion: West and East, Collected Works*, Vol. 11, 2d ed., pp. 3–105; Carl Gustav Jung, "The Undiscovered Self," in *Civilization in Transition*, pp. 245–305. Also, Erich Neumann, *The Origins and History of Consciousness*, trans. R.

useful insights into Jewish mystical symbols and ideas. Although the Kabbalists did not subscribe to the view that a psychological interpretation is the only reasonable and valuable perspective upon their symbols, they, surprisingly, often made such interpretations themselves.

One of the earliest Kabbalists, Azriel of Gerona (early thirteenth century), for example, held that the energy of the human soul derives from the heavenly *Sefirot*, the archetypes through which God expresses himself in creation; and he equated each Sefirah with a psychological power or physical organ in man.[80] Moshe Idel has shown how the *ecstatic* Kabbalah, with its focus on the *experience* of the initiate, regarded the *Sefirot* themselves as human spiritual and psychic processes.[81] For example, Abraham Abulafia (1240–after 1291) understood the names of the ten *Sefirot* (Will, Wisdom, Understanding, Mercy, Fear, Beauty, Victory, Splendor, etc.) as referring to processes taking place in the mind and body of man, and thought it possible for man to cleave to these attributes through proper meditation.[82] An even more radical viewpoint was advocated by R. Meir ibn Gabbay (1480–1540), who interpreted an ancient midrash to mean that God's anthropomorphic structure was itself copied from a human original![83] According to Idel, the psychological understanding of the Kabbalah was eclipsed with the advent of Lurianism, with its emphasis upon the theosophical structure of the godhead and divine worlds; though even in the most thoroughgoing Lurianic Kabbalist, Chayyim Vital, we find the doctrine that the *Sefirot* are mirrored in man's body and soul.

The notion that the divine macrocosm is mirrored in the mind of man was emphasized by the founders of the Hasidic movement, who, as we have seen, can be said to have "psychologized" the Lurianic Kabbalah for their numerous disciples. For example, R. Jacob Joseph of Polonnoye (1704–1794) stated in the name of the Baal Shem Tov (1700–1760), the founder of Hasidism, that the ten *Sefirot* appear in man as a result of a divine contraction, whereby the deity progressively instantiates himself in a series of personal structures until, upon reaching man, he (and man himself) is called

---

F. C. Hull (Princeton, NJ: Princeton University Press, 1970) and Segal, *The Gnostic Jung*, esp. pp. 11–19.

80. Scholem, *Origins of the Kabbalah*, p. 95.
81. Idel, *Kabbalah: New Perspectives*, p. 146.
82. Ibid., p. 147.
83. Ibid., p. 176.

Microcosmos (*Olam Katan*).[84] Rabbi Levi Yitzchak of Berdichov (1740–1809) held that "Man is a counterpart of the Attributes on high," and he provided a one to one correspondence between these attributes and parts of the human body.[85] Similarly, the Apter Rebbe, Rabbi Yehoshua Heschel (1745–1825) held that man is a microcosm, a miniature universe, and his body therefore constitutes a complete structure. According to Heschel, all universes, both spiritual and physical, have a similar structure. Entire universes therefore parallel the various parts of the human body. Some universes correspond to the head, others to the brain, nose, eyes, ears, hands, feet, and the various other parts of the body. Each of these universes contains thousands upon thousands of worlds.[86]

Rabbi Dov Baer, the Maggid of Mezrich (1704–1772), who succeeded the Baal Shem Tov as the leader of the early Hasidic movement, taught "that everything written in (Vital's) *Sefer Etz Chayyim* (the major exposition of the Lurianic Kabbalah) also exists in the world and in man."[87] The "Maggid" went so far as to hold that the very significance of divine thought is contingent upon this thought making its appearance in the mind of man, a viewpoint that is surprisingly premonitory of Jung. The *Tzimtzum*, the act of contraction/concealment through which God created the world is, according to the Maggid, the process by which divine thought is condensed into the human intellect; and it is through this very process that divine thought becomes actual and real. The Godhead himself is the foundation and source of thought, but actual thinking can only occur within the framework of the human mind.[88] Thus, for the Maggid, the psychologization process is one that is necessary for the completion and fulfillment of God himself. For the Kabbalists, there is a reciprocal relationship between the psyches of God and man. God is the ultimate source of the human attributes of thought and emotion, but the psyche of man is the realization of what is only potentiality within God. Like Jung, who was to expound this view two centuries later

---

84. Rabbi Jacob Joseph of Polonnoye, *Toldot Ya'akov Yoseph*, fol. 86a, quoted and translated in Idel, *Kabbalah: New Perspectives*, p. 150 (see also note 366, p. 352).

85. Rabbi Levi Yitzhak of Berdichov, *Kedushat Levi, Bo*, p. 108. In Kaplan, *Chasidic Masters*, p. 78.

86. Rabbi Yehoshua Heschel, *Ohev Yisrael*, Va Yetze 15b; Kaplan, *Chasidic Masters*, p. 150.

87. Maggid, Dov Baer of Mezrich, *Or ha-Emet* (Light of Truth), fol. 36 c–d. Quoted and translated in Idel, *Kabbalah: New Perspectives*, p. 15.

88. Schatz-Uffenheimer, *Hasidism As Mysticism*, p. 207.

with respect to the collective and personal unconscious, the Maggid held that the Godhead has a hidden life within the mind of man.[89]

THE WEDDING SYMBOLISM:
JUNG'S KABBALISTIC VISION

Jung, in his *Memories, Dreams, Reflections*, records a series of visions that he describes as "the most tremendous things I have ever experienced." The visions, which occurred in 1944 when Jung, nearing the end of his seventh decade, was stricken with a heart attack and "hung on the edge of death,"[90] They involve the divine wedding between *Tifereth* and *Malchut*, which, in the Kabbalah, are the masculine and feminine divine principles. Jung describes these visions as occurring in a state of wakeful ecstasy, "as though I were floating in space, as though I were safe in the womb of the universe."[91] He further describes his experience as one of indescribable "eternal bliss." He reports:

> Everything around me seemed enchanted. At this hour of the night the nurse brought me some food she had warmed . . . For a time it seemed to me that she was an old Jewish woman, much older than she actually was, and that she was preparing ritual kosher dishes for me. When I looked at her, she seemed to have a blue halo around her head. I myself was, so it seemed, in the Pardes Rimmonim, the garden of pomegranates, and the wedding of Tifereth with Malchuth was taking place. Or else I was Rabbi Simon ben Jochai, whose wedding in the afterlife was being celebrated. It was the mystic marriage as it appears in the Cabbalistic tradition. I cannot tell you how wonderful it was. I could only think continually, "Now this is the garden of pomegranates! Now this is the marriage of Malchuth with Tifereth!" I do not know exactly what part I played in it. At bottom it was I myself: I was the marriage. And my beatitude was that of a blissful wedding.[92]

---

89. Ibid. Also see Rabbi Schneur Zalman's commentary in *Likutei Amarim-Tanya*, bilingual edition (Brooklyn, NJ: Kehot Publication Society, 1981), Chapter 36, p. 163.
90. Jung, *Memories, Dreams, Reflections*, p. 289.
91. Ibid., p. 293.
92. Ibid., p. 294.

Jung relates that the vision changed and there followed "the Marriage of the Lamb" in Jerusalem, with angels and light. "I myself," he tells us "was the marriage of the lamb." In a final image Jung finds himself in a classical amphitheater situated in a landscape of a verdant chain of hills. "Men and women dancers came onstage, and upon a flower-decked couch All-father Zeus consummated the mystic marriage, as it is described in the Iliad."[93]

As a result of these experiences Jung tells us, he developed the impression that this life is but a "segment of existence." During the visions past, present, and future fused into one. According to Jung, "the visions and experiences were utterly real; there was nothing subjective about them."[94]

It is remarkable that Jung, in what he describes as the most tremendous and "individuating" experience of his life, should find himself in the "garden of pomegranates," an allusion to a kabbalistic work of that name by Moses Cordovero, and should identify himself with the *coniunctio* of *Tifereth* and *Malchuth* as it is described in the Kabbalah. In this vision, which can only be described as "kabbalistic," Jung further identifies himself with Rabbi Simon ben Yochai, who in Jewish tradition is regarded as the author of the Zohar. Here, on the brink of death, Jung has a mystical experience in which the truth of the kabbalistic wedding is equated with the truth of the *hierosgamos*, the divine wedding in Greek mythology. The sexual union of male and female is mystically experienced as the source of both immortality and personal individuation and redemption. Jung tells us that such experience involves an "objective cognition" in which all emotional ties, "relationships of desire, tainted by coercion and constraint" are transcended in favor of a real *coniunctio*, a relationship with oneself, others, and the world that is beyond yet also *behind* desire.[95] Only after this kabbalistic experience was Jung able to compose the *Mysterium Cioniunctionis* and other major works of his final years.

If nothing else, these visions should alert us to the possibility that kabbalistic and other Jewish mystical themes play a significant role in Jung's conception of psychology. And indeed Jung, in his later works, turns to the kabbalistic and alchemical symbols of the "wedding" or sexual intercourse to express the union of opposites that is necessary for the realization of both God and man.

---

93. Ibid., p. 294.
94. Ibid., p. 295.
95. Ibid., p. 297.

The Kabbalists made prolific use of such symbolism to express both the original unification in the Godhead, which was rent apart in the Breaking of the Vessels, and also the reunification that will be brought about in *Tikkun*. Such unifications are expressed in the Zohar and later writings as the union of the *Sefirot Chochmah* (Wisdom) and *Binah* (Understanding), which are personified as the *Partzufim Abba* (Father) and *Imma* (Mother), and in the incestuous passion between the *Sefirot Tiferet* (Beauty) and *Malchut* (Royalty). *Tiferet* and *Malchut* are in turn personified as the *Partzufim Zeir Anpin* (the Short-Faced One) and Nukvah (the Daughter). Their relationship is frequently expressed as the "unification of the Holy One Blessed Be He and His feminine presence (or consort, the *shekhinah*)," and their union is conceptualized as the vehicle through which the fault and disorder in the cosmos will be set aright. Other cosmic conjugal unions are expressed in the Kabbalah in terms of the sexual influx from the *Sefirah Yesod* (identified with the phallus) into *Malchut*, often identified with the earth, or created world.

Both the world and man, according to the Zohar, can be made whole only through a harmonious integration of the masculine and feminine. Man without woman, according to the Zohar, is defective, a mere "half body."[96] Sometimes the female that completes "man" is understood as an actual woman; but at other times it is conceived of, as Jung later conceived the *anima* archetype, as a female "image" that arises within a man's soul and is viewed as his spiritual counterpart or completion. The Zohar speaks of such a counterpart accompanying a man, and making him "male and female," when, for example, he is on a journey away from his wife and home.[97]

Jung was aware of such sexual symbolism in the Kabbalah[98] and occasionally cited examples in which the *Zoharic* symbols were quoted or adapted by the alchemists Knorr Von Rosenroth[99] and Vignerius[100]. In *Mysterium Coniunctionis* he discusses at length a text by the Jewish alchemist Abraham Eleazar in which such kabbalistic unifications are elucidated.[101] There Jung also takes a lively interest in this kabbalistic symbolism independently of its relationship to alchemy, citing the Mueller (German) translation

96. Tishby and Lachower, *The Wisdom of the Zohar*, Vol. 1, p. 298.
97. Zohar I, 49b–50a. See Sperling and Simon, *The Zohar*, Vol. 1, p. 158.
98. Jung, *Letters*, Vol. 1, p. 356; Vol. 2, p. 292.
99. Jung, *Mysterium Coniunctionis*, p. 22.
100. Ibid., pp. 24, 396.
101. Ibid., pp. 432–445.

of the Zohar,[102] quotations from the Zohar in Knorr's *Kabbalah Denudata*,[103] and even the writings of Gershom Scholem.[104] For example, in discussing the *Sefirah Malchut*, which as the widow *Shekhinah* was abandoned by the *Sefirah Tifereth*, Jung writes: "Our current state of disequillibrium results from a rupture between the King and the Queen, who must be reunited to restore God his original unity."[105]

We should note that for the Zohar and later Kabbalists, those sexual acts, such as incest, which are forbidden to man on earth, are permitted, and even necessary, on the divine level, in order to restore the cosmic order. In *Tikkunei ha-*Zohar we learn, for example, that among the *Sefirot* incest is not forbidden: "In the world above there is no "nakedness," division, separation or disunion. Therefore in the world above there is union of brother and sister, son and daughter."[106] The same idea makes its appearance in alchemy. Jung notes that in contrast to Christianity, which allegorized or demonized sexuality, the alchemists "exalted the most heinous transgression of the law, namely incest, into a symbol of the union of opposites, hoping in this way to bring back the golden age."[107]

According to Jung, incest has always been the prerogative of gods and kings and is an important archetype that for modern man has been forced out of consciousness into criminology and psychopathology. For Jung, the alchemical union of King and Queen, and Sun and Moon, are archetypal symbols that express the incestuous union of opposites.

The Zoharic notion that man must be completed by his feminine half is also, according to Jung, echoed in alchemy. As we have seen, Jung held that it is "the moral task of alchemy to bring the feminine background of the masculine psyche, seething with passions, into harmony with the principle of the rational spirit."[108] This, Jung intimates, is another, perhaps deeper, psychological meaning of the alchemical symbols uniting King and Queen, Adam and Eve, brother and sister.

The unification of male and female plays a decisive role in the Lurianic symbols of the "Breaking of the Vessels" and *Tikkun*, the Restoration of the

---

102. Ibid., p. 23.
103. Ibid., p. 442.
104. Ibid., p. 442.
105. Ibid., p. 23.
106. Tishby and Lachower, *The Wisdom of the Zohar*, Vol. 3, p. 1369.
107. Jung, *Mysterium Coniunctionis*, p. 91.
108. Ibid., p. 39.

World. These symbols call out for explication within a Jungian framework. The "Vessels," as described by Luria's most important disciple, Chayyim Vital, are located in the womb of the feminine *Partzuf*, the Cosmic Mother, a symbol of the feminine as "vessel," "receptacle," and "container." The shattering of these vessels brings about a state of affairs in which the masculine and feminine aspects of the cosmos, which had hitherto been in a "face-to-face" sexual conjunction, turn their backs upon one another and become completely disjoined.[109] The "chaos" brought about by the Breaking of the Vessels is one of sexual and erotic alienation, a condition that can only be remedied through a rejoining of opposites through a renewed *coniunctio* of the sexes. At the same time, like the water that breaks signaling the birth of a new human life, the Breaking of the Vessels heralds a new birth, that of a new personal and world order to be completed by man in the process of *Tikkun* (restoration).

The details of this process are as follows. According to Vital, with the original emanation of the worlds, the *Sefirot Chochmah* and *Binah*, which ultimately come to represent the *Partzufim* Father and Mother, were in a state of erotic union ("face to face"). Male and female were in a state of continuous, harmonious conjunction, and the facets of the ideal or intellective realm represented by the *Sefirot Chochmah* and *Binah* were unified as well. Vital describes how the face-to-face (*panim a panim*) status of the Father and Mother visages was maintained by "feminine waters" (*mayim nukvim*) emanating from the interior of the Mother. However, with the Breaking of the Vessels, the cosmic Mother and Father turn their back upon one another. It is only with the advent of *Tikkun*, whereby man, through his ethical and creative acts, provides the "masculine waters" for a renewed *coniunctio* between the feminine and masculine aspects of the cosmos, that the Father and Mother are renewed in their face-to-face relationship and the harmony of the cosmos is restored. Vital's description of this process illustrates the Jungian notion that the sexual can itself be symbolic of spiritual ideas.

In this context we should note that Jung presents an interesting and important discursus on the ultimate significance of the sexual symbolism in the Kabbalah (and by extension alchemy). In discussing the sexual symbolism of *Yesod* in the Zohar Jung writes:

---

109. Chayyim Vital, *Sefer Etz Chayyim*, 2:2 (*Sha'ar Shevirat ha-Kelim*, the Breaking of the Vessels).

Insofar as the Freudian School translates psychic contents into sexual terminology there is nothing left for it to do here, since the author of the Zohar has done it already. This school (Freud's) merely shows us all the things that a penis can be, but it never discovered what the phallus can symbolize. It was assumed that in such a case the censor had failed to do its work. As Scholem himself shows and emphasizes particularly, the sexuality of the Zohar, despite its crudity, should be understood as a symbol of the "foundation of the world."[110]

Jung's (and Scholem's) position raises the question of the full significance of sexual imagery and symbols. Does this view mean that sexuality is simply a vessel or allegory for cosmic creative events; or does it suggest what the Zohar and the later Kabbalah itself implies, that the universe itself is erotic in its own essence?

THE COINCIDENCE OF OPPOSITES IN THE KABBALAH AND JUNGIAN PSYCHOLOGY

For Jung, the key to understanding both the "wedding" and erotic symbolism in the Kabbalah and alchemy is the psychological principle of *coincidentia oppositorium*. In fact, it would not be an exaggeration to say that for Jung the "coincidence of opposites" is not only the key to his interpretation of alchemy, but the cornerstone of his entire psychology. Jung goes beyond the basic Freudian insights that there are no contradictions in the unconscious and that personality develops as a result of psychological conflict. He articulates the notion of a whole "Self," which unifies the conscious and the unconscious, the personal and the impersonal, and a whole host of other oppositions (e.g., between anima and animus, good and evil, light and dark, etc.). "The self," Jung tells us, "is made manifest in the opposites and the conflicts between them; it is a *coincidentia oppositorum*."[111] For Jung, the measure of both an individual and an entire culture is the ability to recognize polarity and paradox and to balance and unify oppositions.[112] "The union of opposites on a higher level of consciousness is not," according to Jung, "a rational thing, nor is it a matter of will; it is a process of psychic development

---

110. Jung *Mysterium Coniunctionis*, p. 442.
111. Jung, *Psychology and Alchemy*, ibid., p. 186.
112. Jung, Commentary on *The Secret of the Golden Flower*, p. 21.

that expresses itself in symbols."[113] It is, I believe, fair to say that Jung attempts in the realm of the symbolic, mythological, and psychic what Hegel attempted in the sphere of reason: a dialectic of oppositions and antinomies leading to the full development of psyche or "mind." This is evident, for example, in the fact that the *Mysterium Coniunctionis* is subtitled "An Inquiry Into The Separation and Synthesis of Psychic Opposites In Alchemy." As we have seen, the coincidence of opposites is a quintessentially kabbalistic idea.

The coincidence of opposites is, however, hardly an exclusive provenance of the Kabbalah. As we have also seen, the notion that oppositions are dissolved in the plenum of the Infinite or Absolute is common to Indian thought, Gnosticism, and mystical thought in general. Nicholas of Cusa defined God as a *coincidentia oppositorum*. A similar idea is also present in the philosophies of Eckhardt, Boehme, and the German Romantics, reaching its full rational articulation, as we have seen in Chapter 6, in the philosophy of Hegel. Still, the Kabbalah, with its dialectical scheme of the unifications of various opposing *Sefirot*; its views that man himself is incomplete unless he is both male and female; that God himself as the absolute being is also nothingness; that the cosmos is, in effect, completed by the "Other Side"; that man, in order to reach his own salvation, must pay his due to the realm of evil; that creation is negation (and vice versa); that destruction (the Breaking of the Vessels) is the condition of progress; and with its theory that the dialectical tensions of the cosmos are mirrored in the psychology of man; provided what was perhaps the Western world's richest symbolic scheme for expressing the "coincidentia" idea.

Jung bases his discussion of the "coniunctio" in alchemy on the indisputable datum that the alchemists themselves viewed their activity as bringing about both a symbolic and material union of opposite tendencies and contradictory ideas. The alchemists not only conceived their melting pots as vessels for the separation and unification of various metals, but also as vessels for the reunification of spiritual wholes that had been rent apart in the material world. The alchemist Barnaud, for example, speaks of: "soul, spirit, and body, man and woman, active and passive, in one and the same subject, when placed in the vessel heated with their own fire and sustained by the outward majesty of the art . . ."[114]

---

113. Ibid.
114. Jung, *Mysterium Coniunctionis*, p. 65.

Among the symbols of unification used by the alchemists are the *coniunctio* of *solis* and *lunae*,[115] the marriage (and identity) of water and fire,[116] the fertilization of earth by heaven,[117] the incestuous marriage of brother and sister,[118] the "chymical" wedding of King and Queen[119] and the conjunction of *Nous* (Mind) and *Physis* (Matter).[120] Jung in his book *Psychology and Alchemy* presents a wonderful collection of mostly medieval illustrations of these ideas, which can have the impact of producing in the viewer a sense of the harmony of soul brought about when a unified peace obtains between these oppositions.

The alchemists also expressed the fundamental *coincidentia* idea through the articulation of a number of paradoxes that have a jarring and ultimately unifying effect on the listener:

> In lead is the dead life.
> Burn in water and wash in fire
> Seek the coldness of the moon and ye shall find
>   the heat of the sun.[121]

According to Jung, this alchemical juxtaposition and mixture of opposites corrects a basic tendency in the human spirit to rend itself apart between conscious and unconscious, or, in Jungian terms, between persona and shadow:

> The essence of the conscious mind is discrimination; it must if it is to be aware of things, separate the opposites.[122]

or,

> Since conscious thinking strives for clarity and demands unequivocal decisions, it has constantly to free itself from counterarguments and contrary tendencies, with the result that especially incompatible contents

---

115. Jung, *Psychology and Alchemy*, p. 84.
116. Ibid., p. 147.
117. Ibid., p. 151.
118. Ibid., p. 153, note.
119. Ibid., p. 232.
120. Ibid., p. 338.
121. Jung, *Mysterium Coniunctionis*, p. 59.
122. Jung, *Psychology and Alchemy*, p. 25.

either remain totally unconscious or are habitually and assiduously over-looked. The more this is so, the more the unconscious will build up its counterposition.[123]

According to Jung, such unconscious contents "stand in compensatory relation to the conscious mind"[124] and, in effect, form a "shadow" that expresses itself in dreams, symptoms etc., all in an effort to balance the individual's "persona."

Jung points out that for the alchemists the tendency to separate opposites within the human psyche reflects an even deeper philosophical principle that "every form of life, however elementary, contains its own inner antithesis."[125] According to Jung, this idea itself is but one example of a perennial worldwide philosophy that takes as its basic axiom the universal idea of "the antithetical nature of the *ens primum*." He points out that in China, for example, this axiom is expressed in the notion of yin/yang, heaven and earth, odd and even numbers.[126] The list can be extended to include all the basic oppositions of language and thought that in various cultures the world over have been incorporated as essential expressions of the world-creative process. The biblical creation story, with its distinctions between the firmaments, light and darkness, night and day, being and void, is only the most familiar example.

Because man's essence as a finite being is, as Jung affirmed in his *Seven Sermons to the Dead*, "distinctiveness," man's psychological propensity is to identify with one pole of any given dichotomy and neglect the other. As such, the oppositions between male and female, good and evil, reason and emotion, etc., are expressed within man's own being.[127] This is a necessary but ultimately unhappy state that the alchemical "conjunctions" are meant to correct.

Jung holds that the alchemical concept of *solve et coagula*, which I will discuss later in relation to the Kabbalists' "Breaking of the Vessels," provides a metaphor for a dialectic in which an original unity in God, being, or the

123. Jung, *Mysterium Coniunctionis*, p. xvii.

124. Carl Gustav Jung, "The Relations Between the Ego and the Uncon-scious," in *Two Essays on Analytical Psychology, Collected Works*, Vol. 7.

125. Jung, *Psychology and Alchemy*, p. 280. This notion is in many ways similar to (but more comprehensive than) Freud's articulation of *thanatos*, the death instinct.

126. Ibid., p. 330.

127. Ibid., p. 25.

unconscious, is separated into component oppositions, and then reunited in an act that brings about a superior wholeness. This is precisely the dialectic expressed by the Lurianic Kabbalists in their concepts of *Sefirot* (archetypes), *Shevirah* (Breakage), and *Tikkun* (Restoration). With *Tikkun ha-Olam* (the Restoration of the World), the unity provided by man is superior to the unity that existed in the godhead prior to creation.

According to Jung, the "self" that is the goal of man's development can only be achieved through a confrontation with the "abysmal contradictions of human nature."[128] Without this confrontation there can, on Jung's view, be no experience of either wholeness or the sacred. Religious orthodoxy, with its efforts to maintain firm distinctions between good and evil, rational and irrational, masculine and feminine, is actually a tool of the ego and an impediment to spiritual and psychological progress. According to Jung, alchemy became an undercurrent to Christianity; and thereby maintained a dim consciousness of the "even numbers" of earth, female, chaos, the underworld, the feminine, and evil, over against the "odd numbers" of Christian dogma. It is just a such an excursion into the rejected aspects of the human psyche that brings about a combination of the universal and the particular, the eternal and the temporal, the male and the female, etc., which is experienced as the archetype of the Self or God. This archetype is expressed in alchemy in the figure of Mercurius, who apart from being the metal quicksilver, is the "world-creating spirit." Mercurius is

> the hermaphrodite that was in the beginning, that splits into the classical brother-sister duality and is reunited in the *coniunctio* to appear once again at the end in the radiant form of the *lumen novum*, the stone. He is metallic yet liquid, matter yet spirit, cold yet fiery, poison and yet healing draught—a symbol uniting all opposites.[129]

According to the alchemists, Mercurius is both good and evil, father and mother, young and old, strong and weak, death and resurrection, visible and invisible, dark and light, known and yet completely nonexistent.[130] Mercurius, who some alchemists equated with the Kabbalists' Primordial Man (*Adam Kadmon*), "truly consists of the most extreme opposites; on the one

128. Ibid., p. 19.
129. Ibid., pp. 294–295.
130. Carl Gustav Jung, "The Spirit Mercurius," *Alchemical Studies, Collected Works*, Vol. 13, p. 221.

hand he is undoubtedly akin to the godhead, on the other hand he is found in sewers."[131]

ADAM KADMON

Jung takes a particular interest in the kabbalistic symbol of *Adam Kadmon* (Primordial Man), which he understands to be both the archetype of all psychological being and an expression of the archetype of the Self, which is man's goal. This primal or original man is spoken of directly by the alchemists, and is taken by them to be an equivalent of the *prima materia*,[132] Mercurius,[133] and the philosopher's stone. Jung sees the symbol of Christ as an expression of the Primordial Man or Self archetype.[134]

As we have seen, the symbol of Primordial Man, the first being to emerge with the creation of the cosmos is common to a number of religious and philosophical traditions. In the Kabbalah, the Primordial Man is spoken of as *Adam Kadmon*, and in the Lurianic Kabbalah this symbol becomes a pivotal notion linking God, Man, and the World. *Adam Kadmon*, as the first being to emerge from the infinite godhead, *Ein-sof*, is essentially indistinguishable from the deity. Yet at the same time, the body of *Adam Kadmon* is said to both emanate and constitute the world. Man, having been created in God's image, is according to the Kabbalists, comprised of the very same cosmic elements, the *Sefirot*, which comprise the "body" of *Adam Kadmon*. The Primordial Man is said to play a critical role not only in the creation of the world but in its redemption as well. Acording to the Lurianists, lights from *Adam Kadmon's* forehead act upon the broken vessels and restore them as *Partzufim* or visages of God. The symbol of *Adam Kadmon* can also be said to express the idea that the cosmos itself has both a soul and body very much like that of man; and that the world too is garbed in the interest, value, and Eros that is normally thought to be the exclusive province of mankind.

For Jung, *Adam Kadmon* is the invisible center in man, the hidden unified self that gives full personal expression to the *coincidentia oppositorum*. Jung quotes a purportedly Jewish alchemical text by Abraham Eleazar:

131. Ibid., p. 222.

132. Jung, *Psychology and Alchemy*, p. 319.

133. Jung, *Mysterium Coniunctionis*, p. 10.

134. Carl Gustav Jung, "Christ, A Symbol of the Self," in *Aion: Researches Into the Phenomenology of the Self*, pp. 36–71.

Noah must wash me . . . in the deepest sea, that my blackness may depart . . . I must be fixed to this black cross, and must be cleansed therefrom with wretchedness and vinegar, and made white, that. . . . my heart may shine like a carbuncle, and the old Adam come forth from me again. O! Adam Kadmon, how beautiful art thou.[135]

Adam, Jung relates, is equated with the alchemist's transformative substance, because he was made from clay, a piece of the original "chaos," yet infinitely formable and moldable.[136] Jung makes reference to the Midrash, *Pirke De Rabbi Eleazar*, which held that Adam was made from the dirt of the four corners of the earth.[137] In a rare reference to Isaac Luria, Jung (who held that the mind was to be understood in terms of a quaternity of basic functions) says: "We can therefore understand why Isaac Luria attributed every psychic quality to Adam: he is psyche par excellence."[138] He quotes a passage from Knorr Von Rosenroth to the effect that *Adam Kadmon* contains all ideas from the lowest, most practical levels of the soul to the highest levels (the *yechidah* of *Atzilut*).[139] *Adam Kadmon*, we are told, is the equivalent of Plato's sphere-shaped "original man,"[140] and like Plato's man and Mercurius he is an apt symbol of the Self because he is androgynous.

Adam Kadmon, Jung informs us, is the universal soul, the soul of all men. Jung reviews the midrashic and kabbalistic notions that suggest that all the righteous come from the different parts of Adam's body: his hair, forehead, eyes, nose, mouth, ears, and jawbone.[141] A midrash, Jung relates, describes the first Adam as extending from one end of the world to the other until God took away pieces from his limbs, instructing him to scatter these pieces to all ends of the earth, so that they can become the souls and body of all future men.[142] *Adam Kadmon* is the equivalent of Mercurius in alchemy, because the metallic element mercury has been disseminated throughout the physical world.[143]

---

135. Jung, *Mysterium Coniunctionis*, p. 50. On Eleazar's being Jewish, see ibid., p. 415.

136. Ibid., p. 394; Jung, *Psychology and Alchemy*, p. 319.

137. Jung, *Mysterium Coniunctionis*, p. 386.

138. Ibid., p. 390.

139. Ibid., p. 390, note 47.

140. Ibid., p. 407.

141. Ibid., p. 390.

142. Ibid., p. 409.

143. Ibid., p. 16.

Jung considers the concept of "Old Adam," which appears in the writings of Abraham Eleazar and which Jung relates to the sinful, unredeemed man in Romans but which could also readily be juxtaposed to the worthless man, Samael, a counterimage of *Adam Kadmon* in the Kabbalah.[144] According to Jung, this "Old Adam" corresponds to the primitive man at the opposite extreme from *Adam Kadmon* but who is also sometimes equated with him.[145] This counter-Adam suggests a primitive identification of God and the Self with an animal consciousness, and, according to Jung, corresponds to the "shadow" archetype. There is a compensatory relationship between the highest spiritual image and the lowest instinct, and when their interdependence is lost, religion, on Jung's view, becomes petrified in formalism and compensation is converted to neurotic conflict.[146]

It is significant for Jung that "in the cabalistic view *Adam Kadmon* is not merely the universal soul or, psychologically, the "self," but is himself the progress of transformation . . ."[147] Jung quotes Knorr Von Rosenroth's Latin translation of a passage from the Kabbalist Abraham ha Cohen De Herrera:

> *Adam Kadmon* proceeded from the simple and the one, and to that extent he is Unity, but he also descended and fell into his own nature, and to that extent he is Two. And again he will return to the One, which he has in him, and to the Highest; and to that extent he is Three and Four.[148]

This passage is particularly noteworthy for its dynamic, or dialectical view of God (or in Jung's terms the Self) which must as it were become estranged from itself (in distinction and consciousness) in order to become itself (as man or ego) only to return to itself (in a unity between man and God, or consciousness and the unconscious). For Jung, as for the Kabbalah, the God archetype completes itself only in this dynamic process, a view that each shares with the philosopher Hegel.[149] Because *Adam Kadmon* is dynamic or transformative "in its very essence, the alchemists could equate Mercurius

---

144. Scholem, *Kabbalah*, pp. 385–388.
145. Jung, *Mysterium Coniunctionis*, pp. 415–417.
146. Ibid., p. 418.
147. Ibid., p. 429.
148. Ibid., p. 429.
149. As outlined in Chapter Six.

and the Philosopher's Stone with the Primordial Man of the Kabbalah.[150] Jung is aware that the symbol of Primordial Man is common to other religious traditions and he makes particular reference to the Taoist P'an Ku, a primal man who is said to have transformed himself into the earth and all its creatures.[151]

For Jung "the archetype of Man, the Anthropos, is constellated and forms the essential core of the great religions." He relates, "in the idea of the homo maximas the Above and Below of creation are united."[152] It is significant that Jung, in exploring this "essential core," works his way through its material representation in alchemy as the "stone" or "Mercurius" to its spiritual and psychological representation in the Kabbalah as *Adam Kadmon*. That the notion of Primordial Man (and his various *coniunctios*) reaches its height of development in the Lurianic Kabbalah should recommend this Kabbalah to Jungians as an essential historical/symbolic support for analytical and archetypal psychology.

THE RAISING OF THE SPARKS

The notion of a spark of divine light trapped in a world of matter where the spark's escape from that world is linked to human salvation is a quintessentially Gnostic idea.[153] It is an idea that remains largely unarticulated in the Kabbalah until it erupts with great force in the system of Isaac Luria in the seventeenth century. Jung's interest in the symbol of the "sparks" is largely centered about its appearance in Gnosticism, alchemy, and Christian theology; but his interpretation of its meaning is again essentially kabbalistic, as he sees the raising of the sparks as a metaphor for psychological redemption in (as opposed to an escape from) the world of individual human existence.

Jung makes brief mention of the theory of the sparks in *Psychology and Alchemy*, where, in speaking about the early (third-century) alchemist Zosimos, he considers the idea of "the pneuma as the Son of God, who descends into matter and then frees himself from it in order to bring healing and salvation to all souls."[154] Jung, in a footnote, relates that "the cabalistic

---

150. Ibid., p. 383.
151. Ibid., p. 400.
152. Ibid., p. 420.
153. On the Gnostic theory of the sparks see Chapter Five.
154. Jung, *Psychology and Alchemy*, p. 301.

idea of God pervading the world in the form of soul sparks (scintillae) and the Gnostic idea of the spinther (spark) are similar."[155] Jung tells us that these ideas suggest a parallel to the unconscious. Indeed, the notion of a buried psychic or spiritual energy that must be freed and returned to its source, is the basic psychoanalytic idea. Jung had early on recognized the image of the spark to be a symbol of the unconscious. In his Commentary on "The Secret of the Golden Flower," a Chinese alchemical text, Jung had interpreted the sparks and fire within the refining furnace as the unconscious impetus to the emergence of the "golden flower" from the "germinal vesicle."[156]

Jung pursues the doctrine of the sparks or scintillae in depth in *Mysterium Coniunctionis*, relating this symbol to his theories of the archetypes, the collective unconscious, and the self. Early in this work he quotes a passage from the presumably gnostic *Gospel of Phillip*, which states the theme of a God/Self dispersed throughout mankind and the world: "I am thou and thou art I, and wherever thou art, there I am, and I am scattered in all things, and from wherever thou wilt thou canst gather me, but in gathering me thou gatherest together thyself."[157] This passage, Jung tells us, reflects man's nature as a microcosm, and he interprets it through the words of the early Christian theologian, Origin: "Understand that the fowls of the air are also within thee. Marvel not if we say that these are within thee, but understand that thou thyself art another world in little, and hast within thee the sun and the moon, and also the stars . . ."[158] When Jung comes to consider the theory of the scintillae in alchemy it is this background of man as microcosm, reflected in his own theory of the archetypes of the collective unconscious, which informs his interpretation.

Jung reviews the history of the spark doctrine as it is manifest in the teachings of the Gnostics, Sethians, Simon Magus, and later thinkers such as Meister Eckhardt. He notes that, for at least the Gnostics, man carries within himself a spark from the "world of light" that enables him to ascend and dwell with "the unknown father and the heavenly mother."[159] Jung takes particular interest in the Sethian notion, as reported by Hippolytus, that darkness "held the brightness of the spark in thrall" and that the "smallest of

---

155. Ibid., p. 301, note 26.
156. Jung, Commentary on *The Secret of the Golden Flower," p. 24*.
157. Jung. *Mysterium Coniunctionis*, p. 8, note 26.
158. Ibid.
159. Ibid., p. 48, and 48, note 55.

sparks" was finely mingled with the dark waters."[160] This idea, which is echoed in alchemy, is also premonitory of the notion of the *Kelippot* (sparks entrapped in dark "shells") in the later Kabbalah.

Jung quotes Abraham Eleazar to the effect that the sparks are to be identified with *Adam Kadmon*[161] and describes how for the alchemists the "scintillae" are often "golden and silver" or are called "fishes eyes," which appear in clouds, water, and earth, and symbolize the omnipresence of the philosopher's stone, and the equivalence of that stone to the heavenly sparks.[162] Eyes, sparks, light, and sun are according to Jung, symbols of consciousness. The Gnostics, in their efforts to reintegrate sparks to reach "the father," and the alchemists who put scintillae together to form gold, are projectively attempting to reintegrate consciousness itself.

The alchemist Dorn gives a spiritual interpretation to the scintillae that is quite similar to that of the Kabbalists. Wisdom, according to Dorn, is an awareness of these sparks, for such sparks are the equivalent to the image of God within man. In man, according to Dorn, there is an "invisible sun."[163] This "sun," however, also contains a dark side, for, according to Dorn, "there is nothing in nature that does not contain as much good as evil."[164] Jung considers the following passage in Dorn, which he interprets as evidence that according to the alchemists the scintillae contain as much potential for evil as for good: "Man is the bait, wherein the sparks struck by the flint, i.e. Mercurius, and by the steel, i.e. heaven, seize upon the tinder and show their power."[165] From the "nuptial" impact between the feminine Mercurius and the masculine heaven (steel), Jung informs us that a "fire point" is created in man that has potential as both danger and panacea. This, we might suppose, is the burning passion that resides in the heart of man.

Jung next considers the work of Heinrich Khunrath (1560–1605) who, as we mentioned earlier, was both an alchemist and Christian Kabbalist. Khunrath was a contemporary of Luria and Vital who studied medicine in Basel and died in Leipzig.[166] It is in regard to Khunrath that Jung notes that

---

160. Ibid., pp. 48–49.
161. Ibid., p. 50.
162. Ibid., p. 51.
163. Ibid., p. 54.
164. Ibid., p. 55.
165. Ibid., p. 54.
166. Ibid., p. 55, note 113; Jung, *Psychology and Alchemy*, p, 509.

Gnostic ideas reemerged independently after many centuries,[167] the same hypothesis that Scholem has made with regard to Luria.[168] According to Khunrath: "There are . . . fiery sparks of the World-Soul, that is, of the light of nature, dispersed or scattered at God's command in and through the fabric of the great world into all fruits of the elements everywhere." Khunrath associates the theory of the sparks with the Cosmic Anthropos or Primordial Man: "The son of the Great World . . . is filled, animated and impregnated . . . with a fiery spark of *Ruach Elohim*."[169] Further, for Khunrath the "fiery sparks of the World-Soul were already in the chaos, the prima materia, at the beginning of the world."[170]

Thus in Khunrath we find a peculiar mixture of Jewish kabbalistic elements intermingled with alchemical concepts in the formation of a theory of the sparks that is remarkably similar to that of Luria, who also held that sparks of the Primordial Man or World-Soul were scattered throughout every corner of the universe. Jung, of course, provides a psychological interpretation of Khunrath's symbolism, noting that "the filling of the world with scintillae is probably a projection of the multiple luminosity of the unconscious."[171]

Elsewhere Jung is more explicit, equating the sparks with the archetypes of the collective unconscious: "In the unconscious are hidden those "sparks of light" (scintillae), the archetypes, from which a higher meaning can be 'extracted'."[172] Jung equates the sparks with the alchemist's Mercurius and with the *anima mundi* or World-Soul of the Neoplatonists, referring to the hermetic doctrine that this soul is "that part of God which, when he 'imagined' the world, was as it were left behind in his creation,"[173] a wonderful metaphor that recalls the kabbalistic notion of the *Reshimu* or trace of divinity that remains in the cosmic void after the first creative act of *Ein-Sof*.[174] Such metaphors resonate deeply with our experience of human

---

167. Jung, *Mysterium Coniunctionis*, p. 56.

168. Scholem, *Major Trends*, p. 260, and Scholem, *Kabbalah*, p. 143. Scholem holds that there is no direct Gnostic influence upon the Lurianists.

169. *Ruach Elohim*, the breath or spirit of God. Jung, *Mysterium Coniunctionis*, p. 56.

170. Ibid.,

171. Ibid., p. 55, note 116.

172. Jung, *Mysterium Coniunctionis*, p. 491.

173. Ibid., p. 491.

174. Scholem, *Kabbalah*, p. 130 ff.

creativity, for who has not felt that a part of a writer or artist is left behind, even long after his death, in his work.

Jung's idea of "extracting" significance from the sparks of light recalls the Lurianic notion of *Birur*, the extraction of the sparks themselves from the *Kelippot* or lifeless "husks" that contain them as a result of the "Breaking of the Vessels." This idea has its alchemical parallel in the concept of the *caelum*, which as Jung explains, was for the alchemist Dorn the celestial substance hidden in man, "the secret truth," the sum of virtue," the "treasure which is not eaten into by moths nor dug out by thieves." According to Dorn, to the world this *caelum* is the cheapest thing, but to the wise it is more precious than gold: the part of man's soul that survives his death.[175] It is precisely this *caelum*, this piece of "heaven," that is symbolically extracted by the alchemists in their procedures. Jung tells us that as a result of this extraction what remains is a *terra damnata*, "a dross that had to be abandoned to its fate."[176] The parallel to the Lurianic notions of *Kelippot* (the "husks") and *Birur* ("extraction") should be apparent.

Jung makes reference to a passage in St. Augustine's "Reply to Faustus the Manichean" in which a very early version of this theory of extraction is described in fantastic terms. According to Augustine's report, the divine spirit is, for the Manicheans, imprisoned in the bodies of the "princes of darkness" who are seduced by angelic male and female beings from the sun and the moon. By exciting their desire these angels cause the wicked to break out into a sweat, which releases the divine spirit and falls upon the earth to fertilize its plants.[177] This description is noteworthy, for in contrast to the Gnostic theory of divine sparks escaping from a useless and damned world this Manichean image has the divine spirit returning to restore it, an idea that is far more compatible with the Kabbalah and Jung than it is with the general tenor of Gnostic thought.

The alchemists, of course, believed that through their procedures they could extract Mercurius or the *lapis*, the philosopher's stone, which were conceived by them as the material representations of both Primordial Man[178] and the heavenly sparks or scintillae.[179] The *lapis* combines, in *coincidentia oppositorum*, elements that are "base, cheap, immature, and volatile" with

175. Jung, *Mysterium Coniunctionis*, p. 487.
176. Ibid., p. 453.
177. Ibid., pp. 39–40.
178. Ibid., p. 383.
179. Jung, *Mysterium Coniunctionis*, p. 51.

those that are "precious, perfect, and solid"[180] in such a manner as to create both a "figurative death" and a panacea for the disharmonies of both the physical world and the human spirit.[181] Jung sees this panacea as a unification of the ego with the shadowy and repressed contents of the unconscious mind, but the alchemists understood their procedure in metaphysical terms, as the extraction or distillation of the *lapis* that is none other than the foundation stone of the world. Knorr Von Rosenroth and other alchemists saw a justification for this view of the *lapis* in the Zohar, which relates:

> The world did not come into being until God took a certain stone, which is called the foundation-stone, and cast it into the abyss so it held fast there, and from it the world was planted. This is the central point of the universe, and on this point stands the Holy of Holies. This is the stone referred to in the verses "who laid the cornerstone thereof?" (Job 38:6), "a tried stone, a precious cornerstone" (Isaiah 28:16) and the stone which the builders rejected has become the head of the corner" (Psalm 118:22). This stone is compounded of fire, water, and air, and rests on the abyss . . . "This stone has on it seven eyes . . ." (Zech. 3:9). It is the rock Moriah, the place of Isaac's sacrifice. It is also the navel of the world.[182]

That the alchemists related their concept of the *lapis* directly to those elements in the Zohar that were to evolve into the Lurianic notion of *Tikkun* (restoration/redemption) is evident from Vigenerus' reference to and interpretation of a passage in the Zohar that comments on Genesis 28:22: "And this stone, which I have set for a pillar, shall be God's house."[183] Vigenerus holds that *Malchut* is called the "statue" (i.e., for Vigenerus the *lapis*) when it is united with *Tifereth*.[184] In the Kabbalah, this union of *Tifereth* with *Malchut* (the masculine with the feminine aspects of God) is a prime metaphor for *Tikkun ha-Olam*. Jung, of course, sees this union of male and female as a bringing together of the *animus* and *anima* or of the masculine (conscious, ego) elements of the psyche with those that are feminine (unconscious and ego-alien).

---

180. Ibid., p. 42.
181. Ibid., p. 474.
182. Ibid., p. 447.
183. Ibid., p. 396, quoting Zohar *Chaye Sarah* on Genesis 28:22.
184. Ibid., p. 396.

ARCHETYPES, ADAM KADMON, MERCURIUS, AND THE SPARKS

As we have seen, throughout both *Psychology* and *Alchemy* and *Mysterium Coniunctionis* Jung variously equates *Adam Kadmon*, the Scintillae, Mercurius, and the philosopher's stone with his own archetypes of the collective unconscious. At other times, Jung equates various of these archetypes either with the *Sefirotic* "Tree,"[185] or with specific kabbalistic *Sefirot*, e.g., *Yesod* with sexuality and *Malchut* with the anima or underlying feminine principle. An evaluation or even detailed discussion of Jung's notion of the archetypes is obviously beyond the scope of this book. Nevertheless, certain essentials must be addressed if we are to make full sense of Jung's interest in and interpretation of the Kabbalah.

The concept of "archetype" is never clearly and unequivocally defined in Jung. As "the contents of the collective unconscious," archetypes are by definition notions that can never be completely known and circumscribed. According to Jung, an archetype is itself an "irrepresentable model" that can, at times, however, be represented in consciousness by "archetypal ideas."[186] These ideas are indeterminately vast in number, yet certain basic archetypes play a recurrent and profound role in both the history of mankind and in individual human development. Among these are the archetypes of the *anima* (feminine principle) and *animus* (masculine principle), the *persona* (the presentation of one's personality to self and others), the shadow (the unconscious converse of the persona that balances or compensates for it), the self (the unity of ego and shadow and the psychic equivalent of God), the *Senex* (the old man), *Puer* (the young man), the mother, the father, the hero, the trickster, etc. The Jungian project is in part an elaboration of the various archetypes, as they are expressed in folklore and myth and as they appear in dreams and other fantasy productions of patients. According to Jung, there are important archetypal ideas corresponding to the phenomenon of human society (King, Queen, Fool, etc.), and also of nature. He relates:

> the mythological processes of nature, such as summer and winter, the phases of the moon, the rainy seasons, and so forth, are in no sense allegories of these objective occurrences, rather they are symbolic expres-

---

185. Jung, *Mysterium Coniunctionis*, p. 43.
186. Carl Gustav Jung, "Archetypes of the Collective Unconscious," in *The Archetypes and the Collective Unconscious, Collected Works*, Vol. 9, p. 5.

sions of the inner, unconscious drama which becomes accessible to man's consciousness by means of projection—that is mirrored in the events of nature.[187]

While there is an archetype corresponding to every significant event in the natural order, such archetypes are not merely the ideas (denotations) of such events but are rather the full panoply of (largely unconscious) associations and meanings (connotations—what Jung calls "projections") that humanity as a whole experiences in relation to these events. Such generic associations or projections are what make the archetypes the content of the *collective* unconscious; personal associations are what Jung calls the Freudian or *personal* unconscious. Because an archetypal idea is always experienced and expressed by individuals, "it takes its colour from the individual consciousness in which it happens to appear."[188]

Archetypes are, according to Jung, related closely to the Platonic ideas. In one place he calls the archetypes "an explanatory paraphrase of the Platonic *eidos.*[189] In *Mysterium Coniunctionis* he states

> . . . within the limits of psychic experience, the collective unconscious takes the place of the Platonic realm of eternal ideas. Instead of these models giving form to created things, the collective unconscious, through its archetypes, provides the *a priori* condition for the assignment of meaning.[190]

This is an extremely important distinction for Jung, because the concept of "archetypes" enables him to shift the whole discussion of ideas from the realm of being (as it was in Plato) to the realm of meaning and significance (which is more amenable to psychology). Archetypes are, in effect, the "human significances" of the things in the world. But because these significances are largely transpersonal and unconscious they are frequently understood as elements of a "higher world." According to Jung:

> This higher world has an impersonal character and consists on the one hand of all those traditional, intellectual and moral values which educate and

187. Ibid., p. 302.
188. Ibid., p. 301.
189. Ibid., p. 300.
190. Jung, *Mysterium Coniunctionis*, p. 87.

cultivate the individual, and on the other hand the products of the unconscious, which present themselves to consciousness as archetypal ideas.[191]

Interestingly, Jung holds that Freud correctly recognized the "traditional values," calling them the superego, but because "the belief in reason and the positivism of the nineteenth century never relaxed their hold [on him]" he remained unaware of the archetypal ideas.[192]

Jung claims that the archetypes are an empirical discovery rather than a metaphysical speculation or creative invention, and that the archetypes are "symptoms of the uniformity of *Homo Sapiens.*"[193] They proceed from the structure and function of the human brain, which, in Jung's view, will in principle produce the same forms of thought in men the world over. He views the production of certain myths and ideas (for example, Primordial Man, the theory of the sparks) in various times and cultures as evidence for the spontaneous production of ideas from an archetypal foundation.[194] Another piece of evidence for the uniformity of the collective unconscious is the appearance of universal archetypal symbols in insanity and dreams.[195]

This is not the place to enter into the debate in the existence or nature of the collective unconscious as conceived by Jung. My own view of the archetypes is even more empirical than Jung's. I do not believe, for example, that the archetypes and collective unconscious must somehow be hard-wired into man's brain. An equally plausible view is that they are symbolic forms that arise spontaneously simply as a result of our psychic interaction with the world, and have a universal existence in the same way as do numbers and mathematical concepts. No one need point to a special brain process (over and above normal human intellect) to account for the existence of counting, addition, subtraction, etc., in societies the world over. Similarly, no one need to point to a special psychic apparatus underlying a collective unconscious to account for the fact that human beings spontaneously experience common meanings and significances (the archetypes) throughout the world and at various times in history.

The question, however, that concerns us here is not the origin of the

191. Ibid., p. 473.
192. Ibid., p. 473.
193. Ibid., p. xiv.
194. Ibid., p. 438.
195. Jung, "Archetypes of the Collective Unconscious," p. 39.

archetypes themselves but rather their purported equivalence to such kabbalistic notions as *Adam Kadmon*, the *Sefirot*, and the sparks. Having considered the nature of Jung's archetypes in general we are now in a position to explore the meaning of these alleged equivalencies.

The kabbalistic symbols of the infinite divine light (Or *Ein-Sof*) and the *Sefirot*, which are themselves comprised of this light, can perhaps best be understood as representing consciousness, significance, and value. Indeed, many of the names of the *Sefirot*—*Ratzon* (Will), *Chochmah* (Wisdom), *Chesed* (Loving-kindness), and *Din* (Judgment)—suggest basic meanings or values in human experience. These values, however, are organized into a system of "worlds" and set in the context of a dynamic in which, as we have seen, most of them have shattered and fallen into a nether realm—the *Sitra Achra*, which is analogous to the unconscious. As such, the *Sefirot* come very close to the Jungian concept of the archetype as an unconscious source of meaning. Further, once the *Sefirot* have been restored (in part as a result of the efforts of mankind), they are reorganized into five *Partzufim Attika Kaddisha* (the Holy Ancient One), *Abba* (father), *Imma* (mother), *Zeir Anpin* (the short-faced one), and *Nukvah* (the female), which bear a remarkable resemblance to specific archetypes that Jung held to be foundational for the collective unconscious. These *Partzufim* correspond almost exactly to the Jungian archetypes of the *Senex*, Father, Mother, *Puer*, and *Anima*, with the *Sitra Achra* itself corresponding to the Jungian shadow.

The kabbalistic notion of *Adam Kadmon* (Primordial Man) spontaneously emanating and also completely containing the light of the ten *Sefirot*, *Partzufim*, and Worlds certainly provides a parallel to the idea of the archetypes being spontaneously created and contained within man. Indeed, various phases in the Lurianic dynamic, e.g., the original divine contraction and the Breaking of the Vessels, correspond to archetypal patterns in human relationships and experience.[196] In short, Jung has sufficient warrant to regard his own archetypes as very similar to, and in some ways illuminative of, the kabbalistic symbols of *Adam Kadmon*, the *Sefirot*, higher worlds, *Partzufim*, etc. He also, I believe, has warrant for regarding the sparks (*netzotzim*) as buried unconscious meanings or archetypes that can erupt into consciousness with powerful effect. As we have seen, according to the Kabbalists these sparks are complexes of divine light that are entrapped in the nether realm of the "Other Side" and that must be released in order to repair the personality of both God and humanity.

---

196. See my *Symbols of the Kabbalah*, Chapter Seven.

FRAGMENTATION AND RESTORATION

We have seen that for the Lurianists the universe as we know it exists in a fragmented, partially displaced, and chaotic state, which resulted from the Breaking of the Vessels (*Shevirat ha-Kelim*). The *Shevirah*, which, according to the Lurianists, is reflected over and over in a multitude of worlds, is also repeated in history and in the psychic structure of the individual. The Breaking of the Vessels (or what the Kabbalists sometimes referred to as the "Death of the Kings") is an archetypical event, which reflects the belief that the original positive unity of the world must be broken and a portion of the original chaos reintroduced in order for humanity to perform the restorative acts that will complete and perfect both God and humankind. The Kabbalists provide a variety of mythological descriptions of the Breaking of the Vessels. On the simplest of levels, they relate how the ten *Sefirot*, which were meant to contain the divine emanation, shattered from the impact of God's light. The broken shards tumbled through the metaphysical void, becoming the negative elements of both the "Other Side" and our world. On a deeper level, the Breaking of the Vessels caused a rupture in the bond between the Celestial Father and Mother (the *Partzufim Abba* and *Imma*), causing them and the other *Partzufim* to turn their backs upon one another, thus disrupting the flow of masculine and feminine "waters" that maintain the harmony of the worlds.[197]

Jung reports that he was not aware of these Lurianic ideas until 1954, probably after the completion of *Mysterium Coniunctionis*, at which point he was excited over having found a confirmation of his own thoughts.[198] Prior to this time, however, he had considered analogues of the Breaking (*Shevirah*) and Restoration (*Tikkun*) concepts in alchemy and elsewhere. For example, the alchemical formula *solve et coagula* calls attention to the fact that for alchemy a premature unity must first be separated and broken apart before the alchemical synthesis can achieve its desired effect. Jung informs us that the initial state in which opposite forces are in conflict is known in alchemy as *chaos*, and is considered the equivalent of the *prima materia*.[199]

---

197. Luzatto, *General Principles of the Kabbalah*, Chapters 3–8, Part II, Ch. 10.

198. Jung, *Letters*, Voil. II, pp. 155, 157.

199. Jung, *Psychology and Alchemy*, pp. 202, 230, 254, 317, 340, 344; Jung, *Mysterium Coniunctionis*, pp. xiv, 156, 385.

It is identical to the "chaotic waters" at the beginning of creation[200] before the separation of opposites as symbolized by the "firmament." According to Jung: "The alchemists understood the return to chaos as an essential part of the opus. It was the stage of *nigredo* [blackness] and *mortificatio*, which was then followed by the "purgatorial fire" and the *albedo* (whiteness).[201] Jung informs us that an element of chaos, negativity, or evil (often symbolized in alchemy by the element "lead"), which can also, by the way, drive the adept mad,[202] must enter into the alchemical work as *solve*.

"Chaos" is symbolized for the alchemists by the sea,[203] the serpent,[204] and the anima, or feminine aspect of the world.[205] The alchemists paradoxically held that all material transformation and psychic healing comes about through chaos. A similar idea is expressed in the Kabbalah of Joseph Ben Shalom of Barcelona (c.1300) who held that there is no creation, alteration, or change in which the abyss of nothingness does not, at least for "a fleeting moment," become visible.[206]

An idea that in some respects parallels the kabbalistic symbol of the *Shevirah* is reflected in the alchemists' view that healing results from the "destruction of the bodies." Jung points out that, according to the alchemist Dorn, bodily and spiritual healing results when Mercurius (as quicksilver) destroys copper, to the point of transforming it into powder. A battle between the elements is set up that brings about an alchemical *separatio, divisio, putrefacio, mortificacio,* and *solutio*, each representing an element of chaos, resulting in physical change in the substances and, more importantly, spiritual healing for the alchemist.[207]

Making reference to the "hermetic vessel" that is said to contain a portion of the original chaos from before the world's creation,[208] the alchemist Dorn writes: "Man is placed by God in the furnace of tribulation, and like the hermetic compound he is troubled at length with all kinds of straits, divers calamities, anxieties, until he die to the old Adam and the flesh

200. Jung, *Mysterium Coniunctionis*, pp. 156, 198.
201. Ibid., p. 197.
202. Ibid., p. 156.
203. Ibid., p. 9.
204. Ibid., p. 80.
205. Ibid., pp. 302, 359.
206. Scholem, *Major Trends*, p. 217.
207. Jung, *Mysterium Coniunctionis*, p. 353.
208. Ibid., p. 279.

and rise again as in truth a new man."[209] Similarly, the British alchemist and cleric Ripley (1415–1490) held in his *Cantilena*[210] that in order to enter the Kingdom of Heaven the "king" must transform himself into the *prima materia* in the body of his mother and return to a state of primal chaos.[211]

According to Jung, the psychological equivalent of these transformations by chaos is a confrontation with one's own unconscious.[212] He writes: "The meeting between the narrowly delimited, but intensely clear, individual consciousness and the vast expanse of the collective unconscious is dangerous, because the unconscious has a decidedly disintegrating effect on consciousness."[213] Yet the process of confronting the chaos of one's unconscious is a necessary, if dangerous, prerequisite to psychological growth. Jung tells us: "We must not underestimate the devastating effect of getting lost in the chaos, even if we know it is the *sine qua non* of any regeneration of the spirit and personality."[214]

This process of regeneration of the spirit, according to Jung, is symbolized by an egg, which stands for the primal chaos containing the divine seeds of life,[215] but which at the same time holds the world-soul captive. Out of this egg will arise the phoenix, which symbolizes a restored Anthropos who had been "imprisoned in the embrace of *Physis*."[216] This egg and captive world-soul parallel the Kabbalists' conception of the state of affairs existing after the Breaking of the Vessels, when sparks of the divine light that had been emanated from *Adam Kadmon* are captured and contained by the *Kelippoth* or husks. The birth of the phoenix can be understood as a symbolic equivalent to *Tikkun*. We have also already made reference to the alchemical equivalents to the kabbalistic concept of *Birur* (extraction). According to Jung, the typical Gnostic and alchemical theory of "composition and mixture" involves a "ray of light from above," which mingles with the dark chaotic waters "in the form of a minute spark." He points out that "at the death of the individual, and also at his figurative death

209. Ibid., p. 353, note 70.
210. Ibid., p. 274.
211. Ibid., p. 283.
212. Ibid., p. 253.
213. Jung, Commentary on "The Secret of the Golden Flower," p. 29.
214. Jung, *Psychology and Alchemy*, p. 74.
215. Ibid., pp. 194–195.
216. Ibid., p. 202.

in mystical experience, the two substances unmix themselves."[217] "Like iron to a magnet," the Sethians held, the spark is drawn to its proper place. This procedure, according to Jung, is perfectly analogous to the process of *divisio* and *separatio* through which the alchemists sought to extract the *anima* or world-soul from the *prima materia* or chaos.[218] It is also analogous to the Lurianic process of *birur* (extraction), in which sparks of divine light are separated from their evil, dark containers.

Jung held that all of these processes of healing, separation, and extraction, after an experience of chaos, represent efforts on the part of man to restore his own soul, or (in a theological language that is very close to the Lurianic Kabbalah) efforts to complete and perfect God. In a letter to Erich Neumann in January of 1952, Jung wrote:

> God is a contradiction in terms, therefore he needs man in order to be made one. Sophia is always ahead, the demiurge always behind. God is an ailment man has to cure. For this purpose God penetrates man. Why should he do that when he has everything already? In order to reach man, God has to show himself in his true form, or man would be everlastingly praising his goodness and justice and so deny him admission. This can be effected only by Satan, a fact which should not be taken as a justification for satanic actions, otherwise God would not be recognized for what he really is.
>
> The advocate seems to me to be Sophia or omniscience. Ouranus and Tethys no longer sleep together. Kether [Jung's spelling] and Malkhuth are separated, the *shekhinah* is in exile; that is the reason for God's suffering. The *mysterium coniunctionis* is the business of man. He is the nymphagogus of the heavenly marriage.[219]

In this passage, Jung seems to make passing reference to the Lurianic doctrine of "feminine waters" in service of reuniting a divided God. One need not comment on every image in this significant passage to note its patently kabbalistic character. The theodicy presented here, as the one outlined in Jung's *Answer To Job*, is that in order for man (and hence God) to become complete, man must come face to face with the negative and evil aspects of the deity and his own soul. Only in so doing can man perform those acts that facilitate the union of opposites necessary to complete himself

---

217. Jung, "Gnostic Symbols of the Self," in Segal, *The Gnostic Jung*, p. 191.
218. Ibid.
219. Jung, *Letters*, Vol. 2, p. 34.

and God. Presumably only by attending to one's evil can man be secure in the attainment of his good. When the Holy One is reunited with his *Shekhinah*, *Tikkun ha-Olam* is achieved and the cosmic balance is restored.

OTHER PARALLELS

Jung explores a number of other early Christian, Gnostic, and alchemical symbols that are parallel to important kabbalistic ideas. For example, the words of St. Ambrose are in some ways premonitory of the Lurianic doctrine of *Tzimtzum*: "Luna is diminished that she may fill the elements . . . He emptied her that he might fill her, as he also emptied himself that he might fill all things."[220] St. Ambrose intends this passage as a homily on Christ. However, the notion of the deity's movement from the level of the divine to the level of the human via an "emptying" is echoed in Luria's theme of creation as a contraction and withdrawal of the infinite *Ein-Sof.*

Among other notions explored by Jung are the Gnostic concepts of alienation and exile[221] and the doctrine of "higher worlds," each of which have obvious kabbalistic parallels. In addition, Jung explores directly and in more detail than I have related in this chapter, the kabbalistic doctrine of the *Sefirot*, dwelling particularly on the metaphor of the *Sefirotic* tree, which is equivalent to *Adam Kadmon*, and which in some sources is described as having its roots in the air,[222] a fact that Jung takes to be a symbol of the equivalence of heaven (the air) with the unconscious (wherein the human psyche is rooted). Jung wrote a major essay on "The Philosophical Tree"[223] in which he acknowledged that the *arbor inversa* (the inverted tree) "found its way into alchemy via the Cabala."

JUNG AND JUDAISM

The striking parallels between Jungian psychology and the Kabbalah raise the question of the actual degree to which Jung was influenced by kabbalistic ideas. As we have seen, in his later works Jung acknowledges a certain debt to Jewish mysticism and recognizes the impact of the Kabbalah on alchemy,

---

220. Jung, *Mysterium Coniunctionis*, p. 35.
221. See Segal, *The Gnostic Jung*, p. 18.
222. See Jung, *Mysterium Coniunctionis*, pp. 43, 455.
223. Carl Gustav Jung, "The Philosophical Tree," p. 340.

which served as a source of many of his ideas. I have argued, however, that Jung did not provide a complete account of the influence of the Kabbalah on alchemy; and that Jung, in extracting the "psychological gold" from the alchemist's material formulations, was actually recovering essentially kabbalistic ideas. Given Jung's highly ambivalent and at times clearly negative attitude toward Judaism, is it possible that Jung could have intentionally downplayed his reliance upon Jewish mystical ideas?

While a full discussion of the controversy regarding Jung's personal and professional stance regarding Judaism and his relationship with the Nazis during the 1930s is beyond the scope of this work,[224] it is important to recall that during this period (the very period of his initial fascination with alchemy) Jung expressed certain negative views about "Jewish psychology." In the 1930s, during the rise of Nazi anti-Semitism, Jung chose to highlight what in his view were the differences between Jewish and German psychology.[225] His statements were understood by many to be anti-Semitic and as playing directly into the hands of those who would view Jews as a threat to, or parasites upon, Germany and other European states.

Jung's observations that the "Jewish race as a whole . . . possesses an unconscious which can be compared with the 'Aryan' only with reserve" and that "the Aryan unconscious has a higher potential than the Jewish"[226] were seen as reinforcing Nazi ideology (despite a context that could be understood as praising the Jewish mind in other respects). Further, in his polemic against Freud, Jung, as early as 1928, wrote, "it is quite an unpardonable mistake to accept the conclusions of a Jewish psychology as generally valid."[227] In a letter to B. Cohen he later explicitly stated: "In so far as his (Freud's) theory is based in certain respects on Jewish premises, it is not valid for non-Jews."[228]

It was during the period of Jung's early, and perhaps greatest, involve-

---

224. See Amiela Jaffe, "C. G. Jung's National Socialism," in Aniela Jaffe, *From the Life and Work of C. G. Jung,* trans. R. F. C. Hull (New York: Harper: 1971); F. McLynn, *Carl Gustav Jung* (New York: St. Martin's Press: 1996); and A. Maldenbaum and S. A. Martin (eds.), *Lingering Shadows: Jungians, Freudians and Anti-Semitism* (Boston: Shambhala, 1991).

225. Carl Gustav Jung, "The State of Psychotherapy Today," in *Civilization in Transition, Collected Works,* Vol. 10.

226. Ibid., p. 166.

227. C. G. Jung, "The Relations Between the Ego and the Unconscious," p. 148, note 8. See also Jung, "The State of Psychotherapy Today," p. 544.

228. Jung, *Letters,* Vol. 1, p. 154.

ment with alchemy that he chose to distance the Western/Christian psyche from Judaism. In 1935 Jung wrote to Neumann (who had written to Jung about Judaism), "analytical psychology has its roots in the Christian Middle Ages, and ultimately in Greek philosophy, with the connecting link being alchemy."[229] Given Jung's need in the 1930s to distinguish his Western/ Christian psychology from the Jewish psychology of Freud, one wonders whether Jung underemphasized the huge impact of Judaism (via the Kabbalah) on alchemy, and thereby upon his own thinking. It is not until after the war that Jung begins to make numerous references to the Kabbalah, and notes the importance of the Kabbalah for alchemy.

I do not know for a fact that Jung suppressed the Jewish mystical origins of some of his ideas. However, given his polemic against Freud, his characterizations of the Jewish psyche, his desire to distinguish his psychology from "Jewish psychology," and the situation in Europe during the 1930s, he had a powerful motive for doing so. If indeed Jung had consciously or unconsciously suppressed the Jewish mystical sources of some of his ideas, his kabbalistic visions during his apparently mortal illness in 1944 can be understood (in Jungian terms) as a powerful compensation for that suppression, or more generally, as an atonement for his anti-Jewish writings and sentiments.

It is important to note that Jung's attitude toward Judaism, even in the 1930s, was by no means always pejorative. During that period Jung steadfastly defended himself against any accusations of antisemitism and worked to prevent Jewish psychotherapists from being pushed out of their profession. While it is also clear that Jung later regretted even the appearance of having flirted with National Socialism[230] he never, as far as I can tell, provided a full and satisfactory accounting of his earlier views on Jewish psychology. His disciple and confidant, Aniela Jaffe, later wrote that Jung's early statements about the Jewish mind "spring from a lack of comprehension of Judaism and Jewish culture which is scarcely intelligible today."[231] In a letter to Jaffe, Gershom Scholem relates that after the war Jung was confronted by the Jewish scholar Leo Baeck on these matters, and the two ultimately made peace after Jung's confession that he had "slipped up." This,

---

229. Ibid., p. 206.
230. See discussions in Jaffe, "C. G. Jung's National Socialism" and McLynn, *Carl Gustav Jung.*
231. Jaffe, "Jung's National Socialism," p. 85.

Scholem relates, was sufficient for both Baeck and Scholem to, in effect, forgive Jung and continue their relationship.

I am deeply troubled by Jung's apparent duplicity and opportunism with respect to what he himself termed the "Jewish question." However, none of the above considerations should, in my opinion, prevent us from either appreciating the affinities between the Kabbalah and the position Jung eventually arrived at, nor in noting the influence of kabbalistic ideas both directly and indirectly (through alchemy) on Jungian psychology. Nor should these considerations prevent us from embarking on the fascinating task of examining the vast kabbalistic literature that has come to light in the past sixty years from a Jungian perspective, thereby enriching our understanding of both the Kabbalah and the human psyche.

I believe it is fair to say that a Jungian approach to the corpus of kabbalistic symbols can yield further insights that are not only psychological, but, on the Kabbalist's own principle that the microcosm mirrors the macrocosm, "kabbalistic" as well. For several reasons, Jung himself never undertook such a systematic exploration of the Kabbalah. It is incumbent upon others, more familiar with the kabbalistic corpus and more sympathetic to Jewish mysticism, to provide a contemporary psychological interpretation of a system of thought that promises not only to unlock the secrets of God, but to provide considerable insight into the nature of man as well.

References

Altizer, Thomas J. J. "Science and Gnosis in Jung's Psychology." *Centennial Review* 3 (Summer 1959).

Applebaum, S., and A. Metzger. "Hasidism and Psychotherapy: An Overview." *Intercom* 16(2) (1976).

Aron, W. "Furzeichnugen Wegen Opshtam fun Sigmund Freud in wegan sien Yiddishkeit" [Notes concerning the genealogy of Sigmund Freud and concerning his Jewishness]. *Yivo Bleter* 40.

Azriel. "The Emanation of the Ten *Sefirot*." In Joseph Dan, *The Early Kabbalah*. Texts trans. by Ronald C. Kieber. New York: Paulist Press, 1966.

Bakan, David. *Sigmund Freud and the Jewish Mystical Tradition*. Boston: Beacon Press, 1971. (Originally published in 1958.)

Bergmann, Martin S. "Moses and the Evolution of Freud's Jewish Identity." *Israel Annal of Psychiatry Disciplines* XIV (March 1976).

Berkowitz, Eliezer. *God, Man, and History*. Middle Village, NY: Jonathan David, 1959.

Bettelheim, Bruno. *Freud and Man's Soul*. New York: Vintage Books, 1984.

Biale, David. *Eros and The Jews*. New York: Basic Books, 1992.

———. "Gershom Scholem's Ten Unhistorical Aphorisms in Kabbalah: Text and Commentary." *Modern Judaism* 5 (1985).

Birnbaum, David. *God and Evil*. Hoboken, NJ: Ktav, 1989.

Blackman, Philip, trans. *Tractate Avoth: The Ethics of the Fathers*. Gateshead, England: Judaica Press, 1985.

Breuer, Joseph. "Studies on Hysteria. Chapter II. Case study of 'Anna O.' (1895). In Sigmund Freud, *Standard Edition of the Complete Psychological Works of Sigmund Freud*, ed. James Strachey. Vol. 2. London: Hogarth Press, 1955–1967.

Buber, Martin. *The Eclipse of God: Studies in the Relation Between Religion and Philosophy*. Trans. Maurice Friedman et al. New York: Harper & Brothers, 1952.

———. "God and the World's Evil." In *Contemporary Jewish Thought*, ed. Simon Noveck. New York: B'nai Brith, 1963.

Buber, Martin. *I and Thou*. Trans. R. G. Smith. New York: Charles Scribner's & Sons, 1937.

Copleston, Friedrich. *A History of Philosophy*. Garden City, NY: Image Books, 1962.

Corbin, Henry. *Creative Imagination in the Sufism of Ibn 'Arabi*. Trans. Ralph Manheim. Bollingen Series 91. Princeton, NJ: Princeton University Press, 1969.

Cordovero, Moses. *The Palm Tree of Deborah*. Trans. Louis Jacobs. New York: Hermon Press, 1974.

Dan, Joseph. *Gershom Scholem and the Mystical Dimension of Jewish History*. New York: New York University Press, 1987.

Dan, Joseph, ed. *The Early Kabbalah*. Texts trans. by Ronald C. Kieber. New York: Paulist Press, 1966.

Drob, Sanford. The Dilemma of Contemporary Psychiatry. *American Journal of Psychotherapy* 43 (1989).

———. Foreword to *God and Evil* by David Birnbaum. 4th ed. Hoboken, NJ: Ktav, 1989.

———. "Freud and the Chasidim: Redeeming the Jewish Soul of Psychoanalysis." *Jewish Review* 3(1) (Sept. 1989).

———. "Hasidus and Contemporary Psychology: A Dialogue with Rabbi Alter Metzger." *New York Jewish Review* 2(2) (Nov. 1988).

———. "Jung and the Kabbalah." *History of Psychology*. 2(2) (May 1999).

———. "The Mystic as Philosopher: An Interview With Rabbi Adin Steinsaltz." *Jewish Review* 3(4) (March 1990).

———. *Symbols of the Kabbalah: Philosophical and Psychological Perspectives*. Northvale, NJ: Jason Aronson, 2000.

Eigen, Michael. "The Area of Faith in Winnicott, Lacan, and Bion." *International Journal of Psychoanalysis* 62 (1981).

Elior, Rachel. "Chabad: The Contemplative Ascent to God." In *Jewish Spirituality: From the Sixteenth Century Revival to the Present*, ed. Arthur Green. New York: Crossroads, 1987.

———. *The Paradoxical Ascent to God: The Kabbalistic Theosophy of Habad Hasidism*. Trans. J. M. Green. Albany: State University of New York, 1993.

Enoch, Slavonic Book of. *Encyclopedia Judaica* 6:797. Jerusalem: Keter, 1972.

Erikson. Erik. "Identity and the Life Cycle." *Psychological Issues* 1 (1959).

Filoramo, Giovanni. *A History of Gnosticism*. Trans. Anthony Alcock. Cambridge: Basil Blackwell, 1990.

Findlay, J. N. *Ascent to the Absolute*. London: Allen & Unwin 1970.

———. *The Discipline of the Cave*. London: Allen & Unwin, 1966.

———. *Hegel: A Re-examination*. New York: Oxford University Press, 1958.

———. *Plato: The Written and Unwritten Doctrines*. London: Routledge & Kegan Paul, 1974.

———. *The Transcendence of the Cave* London: Allen & Unwin, 1966.

———. *Values and Intentions*. London: Allen & Unwin, 1961.

Fine, Lawrence. "The Contemplative Practice of Yihudim in Lurianic Kabbalah." In *Jewish Spirituality: From the Sixteenth Century Revival to the Present*, ed. Arthur Green. New York: Crossroads, 1987.

Fisher, Seymour, and Roger O. Greenberg. *The Scientific Credibility of Freud's Theories and Therapy*. New York: Basic Books, 1977.

Fluegel, Maurice. *Philosophy, Qabbala and Vedenta*. Baltimore: H. Fluegel & Company, 1902.

Frankl, Victor. *Man's Search For Meaning: An Introduction to Logo Therapy*. New York: Washington Square Press, 1963.

Freud, Anna. "Inaugural Lecture." *International Journal of Psychoanalysis* LIX (1978).

Freud, Ernst, Lucie Freud, and Ilse Grubrich-Simitis, eds. *Sigmund Freud—His Life in Picture and Words*. New York: Harcourt, Brace Jovanovich, 1978.

Freud, Sigmund. "Address to the Society of B'nai Brith" (1926). In *Standard Edition of the Complete Psychological Works of Sigmund Freud*, ed. James Strachey. Vol. 20. London: Hogarth Press, 1955–1967.

———. "Analysis Terminable and Interminable." In *Standard Edition of the Complete Psychological Works of Sigmund Freud*, ed. James Strachey. Vol. 23. London: Hogarth Press, 1955–1967.

————. "An Autobiographical Study" (1925). In *Standard Edition of the Complete Psychological Works of Sigmund Freud*, ed. James Strachey. Vol. 23. London: Hogarth Press, 1955–1967.

————. "Beyond the Pleasure Principle." In *Standard Edition of the Complete Psychological Works of Sigmund Freud*, ed. James Strachey. Vol. 18. London: Hogarth Press, 1955–1967.

————. "Civilization and Its Discontents." In *Standard Edition of the Complete Psychological Works of Sigmund Freud*, ed. James Strachey. Vol. 21. London: Hogarth Press, 1955–1967.

————. "The Ego and the Id." In *Standard Edition of the Complete Psychological Works of Sigmund Freud*, ed. James Strachey. Vol. 19. London: Hogarth Press, 1955–1967.

————. "The Future of an Illusion." In *Standard Edition of the Complete Psychological Works of Sigmund Freud*, ed. James Strachey. Vol. 21. London: Hogarth Press, 1955–1967.

————. "The Interpretation of Dreams." In *Standard Edition of the Complete Psychological Works of Sigmund Freud*, ed. James Strachey. Vols. 4 and 5. London: Hogarth Press, 1955–1967.

————. "Introductory Lectures on Psychoanalysis" (1916–1917). Lecture 28: Analytic Therapy. In *Standard Edition of the Complete Psychological Works of Sigmund Freud*, ed. James Strachey. Vol. 16. London: Hogarth Press, 1955–1967.

————. "Letter to the Editor of the Jewish Press Centre in Zurich" (1925). In *Standard Edition of the Complete Psychological Works of Sigmund Freud*, ed. James Strachey. Vol. 19. London: Hogarth Press, 1955–1967.

————. "Moses and Monotheism." In *Standard Edition of the Complete Psychological Works of Sigmund Freud*, ed. James Strachey. Vol. 23. London: Hogarth Press, 1955–1967.

————. "The Moses of Michelangelo." In *Standard Edition of the Complete Psychological Works of Sigmund Freud*, ed. James Strachey. Vol. 23. London: Hogarth Press, 1955–1967.

————. *New Introductory Lectures on Psychoanalysis*. New York: W. W. Norton, 1965. (Originally published in 1933). Also see *Standard Edition of the Complete Psychological Works of Sigmund Freud*, ed. James Strachey. Vol. 16. London: Hogarth Press, 1955–1967.

————. "Notes Upon a Case of Obsessional Neurosis." In *Standard Edition of the Complete Psychological Works of Sigmund Freud*, ed. James Strachey. Vol. 10. London: Hogarth Press, 1955–1967.

————. *The Origins of Psychoanalysis: Letters to Wilhelm Fliess, Drafts and Notes: 1887–1902.* Ed. Marie Bonaparte and trans. Anna Freud and Ernest Kris. New York: Basic Books, 1954.

————. "An Outline of Psychoanalysis" (1940). In *Standard Edition of the Complete Psychological Works of Sigmund Freud,* ed. James Strachey. Vol. 23. London: Hogarth Press, 1955–1967.

————. "Psychoanalytic Notes Upon An Autobiographical Account of A Case of Paranoia (Dementia Paranoides)." In Freud: *Three Case Histories.* New York: Collier Books, 1972.

————. "Resistances to Psycho-Analysis." In *Standard Edition of the Complete Psychological Works of Sigmund Freud,* ed. James Strachey. Vol. 19. London: Hogarth Press, 1955–1967.

————. "Shorter Works." In *Standard Edition of the Complete Psychological Works of Sigmund Freud,* ed. James Strachey. Vol. 23. London: Hogarth Press, 1955–1967.

————. "Studies in Hysteria, Case Histories: Frau Emmy Von N." (1895). In *Standard Edition of the Complete Psychological Works of Sigmund Freud,* ed. James Strachey. Vol. 2. London: Hogarth Press, 1955–1967.

Fromm, Erich. *Man for Himself.* New York: Holt, Rinehart & Winston, 1947.

————. *Psychoanalysis and Religion.* New Haven: Yale University Press, 1950.

Gaster, Theodore H., trans. and ed. *The Dead Sea Scriptures.* Garden City, NY: Doubleday, 1956.

Gay Peter. *Freud: A Life for Our Time.* New York: W. W. Norton, 1988.

————. *A Godless Jew: Freud, Atheism and the Making of Psychoanalysis.* New Haven: Yale University Press, 1987.

Gikatilla, Joseph. *Sha'are Orah* [*The Gates of Light*]. Trans. Avi Weinstein. San Francisco: HarperCollins, 1994.

Goodman, Len, ed. *Neoplatonism in Jewish Thought.* Albany: State University of New York Press, 1992.

Graetz, Heinrich. *Popular History of the Jews.* 5th ed. New York: Hebrew Publishing, 1937.

Graf, Max. "Reminiscences of Professor Sigmund Freud." *Psychoanalytic Quarterly* 11 (1942): 465–476.

Grunwald, Max. *History of the Jews in Vienna.* Philadelphia: Jewish Publication Society of America, 1936.

Haley, Jay. *Problem-Solving Therapy.* New York: Harper & Row, 1976.

Handelman, Susan. *Fragments of Redemption: Jewish Thought and Literary Theory in Benjamin, Scholem and Levinas.* Bloomington and Indianapolis: Indiana University Press, 1991.

Hegel, G. W. F. *Lectures on the Philosophy of Religion.* Ed. Peter C. Hodgson. Berkeley: University of California Press, 1985.

———. *The Phenomenology of Mind.* Trans. J. B. Baille. New York: Macmillan, 1931.

———. *The Philosophy of History.* Trans. J. Sibree. New York: Dover, 1956.

———. *Philosophy of Mind.* Trans. A. V. Miller. Oxford: Clarendon Press, 1971.

———. *Science of Logic* I. Trans. A. V. Miller. New York: Humanities Press, 1968.

Heidegger, Martin. *Being and Time.* New York: Harper & Row, 1962.

Heller-Wilinsky, Sarah. "Isaac ibn Latif—Philosopher or Kabbalist." In *Jewish Medieval and Renaissance Studies,* ed. Alexander Altmann. Cambridge, MA: Harvard University Press, 1967.

Herrera, Abraham Kohen De. *Encyclopedia Judaica* 8: 391–392. Jerusalem: Keter, 1972.

Hillman, James. *Re-visioning Psychology.* New York: Harper & Row, 1976.

Idel, Moshe. *Golem: Jewish Magical and Mystical Traditions on the Artificial Anthropoid.* Albany: State University of New York Press, 1990.

———. *Hasidism: Between Ecstasy and Magic.* Albany: State University of New York Press, 1995.

———. "Jewish Kabbalah and Platonism in the Middle Ages and Renaissance." In *Neoplatonism and Jewish Thought.* ed. Lenn E. Goodman. Albany: State University of New York Press, 1992.

———. *Kabbalah: New Perspectives.* New Haven: Yale University Press, 1988.

———. *Language, Torah and Hermeneutics in Abraham Abulafia.* Trans. Menahem Kallus. Albany: State University of New York Press, 1989.

———. *Messianic Mystics.* New Haven: Yale University Press, 1998.

Jacobs, Louis. "The Uplifting of the Sparks in Later Jewish Mysticism." In *Jewish Spirituality: From the Sixteenth Century Revival to the Present,* ed. Arthur Green. New York: Crossroads, 1987.

Jaffe, Aniela. "C. G. Jung's National Socialism." In Aniela Jaffe, *From the Life and Work of C. G. Jung.* Trans. R. F. C. Hull. New York: Harper and Row, 1971.

Johnson, Paul. *A History of the Jews.* New York: Harper & Row, 1987.

Jonas, Hans. *The Gnostic Religion,* 3rd ed. Boston: Beacon Press, 1970.

————. "Gnosticism and Modern Nihilism." *Social Research* 19 (1952).

Jones, Ernest. *The Life and Work of Sigmund Freud*. New York: Basic Books, 1953.

Jung, Carl Gustav. *Aion: Researches into the Phenomenology of the Self*. In *The Collected Works of C. G. Jung*, Vol. 9. Trans. R. F. C. Hull. Princeton, NJ: Princeton University Press, 1969.

————. *Alchemical Studies. The Collected Works of C. G. Jung*, Vol. 13. Trans. R. F. C. Hull. Princeton, NJ: Princeton University Press, 1967.

————. *Answer To Job*. New York: Meridian, 1960.

————. "Archaic Man." In *Civilization in Transition, The Collected Works of C. G. Jung*, Vol. 10. Trans. R. F. C. Hull. Princeton, NJ: Princeton University Press, 1964.

————. "Archetypes of the Collective Unconscious." In *The Archetypes and the Collective Unconscious. The Collected Works of C. G. Jung*, Vol. 9. Trans. R. F. C. Hull. Princeton, NJ: Princeton University Press.

————. "Christ, A Symbol of the Self." In *Aion: Researches into the Phenomenology of the Self*. In *The Collected Works of C. G. Jung*, Vol. 9. Trans. R. F. C. Hull. Princeton, NJ: Princeton University Press, 1969.

————. Commentary on "The Secret of the Golden Flower." In *Alchemical Studies, The Collected Works of C. G. Jung*, Vol. 13. Trans. R. F. C. Hull. Princeton, NJ: Princeton University Press, 1967.

————. "Flying Saucers: A Modern Myth." In *Civilization In Transition, The Collected Works of C. G. Jung*, Vol. 10. Trans. R. F. C. Hull. Princeton, NJ: Princeton University Press, 1970.

————. "Gnostic Symbols of the Self." In *Aion: Researches into the Phenomenology of the Self*. In *The Collected Works of C. G. Jung*. Bollingen Series XX. Princeton, NJ: Princeton University Press, 1969.

————. *Letters*. Ed. Gerhard Adler. Vols. 1 and 2. Princeton, NJ: Princeton University Press, 1975.

————. *Memories, Dreams, Reflections*. Recorded and edited by Aniela Jaffe. New York: Random House, 1961.

————. *Modern Man in Search of a Soul*. Trans. W. S. Dell and Cary F. Baynes. New York: Harcourt, Brace & World, 1933.

————. *Mysterium Coniunctionis. The Collected Works of C. G. Jung*. Vol. 14. Trans. R. F. C. Hull. Princeton, NJ: Princeton University Press, 1963.

————. "Paracelsus as a Spiritual Phenomenon." In *Alchemical Studies, The Collected Works of C. G. Jung*. Vol. 13. Trans. R. F. C. Hull. Princeton, NJ: Princeton University Press, 1967.

———. "The Philosophical Tree."In *Alchemical Studies, The Collected Works of C. G. Jung.* Vol. 13. Trans. R. F. C. Hull. Princeton, NJ: Princeton University Press, 1968.

———. *Psychology and Alchemy. The Collected Works of C. G. Jung.* Vol. 12. Trans. R. F. C. Hull. Princeton, NJ: Princeton University Press, 1968.

———. "Psychology and Religion." In *Psychology and Religion: West and East, The Collected Works of C. G. Jung.* 2d ed. Vol. 11. Trans. R. F. C. Hull. Princeton, NJ: Princeton University Press, 1969.

———. "The Relations between the Ego and the Unconscious." In *Two Essays on Analytical Psychology, The Collected Works of C. G. Jung.* Vol. 7. Trans. R. F. C. Hull. Princeton, NJ: Princeton University Press, 1966.

———. "Seven Sermons to the Dead." In *The Gnostic Jung*, ed. Robert Segal. Princeton, NJ: Princeton University Press, 1992.

———. "The Spirit Mercurius." In *Alchemical Studies, The Collected Works of C. G. Jung.* Vol. 13. Trans. R. F. C. Hull. Princeton, NJ: Princeton University Press, 1968.

———. "The State of Psychotherapy Today." In *Civilization in Transition, The Collected Works of C. G. Jung.* Vol. 10. Trans. R. F. C. Hull. Princeton, NJ: Princeton University Press: 1970.

———. "The Undiscovered Self." In *Civilization In Transition, The Collected Works of C. G. Jung.* Vol. 10. Trans. R. F. C. Hull. Princeton, NJ: Princeton University Press, 1970.

Kant, Immanuel. *The Critique of Practical Reason.* Trans. Lewis W. Beck. Indianapolis: Bobbs-Merrill, 1956.

———. *Critique of Pure Reason.* Trans. Norman Kemp Smith. New York: St. Martin's Press, 1965.

———. *Religion Within the Limits of Reason Alone.* Trans. T. M. Greene and H. H. Hudson, with introductory essays by T. M. Greene and J. R. Silber. New York: Harper & Brothers, 1960.

Kaplan, Aryeh. *The Bahir: Illumination.* York Beach, ME: Samuel Weiser, 1989.

———. *Chasidic Masters.* New York: Maznaim, 1984.

———. *Jewish Meditation: A Practical Guide.* New York: Schocken, 1985.

———. *Meditation and Kabbalah.* York Beach, ME: Samuel Weiser, 1982.

———. *Sefer Yetzirah: The Book of Creation.* Rev. ed. York Beach, ME: Samuel Weiser, 1997.

Katz, Steven T. "Utterance and Ineffability" in Jewish Neoplatonism." In *Neoplatonism in Jewish Thought*, Ed. Lenn E. Goodman. Albany: State University of New York Press, 1992.

Klein, Dennis. *Jewish Origins of the Psychoanalytic Movement.* Chicago: University of Chicago Press, 1985.

Klein, George S. *Psychoanalytic Theory: An Exploration of Essentials.* New York: International Universities Press, 1976.

Knorr von Rosenroth, Christian. *Kabbala Denudata,* "The Kabbalah Uncovered, or, The Transcendental, Metaphysical, and Theological Teachings of the Jews." (Sulzbach, Latin, 1677–1684).

Kohut, Heinz. *The Restoration of the Self.* New York: International Universities Press 1977.

Layton, Bentley. *The Gnostic Scriptures.* New York: Doubleday, 1987.

Liebes, Yehuda. *Studies in Jewish Myth and Jewish Messianism.* Trans. Batya Stein. Albany: State University of New York Press, 1993), p. 10.

———. "Christian influences on the Zohar." In Yehuda Liebes, *Studies in the Zohar.* Trans. Arnold Schwartz, Stephanie Nakache, and Penina Peli. Albany: State University of New York Press, 1993.

Luzzatto, Moses. *General Principles of the Kabbalah.* Trans. Phillip Berg. Jerusalem: Research Centre of Kabbalah, 1970.

Maidenbaum, Aryeh and Stephen H. Martin, eds. *Lingering Shadows: Jungians, Freudians, and Anti-Semitism.* Boston: Shambhala, 1991.

Markus, Steven. *Freud and The Culture of Psychoanalysis.* London: 1984.

McGuire, W., ed. *Freud-Jung Letters.* Princeton, NJ: Princeton University Press, 1974.

McLynn, F. *Carl Gustav Jung.* New York: St. Martin's Press: 1996.

Meltzer, David. *The Secret Garden: An Anthology in the Kabbalah.* Barrytown, NY: Stanton Hill, 1998.

Menzi, Donald Wilder and Padeh, Zwe, trans. *The Tree of Life: Chayyim Vital's Introduction to the Kabbalah of Isaac Luria, The Palace of Adam Kadmon.* Northvale, NJ: Jason Aronson, 1999.

Mindel, Nissan. *The Philosophy of Chabad.* Vol. 2. Brooklyn, NY: Kehot, 1973.

Moore, Thomas, ed. *A Blue Fire: Selected Writings of James Hillman.* New York: Harper & Row, 1989.

Neumann, Erich. *The Origins and History of Consciousness.* Trans. R. F. C. Hull. Princeton, NJ: Princeton University Press, 1970.

Novak, David. "Self-Contraction of the Godhead in Kabbalistic Theology." In *Neoplatonism in Jewish Thought* ed. Lenn E. Goodman. Albany: State University of New York Press, 1992.

Nozick, Robert. *Philosophical Explanations.* Cambridge, MA: Harvard University Press, 1981.

O'Regan, Cyril. *The Heterodox Hegel.* Albany: State University of New York Press, 1994.

Otto, Rudolph. *The Idea of the Holy.* London: Oxford University Press, 1970. (Originally published 1923.)

Patai, Raphael. *The Jewish Alchemists.* Princeton, NJ: Princeton University Press, 1994.

"Plato and Platonism." *Encyclopedia Judaica* 13. Jerusalem: Keter, 1972.

Plato. *Letters.* Trans. R. G. Bury. Cambridge, MA: Harvard University Press, 1929.

———. *Republic.* Trans. F. M. Cornford. New York: Oxford, 1945.

———. *The Timaeus.* Trans. B. Jowett. In *The Great Books of the Western World*, Vol. 6. Chicago: Encyclopedia Britannica, 1952.

Plotinus. *The Six Enneads.* Trans. Stephen Makenna. In *The Great Books of the Western World*, Vol. 11. Chicago: Encyclopedia Britannica, 1952.

Popkin, Richard. "Spinoza, Neoplatonic Kabbalist?" In *Neoplatonism and Jewish Thought* ed. Lenn E. Goodman. Albany: State University of New York Press, 1992.

Puner, H. W. *Freud: His Life and His Mind.* New York: Crown, 1949.

Radhakrishnan, Sarvepalli, and Charles A. Moore. *A Source Book of Indian Philosophy.* Princeton, NJ: Princeton University Press, 1957.

Rank, Otto. *The Myth of the Birth of the Hero.* New York: Brunner, 1952.

Reich, Wilheim. *The Function of the Orgasm.* New York: Noonday Press, 1942.

Renou, Louis, ed. *Hinduism.* New York: Braziller, 1962.

Reuchlin, Johann. *De Arte Cabalistica. [On The Art of the Kabbalah].* Trans. M. and S. Goodman. Introductions by G. L. Jones and Moshe Idel. Lincoln: University of Nebraska Press, 1993.

Rice, Emmanuel. *Freud and Moses: The Long Journey Home.* Albany: State University of New York Press, 1990.

———. "The Jewish Fathers of Psychoanalysis." *Judaism* (36) 1 (1987).

Ricouer, Paul. *Freud and Philosophy.* New Haven: Yale University Press, 1970.

Roazan, Paul. *Freud and his Followers.* New York: Alfred A. Knopf, 1971.

Roback, A. A. *Freudiana.* Cambridge, MA: Sci-Art Publishers, 1957.

———. *Jewish Influence in Modern Thought.* Cambridge, MA: Sci-Art Publications, 1929.

Robinson, Ira. *Moses Cordovero's Introduction to Kabbalah: An Annotated Translation of His* Or Ne'erav. Hoboken, NJ: Ktav, 1994.

Robinson, J. M., ed. *The Nag Hammadi Library*. 3d ed. San Francisco: Harper & Row, 1988.

Rudolph, Kurt. *Gnosis: The Nature and History of Gnosticism*. Trans. R. M Wilson. San Francisco: Harper, 1987.

Sachs, Hans. *Freud, Master and Friend*. Cambridge, MA: Harvard University Press, 1944.

Schachter, Zalman. "The Dynamics of the Yehidut Transaction." *Journal of Psychology and Judaism* 3 (1978): 7.

Schaefer, Peter. *The Hidden and Manifest God: Some Major Themes in Early Jewish Mysticism*. Trans. Aubrey Pomerantz. Albany: State University of New York Press, 1992.

Schatz-Uffenheimer, Rifka. "Hasidism." *Encyclopedia Judaica* Jerusalem: Keter, 1972.

———. *Hasidism As Mysticism: Quietistic Elements in Eighteenth-Century Hasidic Thought*. Jerusalem: Hebrew University, 1993.

Schochet, Immanuel. "Mystical Concepts in Chasidism." Appendix to Schneur Zalman, *Likutei Amarim-Tanya* Brooklyn: Kehot, 1983.

Scholem, Gershom. "Adam Kadmon." *Encyclopedia Judaica* 2 Jerusalem: Keter, 1972.

———. "The Four Worlds." *Encyclopedia Judaica* 16. Jerusalem: Keter, 1972.

———. *Jewish Gnosticism, Merkabah Mysticism and Talmudic Tradition*. New York: Schocken, 1965.

———. *Kabbalah*. Jerusalem: Keter, 1974.

———. "Kabbalah and Myth." In Gershom Scholem, *On The Kabbalah and Its Symbolism*, trans. Ralph Manheim. New York: Schocken, 1965.

———. *Major Trends in Jewish Mysticism*. New York: Schocken, 1941.

———. *Mystical Shape of the Godhead*. New York: Schocken, 1991.

———. "The Meaning of the Torah in Jewish Mysticism." in Gershom Scholem, *On the Kabbalah and Its Symbolism*. New York: Schocken, 1969.

———. *On the Kabbalah and Its Symbolism*. Trans. Ralph Manheim. New York: Schocken, 1969.

———. *Origins of the Kabbalah*. Trans. R. J. Zwi Werblowski. Princeton, NJ: Princeton University Press, 1987.

———. *Sabbatai Sevi: The Mystical Messiah*. Trans. R. J. Zwi Werblowski. Princeton, NJ: Princeton University Press, 1973.

———. "Yezirah, Sefer." *Encyclopedia Judaica* 16. Jerusalem: Keter, 1972.

Schreber, Daniel Paul. *Memoirs of My Nervous Illness.* Trans. Ida Macalpine and Richard Hunter. Cambridge, MA: Harvard University Press, 1988.

Schur, Max. *Freud: Living and Dying.* New York: International Universities Press, 1972.

Schwaaber, Paul. "Title of Honor: The Psychoanalytic Congress in Jerusalem." *Midstream,* 24 (March 1978).

Segal, Robert A., ed. *The Gnostic Jung.* Princeton, NJ: Princeton University Press, 1992.

Smart, Ninian. "Boehme, Jakob." In *Encyclopedia of Philosophy,* ed. Paul Edwards. New York: Macmillan, 1967.

———. "Eckhardt, Meister." In *Encyclopedia of Philosophy,* ed. Paul Edwards. New York: Macmillan, 1967.

———. "Jainism." In *Encyclopedia of Philosophy,* ed. Paul Edwards. New York: Macmillan, 1967.

———. "Indian Philosophy." In *Encyclopedia of Philosophy,* ed. Paul Edwards. New York: Macmillan, 1967.

———. "Nagarjuna." In *Encyclopedia of Philosophy,* ed. Paul Edwards. New York: Macmillan, 1967.

———. "Sankara." In *Encyclopedia of Philosophy,* ed. Paul Edwards. New York: Macmillan, 1967.

Smith, Richard. "The Modern Relevance of Gnosticism." In *The Nag Hammadi Library* ed. J. M. Robinson. San Francisco: Harper and Row, 1988.

Solomon, Wisdom of. *Encyclopedia Judaica.* Jerusalem: Keter, 1972.

Solomon, Robert. *In The Spirit of Hegel: A Study of G. W. F. Hegel's Phenomenology of Spirit.* New York and Oxford: Oxford University Press, 1983.

Soloveitchik, Joseph. *Halakhic Man.* Trans. Lawrence Kaplan. Philadelphia: Jewish Publication Society, 1983.

———. "The Lonely Man of Faith." *Tradition* 7 (Summer 1965): 7(2).

Sperling, Harry, Maurice Simon, and Paul Levertoff, trans. *The Zohar.* London: Soncino Press, 1931–1934.

Stace, W. T. *The Philosophy of Hegel.* New York: Dover 1955. (Originally published 1924.)

Steinsaltz, Adin. "Hasidism and Psychoanalysis." *Judaism* 19(3). (1960).

———. *The Long Shorter Way: Discourses on Chasidic Thought.* Northvale, NJ: Jason Aronson, 1988.

———. *The Strife of the Spirit.* Northvale, NJ: Jason Aronson, 1988.

———. *The Thirteen Petalled Rose.* Trans. Yehuda Hanegbi. New York: Basic Books, 1980.

———. "Worlds, Angels and Men." In Adin Steinsaltz, *The Strife of the Spirit.* Northvale, NJ: Jason Aronson, 1988.

Suler, B. "Alchemy." *Encyclopedia Judaica* 2. Jerusalem: Keter, 1972.

Taylor, Charles. *Hegel.* Cambridge, MA: Cambridge University Press, 1975.

Thompson, M. Guy. *The Death of Desire.* New York: New York University Press, 1985.

Tishby, Isaiah, and Fischel Lachower. *The Wisdom of the Zohar: An Anthology of Texts.* Trans. David Goldstein. 3 vols. Oxford: Oxford University Press, 1989.

Verman, Mark. *The Books of Contemplation: Medieval Jewish Mystical Sources.* Albany: State University of New York Press, 1992.

Wallace, William, trans. *Hegel's Logic.* Oxford: Clarendon Press, 1975.

Weiss, Friedrich G. *Hegel: The Essential Writings.* New York: Harper & Row, 1974.

Wilson, R. M. "Jewish 'Gnosis' and Gnostic Origins: A Survey." *Hebrew Union College Annual* 45 (1974).

Wittgenstein, Ludwig. *Tractatus Logico-Philosophicus.* Trans. D. F. Pears and B. F. McGuinness. London: Routledge & Kegan Paul, 1961.

Wolfson, Elliot R. "The Tree that is All: Jewish Christian Roots of a Kabbalistic Symbol in *Sefer Ha-Bahir.*" In Elliot R. Wolfson, *Along the Path: Studies in Kabbalistic Myth, Symbolism and Hermeneutics.* Albany: State University of New York Press, 1995.

Zaehner, R. C., ed. *Hindu Scriptures.* Rutland, VT: Charles E. Tuttle, 1966.

Zalman, Schneur. *Likutei-Amarim-Tanya.* Bilingual edition. Brooklyn, NY: Kehot Publication Society, 1981.

Zimmer, Heinrich. *Philiosophies of India.* Princeton, NJ: Princeton University Press, 1971.

Index

About the Author

Sanford L. Drob is Director of Psychological Assessment and the Senior Forensic Psychologist at Bellevue Hospital in New York. He holds doctorate degrees in Philosophy from Boston University and in Clinical Psychology from Long Island University. In 1987 he co-founded, and for several years served as editor-in-chief of, the *New York Jewish Review*, a publication addressing the interface between traditional Judaism and contemporary thought. In addition to numerous publications in clinical, forensic, and philosophical psychology, Dr. Drob's articles on Jewish philosophy have appeared in such journals as *Tradition, The Reconstructionist*, and *Cross Currents*. His philosophical and psychological interests originally led him to the study of Chassidus. For the past fifteen years he has engaged in intensive study of the Kabbalah, the problems of God, Mind, and Evil, and the relationship between Jewish Mysticism and other traditions in the history of Western and Eastern thought. Contact Sanford Drob at www.newkabbalah.com.

Recommended Resources

The Alef-Beit: Jewish Thought Revealed through the Hebrew Letters
by Yitzchak Ginsburgh   1-56821-413-8

**Ascending Jacob's Ladder: Jewish Views of Angels, Demons,
and Evil Spirits**
by Ronald H. Isaacs   0-7657-5965-9

In the Beginning: Discourses on Chasidic Thought
by Adin Steinsaltz   1-56821-741-2

**Demystifing the Mystical: Understanding the Language and Concepts
of Chasidism and Jewish Mysticism—A Primer for the Layman**
by Chaim Dalfin   1-56821-453-7

**The Fundamentals of Jewish Mysticism: The Book of Creation
and Its Commentaries**
by Leonard R. Glotzer   0-87668-437-1

Inner Rhythms: The Kabbalah of Music
by DovBer Pinson   0-7657-6098-3

Jewish Mystical Leaders and Leadership in the Thirteenth Century
by Moshe Idel and Mortimer Ostow   0-7657-5994-2

The Jewish Mystical Tradition
by Ben Zion Bokser   1-56821-014-0